An Introduction to
Real Estate Finance

An Introduction to Real Estate Finance

Edward A. Glickman

ELSEVIER

Amsterdam • Boston • Heidelberg • London • New York • Oxford
Paris • San Diego • San Francisco • Singapore • Sydney • Tokyo

Academic Press is an imprint of Elsevier

Academic Press is an imprint of Elsevier
225 Wyman Street, Waltham, MA 02451, USA
The Boulevard, Langford Lane, Kidlington, Oxford, OX5 1GB, UK

First edition 2014

Notice
No responsibility is assumed by the publisher for any injury and/or damage to persons or property as a matter of products liability, negligence or otherwise, or from any use or operation of any methods, products, instructions or ideas contained in the material herein. Because of rapid advances in the medical sciences, in particular, independent verification of diagnoses and drug dosages should be made

Library of Congress Cataloging-in-Publication Data
A catalog record for this book is available from the Library of Congress

British Library Cataloguing-in-Publication Data
A catalogue record for this book is available from the British Library.

ISBN: 978-0-12-378626-5

For information on all Academic Press publications
view our website at books.elsevier.com

Dedication

For your support, encouragement, love and patience: Diana, Eric, Alex you are my luv-luvs.

For inspiration, my mother Constance Glickman who brought me up to believe that writing was a noble pursuit, my uncle Dr. Lewis Glickman and my father-in-law Dr. Paul Keat, all great authors who made me aspire to write this book. To my father Paul and brother Jon, thanks for being there for me. Michael Berman, Ken Freeling, Marc Grant, Barry Katz, Alan Silverstang, Bobby Tarasowsky, Jon Warren, Paul Weinberg and Donna Zuccarini, thank you for being there.

Contents

Preface

NOTE FOR THE PRACTITIONER

Goals of this Book

After thirty plus years in finance I can still say I learn something new every day. In preparing to teach this subject matter, I attempted to organize much of the information and experience that I had gathered in my career in a form that I hoped would appear logical to my students.

I was told by a number of practitioners and academics that you never really understand a subject until you try to teach it. I now know what they meant.

To write this book, I reviewed the material that I was teaching again and again. I subjected it to additional level of outside review and scrutiny. I let my brilliant and highly opinionated students have at it and provide their comments to draft chapters. Any individual practitioner's experience is somewhat random and there were gaps in the material. I have attempted to fill these in with the help of some good friends. There were also many things that I did not fully understand and I sought guidance from a number of experts. What you have is the product of this adventure. It was a great experience.

I mention this because you are probably asking yourself, what does he know that I do not already know?

Good question. The likely answer is that in some areas, not much, in other areas , a good amount, depending on how you spend your time and in what area of the real estate market you are focused. I think you will find this book a good reference and, as I did, a way to answer some of the nagging questions that all of us in the business have that we do not have the time to research.

Please let me know what you think and how I can make this book and the companion website a more valuable tool for you and your colleagues. I look forward to your comments and advice.

NOTE FOR THE STUDENT

Goal of this Textbook

Real Estate is one of the largest stores of wealth for the US economy and represents the most significant investment held by many American families. It is almost a certainty that during the course of your life you will interact with the real estate industry as a buyer or renter of residential property. Many of you are contemplating careers in finance and given the size of the country's investment in property it is quite likely that the health of the real estate industry will impact your career. This book is intended to give you broad exposure to the fundamentals of real estate finance as well as insight into the way the real estate industry is organized. Since real estate is capital intensive, this book will also serve as a great review of classwork that you have taken in basic finance, accounting and capital markets. Many of my students have commented that this text helped them to see the practical application of much of the theory that they learned in their "core" classes.

What to learn

Many famous real estate people will give you sage advice about the business. One theme that I have heard repeated again and again is "It's all about how you buy". By that it is meant that a big determinant of successful investing is paying the right price for the property. Accurate valuation is critical. The first section of this book is all about valuation.

The second piece of advice you will hear is to "lock in a spread". This means that you should finance the property with an optimal capital structure and hopefully source capital at below the yield you make on your investment. The second section is all about sourcing and structuring capital.

The third section of this book illustrates the above concepts with a series of real world examples by exploring in depth a few of the most critical segments of the real estate industry. We look at their drivers, metrics, and financing structures.

At the end of this book and the course that uses it, you will have a good background in real estate fundamentals, excellent preparation for further study and enough momentum to try your hand at the one of the world's oldest professions!

How to use this book

This book explains concepts, the exercises show you how to implement them, they fit together. You cannot learn how to cook by reading recipes; you need to go into the kitchen and get your hands dirty. All of the chapters end with "thought questions" . These questions require you to integrate what you have learned and defy simple solutions. Al l of the chapters also have multiple choice questions that review facts taken from the text To get these right you must read the material carefully.. In the chapters that require math, do the problems and check your answers.

Web Site

In today's world, textbooks are no longer static, they represent a snapshot in time of an organic body of knowledge. The companion web site http://booksite.elsevier.com/9780123786265 is meant to expand and extend the book. It also serves as a way for us to communicate. Explore the resources that I post for your reference and tell me if you find them useful. Please tell me what you like and dislike about the book.

I look forward to hearing from you.

Prerequisites

Each semester a number of students from the law, public policy, economic, architecture and design programs take my class. While most of them have taken some basic business classes a few have no background in finance and accounting whatsoever.

In my opinion, this is a mistake, not because it is impossible, but because real estate finance builds on core concepts from general finance and accounting. Learning this material l from a "cold start" is very difficult and I suggest that you will have a more rewarding experience with at least some knowledge of the fundamentals.

Real Estate as a Career Choice

If you look at the Forbes 400 or another list of the wealthiest individuals on the planet you will see that investment in real estate is a source of much of that wealth. Many of my students get very excited about real estate, finish class, raise money from friends and family and purchase a property. Many go onto careers in banks, investment banks and funds working in the real estate capital markets. For this reason I spend time in this text on how the industry is organized. If you are a budding entrepreneur use this information to design your company, if you go corporate, use it as a road map in your recruiting activities.

NOTE FOR THE INSTRUCTOR

Goal of this Textbook

The goal of this textbook is to give the MBA or upper-level Undergraduate a complete overview of the fundamental concepts in modern real estate finance as they are currently being practiced at real estate companies operated in the United States.

This book is designed for use in a single semester course. It is not a deep theoretical treatise on any of the individual disciplines as that would require significantly more contact hours than are typically available in a single semester.

This text is intended to be used alongside the associated website http://textbooks.elsevier.com/web/manuals/9780123786265. Sample class layouts are included on the web site along with matching syllabi and power point slides.

Suggested Pre-requisites and *Co-requisites*
Pre-requisites
Managerial Economics or Introduction to Finance

This text assumes that students have been exposed to the basic concepts of interest rates and present value theory.

Intro to Financial Accounting

The assumption is also made that students understand the basic principles of dual-entry accounting and are familiar with the layout of a traditional income statement, balance sheet and cash flow statement.

Co-requisites
Business Law

The material in this text would be enhanced by a student's understanding of basic concepts in business law including the structure of business entities and the fundamentals of property ownership. These topics are discussed briefly in the text.

Recommended Companion Texts

There are many fine books that cover the three topics listed above. Here are some that I recommend:

Managerial Economics: Keat and Young

Finance:

Financial Accounting: Stickney and Weil

Property:

Book Format

There are three sections to the text:

Section one: Financial Mechanics

The goal of this section is to provide the student with the skills needed to analyze and value a property. This task can be highly granular, when dealing with complex assets such as regional malls and mixed use developments, or quite straightforward, when analyzing certain triple net leased assets.

Most students taking this class should have a familiarity with the basic theory behind accounting, finance and valuation from prerequisite classes and this section is designed to refocus that knowledge on real estate.

At the end of this section the student should be able to come to an estimate of a property's value from source materials such as economic reports, market updates, property set-up sheets and financial statements.

Section two: Financial Tools

The second section of the book includes information on the common vehicles used to invest in real estate. The capital markets chapter can be thought of as a transition between Financial Mechanics and Financial Tools. Real Estate is a capital intensive industry and the financial markets are the source of that capital. Understanding the sources and uses of capital in the industry can help give the student perspective on valuation metrics. Understanding the instruments that we use to package capital can give the student perspective on structuring transactions.

Section three: Examples of Implementation

In section three, the focus is on how to apply the methods and metrics of real estate finance to different segments of the real estate market. REITs are a transitional chapter as they can be thought of as both an example of a financing tool and an investment vehicle. Development is the real estate industry's manufacturing business. Corporate real estate shows real estate as a factor of production in a larger context. International gives the student a chance to reflect on the US market by comparing it to world markets. Residential is perhaps the most important chapter in the book as housing is both a fundamental requirement of modern life and one of the largest stores of wealth in the US economy.

Not in this book

This book is intended as a survey of real estate finance not an in depth treatise. In the financial mechanics section, accounting and tax theory is described at a high level. Look to web content for a path to greater depth. In the discussion of financing instruments, derivatives are discussed at a superficial level, again look to the web for a path to greater depth. Last, with the exception of residential, which by some estimates accounts for over three quarters of our country's investment in real estate, no individual property types are described. A path to this information is also on the web.

Dated Material

A number of the chapters contain time series information on aspects of the real estate market. The real estate industry is in a period of great flux and this information is changing daily. It gives context to the book to have a set of data to illustrate concepts and relationships as they existed at the moment the chapter was written. Comparing the data in the book with data available at the time the course is taught and discussion the direction of the market is a great way to engage students in the dynamic follow of our industry.

Chapter Format

The goal of each chapter is to cover its topic at a depth that provides the student with a broad introduction to the subject matter and that can be covered in either a single 3 hour graduate level seminar or two bi-weekly undergraduate 1.5 hour classes.

Each chapter is followed by a Glossary of Terms drawn from the chapter. Definitions for these terms are aggregated on the website.

There are three type of questions posed at the conclusion of each chapter:

Thought questions: Open ended topics that can be used in class to promote discussion or as prompts for short essays. They can also be combined with multiple choice and review questions to form exams.

Multiple Choice questions: Based on specific facts or concepts contained in the chapter. Can be used by students to review the material they have read or as part of quizzes or exams. These questions are easy to grade and brief weekly quizzes can check whether students are keeping up with class.

Review Questions: These questions typically require some simple calculations. They intended to review the concepts presented in the chapter. They are not in-depth case studies.

Answers to all questions are on the instructor's web site. The following is a brief guide to the organization of the website:

Student Website http://booksite.elsevier.com/9780123786265

> Glossary
> Annotated Resource List
> Professional Real Estate Organizations
> Relevant Job Sites

Instructor Website http://textbooks.elsevier.com/web/manuals/ 9780123786265

> Suggested Course Layouts
> Syllabi Template
> Power Point Slides
> Glossary
> Review Questions and Answers
> Suggested Class Projects

Suggest Course Layouts

>   12 Week Undergraduate
>   15 Week Undergraduate
>   12 Week Graduate
>   15 Week Graduate

Syllabus Templates

>   12 Week Undergraduate
>   15 Week Undergraduate
>   12 Week Graduate
>   15 Week Graduate

Chapter Summaries

>   Synopsis
>   Teaching objectives
>   Related resources
>   Activities

Power Point Slides

Acknowledgments

There were many people involved in the evolution of this book, to the extent that it exceeds your expectations they deserve much of the credit. I reserve the responsibility for its shortcomings and will endeavor to improve and extend this book through the companion web site.

My deep gratitude to Scott Bentley, PhD. a patient, wise and thoughtful publisher, without you this book would not exist. Special thanks to my editor Katie Price of the English Department of the University of Pennsylvania and Pauline Wilkinson, Production Project Manager, and all of her colleagues at Elsevier, for baking the cake.

Thank you to Dean Peter Henry and Professors Robert Whitelaw, Richard Levich, Yakov Amihud, Aswath Damodaran and David Bosch of NYU Stern, for your gracious welcome, support and encouragement. To Professor Stijn Van Neiuwerburgh, a special thank you for being an extraordinary partner in the Center for Real Estate Finance Research. To Professor William Fruhan, my amazing finance professor at HBS, thank you for making a difference in my life. To Professor Robert C Higgins, you set a high bar.

To the many real estate professionals, analysts, bankers, lawyers and accountants who I had the privilege of working with over the past 30 years, thank you for making our industry so exciting. To my friends at Econsult Solutions and FG Asset Management thanks for your support.

To my NYU Stern Real Estate Finance students, who read through many drafts, your dedication, your energy and your optimism inspire me. Go forth and build things. To my industry and academic reviewers, who gave me more time than I deserved, my deepest thanks, your suffering was not in vain:

Crager Boardman, Waterfall AM

Saumya Bhatnagar, Met Life

Dan Friedlander, Pfizer

Eric Fuhrman, HGK AM

Steven Hentschel, Hentschel &Co.

Ian Hunter, Sumitomo

Karen Hunter, Harvard GSD

Paul Keat, Thunderbird

Michael Lavelle, Appraisal Economics

Edward Liva, KPMG

Steven Mullin, Econsult

Thomas Opdyke

Erin Pearte, Wells Fargo

Jacob Reiter, Firstrust

Wendy Rowden, Jonathan Rose Associates

Michael Silverman, Integra

Gavin Steinberg, Newcastle

Reviewers and contributors:
    Paul Keat
    Steve Mullins
    Liz Karch for the Real Estate Roundtable

Edited by Katie Price

Principles of Real Estate Finance

INTRODUCTION

The real estate industry is a very important part of the US economy and a highly capital intensive business. Capital flows in this industry are measured in the trillions of dollars and the economic health of the property markets has a major impact on the entire economy. The purpose of this textbook is to give the student a broad understanding of real estate finance from the individual property operating level up to the macro economic trends that impact the global real estate capital markets. Many types of properties are discussed, from single family housing to major commercial buildings and they are discussed at various points in the property lifecycle from development to functional obsolescence. A wide range of debt and equity financing techniques are considered individually as well as in the context of creating a coherent capital structure for a property investment. While the primary focus of this book is the US real estate industry, the principles discussed are applicable in all property markets.

0.1 The US Real Estate Industry

The US Real estate industry is a vibrant business impacting every sector of American life. By definition, the industry includes all aspects of the ownership of land and buildings. Residential and commercial properties house almost all of our daily activities. The quality of our built environment impacts the competitive position of our country and the *quality* of our daily lives.

Ownership of real property has long been a sign of wealth and status. In our current society, many of our wealthiest families have made or extended their fortunes by investing in real estate. For many Americans, the ownership of a home remains a principal goal that over 65% of families have achieved. For most US families with annual incomes below $100,000, their investment in real estate is their largest financial asset,

The real estate industry is asset intensive and property investment requires large amounts of capital. Given the high unit cost of property and the large size of our built environment, the amount of capital invested in real estate is very large, well over $20 trillion. Aggregating the required capital from investors and deploying it to finance residential and commercial real estate is a critical function of our financial system.

The real estate and related construction industries employ over 7 million workers and generate about 30% of our country's GDP. The Real Estate Roundtable, a major trade organization, publishes the following statistics that speak to the depth and breadth of the US Real estate industry:

Exhibit 01.

Real Estate and the Economy:

- *America's real estate creates or supports approximately 9 million jobs.*
- *The construction industry includes 1.6 million self-employed and 6.7 million wage and salary jobs; by the year 2012, there will be a need for an additional 1.1 million special trades contractors.*
- *U.S. commercial real estate is worth approximately $5 trillion, including 4 billion sq. ft. of office space; 13 billion sq. ft. of industrial property; almost 9.5 billion sq. ft. of shopping center space; 4.4 million hotel rooms; and 33 million sq. ft. of rental apartment space.*
- *In 1900, 75 percent of urban Americans lived in rented apartments or flats. In contrast, U.S. home ownership in 2006 reached a record high of 68 percent. Housing accounts for about 15 percent of gross domestic product (GDP) in a typical year.*
- *In 2006, U.S. shopping centers generated $2.25 trillion in sales, and $124 billion in state sales tax revenues.*
- *The nation's multifamily housing provides homes for over 23 million households.*
- *There are approximately 200 publicly traded real estate investment trusts (REITs) in the U.S. today, with a total equity market capitalization of $312 billion (as of Dec. 2007). Tens of thousands of individual investors own shares of REITs.*
- *Spending by resident and international travelers in the U.S. averages $1.9 billion a day. One out of every seven Americans is directly or indirectly employed in the lodging and tourism industries.*

0.2 Historic Store of Value

The reason we are attracted to real estate stems from its combination of utility and its use as a store of value. First, it is an asset class that has historically provided inflation adjusted returns. Second, real estate investments have a low correlation with other asset classes providing good portfolio diversification. Third, in many cases our property investment gives us utility in our daily lives. You cannot sleep in a bar of gold, vacation in a mutual fund or house office workers in a municipal bond. You can do all of those things with property investments. Real Estate provides a unique combination of tangible and intangible benefits that have attracted investors for thousands of years.

Throughout history the ownership of property has brought with it unique rights and privileges. Owning property gave an individual the ability to grow and harvest crops, to consume wildlife, to drink water and to mine for natural resources. Wealth came with the ownership of real estate and many battles have been fought to control property.

In the past, in recognition of its unique value, many societies limited property ownership to the nobility and individuals of stature. Thus to become a property owner was a great accomplishment as well as a great responsibility. If the owner could not exploit the land efficiently there was always another party who would challenge for control.

Today, although the weapons used to gain control of property have become more economic than militaristic, the objectives are still the same: to control and exploit the land and its resources.

Limited Supply

According to the U.S. NAOA approximately 71% of the earth's surface is covered with water. Of the remaining 29%, much is inaccessible or undevelopable due to its topology or geography. Because of this, a limited quantity of land is available for development to serve a growing population that needs to exploit this land for living quarters, food and natural resources. The real estate industry concerns how we utilize this limited resource for our collective needs.

0.3 Rationale for Real Estate as Part of an Investment Portfolio

Income plus Appreciation

Many investors, especially those who are retired, count on their investments to provide them with income to sustain their daily needs. Real estate investments generate a stream of cash flow from the rent payments received from tenants. These rents are generally sufficient to cover the expenses associated with owning the property and to provide the owner with a return on the capital invested in the property. A successful real estate investment can provide the owner with a steady income stream and the potential for appreciation as rents rise over time.

Inflation Protection

Real estate is typically rented to tenants for limited periods of time. At the end of the specified period, the property is vacated and the owner looks for another tenant to occupy the space. This new tenant will pay a rent in keeping with the market at the time of lease. The same economic activity that drives inflation in the broad marketplace increases the demand for real estate and the rents that can be earned on a property. If prices of goods and services are increasing, rents will likely rise as well and even after paying inflated property operating costs owners will be left with a rising residual. Given that the cash flow from a real estate investment adjusts to mirror economic activity, real estate is said to provide its investors with a hedge against inflation.

Counter Cyclicality with Securities Markets

Professional money managers structure portfolios by allocating their capital across many types of investments. The different types of investments are referred to as "asset classes." The predominant asset classes used by most investors are publicly traded debt and equity securities. In the US the public securities markets are very active and investors can rapidly invest and divest large quantities of capital.

Investors add other asset classes to their portfolios to achieve greater diversification. The performance of real estate investments has historically had a low correlation with the public securities market. By allocating a portion of an investment portfolio to real estate, an investor has been able to improve a portfolio's return while limiting its risk.

In times of rapid economic growth, assuming a strong property market, the landlord has the ability to adjust rents upwards and increase cash flow. The ability to increase rent levels in response to inflation is a unique attribute of real estate investments and can preserve the value of property in the face of inflation. In contrast, higher interest rates increase the return expectations used to value many types of publicly traded securities and drive values lower. For this reason, real estate investments and publicly traded securities can move in a countercyclical fashion.

0.4 Importance of Housing to US Economy

The largest segment of the US real estate market is the residential property market, which the Federal Reserve Bank estimates as worth over $16 trillion. The US Census estimates that there are 130 million housing units in the country of which 112 million are occupied and 18 million are vacant. Of the occupied units, 75 million units (67%) are owner occupied and the remaining (33%) are rented.

The majority of U.S. housing units are single family units (90 milion or 70%) and the balance are either multifamily (32 million or 25%).or mobile/manufactured homes (8 million or 5%). At the end of 2010, the average American single family house was valued at $170,600.

The multifamily residential market, including properties housing more than four families, totaled approximately 21 million or 17% of all housing units. Over 85% of multifamily units are owned by investors and for this reason most analysts include multifamily housing as a sector of the commercial property market.

The vast majority of owner-occupied housing in the US is financed with mortgages, long term loans made to homeowners and secured by their ownership in the property. The mortgage market in the US totals over $13.7 trillion.

Since the Great Depression in the 1930's, the US government has supported home ownership with programs that make long term mortgage finance widely available. These programs insure the owner's timely payment of interest and principal on their loans. This government guarantee of payment makes mortgages issued under these programs attractive to investors. Securities backed by portfolios of these mortgages are known as residential mortgage backed securities ("RMBS"). The active market for these securities has provided large quantities of capital to support the growth of homeownership in the US.

Percentage of Americans Who Own Their Own Homes
As a result of the wide availability mortgages, many Americans became homeowners building equity in their homes as they raised their families. The percentage of American families that owned their own homes peaked at over 69.2% in the fourth quarter of 2004. This number dropped to 66.5% by the end of 2010 as a result of the Financial Crisis.

Housing Values
As many American's were building investment in their homes, the price of houses was also growing. As such, the American investment in home owner-ship became a critical store of value. In fact, the primary store of wealth for most American families with incomes under $100,000 per year is the equity in their home.

Wealth Effect
In a 1943 article the economist Arthur Pigou coined the phrase "the Wealth Effect", to measure the changes in consumption based on the change in the values of housing and financial assets. Stated simply, when asset values are high consumers feel wealthy and go shopping: when asset values are low consumers slow spending. As a result of the concentration of American wealth in home equity, the level of housing prices can dramatically impact

consumer confidence. When consumers feel less confident they limit consumption and as consumption falls, economic growth declines. Thus the strength of the housing market has become a great determinant of American prosperity.

Employment in Homebuilding

In the post millennium decade, America's population has been growing at approximately 3 million people per year. Given our average family size of 2.5 people, these additional Americans required approximately 1.2 million housing units per year of which more than two thirds or approximately 800,000 would typically reside in single family houses. To this requirement we must add new houses to replace the approximately 300,000 obsolete or destroyed houses per year. In years when the percentage of home ownership was rising we also needed to house families that desired to switch from rental units into single family houses.

Assuming that the existing housing stock was fully occupied and that housing demand needed to be satisfied from new construction, the annual demand for new single family housing exceeded 1.1 million per year. At an average price per home that was greater than $200,000 for most of the decade, for years we enjoyed a single family housing industry with minimum annual demand of $220 billion.

Economic Multiplier from Home Purchase

The rise in housing values helped many Americans to create personal wealth that they accessed by borrowing against their houses. This feeling of wealth combined with the cash made available from an active home mortgage market lead to increased consumption and helped speed up US economic growth. In addition, the demand for housing created a vibrant homebuilding industry employing millions of Americans to build, equip, furnish and maintain our nation's housing stock.

The economic activity created in the homebuilding supply chain and the ancillary spending related to homeownership results in an aggregate level of economic activity that is measured as a multiple of the initial housing spend. Sectors of the economy impacted by housing construction include manufacturing, real estate, retail, professional services, insurance, wholesale trade, transportation, health care and insurance. The total housing related economic activity divided by the initial purchase price of the home is known as the economic multiplier. Using a multiplier of 2.5 x, the single family housing industry had an annual economic impact of over $600 billion during its growth period which then ended abruptly with the Financial Crisis.

Continued Investment over the Property Lifecycle

As property ages it is subject to deterioration from wear and tear as well as exposure to the elements. Maintaining the housing stock is an ongoing cycle of repair and maintenance. Ultimately, houses age beyond repair and must be demolished and replaced. In the US, over 300,000 houses are lost each year to deterioration, obsolescence and casualty. This can create a base level demand for property construction even in periods of declining housing demand.

0.5 Value of Commercial Real Estate

To view the complete impact of the real estate industry on the U.S. economy we must also include the activity in commercial real estate ("CRE"): properties that are primarily used to facilitate commerce. Typical commercial property types include office, industrial, retail and hotel. Multifamily residential is also considered a commercial property type because renting space to individuals is a commercial activity.

The value of the U.S. commercial real estate market is estimated at over $5 trillion. This investment is financed by equity and debt capital sourced from domestic and foreign investors. The average leverage (percentage of debt to asset value) in the commercial market is estimated at 50%. Major sources of debt capital include financial institutions: commercial banks ($1.4 T) , insurance companies and pension funds that underwrite mortgages and lend to property owners, as well as institutional investors who purchase commercial mortgage backed securities.

The value of real property is directly tied to the cost and availability of investment capital. Commercial real estate had been the target of significant global investment in the early years of the new century, peaking in 2007. Capital availability for the commercial property market was then immediately and severely impacted by the Financial Crisis. As a result, in the period from mid 2007 through mid 2009, property valuations were estimated to have fallen by as much as 40%. Commercial property values have recently started to recover, especially in the top US gateway markets including New York and Washington DC. The recovery has been slower in most other areas of the country

0.6 Importance of the Real Estate Industry to the U.S. Economy

Value of Annual Construction Activity

Construction (1) is an important part of the economy, historically responsible for approximately 5% of U.S. total GDP. Construction activity has declined since the Financial Crisis from $657 billion in 2007 to $505 billion in 2010 as both the demand for new commercial space and the availability of capital to finance new development projects have decreased. It is estimated that employment in the construction sector peaked at approximately 7.7 million in mid 2006 or about 5% of the American workforce falling to approximately 5.5 million by the end of 2010.

In addition to the construction of new property, our commercial property stock requires constant repair, maintenance and ultimately replacement. Commercial property is subject to deterioration, obsolescence and casualty. Even in periods of reduced economic activity property owners must purchase the labor and materials required to service their existing properties.

Employment in Real Estate and Ancillary Sectors

The real estate industry employs over 1.9 million Americans in a wide variety of professional and service jobs to develop, manage and maintain commercial properties. Not including construction, in 2010 the real estate industry contributed approximately $1.9 trillion or 13% of US GDP. Unlike construction, this amount has been steady through the Financial Crisis.

Link between the Real Estate Industry and Other Economic Sectors

The residential real estate market and the commercial property market are influenced by overall US economic activity, which determines the demand for real estate. Real estate is a factor of production in our economy in the same way as labor and capital. The efficient use of real estate can have a major impact on business productivity.

Economic growth can also have a significant impact on the demand for real estate. For example, when the economy prospers and job growth occurs, demand for office space typically rises. When personal incomes rise from these new jobs, individuals have more money to spend on retail purchases, increasing demand for shop space. In addition, newly employed workers are able to afford their own housing and drive demand in the residential market.

The real estate industry also has its own supply chain, including maintenance firms, contractors, building supply companies and many professional service workers. All of these ancillary participants are impacted by growth in the real estate industry and generate economic activity by responding to the increased demand for the goods and services required to develop, operate and manage property.

Notes
(1) References to construction contribution to GDP and employment include activities not directly related to commercial real estate including infrastructure and residential construction.

GLOSSARY

(See web for definitions)

Alternative investments
Asset class
Casualty
Commercial real estate
Contractor
Correlation
Counter cyclicality
Debt capital
Diversification
Economic multiplier
Financial Crisis
Gateway markets
Gross Domestic Product
Leverage
Mortgage backed securities
Multifamily housing
Owner occupied housing
Property lifecycle
Residential real estate
Residential Mortgage Backed Security
Single family housing
Supply chain
Underwrite
Wealth effect

THOUGHT QUESTIONS

a) Upon graduation you join the investment staff of Northern States Pension Fund which invests the retirement funds of public employees in six states. NSPF has previously invested only in publicly traded equity and debt securities. It is now considering moving a portion of its capital into real estate. Prepare a brief position paper on the pros and cons of investment in real estate for consideration by the fund's investment committee .

b) You are a real estate developer in Seattle in 1980. You are approached by a group of young entrepreneurs looking to rent space for their new company. They tell you that they have created a computer program that can change the world. At the moment it only works on this new device called a PC which you have never seen. They suggest that you lease them space at a below market rent and take some stock in their newly formed company as an incentive. Their CEO is pretty impressive but is only 25 years old and by the way you have a mortgage to pay…What do you do?

REVIEW QUESTIONS

1) Which of the following is not considered a type of commercial real estate?
   a) **Single family housing**
   b) Office buildings
   c) Shopping Centers
   d) Hotels

2) If one million homes are sold at a price of $300,000 per home and the housing industry has an economic multiplier of 2.0x what is the total economic impact of the housing industry?
   a) $100 Million
   b) $6.0 Billion
   c) **$600 Billion**
   d) $6.0 Trillion

3) Benefits of investing in Real Estate include all of the following except:
   a) **Guaranteed cash flow**
   b) Income plus growth
   c) Inflation protection
   d) Portfolio diversification

4) The Real Estate and Construction industries bring all of the following benefits to the US economy except:
   a) Job creation for American workers
   b) **Stability for the economy**
   c) Modern infrastructure for industry
   d) Store of value for investors

5) Which is not a benefit of home ownership in the US?
   a) Creation of wealth over long period of time
   b) **The right to vote in local and state elections**
   c) Access to government supported financing program
   d) Potential for capital appreciation

Edward A. Glickman
Adjunct Professor of Finance
Leonard N. Stern School of Business,
New York University
President
Pennsylvania Real Estate Investment Trust

CHAPTER 1

The Real Estate Industry

1.1 TYPES OF REAL ESTATE

The real estate industry is generally organized by property type. The key distinction is between residential and commercial property. Residential property includes single-family houses and multifamily apartments. Commercial property is used for business and includes office, retail, industrial, hotel, and many special purposes such as laboratory space and telecom equipment.

1.1.1 Residential

The main residential property types are single-family homes and multifamily dwellings.

1.1.1.1 Single-Family Homes

The classic American single-family home is a one- or two-story building surrounded by a garden in which a single family resides. In some cases, multiple single-family units may share one or more common walls. These are called attached or semi-attached houses. Groups of these homes may also share recreational amenities.

Single-family residencies are typically owner occupied but may also be rented from a nonoccupant owner.

1.1.1.2 Multifamily

Multifamily housing consists of single or clustered structures that are divided into many separate housing units. Multifamily property is typically classified by structure height into low-rise (fewer than four floors), mid-rise (between four and ten floors), and high-rise (more than ten floors). The most prevalent form of low-rise housing in the United States is the garden apartment complex, in which a number of low-rise structures are grouped around shared recreational amenities such as playgrounds, pools, and community rooms.

In more densely populated areas, multifamily development centers on apartment house complexes instead of garden apartments. Apartment house complexes consist of a number of mid-rise or high-rise structures that are clustered and share amenities such as shopping centers, medical offices, and recreational spaces.

CONTENTS

1

In major urban areas, high-rise apartment buildings are the predominant multifamily property type. Where land costs are very high, building tall vertical structures can amortize the expensive land cost over many units. Although high-rise structures have greater construction costs, the higher value of apartments in major urban areas can support these costs.

Multifamily properties are also classified by form of ownership into for-rent and owner-occupied units. The most typical form of owner-occupied multifamily property is the condominium, in which the owner of each unit is granted a direct interest in the real estate. Another form of multifamily ownership that is less prevalent is the cooperative housing format, in which each occupant owns shares in a corporation that in turn owns the real estate.

1.1.2 Commercial Property
1.1.2.1 Office

Office properties are generally classified by type of location, quality of gradient, and tenancy. The key factors in determining the value of an office building are its location and its quality level. Office market locations are typically classified as being central business district (CBD) or suburban. Within most major cities, the CBD is further broken down into smaller submarkets. A large city may also have a number of distinct suburban submarkets. A submarket can be a very important factor, impacting property desirability. Submarkets differ in access to transportation, amenities such as shopping, restaurants, and cultural institutions and co-location with companies in similar or dependent businesses.

Suburban properties are also classified by location and quality. In many cases, suburban properties are either part of a planned development such as an office park or located in an increasingly common "edge city," which is a crowded developed commercial area on the outskirts of a densely populated urban core city.

The quality level of an office building is generally referred to with a letter grade of A, B, or C. The properties with the highest level of construction quality ("finish"), services, and amenities in a market are graded as "A." The typical "A" asset will have newly renovated elevators, lobbies, bathrooms, and sophisticated climate control and security systems. "B" buildings are yesterday's "A" buildings with nice but not state-of-the-art amenities. "C" buildings are not only lacking in a full complement of amenities and services but are typically in less-attractive locations than the higher-grade buildings.

Office properties are also classified by tenancy. Properties used by a single company are referred to as "single-tenant" or, if occupied by a number of different companies, "multi-tenanted."

1.1.2.2 Retail

Retail properties are differentiated by format and size. There are five common retail formats: malls, shopping centers, power centers, lifestyle centers, and street retail. Depending upon the size of the property and its complement of merchants, a retail property is classified as neighborhood, community, regional, or super regional.

Malls typically consist of two or more major department stores linked by indoor common areas featuring smaller specialty shops. The department stores typically offer a wide range of merchandise and are referred to as "anchor stores" because they are the key merchants. The specialty stores are typically focused on a single type of merchandise and are referred to as "in-line" stores because they line the interior corridors of the mall.

Shopping centers offer stores with individual outdoor entrances. In most cases, these stores surround an outdoor parking area where shoppers can drive and park close to the store entrance. The most common merchants in shopping centers are grocery stores and drugstores.

Power centers and lifestyle centers are relatively new retail property configurations. Both of these concepts offer outdoor drive-up shopping but differ in their lineup of merchants. Power centers are anchored by large-format, value-oriented stores such as Wal-Mart or Target. These anchors are complemented by a number of medium-format stores focused on a single merchandise category. Best Buy and Bed Bath and Beyond are typical of this genre. Collectively, these value-oriented stores are known as "big-box merchants." They are also known as "category killers" because their large selection of merchandise and aggressive pricing can kill off the competition in their merchandise category.

Lifestyle centers are outdoor drive-up shopping centers featuring a collection of specialty merchants that offer higher-priced products that help the customer achieve their aspirations. Many of these properties feature restaurants, cafés, and entertainment venues that complement the shopping experience.

Street retail refers to collections of stores located along a highly trafficked urban street. In the United Kingdom, these streets constitute the main shopping district of a town and are known as High Streets. In the United States, we generally refer to these shopping streets as Main Streets. Each major U.S. city has its well-known retail corridors: Fifth Avenue in New York City, Rodeo Drive in Beverly Hills, and the Miracle Mile along Michigan Avenue in Chicago are among the better known high-end shopping streets in the United States.

In addition to classification by format, retail properties are also referred to with quality grades using an A, B, C scale. "A" assets are market-dominant shopping destinations in major cities featuring the best merchants and upscale amenities and services. "B" assets are generally second-tier assets in better locations or the best properties in lesser locations. Merchants operating in "B" assets typically produce lower sales volumes than those in "A" assets. "C" assets are the second-tier assets in smaller markets and generally feature merchants operating at a low level of sales productivity. In many cases, "C" assets generally suffer from some level of functional obsolescence and deferred maintenance. Owners are unwilling to invest to upgrade these assets, as their limited rent revenues cannot justify high levels of ongoing capital expenditures.

1.1.2.3 Industrial

Industrial real estate is a broad category including warehouse, manufacturing, and assembly space. Flexible or "flex" space can combine a number of industrial activities, such as light manufacturing, assembly, logistics, and office space in a single property. Industrial properties can stand alone or as part of large developments with many similar properties known as industrial "parks."

In recent years, changes in manufacturing and logistics have affected the market for industrial space. Supply chain management including just-in-time inventory management has changed user requirements for warehouse space. Properties that host and facilitate logistics for today's best companies are highly specialized purpose-built structures employing sophisticated processes and systems. This change has resulted in the obsolescence of older space.

In a similar manner, today's manufacturing environment is much more sophisticated and environmentally controlled than in previous years. Many industrial sites from the mid-twentieth century suffered from environmental contamination and required significant cleanup as regulations became stricter.

BROWNFIELD RECLAMATION

In the closing years of the twentieth century, a new real estate field emerged, known as brownfield reclamation. The term "brownfield" typically refers to an industrial site that has previously been used in a manner that resulted in environmental contamination. Most of the reclamation process involves environmental cleanup and repositioning for a new use. In many cases, the new use is for a different type of real estate, such as the conversion of an old mill into a condominium or the repurposing of a warehouse into a retail center.

1.1.2.4 Hotel

Hotel properties are classified by location, intended usage, and level of services.

Resort hotels cater to vacation travelers and feature leisure amenities such as golf courses, tennis courts, and spas. These properties are typically located in a tourism-focused destination with location amenities such as beach or ski area access.

Hotels oriented to the business traveler are typically distinguished by level of services and amenities. Full-service hotels feature restaurants, 24-hour room service, concierge services, and fitness centers. High-end luxury hotels offer many ancillary services such as spas and business centers. Convention hotels focus on hosting meetings for large numbers of guests. In contrast, limited-service hotels may not offer any food service or staff assistance other than basic room cleaning. A limited-service extended stay hotel caters to guests who stay at the property for long time periods—perhaps a month at a time—and may feature larger rooms with kitchen facilities.

Hotels are one area of real estate where brand is a key factor in the tenants' decision making. Hotels are branded or "flagged" by a hotel operating company such as Hilton or Marriott. These companies manage many hotels and market their properties to travelers through proprietary reservation systems. They also provide operating, amenity, and service standards for their properties. In some cases, the hotels are owned by the hotel management company, but more often the hotel is owned by a real estate investment company that hires the hotel management company on the strength of its brand.

1.1.2.5 Other

There are many specialized types of real estate that have captured the attention of property investors. These include properties used by the government and its agencies; properties used to facilitate the hosting of data and telecom equipment; properties used in the health care field, including hospitals, outpatient facilities, medical office, and laboratory and research space; and properties being exploited for their natural resources, such as timber tracts and farmland.

The value of specialized properties is dependent on the performance of the industry in which they are used. For example, properties used in high-growth industries consisting of creditworthy companies can be more valuable than specialized properties aimed at low-growth industries full of troubled companies. Recently, real estate companies have been formed around laboratory properties used by the biotechnology industry and antenna sites leased to telecom providers. A change in the outlook for the tenant's industry can increase or decrease the value of special purpose real estate.

1.2 INTERESTS IN REAL PROPERTY

There are many different types of interests in property; each affords a different set of rights and responsibilities. Understanding the nuances of these interests is critical in determining their value. This determination of value is a predicate to creating any financial strategy involving the asset.

1.2.1 Real versus Personal Property

Real property includes land and structures that are affixed to land. Real property cannot be moved. In contrast, personal property is any property that can be transported by a person. Personal property can be viewed as being attached to its owner, rather than to the land.

Although the distinction between real and personal property seems clear and easily determined by common sense or observation, there are many instances in which we must rely on convention. For example, consider major appliances located in residential property. Most people would consider the heating system and central air conditioning system to be part of the real property. The distinction is less clear when we talk about window air conditioning units, dishwashers, and laundry machines. Are these "built-in" appliances real or personal property? If you tour a house and they are present, are they automatically conveyed to you when you buy the house? This depends on the law and custom in the particular locale where the home is located.

The characterization of property as real or personal has implications not only for the legal form of ownership but also for the tax and accounting treatment of the asset.

1.2.2 Types of Interests in Real Property

The ownership of real property includes certain rights and obligations. The rights include the ability to enjoy the asset, to exploit its resources, and to transfer it to one's heirs. The obligations include maintaining the property and paying taxes. The rights and obligations of property ownership can be divided among certain parties, each of which will have a defined lesser "interest" in the asset.

1.2.2.1 Fee Interest

The most fundamental interest in real property in the United States is a fee simple interest. The fee simple interest is subject only to the powers of the government. The fee simple interest includes a parcel of land defined as an enclosed shape drawn on the surface of the planet, all of the "earth" below it in a cone stretching to the center of the earth, and the "buildable" volume of the sky above the property. The fee simple interest includes the right to utilize this volume of space for one's enjoyment and exploitation in perpetuity. Any buildings and improvements created on this property are included under this interest.

1.2.2.2 Leasehold

A fee simple interest can be divided by its owner into lesser rights that can be granted to other parties for consideration. One way in which a fee interest can be divided is by time. The right to use a property for a discrete period of time is known as a leasehold interest. At the end of the leasehold period the property reverts to the original owner.

Leasehold interests can be subject to a myriad of conditions limiting the use to which any part of a property may be put, any changes to the property which may be made and the requirement to undo these changes at the end of a lease.

In a simple example, a homeowner may lease a room in their home to a student boarder for a period of one semester. In a much more complicated example, a rancher may grant a lease to a mining company to extract minerals from the land subject to environmental protections and the requirement that the surface be restored to its original condition at the end of the lease.

The holder of a leasehold interest is known as the lessee. The lessee's right to use the property is set forth in a legal document known as a lease. Under the lease, the property owner or lessor, grants the lessee rights to use the defined property in return for consideration. The most typical consideration for a lease is the lessee's payment of rent to the lessor. The lease will also document which party is responsible for the payment of property expenses such as taxes, utilities and repairs both major and minor.

At the conclusion of a lease, the property reverts back to the lessor. The lessor's property value includes the cash flow from the rental payments and the value of the reversionary interest in the asset, its expected worth at the conclusion of the lease.

1.2.3 Restrictions on Use

Governments put restrictions on land use for the common good. These restrictions protect the interests of society at large and of adjacent property owners against development which would limit their enjoyment or use of their property. Governmental restrictions on land use can impact valuation and can be contentious between land owners with competing agendas.

1.2.3.1 Zoning

The restrictions on land use imposed on landowners by a governmental agency are codified in a zoning plan. A zoning plan is a detailed map that designates restrictions placed on the use of each piece of property under a government's jurisdiction.

Zoning restrictions can limit the type and amount of development which may take place on a land parcel. For example, zoning may prohibit the construction of a warehouse or industrial plant on a parcel of land in a residential neighborhood. Zoning may also specify the maximum size of the house that may be constructed with limits on height and volume. The zoning regulations may also specify the "setbacks," the distance of any structures from the boundaries of the property.

In the United States, zoning plans are typically drawn by local county or township governments. These regulations are in turn subject to overriding state and federal legislation that can proscribe activities having environmental impacts that transcend local boundaries.

1.2.3.2 Entitlements

Land owners seeking to improve or build upon their land must present a development plan to their local governmental authority that outlines their proposed land usage and building plan. If the plan conforms to the existing zoning and other government regulations, the landowner will be granted permission to proceed. These permissions are collectively referred to as entitlements.

1.2.3.3 Eminent Domain

The U.S. federal, state, and local governments all claim the preemptory right to take property for their use from any landowner after compensating that landowner for the fair market value of the land. This concept, known as eminent domain, was first defined in English Common Law and is present in the Fifth Amendment to the U.S. Constitution.

KELO V. CITY OF NEW LONDON

In 2005, *Kelo v. City of New London* was argued before the Supreme Court. The City of New London had sought to condemn the house of Susette Kelo so that it could include the land on which it sat in a private economic development project. Kelo argued that the taking violated the Fifth Amendment to the U.S. Constitution, which includes the following language "nor shall private property be taken for public use, without just compensation." The city claimed that economic development, even if privately owned, created a public good, which justified the taking of the property.

The Supreme Court agreed with the city in a 5–4 decision. Commentators on the side of the decision argued that the taking facilitated urban redevelopment, which is a critical public endeavor regardless of the sponsorship of a project. The dissenting justices claimed that powerful private parties initiating development projects could unfairly influence government on their behalf and that the constitution should protect citizens against takings for any but clear public uses.

In a strange twist of fate, the proposed redevelopment failed to materialize, and as of the end of 2010, the seized property sits vacant.

---

http://www.supremecourt.gov/opinions/04pdf/04-108.pdf(sourced June 11, 2011).
http://www.archives.gov/exhibits/charters/bill_of_rights_transcript.html

1.2.3.4 Easements

A landlord may grant another party the right to access or transit its property in certain limited circumstances. These rights are known as easements. A typical easement is one that grants an electric utility the right to run a neighborhood power line across a property. In many circumstances, the landlord is required by the government to let certain utilities access its properties to provide essential services.

The government's requirement to let for-profit service providers transit private property without paying consideration to the landlord is an area of property rights that has been particularly controversial in recent years. For example, landlords have contested the rights of telecommunications companies to access their properties to provide services to the landlord's tenants.

1.3 FORMS OF PROPERTY OWNERSHIP

Real property may be owned directly by an individual or group of individuals, or indirectly through an entity created to serve as the property owner. There are a number of common legal structures that define the rights and responsibilities of owners under these structures. Rights to control major decisions regarding the operation of the property, its finances, its tax status, and the ability to transfer the ownership interests in the asset are all allocated among the owners depending on the type of structure chosen. Liabilities resulting from the ownership and operation of a property are also allocated based upon the ownership structure chosen.

The following subsections describe common types of ownership structures.

1.3.1 Direct Ownership

Investors can own an interest in property or in an entity that owns property. When an investor owns an asset, the investor is known as a direct investor. Investors that own interests in entities that in turn own property are known as indirect investors.

1.3.1.1 Single Proprietor

In the simplest form of property ownership, a single individual is the direct owner of a real property. The owner makes all the decisions regarding the asset, controls its finances and disposition, and accepts all legal liability resulting from ownership. Upon death, the property becomes part of the owner's estate and is transferred to the owner's heirs, subject to estate taxes.

1.3.1.2 Tenants in Common

When the ownership of a property is held by a number of different individuals, the owners are called Tenants in Common. Each owner holds a percentage interest in the property and its economic benefits and liabilities. The ownership interests can be transferred and pledged by the individual owners as collateral for debt. Property operating, financing, and disposition decisions are allocated by agreement either amongst the owners or to third-party agents hired for that purpose. Upon death, the property becomes part of the owner's estate and is transferred to the owner's heirs subject to estate taxes.

1.3.1.3 Joint Tenants with Rights of Survivorship

This variant of Tenants in Common is typically used when a property is held by husband and wife. In this ownership structure, each joint tenant technically owns the entire property (rather than just a portion of it as in a tenancy in common). Thus, upon the death of one owner, that owner's interest passes to the surviving owner(s) by law rather than through the deceased owner's estate, thereby avoiding probate and potential tax consequences. After the death of the last surviving owner, the property becomes part of the surviving owner's estate and is transferred to the surviving owner's heirs, subject to estate taxes.

1.3.2 Indirect Ownership

When a legal entity is created for the purpose of owning one or more properties, those properties are held directly by the legal entity and indirectly by their ultimate owners. The most common types of legal entities created to hold real property are the partnership and the corporation. Each of these structures offers unique benefits and implementation issues.

1.3.2.1 Partnership

A partnership is a legal entity created to facilitate the ownership of a property by a group of individuals. All partnerships have similar structural elements set forth in the laws of the state in which they are organized.

The rights and responsibilities of each partner are set forth in a partnership agreement. Partnerships are limited life entities and are dissolved after a specified period of time unless all of the assets are sold or a majority of the partnership interests change hands.

The liability for the actions and obligations of a partnership falls on its general partners. Their liability extends beyond their investment in the partnership to other assets that they may own; for this reason it is said to be "unlimited." The general partners are also given the authority to make all of the partnership's decisions, including asset acquisition, disposition, financing, operations, and management.

Partnerships may also have limited partners. The liability of the limited partners is limited to the amount of their investment. In return for limited liability, the limited partners give up decision-making authority to the general partners. A partnership that includes limited partners is known as a limited partnership.

Interests in a partnership are personal property and may be transferred. The transfer of a partnership interest is generally subject to the approval of the managing general partner.

The tax attributes of a partnership are enumerated in federal, state, and local law. Partnerships are generally tax pass-through entities. In a pass-through entity, there are no taxes paid at the entity level; instead, its profits, losses, and capital gains are attributed directly to its owners.

1.3.2.2 Corporation
A corporation is a legal entity that is granted unique rights and responsibilities by the state in return for paying corporate taxes.

Corporations are owned by their shareholders, who invest by purchasing securities issued in public or private offerings. The shareholders control the corporation by electing a board of directors that in turn selects the corporation's management. Investors in a corporation have no personal liability for its actions or its liabilities. The legal liability for the corporation's actions rests with management and the board of directors.

Shares in a corporation are nonassessable, meaning that the corporation's financial liabilities are backed solely by its assets. If a corporation needs additional funds for its operations or its growth plans, it can reinvest its profits, borrow money, or raise that capital from investors. If it raises additional capital in the form of equity, existing shareholder's interests in a corporation may be "diluted" by the shares issued to the new investors.

Interests in a corporation are generally freely tradable, although the investor may limit its right to sell its shares by contract. Although the investors in a corporation change over time, the corporation itself has an unlimited life-span. A corporation is dissolved when all of its assets are sold or liquidated.

Corporations are subject to "double taxation". They pay corporate taxes on their net taxable income and capital gains. In addition, individual share-holders are assessed taxes when a corporation elects to pay a dividend or when they sell their shares. Gains or losses on the sale of shares are based on the difference between the acquisition price and the sale price, net of transaction costs.

1.3.2.3 Limited Liability Company
A limited liability company (LLC) is an entity that shares attributes of both corporations and partnerships. The owners of an LLC are known as Members. The Members may elect for the LLC to be treated as a proprietorship, part-nership or corporation for tax purposes. It is typically utilized for closely held companies in which the owners desire the limited liability of the corporate form but the taxation of a partnership.

1.3.2.4 Real Estate Investment Trusts

Real estate investment trusts (REITs) are entities typically organized as corporations and limited in their investment program to real estate or mortgages. Like other corporations, they are controlled by their shareholders, who elect a board of directors. REITs are unlimited-life, limited-liability entities, and shares issued by a REIT are nonassessable.

To qualify as a REIT, the entity must be widely held with at least 100 shareholders, no five of whom can own more than 50 percent of the equity. The entity must also distribute at least 90 percent of its taxable "earnings and profits." If the entity meets these and other qualification tests, it may elect to qualify as a REIT. REITs are granted a tax deduction for any dividends that they pay, allowing them to act as pass-through entities for tax purposes. Dividends paid by a REIT are subject to personal income tax.

REIT securities may be issued in public or private offerings. Shares in public REITs are traded on major stock exchanges. The REIT has become a popular form of organization for large publicly held real estate companies in the United States. Many other countries have adopted REIT structures.

1.3.2.5 Real Estate Mortgage Investment Corporations

A real estate mortgage investment corporation (REMIC) is an entity that facilitates investment in mortgages and mortgage-backed securities. A REMIC invests in a pool of mortgages. The REMIC finances its purchase of the mortgage pool by issuing securities backed by the cash flows that it will receive from these mortgage investments.

The REMIC is a passive entity that fulfills the administrative requirements related to the assets it holds and the securities which it has issued. Asset administration functions are typically delegated to mortgage servicing companies. These third party administrators are paid a fee to collect mortgage payments and see that borrowers are compliant with the technical requirements under the mortgage documents.

The REMIC then pays out the cash received to the holders of the securities that it has issued.

1.3.2.6 Special-Purpose Entities

Special-purpose entities (SPEs) are entities that are generally established to hold single properties and isolate them from claims involving the owner's other assets. SPEs are used to protect an asset's lenders from claims made against the owner's other properties that could force the owner into bankruptcy. For this reason, SPEs are often called bankruptcy remote entities. The SPE also benefits the owner in that it limits liability claims that evolve from a particular property to the owner's investment in that property.

Many investors owning multiple properties isolate each one in a separate legal entity. If an owner has not already adopted this legal strategy, most institutional lenders will insist that it is adopted as part of any commercial mortgage financing.

1.3.2.7 Special Investment Vehicles

Special investment vehicles (SIVs) are a type of entity created to hold portfolios of mortgage-backed securities. The SIV finances its assets by issuing commercial paper and other short-term liabilities. The goal of the SIV is to own high-yield, long-term assets and to fund them with lower-cost, short-term paper. For the SIV to achieve its goal, the long-term assets that it holds must pay higher interest rates than the short-term paper that it issues and the long-term paper must remain creditworthy. During the financial crisis, many of the long-term mortgage-backed securities held by SIVs failed and the short-term liabilities that they had issued became worthless. This problem hurt many money market funds that were large investors in SIVs.

1.4 REAL ESTATE FUNCTIONS

1.4.1 Development

Property development is a multiyear process that includes identifying a site for a particular type of property, conceptualizing the way in which the building will serve its intended purpose, and securing the necessary governmental approvals required. The development professional provides project management services during both the planning and the construction phase of a project.

1.4.2 Construction

Construction commences when a site is prepared to accommodate the building of a structure. The level of site work required depends on whether the property contains existing structures that need to be demolished or terrain that needs significant preparation. This preparatory work also includes the creation of infrastructure to serve the buildings such as utilities and roads. Construction continues as structures are erected on the site and the interiors of these structures are prepared. Construction is complete when a local government grants a certificate of occupancy allowing the tenant to use the space.

1.4.3 Property Management

Property management involves the day-to-day operation of a property including housekeeping, security, maintenance, and repairs. The property manager is also responsible for the administration of the property, including billing and collecting rents and paying the property's operating expenses. The property manager may also provide accounting services, preparing periodic financial statements for the property's owners.

1.4.4 Leasing

Leasing professionals are responsible for identifying prospective tenants who require space for their store or business. They help tenants select a particular space that fits their requirements and negotiate the price and terms under which that tenant will occupy that space.

Leasing brokers typically work with landlords to identify tenants for their space. Depending on the property type, the leasing broker may represent one or more properties. Given their size, large properties including apartment complexes, offices, and industrial parks may have onsite brokers. Brokers who represent a number of properties held by a single landlord are known as captive brokers. The captive broker's goal is to direct the tenant to a property in their owner's portfolio. Independent brokerage firms may represent a variety of properties held by many landlords; their goal is to situate the tenant and earn a commission.

Some leasing representatives work for the tenant rather than the landlord. These brokers are called tenant representatives or tenant reps. The tenant rep may help the tenant find a single location or, in the case of a retail chain or multiple office company (i.e., a national law firm), represent the tenant in many locations with a number of different landlords.

1.4.5 Property Brokerage

Property brokerage involves the sale of investment properties. Brokers create liquidity in the property markets by matching buyers and sellers of assets.

The role of the broker is to analyze the asset in the context of the current property market and identify interested investors. Expert brokers assist sellers in determining the optimum audience for their asset. They can suggest target pricing levels and estimate the time that it will take for a property to sell. Brokers trade on their deep knowledge of the property market. They gain their market insight by studying transaction data and by meeting with property users to assess demand for various types of assets.

A good broker will help an owner understand the market value of a property and set reasonable expectations for sale proceeds. Creative brokers can visualize potential uses for a property that may not be immediately apparent and identify new classes of buyers. In difficult markets, astute brokers may help sellers reposition their assets for creative reuse and can help property buyers consider alternative property types that may fill their needs.

The broker organizes property data into a form that can be easily analyzed by potential buyers, creates marketing materials, and helps the owner identify and organize the due diligence information that will be required for an investor to complete a purchase.

The broker typically works on behalf of the seller to identify a potential buyer, although it is becoming more common for buyers to be represented by brokers as well. Because a broker typically works for a seller, when a broker works for a buyer that broker is referred to as a "buyer's broker." Buyer's brokers can help real estate investors identify properties that meet specific investment criteria or help prospective owners identify properties that meet their real estate needs. In many cases, a broker will be able to help the buyer arrange financing sources to complete a transaction.

1.4.6 Asset Management

Asset managers are responsible for developing and implementing a strategic plan that maximizes the value of a property. Asset managers evaluate an asset against the tenant demand present in the real estate market and perform a gap analysis to determine whether the property meets market needs. If the asset needs to be altered to better meet market needs and opportunities, the asset manager will develop and implement a repositioning plan. Once the asset is properly positioned, the asset manager will review potential tenants and lease structures. Asset managers will also perform an analysis of ongoing property maintenance and repair and upgrade expenditures. Asset managers also continually review the asset against the market to determine when to consider a sale of the property.

1.4.7 Portfolio Management

Portfolio managers buy and sell assets to form a portfolio that matches the requirement of an investor. Although this traditional arrangement is slowly changing, many real estate companies focus on a single type of property. This singular focus allows the real estate company to optimize its ability to serve the unique needs of its customers. Portfolio managers may work in a single property type or across a number of property types to create a diversified portfolio.

1.5 TYPES OF REAL ESTATE COMPANIES

1.5.1 Operating Companies

1.5.1.1 Developer/Owner/Manager

The most common form of real estate company is the developer/owner/manager. This type of company creates or acquires the real estate that it ultimately owns and manages. To fulfill its objectives, it is vertically integrated and performs a full range of real estate functions acting as a principal.

1.5.2 Service Companies

1.5.2.1 Brokerage

Real estate brokerage companies employ brokers who work with both buyers and sellers of assets. Brokers are required to hold a Real Estate Salesperson or Brokerage license issued by the state in which they do business. Brokers are paid a fee equal to a negotiated percentage of the sales proceeds.

1.5.2.2 Leasing

Leasing firms typically employ brokers who work with landlords to identify tenants for their vacant space, although they may also work for tenants. In most locations, leasing professionals are also required to be licensed. In general, leasing agents are paid a commission based on a percentage of the value of the rent generated by the leases that they conclude.

1.5.2.3 Property Managers

Property management companies provide outsourced management and administrative services to real estate owners. Property managers are typically paid on a monthly basis. They receive a percentage of the property revenues as a fee and are reimbursed by ownership for their direct costs, including the salaries of any onsite property staff.

1.5.2.4 Diversified

Diversified real estate service companies provide any number of real estate services under one organization. This organizational structure can address most of the service needs of the typical landlord. Smaller landlords benefit from the expertise and scale of an outsourcing relationship with a large diversified service firm. Larger landlords with sizable portfolios tend to create their own service organizations.

1.5.3 Construction Company

Construction companies plan and implement the construction of a property. They hire various subcontractors who specialize in different trades and organize and stage the work of these craftsmen to complete the construction of a building.

1.6 OWNERSHIP OF REAL ESTATE COMPANIES

1.6.1 Private

Until the latter part of the twentieth century, most major properties were in the hands of private owners or financial institutions. These wealthy owners were the only entities that could source the capital required to construct major projects.

1.6.2 Syndications

Prior to 1986, companies known as real estate syndicators raised equity through groups of unrelated investors known as syndicates. Syndicates were typically structured as limited partnerships with the syndicator, also known as the sponsor, serving as the general partner and providing real estate services to the partnership for fee income. Equity capital raised in the syndication was levered with bank debt to develop or acquire property.

Government regulations limited participation in publicly offered real estate partnerships to wealthy individuals who qualified under Regulation D of the Securities Act of 1933. These individuals needed to show either substantial net worth or a high level of continuing annual income. These regulations were instituted to limit participation to investors deemed to be sophisticated and less likely to experience financial distress in the event that the project offered was an economic failure.

Many real estate syndicates' primary goal was the creation of tax-sheltered income. Syndication was a very popular method of real estate investment prior to the Tax Reform Act of 1986, which limited tax sheltered real estate investing. After 1986, the syndication business went out of favor.

1.6.3 Public
1.6.3.1 REITs

On September 14, 1960, President Eisenhower signed the REIT Act and the creation of real estate investment trusts: companies that could aggregate property on behalf of public shareholders. REITS had tax benefits that made them almost economically equivalent to partnerships. With the advent of the REIT, the American public, including the small investor, could make an investment in large commercial properties.

REITs have become a popular investment because they provide a tax-advantaged and liquid vehicle for investment in professionally managed commercial property.

1.6.3.2 Real Estate Operating Companies

Real estate operating companies (REOCs) are public companies that invest in real estate without using the REIT structure. Many of these companies own portfolios of property that are tax efficient and do not require the tax benefits or want the operating constraints of the REIT structure.

1.7 OTHER REAL ESTATE INDUSTRY PARTICIPANTS

There are many financial institutions and professional service companies that support the real estate industry.

1.7.1 Banking

The lifeblood of the real estate business is capital. The banking system is the major provider of capital to the industry.

1.7.1.1 Commercial Banks

Commercial banks aggregate funds from depositors and provide transaction processing services to corporate and individual clients. Commercial banks are allowed to offer deposit accounts that are insured by the Federal Deposit Insurance Company (FDIC), a U.S. government agency. This insurance makes banks an attractive place to store capital. The bank invests a portion of its asset base in loans to borrowers in many industries. A large portion of commercial bank assets are invested in financing real estate construction and acquisition.

1.7.1.2 Investment Banks

Investment banks source capital from investors who are interested in higher returns than are available through government-insured deposits and who can take on greater risk in investing their capital. Investment banks link these investors directly with large corporate issuers of debt and equity securities through the public and private capital markets. In addition, investment banks fashion mutual funds investment opportunities for their clients from diversified portfolios of securities.

In addition to underwriting securities, investment banks create liquidity for the holders of securities by acting as market makers, trading securities, and taking principal positions. Many investment banks also provide investment advice. They advise investors on creating investment portfolios that meet their long-term goals. They also advise corporations on accessing the capital markets and on corporate financial strategy.

In recent years, investment banks have been active participants in the real estate capital markets raising capital for real estate developers and owners by issuing debt and equity securities backed by real property. The investment banks have been very active in the underwriting of mortgages and the aggregation of these mortgages into various forms of mortgage-backed securities. Investment banks have also raised equity capital to finance the growth of real estate investment trusts and other real property companies as well as selling interests in partnerships organized to finance development and acquisition of real property. Investment banks have also been active in the trading of these securities in the secondary market.

1.7.1.3 Mortgage Banks

Mortgage bankers specialize in the underwriting of mortgages on major commercial properties. They then fund these mortgages by placing them with financial institutions, including commercial and investment banks, insurance companies, and pension funds.

By limiting their focus to underwriting commercial mortgages, sophisticated mortgage bankers effectively match real estate investment opportunities with unique capital pools seeking those investments.

1.7.2 Professional Services

A deep pool of professional talent has developed to serve the many specialized needs of participants in the real estate industry.

1.7.2.1 Legal Services

Lawyers structure transactions in which real estate is acquired, developed, leased, and ultimately sold. They also help to structure the entities that own the assets and the relationship between these entities and their investors. Tax lawyers structure transactions in a way that is compliant with regulations yet tax-efficient for the investors.

1.7.3 Accounting Services

Real estate investments are transaction-intensive. Many agreements exist between landlord, tenants, and the real estate industry's supply chain. These relationships result in regular rent-, expense-, and capital-related transactions. Accountants process and aggregate these transactions on a monthly basis into financial statements. The financial reports prepared by the accountants enable owners, bankers, and investors to assess the financial health of their properties.

1.7.4 Appraisers

Investors and capital providers use appraisers to provide an objective estimate of the value of assets. Banks and investors rely on appraisals when making credit and investment decisions.

1.7.5 Insurance Brokers

Property ownership and management subjects the participants to a number of risks. Insurance brokers work with real estate owners to source and implement risk management solutions, including the purchase of insurance products, to protect the property owner against economic losses from these risks.

1.7.5.1 Property and Liability Insurance

Property insurance companies insure the property owner for losses from property damage resulting from natural or manmade disasters. Liability insurance covers the property owner for claims brought by those who are accidentally injured at or on the property.

1.7.5.2 Title Insurance

Title insurance protects the property owners against claims by prior owners. This allows for efficient transfer of title between contracting parties.

1.7.5.3 Personal Lines

Personal line insurers provide health, disability, and life insurance benefits to workers in the real estate business.

1.7.6 Architecture

Architects design buildings to serve a designated purpose on an identified site. They provide conceptual thinking on design and are trained to prepare detailed construction drawings from their conceptual plans.

1.7.7 Surveyors

Surveyors identify land parcels from maps and written description. They also create physical markers on the property by observing landmarks and measuring the land.

1.7.8 Engineering

Engineers are applied scientists who use knowledge from different scientific disciplines to solve real-world problems. Many types of engineers work in the real estate industry.

1.7.8.1 Civil

Civil engineers focus on issues in the built environment. Specialized civil engineers focus on the creation of public infrastructure such as utility systems (electric, water, sewer) and transportation systems, including road networks and traffic management.

1.7.8.2 Environmental

Environmental engineers work prospectively to assure that the built environment does not damage the natural environment. They also work to identify existing environmental damage and propose plans to extract or contain existing contaminants, making land available for productive reuse.

1.7.8.3 Mechanical

Mechanical engineers produce technical plans for the design and construction of buildings including structural elements as well as critical environmental systems. Specialized mechanical engineers working in the real estate industry include structural engineers, electrical system engineers, HVAC (heating, ventilation, and air conditioning) and vertical transportation engineers (elevators and escalators).

Glossary

(See web for definitions)

Appraisal

Brownfield reclamation

Civil engineer

Due diligence

Easements

Eminent domain

Entitlements

Fee interest

Functional obsolescence

HVAC (heating, ventilation, and air conditioning)

Infrastructure

Leasehold

LLC (limited liability company)

Mechanical engineer

REIT (real estate investment trust)

REOC (real estate operating company)

Reversionary Interest

SPE (special-purpose entity)

Structural engineer

Surveyor

Title insurance

Zoning

Thought Questions

1. Real Investments Co. is a pension fund management company seeking to diversify into the ownership of real estate. They have identified a portfolio of twenty properties located across the state of California. They are considering the form of the entity in which they will hold the properties as well as whether to create their own property management company. What are their options and what facts must they consider in making their decisions?

2. Lodging Co. is an owner/operator that has historically invested in mid-priced business hotels. In recent years, this has proven to be a property type with very volatile performance. The company is seeking to diversify its investments to include other types of property. Which other types of property should the company consider? If the company broadens its investment portfolio, what impact will this decision have on their operations?

Review Questions

1. Which of the following is not considered commercial real estate?
   a) single-family housing
   b) shopping center

     c) biotech laboratory

     d) office building

2. At which kind of retail properties can shoppers not drive up to stores?

     a) power center

     b) lifestyle center

     c) regional mall

     d) shopping center

3. Which of the following are not considered direct interests in real estate?

     I) Buying a shopping center

     II) Buying a share in an office building REIT

     III) Buying a 50 percent share of an office building

     IV) Buying a security from a REMIC

     a) I, IV

     b) II, IV

     c) II, III

     d) they are all direct investments

4. Jon intends to build a new convenience store on a property and operate it until he retires in 25 years. Each month, he will pay a fee to his landlord for the use of the land. At the end of the period, he will no longer own either the land or the building. What type of interest does Jon have in the property?

     a) Fee interest

     b) Easement

     c) Leasehold

     d) Syndication

5. Apex Office Building is a circa 1950 mid-rise office building in a rapidly improving commercial corridor in Big City. Which professional has the responsibility for developing a new competitive strategy for this property?

     a) Portfolio manager

     b) Asset manager

     c) Property manager

     d) Commercial banker

6. An office park property has lost occupancy because a large corporate tenant that had space in a number of buildings has decided to relocate to another city. The market for other office properties in the area is good and the property is well located and in good physical condition. Whom at type of expert can help the landlord?

     a) Property brokerage company

     b) Construction company

     c) Leasing company

     d) Law firm

7. An investor has just purchased the office building where her office is located. She is visiting her insurance broker to buy insurance for her new acquisition. What type of insurance is she least likely to buy?
   a) Property casualty
   b) Personal lines
   c) Liability
   d) Title

8. Which type of equity structure offers all of its investors the most protection against personal liability?
   a) Limited partnership
   b) Joint venture
   c) General partnership
   d) Corporation

9. A real estate company has an opportunity to acquire a large portfolio of hotels located along the eastern seaboard. The acquisition will require many different types of financing and sophisticated structuring advice. Which financial institution is best suited to this task?
   a) Commercial bank
   b) Investment bank
   c) Mortgage broker
   d) None of the above

10. Tenants are constantly complaining that the temperature in the office building is either too hot or too cold. Which type of engineering firm should the owner call in order to see if the HVAC design is correct?
    a) Environmental
    b) Civil
    c) Mechanical
    d) Biomedical

For answers to these Problems and Exercises, please visit the companion website: http://booksite.elsevier.com/9780123786265

Market Analysis

2.1 IMPACT OF THE ECONOMY ON THE REAL ESTATE MARKET

The space within commercial properties can be viewed as a product that is subject to market dynamics. Users of commercial space, also known as tenants, require space for offices, retail stores, warehouses, and many other purposes. Suppliers of commercial space, also known as landlords, create or acquire space to satisfy tenant demands.

2.1.1 Importance of Supply and Demand

When customers (tenants) require more space than is currently available in a market, suppliers (landlords) raise prices to ration available supply. If demand cannot be satisfied from existing inventory, suppliers turn to manufacturers (developers) to create more product. Prices stabilize when additional product is produced and demand is satisfied.

When tenants have a surplus of space, they generally attempt to give the excess space back to their landlords. The landlord will then remarket the space to others. If demand is insufficient, the landlord will decrease the price to attract new users. No additional product is requested from developers when the market is oversupplied.

Tenants acquire the use of space by entering into contracts known as leases. These contracts range in length from one day, in the case of a hotel room, to many years, in the case of many office, warehouse, and anchor retail leases. Long-term leases create friction in the marketplace by slowing the property market's response to changes in supply and demand.

The demand for space in commercial properties depends on the overall level of economic activity. Most businesses require space to house their operations, and as their activity level increases, so does their requirement for space. Simply put, economic growth drives the demand for space.

In many cases, the demand is satisfied from the existing inventory of vacant space in completed buildings. When this space is leased, the percentage of the available inventory that is in use increases. This metric is known as the

An Introduction to Real Estate Finance

occupancy rate. The complement of the occupancy rate is the vacancy rate, the percentage of built space that is currently vacant. The sum of the occupancy rate and the vacancy rate is always 100 percent.

As the occupancy rate increases (that is, the vacancy rate falls), rents rise. Ultimately, the increase in occupancy and rent levels encourages landlords to create new space. The price a landlord can pay for new space is a function of market rent levels and the landlord's cost of capital. When landlords demand space at a price that is greater than the cost of construction, developers can build new projects.

Occupancy and rent levels also set the value of property. As these levels rise, the landlord's earning potential increases and the landlord is willing to pay more for a building.

Economic down cycles can reduce demand for space and lead to declines in occupancy and rent levels at existing properties. As demand falls, the cash flow generated from a building and its market value fall. When the decline in value makes existing properties worth less than the cost of constructing new assets (replacement cost), the development of new properties no longer makes economic sense.

Developers are individual actors, each reading the market signals simultaneously. As a result, many developers will perceive the same market demand and seek to fill it without necessarily consulting other developers. Sometimes the banking system, which may have knowledge of many developers operating in the same market, will signal to developers that there is a potential oversupply of space in competing projects by rationing access to capital.

In some cases, the information is not shared efficiently and multiple developers flood the market with new space. The presence of the new space causes prices to drop, capital stops flowing, and development ends until new space users are found. The rate at which users take occupancy of the new space is known as the absorption rate, measured as units of space per period of time, as in square feet per year.

2.1.2 Global and National Economic Factors' Impact on the Overall Market for Real Estate

Although real property by definition cannot be moved, local property markets are nevertheless subject to many global and national influences. Global economic activity affects national economic activity through international trade. Increased national economic activity can boost local business and increase the demand for space. As more industries globalize, it becomes increasingly difficult to distinguish between national and global economic trends, as the impacts of both are now felt in local markets.

Supply is also affected by the level of global and national economic activity. Economic activity in other countries can have an impact on pricing of materials and labor and change the cost of construction. Many commodities required in construction such as steel and timber are sourced globally. Changes in pricing of these materials can impact the cost of construction. Economic activity can also increase the demand for labor and increase wage rates. Capital markets are also becoming global, and the cost of financing a property in any one country can be affected by events taking place far across the globe.

2.1.3 Local Supply and Demand: Determining the Micro Climate for Particular Properties

Although construction costs and the global economy can have an impact on property market dynamics, real properties typically find their primary market among users located in a particular geographic region. Multifamily, office, and smaller retail properties mostly serve local users; major retail complexes and warehouse spaces can serve a larger regional market. Hotels are unique in that although they typically serve distant clients, their demand is derived primarily from the health of the local economy and its ability to draw visitors.

2.2 ECONOMIC INFLUENCES ON SPECIFIC PROPERTY TYPES

As mentioned earlier, the economic health of the nation and the region set a backdrop for property demand. The general economy sets the tone for the real estate market, but principals active in each property sector—through interaction and consultation with economists, market researchers, and capital market experts—develop their own picture of the economic measures that are most predictive of their sector's performance. The following subsections describe a few examples.

2.2.1 Multifamily Housing

Historically, multifamily housing has been attractive to young adults, empty nesters, and those who have frictional needs while relocating or changing family status. Long-term users of multifamily housing primarily included those families and individuals that could not afford home ownership.

Job availability determines the pace at which adolescents leave their parents' homes. When unemployment and underemployment are high, fewer among young people can afford to rent apartments. Interest rates and mortgage availability then determine the rate at which they leave multifamily housing to acquire their own dwellings.

If the market for existing home sales is robust, empty nesters may return to multifamily housing after they sell their primary dwellings. Many enjoy the convenience and amenities of apartment living.

After the financial crisis, a new group of long-term multifamily users is emerging: renters-by-choice. The renter-by-choice has the income to support home ownership but after witnessing the housing bubble does not see the economic benefit of investing in a house. These renters desire a level of quality and amenities commensurate with homeownership and have led multifamily developers to build new communities catering to this demographic.

2.2.2 Retail Properties

Demand for retail property can be affected by factors such as consumer confidence, unemployment levels and credit accessibility. Consumer confidence affects retail spending, which in turn determines demand for retail space. There are many factors that have an impact on consumer confidence. Housing prices and the value of financial assets affect consumers' perception of their wealth. A decline in the perception of wealth causes a shift from discretionary spending to savings. Unemployment levels and length of the period of unemployment directly affect consumer spending. Also directly impacting consumer spending are the availability of and access to credit.

2.2.3 Office Space

GDP growth generally implies economic activity. There are numerous sources of GDP growth predictions. In turn, increased economic activity implies job creation. Job creation statistics are reported by the Bureau of Labor Statistics. To assess office demand, the analyst can multiply the changes in jobs by published metrics for square feet of office space usage per employee.

This formula is only an approximation of office demand, as many factors are affecting the amount of office space used per worker. Worker productivity, the number of labor hours required to complete a task, and telecommuting (working from home) are having significant impacts on the amount of space dedicated to each worker. These changes are having major effects on the demand for office space.

2.2.4 Warehouse Space

Overall levels of inventories and shipments of goods (measured by truck miles) are key indicators of demand for warehouse space.

Sophisticated logistics processes, including just-in-time stocking and inventory control software, have improved the productivity of the supply chain, increasing inventory efficiency and decreasing the need for warehouse space.

2.2.5 Hotels

The U.S. travel business is dominated by leisure travel, which in 2010 included 5 billion trips of over 50 miles, or 77 percent of all U.S. trips. Business trips accounted for 448 million trips or 23 percent of domestic travel. Though leisure trips outnumber business trips by 3 to 1, on the spending side, leisure spending of $526 billion is almost twice as high as business spending of $233 billion.[1]

The key indicators for business room demand are GDP growth and corporate profitability. In good times, businesses see meetings as facilitating interaction between employees and client visits and industry conferences as important tools for business development. Corporate travel executives and meeting planners pull back on hotel bookings when companies institute cost-cutting measures. Through web conferencing the internet can now provide a lower cost alternative to travel especially when budgets are constrained.

In addition to being impacted by the general state of the economy, personal travel has been found to be highly dependent on gasoline prices.[2]

2.3 ECONOMIC AND DEMOGRAPHIC ANALYSIS

2.3.1 National Economic Analysis

The country in which a property is located is one of its defining qualities. To consider an investment in real estate in any country, one must understand its economy and political structure, as both have significant implications for the value of your investment.

2.3.1.1 Metrics for National Economic Analysis

The most typical measure used to estimate the level of national economic activity is GDP, an inclusive measure of any country's total economic output. This metric is generally reported as both an aggregate—country X's GDP is Y billion dollars—or as a directional—country X's GDP grew by 3 percent in the third quarter.

Over the last 50 years, the growth rate of the US economy's real GDP has averaged over 3 percent per year.[3] Rates above 3 percent indicate strong economic growth: below 3 percent represents weak growth. Economists say that a recession occurs if GPD falls for two consecutive quarters.

---

[1] http://www.ustravel.org/sites/default/files/page/2009/11/USTravelAnswerSheet.pdf
[2] Canina, L., Walsh, K., Enz, C. A. (2003). The effects of gasoline-price changes on room demand: a study of branded hotels from 1988 through 2000. Cornell Hotel and Restaurant Administration Quarterly, 44(4), 29-37
[3] Real Gross Domestic Product (GDPCA). Source: Federal Reserve of St. Louis (FRED).

Other important national economic metrics include the unemployment rate and the inflation rate. There are always people out of work in any economy as many individuals normally switch jobs. This is called frictional unemployment. The US economy is generally considered to be at full employment when the unemployment rate is below 5 percent. An unemployment rate exceeding 5 percent indicates that the U.S. economy is not generating enough jobs to employ all of those adults that want to work. When people cannot find work, they lower their consumption and the economy slows.

The inflation rate measures the rise in prices over time. When demand exceeds supply, prices go up. Excess demand can fuel inflation. Demand can be created by rising income, expenditure of savings, and by easy credit. Supply constraints—for example, shortages of commodities and manufactured goods—can also lead to inflation. Governments try to pull back inflation by increasing interest rates to make credit more expensive and to limit demand. When the economy is slow, the government lowers interest rates to reduce the cost of borrowing and to encourage companies and individuals to spend.

2.3.1.2 Breadth of Economic Activity

One fundamental aspect of a country's economy is the breadth of its economic base. The world's largest economies, the G20 countries, are known for the breadth of their economic activities, which include a wide range of manufacturing, service, natural resource, and agricultural industries. Due to their diversification, these economies are resilient to global shifts in supply and demand. In contrast, many less-developed countries may be defined by a single industry. When the single focus of economic activity is on a product that is in high demand, the economy can be quite robust. For example, energy-rich states such as Kuwait and Qatar control significant wealth. Many similar-size countries that rely primarily on producing agricultural commodities are much less wealthy. Regardless of wealth, single-product countries are similar in that their economies are not diversified and are rooted in the demand for a sole product.

A real estate investment in a country or region defined by a single product will likely exhibit a covariance with the demand for that product. In contrast, the performance of a property in a major city in a diversified G20 country will likely perform in keeping with the overall economic activity of that country.

2.3.1.3 Industrial Activity
2.3.1.3.1 Major Industries and Products

In order to analyze the industrial activity in any country, it is necessary to identify the country's primary industries, the scope and scale of their activities, and the direction of their growth.

The Central Intelligence Agency (CIA) publishes *The World Factbook*, which provides a listing of each country's primary industries and agricultural products as well as many macroeconomic metrics on industrial production. The World Bank also publishes country data profiles, which provide basic economic statistics on many of the world's economies. The Economist Intelligence Unit associated with the *Economist* magazine follows 200 countries, publishing in-depth economic analysis. The International Monetary Fund (IMF) publishes the World Economic Outlook each year with data on each country's economy. In addition, the central bank of each country generally publishes information regarding its key industries and their level of activity. Collectively, these reports and statistics can help the investor assess the structure and performance of almost every economy in the world.

2.3.1.3.2 Concentration of Activity
Most developed countries are likely to have stock markets that trade the shares of larger companies. By researching the types of companies that trade on a national stock market, you will gain insight into the most important segments of its economy. A review of companies that are listed on these exchanges will give an indication of industries that are attracting or seeking capital.

2.3.1.3.3 Key Trading Partners
Once the industrial activity is identified, a review of the country's export and import activity can help to identify its trading partners and the level of activity with each partner. This information is helpful in ascertaining whether the economic activity of key trading partners is likely to affect the target country's economy.

2.3.1.4 Economic Advantages
A country's economic success is due to a combination of many factors, natural and manmade, that combine to give it a competitive advantage in the world economy. A country's comparative advantage comes from its ability to produce goods at either a lower cost or higher quality than its trading partners.

2.3.1.4.1 Climate
As man developed the ability to control the environment, the importance of climate has declined. However, climate is still an important factor in the success of certain industries. For example, climate significantly affects agriculture, is a key factor in attracting residents and tourists, and has influenced population movements in many countries—including the United States.

2.3.1.4.2 Natural Features
Natural features such as topology and navigable rivers remain important in defining the ease and cost of transporting goods to and from foreign markets.

Difficulty in transporting raw materials can increase the cost of production, making one nation's products more expensive than those of a competitor.

2.3.1.4.3 Presence of Natural Resources

The availability of natural resources can be a key determinant of industrial activity. Harvesting resources is in itself a major activity. Once the resources are harvested, there may be many advantages to collocating activities that add value to the raw material.

2.3.1.4.4 Availability of Water and Power

In many cases, access to power and water facilitate the exploitation of natural resources through extraction, harvesting, processing, and shipping activities. The availability of power is tied to geothermal activity, moving water, or the location of hydrocarbon deposits.

2.3.1.4.5 Presence of Skilled Workforce

The presence of appropriate human resources is a key factor in developing a competitive advantage. Many industries depend on pools of workers that have unique skills and process knowledge; other industries rely on the presence of low-cost laborers to create products at a lower cost than other markets.

2.3.1.5 Demographics
2.3.1.5.1 Overall Population and Growth

The size of the population determines the demand for many types of real estate. Fast-growing populations require additional space for housing, logistics, retail, and the like.

2.3.1.5.2 Births and Migration versus Death and Emigration

Steady population growth increases demand for goods and services and leads to economic growth. Agrarian societies require offspring to continue food production and support elders when they are no longer able to work. Countries with poor health care and high infant mortality require higher birth rates to ensure the survival of enough offspring to maintain food production. If countries with high population growth improve infant mortality, they can grow rapidly. In certain circumstances, this growth can create dire poverty; in other cases, rapid economic growth. The latter case has recently occurred in many formerly developing nations such as China, India, Brazil, and Malaysia.

2.3.1.5.3 Age Trends

Rapid population growth leads to a country with a young average age. Young populations require creation of new infrastructure including shelter, health care, and schools. If the country has the resources to employ their new labor, the population increase can lead to rapid economic growth. If, on the other hand, the country cannot utilize its workforce productively, then unemployment rises, often leading to civil strife and emigration.

Many industrial economies have birth rates below the level required to replace their existing populations. Low birth rates can lead to a population with a relatively high average age. As populations age, internal consumption declines and any economic growth comes from exporting goods and services. Many industrial countries with slow population growth are also concerned about the burden placed on young workers by the need to care for an aging population. These countries may need to import labor, and the new workers can benefit from utilizing the existing infrastructure and perhaps rekindle growth, which ultimately benefits the country.

2.3.1.5.4 Size and Growth of Workforce

2.3.1.5.4.1 Available Workers. The availability of skilled labor can create a competitive advantage in the production of particular types of goods and services. A concentration of labor with a particular expertise can lead to the rapid growth of an industry and its supply chain. This can foster regional economic development, including a vibrant real estate market. The financial industry in New York and the high-tech industry in Silicon Valley are great examples of this phenomenon.

2.3.1.5.4.2 Employment Levels. When employment opportunities increase faster than the population, the economy moves toward full employment and wage levels rise. Immigration of additional workers and the training of any underutilized workers already in the market combine to satisfy the demand for new employees. These workers demand goods and services, leading to further economic growth. Markets with full employment and expectations for future job creation generally require the creation of infrastructure and all manner of real property, making them highly attractive to real estate investors.

2.3.1.5.4.3 Skills of Workforce. In many cases, pockets of skilled labor develop due to the presence of high-quality educational institutions. The concentration of educated labor with marketable skills spurs entrepreneurial activity that creates economic growth. For those reasons, the regions surrounding major universities are hotbeds of economic activity as faculty and students launch new companies to exploit products and services conceived of in the academic setting.

Higher education is only one necessary component for robust growth. High-quality child care and elementary schools allow parents to participate in the workforce without interruption and facilitate economic growth. High-quality child care can also create the opportunity for children to begin their education at an earlier age.

2.3.1.5.4.4 Impact of Health Care. Another major determinant of the vitality of the labor pool is the widespread availability of quality health care. Easy access to care leads to a higher level of health and well-being, allowing for more productive workers who are less likely to lose work time to either personal illness or the care of sick family members.

The vital role that health care plays in employee productivity makes the presence of quality health care facilities an important consideration to companies when choosing a location for their facilities. It is also a consideration for families considering relocation.

2.3.1.5.5 Productivity

The combination of higher education, child care, and health care helps create an environment that maximizes the productivity of labor and industry. In turn, highly productive economic activity creates competitive advantage and leads to economic growth increasing the potential for a robust real estate market.

2.3.1.6 Economic Scale

When reviewing the economic activity of a country, one must develop a series of metrics that allows for cross-national comparison. The most widely used indicator of economic activity is GDP. In the United States, the GDP estimate is published by the Bureau of Economic Analysis and is defined as the "unduplicated—production of all sectors of the economy as the sum of goods and services sold to final users."[4] In short, GDP is the total output of the economy.

2.3.1.6.1 GDP

2.3.1.6.1.1 Total GDP. The GDP number is viewed both as an absolute amount, which in the case of the United States, peaked at approximately $14.4 trillion in mid-2008,[5] and—perhaps more important—as a time series implying economic growth or decline.

2.3.1.6.1.2 GDP Growth. From 1950 to 2008, GDP in the United States increased each year. The direction of an economy is a key factor in determining demand for commercial property. The fact that U.S. growth has been consistently positive over such a long period has been a key basis of support for using positive growth factors in property income projections.

2.3.1.6.1.3 Per Capita GDP. Per capita GDP, or a nation's economic output per person, is an important statistic derived from relating GDP data to population data. The absolute level of per capita GDP indicates a country's level of economic development and its capacity for consumer spending. The average

---

[4] A Guide to the National Income and Product Accounts of the United States BEA (September 2006).
[5] U.S. Department of Commerce: Bureau of Economic Analysis (GDP series).

citizen in a nation with high per capita income levels can provide for their daily needs and then have additional funds available for purchasing goods and services. In contrast, there are a number of nations with low per capita income whose average citizens cannot afford the basic necessities of life.

The feasibility of commercial property development depends on an assessment of the absolute level and direction of per capita income levels.

2.3.1.6.2 Productivity

Productivity is a measurement of economic output per unit of resource consumed. The most commonly reported economic productivity measurement is labor productivity: the economic output per hour of labor. In the United States, the Department of Labor's Bureau of Labor Statistics reports this information.

Labor productivity is a function of many contributing factors. The training and education of the labor pool combine with the quality of infrastructure that supports production to affect productivity levels. Recent improvements in process technology have had a major impact on productivity in developed nations.

Labor productivity as well as labor cost can combine to give a nation a comparative advantage in an industrial activity and spur significant economic development. For example, in the technology sector, Mumbai, India, has developed global comparative advantage in software development.

The presence of comparative advantage can be a key leading indicator of economic growth and real estate activity.

2.3.2 Regional Economic Analysis

Regional economic analysis applies the same general principles as those of a nation but limits the area of analysis to a particular geographic region. There are various ways to define a region depending on the purpose for which it is used. For example, the Federal Reserve Bank divides the United States into 12 regions, each of which is served by a regional federal reserve bank. The U.S. Federal Court System divides the country into 94 districts and the U.S. Office of Management and Budget defines regions as core-based statistical areas (CBSA) and reports statistics for 942 CBSAs within the United States. Each CBSA is centered around a U.S. city with a core of at least 10,000 people. At present, 366 of the CBSAs qualify as metropolitan statistical areas (MSAs) with populations of at least 50,000.

For the purpose of analyzing real estate markets, regional boundaries are defined by a combination of common geography and shared economic influences. In general, regions surround a core location such as a city, a cluster of cities, or a geographic feature such as a river, lake, mountain, or valley. To be a valid real estate region, properties within the defined area should be influenced by common economic factors.

2.3.2.1 Location of Economic Activity

A common factor that defines a region is the presence of major industries and institutions. Economic development tends to occur because of the presence of a source of abundant or unique resources, natural or human. The demand for the product or service produced and the competitiveness of the quality and cost of production can have a great impact on the economic health of a region and derivatively, the robustness of its real estate market.

For example, steel production in the United States centered around Pennsylvania and Ohio due to the presence of coal and iron ore. The steel industry created a community of interest, including universities (e.g., Carnegie Mellon) where process technology was developed, further enhancing the industry. The industry remained competitive until the 1970s when cheaper offshore labor and natural resources reduced the competitiveness of the U.S. product. This reduction affected the health of the U.S. steel industry and the supply chain that it supported. As a result, growth in the steel-producing regions decreased, and their property markets declined as well.

2.3.2.1.1 Major Industries and Products

Regional chambers of commerce and government economic development agencies report on the largest employers in their regions. These statistics can offer an understanding of the industrial base of any region. The growth or decline of these key industries and institutions can indicate the economic health of the region.

2.3.2.1.2 Concentration of Talent or Skill

Concentrations of individuals with complementary skills can lead to entrepreneurial activity and a vibrant community of interest around a particular industry or industry group. Often, these skill sets develop at local universities whose alumni or faculty start or feed regional economic activity.

The Silicon Valley surrounding Palo Alto, California, is a great example of how the presence of high-level intellectual talent can feed the growth of a local economy. Stanford University, which has a high-ranked engineering school, is located in the heart of this area; its graduates and faculty have provided the inspiration for many entrepreneurial ventures.

2.3.2.1.3 Presence of Natural Resources

The presence of natural resources is a major driver of economic activity. The mining or extraction of resources such as metal ores and hydrocarbons can create large-scale industrial activity. The processing of these commodities may rely on large quantities of energy. This energy may come from hydroelectric or thermal generation. The presence of water or naturally occurring steam can provide the unique concentration of energy that allows for the development of processing activities. For example, because of its geothermal activity, Iceland is the site of the energy-intensive conversion of bauxite into aluminum.

In addition to uses in production, water resources can also create recreational amenities such as lakes that lead to the development of tourism and ancillary service industries. Waterways also facilitate shipping of commodities and processed goods.

2.3.2.1.4 Regional Mobility

The ability to easily move goods and people into and out of a geographic region can determine its attractiveness as a location for commerce. Historically, many cities developed because of their access to waterways, which allowed for straightforward shipment of goods. Others developed at intersections of major land-based trade routes, sometimes at the end or beginnings of mountain passes or at the mouths of rivers.

Today, access to airports, rail networks, and highways can determine the attractiveness of a region. Corporate real estate officers seeking new locations for operations often factor in the variety, proximity, and cost competitiveness of transportation options.

2.3.2.2 Comparison of Region to Nation

2.3.2.2.1 Concentrated versus Diverse Employment Base

An employment base concentrated in a single industry attracts unique talent and resources that can bring about a competitive advantage. Regions with a single industrial focus, however, face the risk of rapid decline if outside forces diminish that advantage, as has happened in the Midwest as successive industries such as steel and automotive production have failed when faced with foreign competition.

2.3.3 Local Market Economic Analysis

Local markets exist within regional markets and the success of these "submarkets" depends upon the same factors affecting inter regional dynamics but on a smaller scale.

2.3.3.1 Location of Economic Activity

2.3.3.1.1 Key Employers

The location of key employers within a region determines centers of economic activity and commuting distances and times. Residential locations that are attractive and accessible to major employers have a competitive advantage.

Residents are also driven by access to schools, cultural and recreational amenities such as museums, theatres, and entertainment venues as well as parks, lakes, and other natural attractions. These amenities attract residents who support commerce and the demand for further development.

2.3.3.2 Population
2.3.3.2.1 Number and Growth
A key factor in assessing a local market is the size and the growth patterns of its population. A young growing population indicates a dynamic real estate market; a declining and aging population may imply decreasing economic activity.

2.3.3.2.2 Net Inward or Outward Migration
Looking at the number of individuals moving into or out of a region is a good indicator of future growth or decline.

2.3.3.3 Income
The income of a local population is a function of its workforce's skills and education as well as the types of employment available. Income levels determine retail spending, the types of products purchased, and the stores that will be able to operate profitably. Low-income areas are generally served by stores providing food, prescription drugs, and value-priced merchandise. These areas also feature basic services such as education and health care. Areas with higher income levels feature these goods and services as well as additional specialty retailers and professional services.

Income levels and population growth levels may not always correlate. Many areas grow by attracting industry because of their low cost of living and available low-wage workers. These high-growth/low-income areas have residents with limited disposable income and may be able to support the development of only basic retail and service businesses.

In contrast, fully developed areas with slow growth and a large complement of highly paid workers may have a large number of consumers with high levels of disposable income. These markets can have high market size growth (income times population) that is very attractive to developers.

2.3.3.4 Comparison of Local Area to Region and Nation
Assuming that one has the freedom to choose a location in which to pursue the real estate business, an analysis of the factors that promote economic growth can help determine the probability of success. In the event that one is constrained in choosing a location, or needs to reposition existing assets, an economic analysis of the marketplace can help determine the type of development that may be most successful.

2.4 GOVERNMENTAL AND POLITICAL FACTORS

2.4.1 National Analysis

There are many aspects of a nation's political institutions and infrastructure that have an impact on suitability for real estate development and investment.

2.4.1.1 Form and Stability of Government

The political ideology of a nation typically affects that government's position on private property rights. The stability of the government in turn implies the duration of the current ideological system. A new government initiating private property rights for the first time may be a risky proposition for investment until that government demonstrates stability. However, returns during this transition period may be very high. Governments with long traditions of respect for private property rights are typically safer markets for investment, but they may not achieve the rapid growth of a newly opened market.

2.4.1.2 Property Rights

Property rights include the right to purchase and hold real property. The rights accorded a property owner vary under different legal systems. These rights can include the right to use the property as is, develop it for other uses, or the right to lease it to others. These rights may be subject to numerous government-imposed limitations.

2.4.1.2.1 Deeds and Titles

Property ownership is typically recorded under a title system that documents ownership and precludes transfer of property without consent of the existing owner. The owner is said to hold title to the property, and this title is evidenced by a deed.

2.4.1.2.2 Free Transferability of Property

Once property ownership is documented under a title system, government sets the terms and conditions under which such ownership can be transferred. In the most liberal cases, there is free transferability of property. In more restrictive regimes, property transfer is also subject to government approval.

Many governments, including that of the United States, reserve the right to seize property for the public good or necessity. This is called the right of eminent domain. Government seizure of property generally involves compensation at market value.

2.4.1.3 Taxation
2.4.1.3.1 Property

Many governments charge administrative fees and taxes on the use and transfer of property. These fees can be a critical component of local government budgets. In the US, annual use taxes are assessed based on the value of property owned. These taxes are used to support the provision of municipal services. In addition, many localities charge a transfer tax when property is sold: if a property sale results in a profit to the seller, the government can claim a capital gains tax—in addition to any income taxes on annual profits derived from the operation of the property. Taxes can impact the profitability of investing in real estate in a particular country.

2.4.1.3.2 Income, Business Privilege, and Sales Taxes

The level of taxes can have a major impact on the ability of a country to attract and maintain businesses. The benefits of locating in the country must outweigh the added cost of operating in a high tax location. When the tax levels become noncompetitive, businesses leave to seek other locations. This is bad for the real estate market. Governments frequently use tax-based incentives to lure businesses to particular regions where they want to promote economic development.

2.4.1.4 Mature Financial Market

Commercial real estate is a capital-intensive business. Sophisticated property investors rely on debt financing. A critical predicate to mortgage lending is the presence of a legal system that recognizes and protects private property ownership rights. In addition to this system, the presence of the risk management infrastructure identified earlier is of critical importance.

Mortgage lenders can either rely on a local banking system to source capital for property loans or on the global capital markets. Countries that have restrictions against currency convertibility and free transfer of funds limit the attractiveness of their market to foreign investment.

2.4.1.5 Risk Management

One of the key underpinnings of a commercial mortgage market is the availability of insurance that will protect the owner—and derivatively, the lender—against the risk of loss outside of the owner's control.

Property and casualty insurance protects against risks such as fire and flood. Liability insurance protects the owner against accidents and injuries occurring to tenants, visitors, and workers at the property. Title insurance provides protection to the owner from other parties who make ownership claims against the insured property, such as when someone asserts a prior, unresolved claim against the land or building in which you have invested.

The presence of an insurance market infers the existence of sophisticated governmental infrastructure, from first responders such as firefighters and police to a system of recording land holdings and transfers. In addition to service provision, the infrastructure must include a court system where claims and counter claims can be adjudicated. Not all countries provide these services at a uniformly high level.

A lack of a functioning insurance market served by well-capitalized insurance companies and the ancillary infrastructure to support modern risk management techniques adds risk to commercial real estate investments.

2.4.2 Regional and Local Analysis

2.4.2.1 Structure of Local Government

Property development decisions depend on the way a country distributes rights to control land use between the local and federal government. In the United States, property entitlement decisions are generally made at the local level.

2.4.2.2 Legal Structure of Tenant Landlord Relationships

In the United States, local governments administer the landlord—tenant relationship and local laws and regulations set the balance of power between the tenant and the landlord. This is particularly true in the residential property market. In many U.S. cities, residential tenants are accorded broad rights and protection under the law, including in some cases limitations on rent increases.

In some other countries, local governments also exert broad controls over the residential property market. In most areas, however, these regulatory constraints are limited significantly in the commercial property market.

2.4.2.3 Land Use Regulation

2.4.2.3.1 Permitting Process

When considering a location for real estate development or investment, it is important to understand the governmental land use philosophy, the nature of restrictions in place, and the permits required to develop or renovate property.

2.4.2.3.2 Pro Economic Development or Antigrowth

Many local governments are torn between the economic benefits of growth and the environmental impacts of that growth. Unchecked growth into previously open space requires the creation of additional infrastructure and the provision of utilities. Increases in population require municipal services and capital investments by government. Loss of green space may be seen as diminishing the quality of life.

Redeveloping existing property for new uses may receive greater support if it can be shown that the creative reuse conserves resources. Depending on the location, local residents may desire growth or actively oppose it. This can significantly alter the course, and the cost, of a real estate development project.

2.4.2.4 Presence of Infrastructure

As mentioned previously, the development of real estate requires the presence or creation of infrastructure. First, roads and other transportation services must provide access to the site. Location near a major highway and access to public transportation can define the value of a project. Second, providing accommodation to workers, residents, and shoppers requires the provision of water, sewer, and power. If these resources are not readily available, they must be created and the cost financed by the developer or municipality.

2.4.2.5 Construction Market

Creating real estate involves the coordinated services of many professionals and tradesmen. The availability, skill, and experience of local contractors and the availability of skilled labor can facilitate development. The absence of these resources can make it more difficult and expensive to construct projects.

Finally, construction requires supplies of building materials. Materials such as steel are sourced on the global market and are subject to competitive pressure from demand in many countries. Other products, such as aggregates, have a low value-to-weight ratio and must be sourced locally. If this material needs to be shipped a great distance to the site, it will make a project very expensive.

2.5 ANALYSIS OF LOCAL SUPPLY AND DEMAND

Though subject to the broad movements and pressures of a global economy, the supply and demand for real estate is a function of local market dynamics.

2.5.1 Determination of a Property's Competitive Market

The first step in determining demand for any property is to determine the market in which it competes. The determination of a project's market involves an assessment of the project's scale and importance. For example, the market for a massive development such as Walt Disney World in Orlando, Florida, may be said to be national or possibly global. The project competes for customers on a wide scale. In contrast, most office buildings and retail centers compete within a region and probably within a submarket inside of a region. As a rule, major developments command attention from a larger geography and small-scale projects serve a local market.

The market will also be segmented by the intended quality level or "position" of the property. When building a new property, one needs a certain rent level to cover costs and earn a return on investment. The required rent level may serve to segment the market place. If one is buying an existing asset, one needs to assess whether it serves the broad market or a particular niche with unique characteristics.

2.5.2 Measurement of Current Market Conditions

Once a property's target market is determined, the existing properties within that segment can be identified. Local governments typically maintain public records of properties in their locale for the assessment of taxes. The local chamber of commerce generally maintains a census of commercial properties by type. Many large property brokerage firms and a number of independent data providers keep annotated databases of commercial properties.

Once you have gained an understanding of the market, it is necessary to gather metrics on supply and demand. What is the existing inventory of property? What are occupancy levels and rent levels at the existing assets?. Are there any trends that can be observed in the marketplace, such as declining occupancy levels or rising rent levels? When recent projects have been brought to the market, how fast have they been leased and at what rent levels? The speed at which a market is absorbing newly created space is known as the historic absorption rates.

If possible, there is no better way to understand a market than to drive through it at different times of the day, observing the flow of traffic and the different types of users who are present.

2.5.3 Determination of Future Supply and Demand
2.5.3.1 Supply
Once the present state of the property's market is understood, it is necessary to bring that view into the future by constructing a forecast. The first step in forecast is to identify competitive projects in planning and construction. This step can be accomplished by researching projects that have been announced in the press. Local government economic development and regional planning offices keep lists of development permits that have been issued. Bankers and real estate lawyers are also a great source of information on projects that are planned or underway in the markets.

Although not all of the identified projects will go forward, they can give you a good idea of the level of future construction that is likely to occur in the market. An understanding of building costs and rent levels required to support new construction can also help predict the likelihood of new market entrants. If market rents and occupancy rates are low, new projects will be less economically viable.

Understanding property obsolescence is best accomplished through observation. If an area experiencing growth has an outdated property stock, this indicates a market opportunity for either rehabilitation of existing assets or new development.

2.5.3.2 Demand
To evaluate the demand for new space, it is necessary to look at expected economic growth in the market and the potential obsolescence of the existing property stock.

Market growth is a function of many economic factors, including population growth and job creation. Major corporations expanding and new corporations and institutions entering into the market create a demand for space. Net population immigration, as measured by government statistics, is also a good indicator of growth. An increase in new residential stock, or permits for the same, and absorption of recently created residential units indicates a growing market.

2.5.3.3 Market Balance

The goal of our work is to forecast the forward condition of the market. This is accomplished by comparing future demand to future supply to ascertain whether the market will remain in balance, develop an oversupply position, or experience net demand.

A market with increasing oversupply is not a sound place to invest capital unless the intention is to apply a niche strategy. Growth markets are exciting, but timing is everything. If many developers or investors share your thinking, a flood of capital can push up prices of existing assets, encourage excessive development, and create a future oversupply position. A steady market can be good for real estate, as returns can be maintained and the threat of new entrance is minimized.

Once the preliminary assessment of the market is complete, there are many ways that the initial forecast can be verified. First, occupancy and rent levels at existing projects can be monitored over time. Next, the absorption of recently completed projects, if any, can be followed. Last, existing demand can be ascertained through discussions with brokers who generally know which tenants are looking for space in the market.

2.6 PROPERTY-SPECIFIC DUE DILIGENCE

2.6.1 Assess Market Dynamics

Economic, political, and market analysis at the national, regional, and local level help inform the real estate investor regarding the broad environment impacting property performance. The results of these "macro-level" inquiries inform investment decisions but are not sufficient. To complete the review, "micro-level" property fundamentals must be considered.

2.6.2 Review of Historic Performance

It is important that a property is acceptable to its marketplace or can be made to be so through improvement. To test acceptance, it is necessary to review a project's historic rent and occupancy metrics against those prevalent in the marketplace. If there are discrepancies, the causes need to be identified: why was the property under leased or why did it achieve above-market rents? Was there a problem with market acceptance of the asset? If so, can it be fixed? Does the property have an exceptional market position? Why does it have a good reputation and can the market position be sustained?

Once the asset's particular market position is identified, the next step is a detailed examination of the current rent role and tenancy. A property with long-term leases to high-quality tenants is valued for its certainty of cash flow. This type of asset may have limited potential growth because of its fixed rent stream. In contrast, a property with short-term tenants in a high-occupancy, rising rental market can be valuable for its growth. Each type of property will have different cash flows and appeal to different classes of investors.

2.6.3 Assess Expenses versus Market

In addition to understanding the property competitiveness on the revenue side, one must also understand its cost side. Is this property comparatively expensive to operate, and if so, why? Can this problem be cured through a change in operations, a technology retrofit, or other means?

2.6.4 Physical Condition

An accurate assessment of the physical condition of a property is a major determinant of investment success. Before purchasing an asset, it is necessary to perform an engineering and environmental inspection. The purpose of the inspection is to determine whether there are any deferred maintenance items that require immediate attention and to develop an estimate of the necessity and cost of expected future capital expenditures. Acquiring an asset requiring repairs is riskier than purchasing one that is in excellent condition, as any construction work involves uncertainty. This risk should be reflected when considering the value of the property.

2.6.5 Assess Availability and Cost of Financing

A large part of the cost structure of real estate is the cost of financing. The availability of financing can be affected by the market in which a property is located and the strength of the local or regional banking market. It is harder to finance assets in unproven markets or newly developing markets, and you may face limited capital availability and higher costs.

2.6.6 Financial Pro Forma

Once property operating costs are estimated, it is necessary to combine that information with a revenue forecast to develop a pro forma. A pro forma is a forecast done to estimate the future financial performance of a property. The pro forma can help determine whether an investment in property can achieve desired return levels.

2.6.7 Legal Review

There are numerous legal documents that define a property's relationship with its many interested parties, including governmental agencies and regulators, tenants, suppliers, and others. It is necessary to carefully review the contents of these documents, as they can have a significant impact on the operating and financial performance of a property.

Before acquiring any asset, it is necessary to review the title. The title reflects your ownership of the asset and any constraints on that ownership imposed by the government or through prior commercial agreements. Financial partners such as mortgage lenders will want to know that you own the proper title to your asset.

2.6.7.1 Outstanding Liens

Part of the work of an attorney in conducting title research is to identify any liens or claims that exist against the property. These claims can result from unpaid taxes or unpaid contractors who look to the asset as security for their payment. For these claims to have legal authority, they must be recorded in government records. A title attorney is hired to search those records and identify any outstanding liens. This process is known as a lien search. Once the search is completed, the buyer typically requires the seller to clear the lien or adjust the price accordingly. Once this is accomplished, an insurance policy is typically purchased by the buyer that protects the buyer against the existence of any other claims at that time.

2.6.7.2 Lease Abstracts

The revenue stream of a property is determined by the leases in place. These leases set forth the financial relationship between the landlord and tenants and may include many other provisions that limit the ability of the landlord to exploit the asset while the tenant is in place. These limitations can reduce the value of an asset and need to be analyzed in advance. This analysis is accomplished by having an abstract of each lease prepared and then reviewing those abstracts with the help of skilled legal counsel.

Glossary

Absorption rate
Capital gains tax
Comparative advantage
CBSA (core-based statistical area)
Cost structure
Deed

Deferred maintenance
Discretionary spending
Emigration
Entitlement
Frictional unemployment
Full employment
Immigration
Infrastructure
Lease abstract
Liability insurance
Lien search
Logistics
Market dynamics
MSA (metropolitan statistical area)
Occupancy rate
Process knowledge
Productivity
Pro forma
Property casualty insurance
Property obsolescence
Recession
Replacement cost
Supply chain
Title insurance
Transfer tax
Vacancy rate
Value-to-weight ratio

Thought Questions

1. You have just attended a real estate conference at which a famous private equity investor has made the case for investing in Brazil and India. Your fund is currently a U.S. domestic real estate investor, but you have been considering an international component as part of your next fund. Build a one-page analysis comparing the economies and political structures of both countries with the United States. What findings are particularly important to a real estate investor?

2. One of your top competitors calls with an intriguing proposition. He wants to sell you a great property at a time when the market is very strong and few quality assets are trading. The metrics for this particular asset are strong as well, but there is only one big problem: it is located in Grand Rapids, Michigan. There is general concern in the media and the property marketplace regarding Michigan and its economic future. Create a one-page comparison that looks at the economy of Grand Rapids, Michigan, placing it in the context of its state and the nation as a whole. What do you think of making a major investment in Grand Rapids?

3. The wealth management practice of your investment bank has asked you to open a client service office in the Washington, D.C., metro area. You will need 10,000 feet of office space. Identify three potential suburban markets and compare them to two submarkets in the area D.C. proper. Develop a one-page comparison of the markets and choose the one that you like best for your intended purpose.

Review Questions

1. The sum of the occupancy rate and the vacancy rate for the same property are:
   a) Always 100 percent
   b) Always greater than 100 percent
   c) Always less than 100 percent
   d) Unrelated

2. Which of the following are considered positive economic indicators for real estate?
   I) GDP growth
   II) Rising unemployment
   III) Rising consumer confidence
   IV) Declining corporate profits
   a) I, II
   b) II, III
   c) I, III
   d) I, IV

3. All of the following are indicators of a strong regional real estate market except:
   a) Broad industrial base
   b) Access to transportation
   c) Abundant natural resources
   d) High unemployment

4. Which of the following is false?
   a) Retail property demand is increased by rising consumer confidence
   b) Hotel demand is decreased by rising corporate profits
   c) Office demand is increased by GDP growth
   d) Multifamily demand is increased by job growth

5. Which of the following is true regarding economies that are heavily dependent on a single industry?
   a) Economic growth is slower than average
   b) Economic growth is faster than average
   c) Economic risk is higher than in diverse economies
   d) Economic risk is lower than in diverse economies

6. Climate, natural features, natural resources, and availability of water and power are examples of factors that determine a country's:
   a) economic advantage
   b) cost of living
   c) level of immigration
   d) political system

7. Which age trends are most favorable for economic growth?
   I) Birth rate < replacement
   II) Birth rate > replacement
   III) Average age increasing
   IV) Average age decreasing
   a) I, III
   b) II, III
   c) I, IV
   d) II, IV

8. Which factor does not contribute to regional concentration within a particular industry?
   a) Concentration of skilled workforce
   b) Location of relevant institution of higher education
   c) Availability of unique natural resources
   d) Geographic isolation

9. Good sources of real estate market information include?
   a) Economic development officers
   b) Regional planning officers
   c) Bankers and real estate lawyers
   d) All of the above

10. Asset-level due diligence for an existing property includes all of the following historic performance metrics except:
    a) Rent
    b) Vacancy
    c) Operating expenses
    d) Time to entitlement

For answers to these Problems and Exercises, please visit the companion website: http://booksite.elsevier.com/9780123786265

Accounting and Tax

3.1 ACCOUNTING STANDARDS

Real estate is a capital-intensive industry. Keeping track of the source, use, and productivity of the capital deployed is a critical aspect of any successful real estate investment. Property companies use sophisticated accounting systems to produce operating and financial statements for their businesses.

3.1.1 Dual-Entry Accounting

All modern accounting systems are based upon the Venetian system of double-entry accounting first codified by the Italian Friar Luca Pacioli in the fifteenth century.

When Pacioli wrote his treatise on dual-entry accounting, most Venetian merchants were involved in trading or banking. The merchant's investments were typically loans to traders. These investments were recorded as the "accounts of debtors" and were said to have "debit" balances. To finance these investments, the merchant borrowed funds from the nobility. Accounts representing amounts owed to creditors were said to have "credit" balances. The merchant's own account — the residual value of the investments, after all amounts were repaid to creditors — is known as the net worth account. This account also has a credit balance. Because all the loans made by the merchant (debits) were sourced from a borrowing or the merchant's own investment (credits), under the dual-entry system debits always equal credits.

Fundamental equation of dual-entry accounting: Debits = Credits

Although business has evolved, the basic conventions of dual-entry accounting remain the same. All accounting transactions are represented as combinations of debits and credits. Every time we record an amount of debits, we must record an equal amount of credits. This recording maintains the basic equation: Debits = Credits.

If an account has a debit balance, a debit entry to that account increases it and a credit entry will reduce it. The opposite is also true: if an account has a credit balance, a credit entry will increase it and a debit entry will decrease it.

An Introduction to Real Estate Finance
Copyright © 2014 Elsevier Inc. All rights reserved.

3.1.2 The Balance Sheet

Today, we refer to the holdings of a business as its assets. We refer to amounts owed to creditors as liabilities. The investment made or earned by ownership, the net worth, is referred to as owner's equity.

> Assets = Liabilities and owner's equity (net worth)
> Things owned by a company = The claims of creditors and owners

Even though the account names have changed since Pacioli, the accounting fundamentals remain the same. Each asset owned by a company represents an amount that either is owed to a creditor (a liability) or is part of the residual due to the owner (owner's equity). Following our fundamental principals, assets are always equal to the sum of liabilities and net worth. Because asset amounts are stored in accounts with debit balances and both liability and net worth amounts are stored in accounts with credit balances, the sum of debit balances always equals the sum of credit balances.

At the end of each accounting period, a balance sheet is prepared that lists the amount of all of the company's assets, liabilities, and net worth. This is a snapshot view of the company at a moment in time. By convention, assets are listed and summed on the left-hand side, and liabilities and net worth are listed and summed on the right. If all of the entries have been properly made, the sums will equal and the balance sheet is considered "in balance."

> Debits   =   Credits
> Assets   Liabilities
>   Owner's Equity

3.1.3 Accounting for Transactions

In business, goods and services are exchanged for payment. These payments are used to acquire the requisite factors of production (labor, raw materials, capital) needed to run the business as well as to provide a profit to the owners.

> Revenues − Expenses = Profits

In the typical sales transaction, an asset owned by the business is sold for cash. The amount of the sale is recorded in a revenue account and the receipt of the payment is recorded in the cash account. Because all sales are made on behalf of the owners of a company, entries in revenue accounts are recorded as credits. The cash account is an asset account with a debit balance. These symmetric entries maintain the fundamental equation of dual-entry accounting: debits equal credits.

SIMPLE SALE OF GOODS

Debit	Asset: Cash
Credit	Revenues: Sales

Once a sale is made, we must record our cost of providing the goods sold by recording a debit entry to the expense account: Cost of Goods Sold. The item sold must also be removed from the assets of the company. To do this, we make a credit entry that reduces the debit balance of the asset account: Inventory. Again, this maintains the fundamental equation of dual-entry accounting: debits equal credits.

Debit	Expenses: Cost of Goods Sold
Credit	Asset: Inventory

3.1.4 The Income Statement
At the end of each accounting period, all of the revenue and expense transactions are aggregated and summed. The difference between total revenues and total expenses is the profit earned. The results of a company's activities are reported on a periodic financial statement known as an income statement.

3.1.5 The Closing Process
The period of time covered by a financial statement is known as the reporting period. The income statement shows the results for business activities that have taken place during a particular period of time. The balance sheet reports the amounts in the accounts at the end of a period.

The first step in preparing financial statements is to sum the activity that has taken place in each of the accounts during the period. This is called taking a trial balance. Following the trial balance, a number of closing entries are made to the accounts.

The income statement accounts are periodic accounts that must be reset to zero balances so that they can be used to aggregate new activity. After the period has ended, each of the revenue accounts is reset to zero and the amounts are transferred to the income account (Debit: Revenue; Credit: Income). The expense accounts are also reset (Credit: Expense; Debit: Income) to zero during the closing process.

If the income account shows a credit balance (credited revenues exceed debited expenses), the company has earned a profit. If it costs the company more to sell its goods or services than it makes (debits exceed credits), the income account will show a debit balance and the company will have a loss.

Also a part of the closing process, at the end of the period, the income account is reset to zero and its balance is transferred to the owner's equity account on the balance sheet (Debit: Income; Credit: Net Worth).

The balance sheet is prepared after the income statement is closed and reflects any profit or loss from the period's activity. The amounts shown on the balance sheet are the ending balances in the asset, liability, and owner's equity accounts "as of" the end of the reporting period. Unlike the income statement accounts, these amounts are not set to zero. The ending balances in these accounts become the beginning balances in the next reporting period.

Summary of Dual-entry Accounting

Account Type	Location	Balance	Increase	Decrease	Source
Asset	Balance Sheet	Debit	Debit	Credit	Cash, property owned
Liability	Balance Sheet	Credit	Credit	Debit	Borrowings
Net Worth	Balance Sheet	Credit	Credit	Debit	Owners investment and profits
Revenue	Income Statement	Credit	Credit	Debit	Sales
Expense	Income Statement	Debit	Debit	Credit	Costs of sales, operations, and interest
Income	Income Statement	Credit	Credit	Debit	Profits

3.1.6 Methods of Accounting

Although all modern accounting methods employ the dual-entry system just described, there are different accounting standards in use. Standards differ in the type of transactions that result in accounting entries. Currently, most businesses in the United States use Generally Accepted Accounting Principles (GAAP) set by the Financial Accounting Standards Board, an association of Certified Professional Accountants (CPAs), as their accounting standard. Under GAAP, transactions are recorded when they have economic effect. Certain industries, including a number of private real estate companies, have histori- cally used cash accounting. Under cash accounting, transaction entries are made only when cash is exchanged. Many companies also maintain separate accounting ledgers for tax accounting. In tax accounting, the tax code determines when transactions are recorded.

3.1.6.1 Cash Accounting

Some real estate companies are run on the cash method of accounting. Under the cash method, transactions are recorded only when they effect the cash account directly – when cash changes hands. For example, revenues are recorded when rent and other charges are received in cash. Expenses are recorded when payments are issued. There are no accruals of revenues or expenses or attempts to match accounting entries to the period of economic effect. In this method of accounting, showing a profit literally means that money is in the bank.

The real estate owner, in choosing cash accounting has a primary focus on seeing what cash is available each month to pay the mortgage and is not interested in the more theoretical net income account as an indicator of profitability.

The major failings of the cash accounting method is that it does not account for either (a) amounts earned but not yet received or (b) for obligations that are owed but not yet paid. As a result, the cash method doesn't represent the fundamental economics of the business as accurately as the accrual method of accounting.

The timing of the receipt of cash payments impacts the results reported under cash accounting, which can lead to periodic returns appearing more volatile than then they would under accrual accounting. This higher volatility means that at any given time, cash accounting may not give an accurate picture of the long-term profitability of the business.

3.1.6.2 GAAP

GAAP is based upon accrual accounting. The fundamental principal of accrual accounting is that financial transactions are recorded in the period in which they have economic effect regardless of whether cash has actually changed hands. Under accrual accounting, revenues are recorded when the company has satisfied its obligation to the buyer, regardless of whether payment has been received. Expenses are recorded when the company has received the goods or services purchased, regardless of whether it has issued a check to its vendors. In this manner, the profit shown during each period will be a more accurate reflection of the economic activity that took place in the period but perhaps a less accurate portrayal of the cash flows.

Comparison of Accounting Methods		
	Cash	**GAAP: Accrual**
Revenue: Rent	When received	When due/earned
Expense	When paid	When owed
Income	Money in bank	Economic profit

3.1.6.3 Tax

Certain accounting transactions are treated differently depending on whether they are used to calculate taxable, GAAP, or cash income. For example, the US government encourages certain economic activities through tax incentives. One such incentive is to reduce the number of years in which various assets can be depreciated. By reducing the depreciation period, the amount of depreciation expense allowed each year increases, which has the effect of lowering taxable income. Lowering current taxes gives businesses an increased incentive to invest in the asset class with the favorable depreciation schedule.

These tax accounting transactions affect the GAAP books because they lower a company's effective tax rate and the amount of tax actually paid. As a result, there will be differences between the profits shown and the tax liabilities as measured under GAAP and those measured for tax reporting. These differences usually relate to the timing of expense and revenue recognition and will resolve over time.

3.1.7 Accounting for the Real Estate Business

Real estate businesses aggregate capital (Credit: Liabilities and Net Worth) to buy or build property (Debit: Assets). They can sell property outright and attempt to make a profit. The profit will be the difference between the adjusted cost of the asset and the net sales price.

The landlord can also rent the property: sell the user a right to use the property for a period of time (Credit: Rent; Debit: Cash). In the case of renting, the expenses are the costs of operating the property and paying lenders for the use of their capital (Credit: Cash; Debit: Interest and Operating Expense). If the company receives more rent than it costs to own and operate its property, it earns a profit.

Most large real estate companies, including all publicly traded companies, use GAAP accounting. Many real estate owners are focused on the monthly cash cycle: collecting rent and paying the mortgage. Some of these owners prefer cash accounting. All real estate owners must maintain separate tax accounting so that they can prepare their tax returns.

3.2 REAL ESTATE INCOME STATEMENT

INCOME STATEMENT

Period Ended xx/xx/xxxx	Net Operating Income
Revenues	Selling General and
Rent	Administrative Expense
Participating Rent	Earnings Before Interest Taxes
Reimbursement of Expenses	Depreciation and Amortization
Ancillary Income	Interest Expense
Early Termination Fees	Depreciation
Expenses	Amortization
Utilities	Earnings Before Taxes
Maintenance	Taxes
Insurance	Net Income
Real Estate Taxes	

3.2.1 Revenues

There are three main classes of revenues received from the operation of real property: rent, or the amounts paid by lessees for the use of a property; expense reimbursements, or the tenant's payment towards the operating costs of the property; and ancillary income, or income from the exploitation of the asset for uses other than the leasing of space. These revenues can include using the property as an advertising vehicle, such as selling the naming rights to a stadium, or earning fees from a telecommunications provider for allowing them to sell services to tenants.

3.2.1.1 Rents

By contract, rents are considered earned on the date that they are due. On that date, generally the first of the month, the landlord makes the following bookkeeping entry:

   Debit: Accounts Receivable
   Credit: Rent

When the rent payment is actually received, the following entry is made:

   Debit: Cash
   Credit: Accounts Receivable

3.2.1.1.1 Revenue Recognition

Lease terms on commercial spaces are quite complex and include both up-front concessions to incentivize a tenant to enter into a lease and escalating payments over time to compensate the landlord for the increasing value of the space. A number of accounting conventions attempt to allocate the tenant's total expected payment over the life of a lease to the accounting periods during the lease term.

3.2.1.1.2 Straight-Line Rent

The amount of rental revenue taken in each period is based upon the terms of the lease. If the rent changes over the lease term, GAAP requires that rental revenue be recorded using the straight-line method. The straight-line method averages the lease payments over the life of the lease. To do this, we sum all of the rent payments expected during the lease term and subtract all of the concessions made. This total value is then divided ratably over the term of the lease.

CALCULATION

Straight-line rent = (Total rent due over lease life less concessions)/lease term

In this example, a five year lease starts with a year of "free rent" which increases to $1,000 for each of the next two years and $1,500 for each of the last two years. The rent revenue recorded under the straight line method ($1,000/year) is the sum of all of the payments due ($5,000) divided by the life of the lease (five years):

Year	One	Two	Three	Four	Five
Rent (cash paid in period)	-0-	1,000	1,000	1,500	1,500
Rent (recorded under straight-line method)	1,000	1,000	1,000	1,000	1,000
Straight-line rent receivable	1,000	1,000	1,000	500	0

The actual cash received from the tenant will vary depending on the time period considered. Early in the lease, straight-line rent exceeds cash received. This direction reverses later in the lease. To account for the difference between the cash received and the straight-line rent, we create an asset known as a straight-line rent receivable. This asset typically builds in the early years of a lease and is then reduced as we receive cash in excess of straight-line rent toward the end of the lease.

When the straight-line rent is greater than the rent due in the period, we make the following entry:

Debit: Accounts Receivable
Debit: Straight-Line Rent Receivable
Credit: Rent

The amount of cash received will be sufficient to cover only the normal accounts receivable and the straight-line rent receivable will remain outstanding:

Debit: Cash
Credit: Accounts Receivable

Later in the lease, the straight-line rent will be less than the amount of rent the landlord will receive. The transaction entry changes to record a debit to accounts receivable that is larger than the straight-line rental revenue and the credit to the rent account is supplemented with a credit that reduces the straight-line rent receivable account:

Debit: Accounts Receivable
Credit: Straight-Line Rent Receivable
Credit: Rent

At the end of the lease, the straight-line rent receivable account goes to zero. If the tenant terminates the lease prematurely, any balance in the straight-line receivable account is expensed at that time.

Debit: Lease Termination Expense
Credit: Straight-Line Rent Receivable

3.2.1.2 Percentage Rent

Landlords may participate in the success of their tenant's business by receiving extra rent calculated as a percent of their tenant's sales revenue. The lease will state the circumstance under which percentage rent is payable. Typically, additional rent is calculated as a set percentage of the tenant's sales above a threshold level known as a Sales Breakpoint. Most tenants subject to percentage rent report their sales to the landlord each month. The additional rent amount is taken into income by the landlord on a monthly basis once the tenant sales exceed the Sales Breakpoint.

CALCULATION

Each month : Cumulative sales = Prior month's cumulative sales plus monthly sales

In the first month of a year during which cumulative sales exceed the sales breakpoint:

Percentage rent due = (Cumulative sales−Sales breakpoint) ∗ Participation percentage

In this month, percentage rent is payable only on the amount by which cumulative sales exceeds the breakpoint.

In all remaining months of the same year, because the breakpoint has already been reached, all additional sales are subject to percentage rent:

Percentage rent due = (Monthly sales ∗ Participation percentage)

In the following year, the tenant's cumulative sales counter is reset to zero and the testing begins again.

Entries made when the landlord bills for percentage rent are as follows:

Debit: Percentage Rent Receivable
Credit: Percentage Rent

When the tenant's check is received:

Debit:　　Cash
Credit:　　Percentage Rent Receivable

In certain cases, the percentage rent is paid and calculated only once a year. If sales exceed the threshold amount, a participation percentage is applied to the excess and the amount is billed to the tenant. The same accounting entries are used.

3.2.1.2.1 Natural Breakpoint

When the sales breakpoint is equal to the annual base rent divided by the sales participation percentage, the breakpoint is known as a natural breakpoint. Leasing agents refer to a lease as having an *X percent participation above a natural break*, meaning that the sales threshold is the annual base rent divided by X percent and the tenant will pay as additional rent X percent of any sales above that amount.

EXAMPLE OF PERCENTAGE RENT OVER A NATURAL BREAKPOINT

Store X pays $90,000 per year in base rent. In addition, the tenant pays percentage rent of 6 percent above a natural breakpoint. This year sales are expected to be $2.0 million. What percentage rent is due?

$$\text{Natural breakpoint} = \text{Rent/Participation percentage} = \$90,000/.06 = \$1,500,000$$

$$\text{Percentage rent} = \text{Participation percentage} * (\text{Sales} - \text{breakpoint}) =$$

$$0.06 * (\$2,000,000 - \$1,500,000) = 0.06 * \$500,000 = \$30,000$$

3.2.1.3 Expense Reimbursements

In many cases, tenants are expected to cover part or all of the operating expenses associated with the property that they occupy. These costs include amounts needed to cover the operation of the tenant's own space as well as a contribution to the cost of the common area of the building called Common Area Maintenance (CAM).

From the landlord's perspective, the receipt of these operating expense reimbursement payments are treated as income in the period received.

When the property is a large multi-tenant building, it is difficult for the landlord to calculate and bill each tenant for each cost of operation each month. In most cases, the tenant is billed a fixed monthly amount based on an annual operating cost estimate.

This estimate is then reconciled at the end of each year to the actual incurred operating costs. This process results in a "true up" payment due from or to the tenant.

If the expense reimbursement payment is based upon an estimate, the landlord will bill the tenant a set amount at the beginning of each month. That amount is recorded as a receivable and is then relieved on receipt of the tenant's check:

Debit: Accounts Receivable
Credit: Expense Reimbursement Revenue

Upon receipt of the payment:

Debit: Cash
Credit: Accounts Receivable

3.2.1.3.1 Common Area Maintenance (CAM) Reconciliation

Many tenants are responsible for reimbursing the landlord for their pro rata share of CAM expenses. Because the landlord typically bills the tenant monthly based on an annual cost estimate, once a year the landlord prepares an accounting of the true costs as incurred and presents the tenant with a reconciliation of their CAM account. This reconciliation may result in an adjustment in either the tenant's or the landlord's favor.

3.2.1.3.2 Alternative Expense Reimbursement Methods

In some cases, operating costs are included in a single rent figure charged to the tenant, which is known as a gross lease, and part of the rent charged must be used to cover the property operating expenses. Similarly, some landlords have offered leases with predetermined expense reimbursement levels. These leases are known as flat CAM leases. Under both gross and flat CAM leases, the landlord absorbs the economic risk that the actual CAM expense will be more than the amount billed (or allocated). An additional benefit of these methods is that expense reconciliation becomes unnecessary.

Another common concept is the inclusion of a "base-year" expense level in the initial rent quoted in the lease. To the extent that the actual CAM exceeds the base-year cost, the tenant is billed for the difference. The amount of expenses included in the base year is called the expense stop:

$$\text{Tenant CAM charge} = \text{Actual CAM} - \text{Expense stop}$$

Tenants that are focused on managing cost but unable to negotiate for a form of lease with fixed expenses may attempt to negotiate for a limit or "cap" on expenses. Expense caps can take many forms. One common form is to limit the amount of expenses charged to the tenant during the current lease term to a set amount. Another is to limit any increases to the change in an objective measure such as the CPI. In both cases, the expenses charged will be the lesser of the actual expenses or the capped amount.

3.2.1.4 Ancillary Income

Ancillary income can come from multiple sources, depending on the type of transactions that the landlord has constructed. In general, these transactions are accounted for as follows:

    Debit: Cash
    Credit: Ancillary Income

3.2.1.5 Early Termination Fees

In some cases, tenants who leave prematurely by their own choice are responsible for paying the landlord an early termination fee. Early termination fees depend on the remaining lease term. They are typically set to compensate the landlord for the expense of releasing the space as well as the lost revenue from having the space remain vacant for a period of time while it is released. This fee is typically taken into income when received.

3.2.2 Expenses

Typical property expenses include utilities (power, water, sewer); maintenance (housekeeping and minor repairs); security (guards and alarm systems); insurance (property, casualty, and liability); and real estate taxes.

Most utility expenses are billed by the vendor on a monthly basis. Maintenance expenses may be billed monthly or as incurred. In either case, when the bill is received, it is recorded as an expense and an account payable is entered to show that the amount must be paid to the vendor.

    Debit: Expense
    Credit: Accounts Payable

When the check is issued, the cash account is decreased (credited) and accounts payable is reduced (debited):

    Debit: Accounts Payable
    Credit: Cash

3.2.2.1 Prepaid and Accrued Expenses

Some expenses, such as insurance, are paid in advance. In this case, a prepaid expense asset account will be created representing the unused or "prepaid" amount of the expense.

    Debit: Prepaid Expense
    Credit: Accounts Payable

When the check is issued, the cash account is decreased (credited) and accounts payable is reduced (debited):

Debit: Accounts Payable
Credit: Cash

Each month as a portion of the prepaid expense is used, the prepaid expense account is reduced (credited) and the expense account is increased (debited):

Debit: Expense
Credit: Prepaid Expense

Providers sometimes bill for goods and services long after they are delivered. In this case, the recipient (the property company) will have to record the expense (debit) and construct a placeholder entry into an accrued expense (credit) account until the invoice arrives:

Debit: Expense
Credit: Accrued Expense

When the invoice arrives, we create an accounts payable (credit) and reduce the accrued expense (debit). When the check is issued, the cash account is decreased (credited) and accounts payable is reduced (debited):

Debit: Accrued Expense
Credit: Accounts Payable

Debit: Accounts Payable
Credit: Cash

3.2.3 Net Operating Income

At the end of each period, the revenue accounts are "closed out" into net operating income (NOI). When an account is closed, its balance is moved into another account and set back to zero. This occurs with the following entry:

Debit: Revenue
Credit: NOI

In a similar manner, expense accounts are closed into net operating income:

Debit: NOI
Credit: Expense

If the account are profitable and revenues exceed expenses, NOI will have a credit balance.

3.2.3.1 Selling, General and Administrative Expense

NOI represents the property level profit. From this we must subtract the costs of managing the assets and the enterprise. These costs are recorded in the selling, general, and administrative expense account (SG&A). These costs include salaries, benefits, and the costs of office overhead, including rent, business supplies, and telecom:

Debit: SG&A Expense
Credit: Accounts Payable

When the SG&A expense is paid (check is issued), the cash account is decreased (credited) and accounts payable is reduced (debited):

Debit: Accounts Payable
Credit: Cash

3.2.3.2 Management Fees

In some cases, property owners outsource management to a third party and incur a management fee instead of the direct costs discussed above. Management fees are typically paid monthly and calculated as a percentage of the property's gross revenue:

Debit: Management Fee
Credit: Accounts Payable

When the management fee is paid (check is issued), the cash account is credited and accounts payable is reduced (debited):

Debit: Accounts Payable
Credit: Cash

3.2.4 Earnings Before Interest Taxes, Depreciation, and Amortization

At the end of each period, NOI and SG&A are closed into Earnings Before Interest Taxes, Depreciation, and Amortization (EBITDA). This metric is important because it represents the return on the property investment independent of the manner in which it is financed:

Debit: NOI
Credit: EBITDA

In the event that we have a net operating loss (NOL), the entry is reversed:

Debit: EBITDA
Credit: NOL

In either case, we close out the SG&A expense or management fee account:

Debit: EBITDA
Credit: SG&A Expense (or management fee)

If NOI exceeds the cost of operating both the properties and the enterprise, then EBITDA is positive (credit balance); if not, we have a loss (debit balance).

3.2.5 Amortization of Capitalized Costs

In addition to the costs of operating the properties, landlords face costs to identify tenants, to negotiate lease agreements, and then to prepare the space for use by the new occupants. Although these costs must be paid in advance of the tenant's occupying the space, they benefit the landlord over the entire period of the lease. As prepaid expenses that create value for the company for a period greater than one year, these costs are capitalized (recorded as assets). The asset is then amortized, or taken as an expense ratably over its useful life:

Debit: Amortization Expense
Credit: Asset Account

This is an example of the "matching principle" of accrual accounting, as the expense is moved from the period when it is paid with cash into the periods when it has economic effect.

3.2.5.1 Leasing Commissions

Fees paid to real estate brokers for identifying tenants and negotiating the business terms of the leases are called leasing commissions. They are typically structured as a percentage of the aggregate revenue payable to the landlord over the term of the lease. Commissions are generally paid at the beginning of the lease term, but they benefit the landlord over the term of the lease. They are capitalized when incurred and amortized over the life of the lease:

Debit: Leasing Commissions
Credit: Cash

Amortization during each period of occupancy:

Debit: Amortization: Leasing Commission
Credit: Leasing Commissions

3.2.5.2 Tenant Allowances

The costs of preparing space for new occupants are known as tenant allowances and are denominated in dollars per square foot. These costs are incurred prior to occupancy but bring benefits to the landlord over the life of the lease. As these expenses bring benefits in more than one year, they are considered capital expenditures. Amounts spent are added to the property investment account and then amortized over the life of the lease:

Debit: Tenant Allowance
Credit: Cash

During each period of occupancy:

Debit: Amortization: Tenant Allowance
Credit: Tenant Allowance

In the event that a tenant leaves before the full amount of either the leasing commission or the tenant allowance has been amortized, any remaining amounts are taken as a lump sum expense during the period in which the tenant vacates the property:

Debit: Amortization: Leasing Commission
Debit: Amortization: Tenant Allowance
Credit: Leasing Commission
Credit: Tenant Allowance

The early termination fee, if any, received by the landlord may mitigate these expenses.

Debit: Cash
Credit: Revenue: Early Termination Fees

3.2.5.3 Depreciation

Property assets other than land are assumed to physically deteriorate over time. Accounting principles reflect this continuing diminishment in value as an expense in each period that the asset is owned by taking a percentage of the building value as a depreciation expense each period. Each period, we reduce the amount of our investment by the amount of depreciation taken. At the end of its useful life, the only remaining amount of our property investment will be the amount allocated to the value of the land component of the property's original purchase price.

Because it is not possible to know the actual time that it will take for any building to fully depreciate, accountants use a standard depreciable life depending on property type, which is currently set by the Internal Revenue Service at 27.5 years for residential property and 39 years for commercial property. To calculate the depreciation expense for any period, a portion of the asset purchase price is first allocated to the value of the land acquired, as land does not depreciate. The remainder (the amount allocated to the improvements) is divided by the depreciable life; this is the amount of annual depreciation. A company takes a depreciation expense in each period based on the length of time contained in the financial statements.

In order to retain the original cost of our property investments, accountants do not reduce the original historical cost of the investment in real estate accounts for each depreciation charge. Instead, depreciation expense is added to an account called accumulated depreciation. Accumulated depreciation is then reported as a special kind of account known as a contra asset. This account has a credit balance and is shown on the balance sheet as reducing the balance of a depreciable asset account.

The bookkeeping entry for depreciation in each period is:

Debit: Depreciation Expense
Credit: Accumulated Depreciation

The balance sheet presentation of these accounts is typically:

Investment in Property at Cost
(Accumulated Depreciation)
Net Investment in Property

EXAMPLE

Investors Corp purchases an apartment building in Big City for $20,000,000. An allocation of 20 percent of the purchase price is made to land. Calculate the depreciation expense that will be taken on a quarterly financial statement:

$$\text{Depreciable amount} = \text{Purchase price} + \text{Improvement} - \text{Land allocation}$$
$$= 20,000,000 + 0 - (.20\% * 20,000,000) =$$
$$= 20,000,000 + 0 - (\$4,000,000) =$$
$$= \$16,000,000$$
$$\text{Depreciation} = (\text{Depreciable amount}/\text{Depreciable life}) * (\text{Months in period}/12)$$
$$= (\$16,000,000/27.5) * (3/12)$$
$$= (\$581,818.18) * (.25)$$
$$= \$145,454.55$$

3.2.5.4 Interest

In each period, interest is paid to providers of debt capital. Interest is calculated as an annual interest rate times an outstanding balance times the fraction of the year the debt is outstanding. This amount is shown as an expense on the income statement.

CALCULATION OF INTEREST ON NONAMORTIZING DEBT

Debt outstanding $*$ Annual interest rate $*$ (Months in accounting period/12)

Calculation of interest on amortizing debt:

$\text{Sum}_{\text{(for each month in period)}} \{\text{Debt outstanding}_{\text{(beginning of month)}} * (\text{Annual interest rate}/12)\}$

Note: The interest calculation for each month of an amortizing debt will generally be specified as part of the loan document.

Both calculations result in the same form of accounting entry:

Debit: Interest Expense
Credit: Cash

3.2.5.5 Earnings Before Taxes

At the end of each period, the balance in the interest, depreciation, and amortization expense accounts are closed along with EBITDA to the income before taxes account:

Debit: EBITDA
Credit: Earnings Before Taxes

If we have a loss, the entry is reversed:

Debit: Earnings Before Taxes
Credit: EBITDA

In either case, we need to close our expense accounts:

Debit: Earnings Before Taxes
Credit: Interest Expense
Credit: Depreciation Expense
Credit: Amortization Expense

3.2.5.6 Income Taxes

A credit balance in the Earnings Before Taxes account represents a profit, and a debit balance represents a loss. The resulting balance in income Earnings Before Taxes is the amount of income on which you must calculate your tax liability; this is done by multiplying the taxes Earnings Before Taxes by the appropriate tax rate:

$$\text{Income Earnings Before Taxes} * \text{Tax rate} = \text{Income tax expense}$$

Debit: Income Tax Expense
Credit: Income Taxes Payable

Depending on the size of the company, income taxes must be paid to the government one or more times per year. When taxes must be paid:

Debit: Income Taxes Payable
Credit: Cash

At the end of the accounting period, income tax expense is closed along with income Earnings Before Taxes into net income.

3.2.5.6.1 Pass-Through Entities

There are a number of common entity forms in the United States, including partnerships, limited liability corporations, subchapter S corporations, REITs, and REMICS, that under specific conditions are not subject to corporate income taxes. These are called pass-through entities and will not show entries for income taxes at the entity level as profits are passed through to investors who are subject to taxation.

3.2.6 Net Income

Net Income for a reporting period is the accounting profit after taxes after all revenues and operating, administrative and financial expenses have been taken into consideration.

At the end of each period, earnings before taxes and income taxes (if any) are closed into net income:

Debit:	Earnings Before Taxes
Credit:	Net Income

Debit:	Net Income
Credit:	Income Tax Expense

3.2.6.1 Dividends

Once the net income is calculated, a decision must be made as to whether to distribute some or all of this profit to the owners. The following entry is made when a dividend is announced:

Debit:	Dividend Declared
Credit:	Dividends Payable

When the dividend is actually paid:

Debit:	Dividends Payable
Credit:	Cash

To calculate the earnings retained by the company for future use, net income is closed to retained earnings. The dividends account is then closed by subtracting the amount of the dividend from retained earnings:

Debit:	Net Income
Credit:	Retained Earnings

Debit:	Retained Earnings
Credit:	Dividend Declared

Retained earnings is an equity account that bridges the income statement to the balance sheet at the end of every accounting period. The retained earnings account reflects the contribution made by the period's business activities to the equity of the company.

After the net income and dividend accounts have been closed, all of the income statement accounts return to a zero balance and are ready to accept transactions related to the next accounting period.

3.3 REAL ESTATE BALANCE SHEET

BALANCE SHEET	
As of xx/xx/xxxx	
Assets	**Liabilities**
Long-Term Assets	Long-Term Liabilities
Investment in Real Property	Bank Line of Credit
Accumulated Depreciation	Notes and Bonds
Net Investment in Real	Mortgages
Property	Total Long-Term Liabilities
Total Long-Term Assets	Short-Term Liabilities
Short Term Assets	Accounts Payable
Cash	Accrued Expenses
Accounts Receivable	Tenant Deposits
Straight-Line Rent	Total Short-Term Liabilities
Receivable	Total Liabilities
Prepaid Expenses	**Net Worth**
Total Short-Term	Owner's Investment
Assets	Retained Earnings
Total Assets	Total Net Worth

3.3.1 Assets

The most significant asset held by a real estate company is its property portfolio. Real estate is classified as a long-term asset because its usable life is greater than one year.

3.3.1.1 Long-term Assets

3.3.1.1.1 Investment in Real Estate

Real estate is accounted for as a long-term asset at its historic cost. This cost is allocated between the building (a depreciable asset) and the land, which does not depreciate. Each year, a portion of the building is depreciated and recorded as a noncash expense.

Typical entries when real estate is acquired:

    Debit: Investment in Real Estate
    Credit: Cash

There are other long-term investments related to situating tenants in a property. These include the cost of leasing, including brokerage commissions, legal costs and leasehold improvements (the fit out of space prior to tenant occupancy). These amounts are reduced each period through amortization expense.

Investment in real estate is followed by accumulated depreciation, which is a contra asset reflecting the total amount of prior depreciation expense taken.

3.3.1.1.2 Landlord as Lender to Lower-Credit Tenants

The landlord plays an important role as a financial intermediary for its tenants. In many cases, the landlord directly or indirectly makes the tenant a loan to pay for the improvements that the tenant uses in its business. This loan is repaid through the rent. This aspect of a lease is most important to the tenant who could not otherwise finance the improvements with their own capital. If the tenant could access capital at rates below the landlord's cost of funds, they would do so in the open market.

3.3.1.1.3 Above/Below-Market Leases

When a landlord acquires an asset with leases in place that are at rents above the current market, part of the acquisition cost must be allocated to an above-market lease account. The net present value of the portion of the rent stream that is over market is recorded as an asset that is amortized over the remainder of the lease term.

Upon acquisition:

Debit: Above-Market Lease Asset
Credit: Investment in Real Estate

As rents are received:

Debit: Cash
Credit: Rent (for rent at market level)
Credit: Above-Market Lease Asset

At the end of the lease term, it is assumed that the lease will renew at the current market rent, which we expect will be lower. At that point, the above-market lease asset account will have amortized to zero, reducing the total investment in the asset. The level of return earned on the residual amount of investment should remain steady, reflecting both the lower rents we expect to earn upon renewal of the leases and the lower investment account.

Leases that carry below-market rents are treated in a similar way, except that the under-market lease account is a contra asset – an asset account with a credit balance:

Debit: Investment in Real Estate
Credit: Under-Market Lease

As rents are received:

> Debit: Cash
> Debit: Under-Market Lease
> Credit: Rent

3.3.1.2 Short-Term Assets
3.3.1.2.1 Cash

The major sources of cash in a real estate company are rents and expense reimbursements. Tenant rent payments are generally received into bank remittance accounts known as lockbox accounts, which are established for this purpose. If a bank has financed a property, it is likely that it will ask that the lockbox for that property be kept at their bank. In many cases, if a landlord defaults on a mortgage, the bank or other lender can require that the lockbox funds be utilized in a prescribed manner: to cover interest and other property operating expenses with the balance, if any, applied to reduce mortgage principal.

If the landlord is in good standing under its mortgages, any available funds are released from the lockbox to the landlord for its use. A company that owns many properties uses a concentration account to aggregate the funds from its many lockbox accounts. Funds are then moved to one or more disbursement accounts against which the landlord writes checks and initiates electronic fund transfers.

Landlords also hold cash security deposits put up by tenants to guarantee their performance under their leases. These accounts are segregated and held in escrow for the tenant.

3.3.1.2.2 Accounts Receivable

By convention, most real estate leases call for rents and other charges to be paid on the first of every month. On that day, the property owner recognizes the revenue (Credit: Rent) and creates a receivable (Debit: Accounts Receivable) for the amount of the payment due from the tenant. This receivable is then reduced (Credit: Accounts Receivable) as the tenant's payments arrive into the lockbox (Debit: Cash).

3.3.1.2.3 Prepaid Expenses

As discussed earlier, it is common by either custom or by contract for landlords to pay for certain goods and services in advance of their receipt. These amounts are called prepaid expenses. (Debit: Prepaid Expense, Credit: Cash). The balance of this account is reduced and the relevant expense account is increased as the goods or services are used. (Debit: Expense, Credit: Prepaid Expense).

A retainer for future legal services is a good example of a prepaid expense. The company pays the law firm an amount in advance for the time they expect to spend working on the company's matters.

3.3.2 Liabilities

As an asset with long-term value, typically supported by many long-term leases, real estate is an asset class that is generally financed with long-term debt. The amount of this debt is reflected in the long-term debt account, which includes liabilities that are due more than one year from the date of the reporting period.

3.3.2.1 Long-Term Liabilities

Long-term liabilities include all amounts due to creditors with a maturity greater than one year from the date of the financial statement. These liabilities can take a number of forms.

3.3.2.1.1 Bank Line of Credit

A bank line of credit (LOC) is a revolving credit agreement with a bank that functions as a corporate credit card. The borrower can draw money against the line and then repay it at will. The bank charges a fee for providing the credit line and interest is owed on any amounts that are outstanding. The amount reported on the balance sheet is the amount outstanding at the end of the accounting period.

To record a borrowing against a LOC:

| Debit: | Cash |
| Credit: | Line of Credit |

To record a payment against a LOC:

| Debit: | Line of Credit |
| Credit: | Cash |

To record a monthly interest payment:

| Debit: | Interest Expense |
| Credit: | Cash |

3.3.2.1.2 Notes and Bonds

Notes and bonds are long-term loans made by financial institutions and investors to a company. In contrast to the line of credit, they are made for a set amount of money, the principal balance, and generally have a stated date on which the balance matures, the maturity date. In the interim, the loan may call for amortization, periodic cash payments to reduce the outstanding principal balance. Loans carry a specified rate of interest, which is accrued each month and payable at intervals set forth in the indenture or loan document.

To record the issuance of a note or bond:

| Debit: | Cash |
| Credit: | Long-Term Debt |

To record a monthly interest payment:

> Debit: Interest Expense
> Credit: Cash

To record monthly interest to be paid at a later date:

> Debit: Interest Expense
> Credit: Accrued Expense (short-term liability)

Then later, when payment is made:

> Debit: Accrued Expense
> Credit: Cash

To record a periodic amortization payment:

> Debit: Long-Term Debt
> Credit: Cash

3.3.2.1.3 Mortgages

Mortgages are long-term borrowings secured by an interest in real property. Mortgages are typically made for a set amount of money at interest rates that are either fixed or that may float against a market interest rate index. Interest is typically due monthly, and many mortgages require periodic principal reduction payments.

The most common form of a mortgage loan is a fixed-rate self-amortizing loan that calls for level monthly debt service payments that include both interest and principal. If paid through the end of the amortization period, the principal outstanding will be completely repaid.

Many commercial real estate loans have a maturity date before the end of the stated amortization period. At this time, there will be a remaining balance due that must be refinanced by the borrower.

To record the issuance of a mortgage:

> Debit: Cash
> Credit: Mortgage Debt

To record a monthly debt service payment:

> Debit: Mortgage Debt
> Debit: Interest Expense
> Credit: Cash

3.3.2.2 Short-Term Liabilities

Short-term liabilities are amounts owed by a company that are due within the next year.

3.3.2.2.1 Accounts Payable

Accounts payable are amounts due to vendors of goods and services.

3.3.2.2.2 Tenant Deposits

Tenant deposits are amounts placed in escrow with the landlord that are pledged against the tenant's performance of its obligations under a lease agreement. If the tenant performs, then the deposit will be released at the end of the lease term. By custom, and in many localities by statute, tenant deposits are segregated from other landlord funds and kept in special interest bearing bank accounts known as escrow accounts.

3.3.2.3 Net Worth

The net worth accounts record the owner's equity in the entity, including the owner's investments and retained earnings. Depending on the entity structure (partnership or corporation), this group of accounts may be referred to as shareholder's equity or partner's capital.

3.3.2.4 Owner's Investment

The owner's investment account stores equity contributed to the enterprise by its owners. As with the investment in real estate accounts, the owner's investment account typically records the owner's investments in the same amounts as they were originally contributed. Transactions that later affect these contributions, such as company profits, losses, and distributions, are made to the retained earnings account.

To record a cash investment:

Debit:	Cash
Credit:	Owner's Investment

Not all investments are made in cash. Sometimes an investment is made by contributing a property.

To record an investment via the contribution of an asset:

Debit:	Asset
Credit:	Owner's Investment

3.3.2.5 Retained Earnings

As the real estate entity generates profits or losses, these amounts are closed at the end of each period to the retained earnings account.

To close a profit into retained earnings:

Debit:	Net Income
Credit:	Retained Earnings

To close a loss into retained earnings:

> Debit: Retained Earnings
> Credit: Net Loss

3.3.2.6 Dividends and Distributions

Real estate is typically an asset class that is expected to generate cash flow for its investors. Management decides on what level of cash on hand is required to support the operation and maintenance of the assets as well as debt repayment requirements. The balance, if any, is available for distribution to the owners.

3.3.3 Balance Sheet Issues

3.3.3.1 Working Capital

Many of the transactions affecting both the short-term asset and the short-term liability accounts originate in the day-to-day operation of the business. For this reason, short-term asset and short-term liability accounts are known as working capital accounts. A company's working capital is equal to its short-term assets minus its short-term liabilities.

3.3.3.2 Historical Cost versus Market Values

There is a dynamic tension in accounting between reporting useful information and reporting accurate, objective information. The most relevant information regarding the value of an asset is what an unrelated party will pay for it. The last third-party transaction for the property occurred when the asset was acquired. When we use the acquisition price as the basis for the reported property value, this is called the historical cost method.

Although acquisition price information is both accurate and objective, the transaction could have taken place in a different market environment, and the property's market position could have changed significantly. Though less accurate, a current estimate of value by an objective party may be more informative to an investor. This is called the mark-to-market method. Under this method, the value of an asset is evaluated at the end of each reporting period and, if necessary, adjustments are made to the financial statements.

To increase value:

> Debit: Investment in Real Estate
> Credit: Income: Gain from Asset Valuation

To decrease value:

> Debit: Income: Loss from Asset Valuation
> Credit: Investment in Real Estate

At present, US GAAP generally relies on the historical cost method. The International Financial Reporting Standards (IFRS) call for the mark-to-market accounting method. Over time, the United States intends to move to the IFRS and implement the mark-to-market method of accounting.

3.3.3.3 Expense versus Capitalize

An area that remains uncertain in accounting is the types of costs that should be capitalized and then expensed over a period of time versus the types of costs that should be expensed immediately. Immediate expensing of costs lowers near-term income and taxes and is good for private tax-paying companies that are not concerned with reporting high levels of income. REITs, which are generally public entities that are sensitive to reported earnings and pay limited taxes, would generally capitalize costs whenever possible.

3.3.3.4 Component Depreciation

In addition to allocating part of a real estate purchase to land, component depreciation seeks to divide the acquisition cost across the physical components of a structure and apply more accurate depreciable lives to each component. Component depreciation is an acceptable method of accounting but entails more work and may not result in a significantly different financial outcome.

3.3.3.5 Asset Impairment

Even when using the historical cost method, companies have a responsibility to lower the reported value of assets if they are considered impaired, which means that the asset is worth significantly less than its stated book balance (historical cost less accumulated depreciation). The impairment assessment is typically done annually and tests the expected cash flow from the asset over a future period against the asset's book balance. If its book balance exceeds the assets ability to generate cash flow over time, it must be written down.

Assets being held for sale must also be evaluated for impairment, and if the expected sales price is significantly lower than the book balance, the asset must be revalued.

Debit: Asset Impairment Expense
Credit: Asset

3.3.3.6 Variation for Partnership Structure
3.3.3.6.1 Partnership Capital versus Equity

The income statement for a partnership holding real property will not differ significantly from the income statement for a corporation holding similar assets. The significant differences will occur in the equity accounts on the balance sheet. The equity contributed by each partner is recorded in that partner's capital account.

3.3.3.6.2 Earnings added to Partnership Capital

The partner's capital account is increased for the income earned by the partnership and reduced for losses. Distributions of cash or property to a partner are treated as a reduction of the account.

3.3.3.6.3 No Federal or State Income Taxes at Partnership Level

Partnerships do not pay income taxes, so the income tax account will not exist on the income statement. (Although the entity itself does not pay taxes, the income or loss passes through to the partners, who may be liable for taxes.)

3.3.3.6.4 Distributions versus Dividends

In the same way that corporations pay dividends to shareholders, partnerships pay out distributions. Distributions can take the form of cash or property and are treated as a reduction of the partner's capital account.

3.4 REAL ESTATE CASH FLOW STATEMENT

CASH FLOW STATEMENT

Period Ended xx/xx/xxxx

Cash Flow from Operations	Cash Flow from Financing
Net Income (source)	Additional Borrowings (source)
Depreciation (source)	Debts Repaid (use)
Change in Working Capital (use)	Dividends/Distributions Paid (use)
Cash Flow from Investment	Beginning Cash Balance
Long-term Assets Purchased (use)	Change in Cash
Long-term Assets Sold (source)	Ending Cash Balance

The typical cash flow statement used in GAAP reporting has three separate sections: cash flow from operations, cash flow from investment, and cash flow from financing. The sum of the cash flows recorded on these three sections equals the entity cash flow or change in the cash account during the reporting period.

3.4.1 Source of Cash versus Accrual Differences

Under GAAP, cash flow and net income are unlikely to be equal, as there are many transactions with economic effect in which cash does not immediately change hands. A few of these are illustrated here in the following subsections.

3.4.1.1 Cash versus Accrual Rents

Under GAAP, certain lease agreements result in accounting income that differs from the cash received in the same period. The difference results in an increase or decrease in the straight-line rent accrual account.

In other cases, tenants who are late in paying their rent will cause the accounts receivable account to increase. Receipt of the tardy rents will reduce this account.

3.4.1.2 Cash versus Accrual Expenses

Certain expenses are incurred prior to the requirement for payment, resulting in an increase in accrued expenses.

3.4.1.3 Depreciation

Depreciation expense represents the decline in value of physical assets that were paid for in prior periods but are being used in the current period. Depreciation affects accounting income but is not a cash cost.

3.4.1.4 Amortization of Capital Costs

Amortization represents the declining value of expenditures that were incurred and paid for in prior periods but that have value for future periods. Amortization affects accounting income but is not a cash cost.

3.4.2 Cash Flow from Operations

Cash flow from operations looks at the cash generated by operating the business. It may be different than the net income of the business due to many noncash transactions that are recorded on the income statement, which is based on the accrual method of accounting.

3.4.2.1 Net Income

Cash flow from operations starts with net income, the profit earned by an entity determined using the accrual method of accounting.

3.4.2.2 Depreciation and Amortization

Depreciation and amortization expenses represent the economic cost of deteriorating assets and are subtracted in calculating net income. These expenses have had no impact on cash during the current period and must therefore be added back to net income when determining cash flow.

3.4.2.3 Change in Working Capital

Short-term assets and liabilities are known as working capital accounts. Short-term assets include amounts owed to the entity from customers and vendors such as accounts receivables and prepaid expenses. Short-term liabilities include amounts that the entity owes to customers and vendors, such as accrued expenses and accounts payable.

To create short-term assets, the entity has "used" cash to acquire goods or to make a loan to a vendor or customer. For example, if the entity has an accounts receivable from a tenant in place of a cash rent payment, it is equivalent to accepting a note from the tenant in place of cash.

This effect can be traced through the income statement. Under GAAP, when rent is due, revenue is increased, which affects net income. This increase in net income is then reflected in cash flow from operations. The assumption is that rent results in cash for the business. However, if accounts receivable has also increased, we know that the entity did not receive cash for the rent but instead a tenant's promise to pay. In effect, the entity has received a note rather than the cash that was expected. The increase in accounts receivable must be reflected as a decrease in cash flow from operations to cancel out the expected cash from the rent. Therefore, cash flow from operations correctly shows a net zero change in cash.

> An increase in short-term assets is a use of cash and reduces cash flow from operations.

Short-term liabilities represent credit that has been extended to the entity by its vendors and suppliers. It is as if vendors have given the entity cash to purchase goods and taken back notes for that cash. For this reason, increasing a short-term liability is seen as a source of cash. The entity has traded its paper for cash.

This effect can be also traced through the income statement. When an expense is recorded, net income is decreased, and this decrease is also reflected in cash flow from operations. Payment for the expense is expected to reduce cash. However, if accounts payable has increased, the entity has sourced cash by increasing a short-term liability. The increase in short-term liabilities is reflected as an increase in cash flow from operations, canceling out the expected use of cash for the expense. Cash flow from operations therefore properly shows a net zero change in cash.

> An increase in short-term liabilities is a source of cash and increases cash flow from operations.

In summary, an entity uses cash to generate its short-term assets and sources cash from its short-term liabilities. If an entity's working capital is increasing, it is using cash, and if it is decreasing, it is generating cash. Entities that are using cash may need to look for external capital to fund their growth. Entities that are generating cash can invest in the business, repay debts, or pay a dividend.

When the short-term assets exceed the short-term liabilities, the entity is said to have positive working capital. The opposite is true when the entity owes more than it is due.

3.4.3 Cash Flow from Investments

Cash flow from investment is affected by sales or purchases of long-term assets.

3.4.3.1 Change in Long-term Assets

As our real estate business grows, we invest in additional properties, related equipment, and perhaps mortgages and other securities backed by real property. These investments require us to use our cash. Selling these assets provides us with liquidity and is a source of cash. As previously mentioned, depreciation lowers the amount of long-term assets shown on the balance sheet but has no effect on cash from investment.

In any period during which we have bought more property than we have sold, we have used cash.

3.4.3.2 Capital Expenditures and Tenant Allowances

Major repairs that have a useful life of more than one year are considered capital expenditures and are classified as long-term assets. Tenant replacement costs including leasing commissions and tenant allowances, if they are tied to leases with a life of over one year, are also considered long-term assets. Capital expenditures and tenant costs are uses of cash that impact cash from investment.

3.4.4 Cash Flow from Financing

Cash flow from financing is typically affected by borrowing or repaying long-term corporate debt or by issuing or repurchasing equity securities.

3.4.4.1 Change in Long-Term Liabilities

When an entity issues debt, it exchanges a note for cash. Raising long-term liabilities is a source of cash. Later, an entity must use its cash to repay its liabilities.

3.4.4.2 Changes in Equity

Real estate is a capital-intensive business, and many real estate firms frequently access the capital markets to source equity. These transactions raise or source cash for the entity. Investors typically look to real estate investments to generate income. Dividend payments, or distributions of partner's capital, although actually generated by operations, are considered changes to the equity account and are shown as affecting cash from financing.

3.4.5 Cash Flow Metrics
3.4.5.1 Funds from Operations

Rather than looking at net income, which some analysts consider distorted by depreciation expense, many real estate investors are more interested in looking at cash flow from operations. Real estate investment trusts have developed a measure of cash flow from operations that is known as funds from operations (FFO).

FFO is typically defined as net income plus depreciation and is reported both as an aggregate and on a per-share basis.

3.4.5.1.1 Adjusted FFO

Adjusted FFO (AFFO) or funds available for distribution (FAD) is a metric that looks to adjust FFO for the costs of annual non-revenue-generating capital expenditures, including major repairs and tenant replacement costs. Some analysts consider these costs the "true" depreciation expense because they reflect the real annual cost of keeping the asset at peak performance.

3.4.6 Coverage Ratios

3.4.6.1 Fixed Charge

Credit analysts who work for debt investors like to look at the ability of an entity's income stream to pay for its fixed charges, such as the interest and principal payments due on its long-term liabilities. The ratio is generally stated as EBITDA divided by the sum of interest expense and periodic principal amortization. The higher the fixed charge coverage ratio, the more likely it is that the entity will be able to manage its debt load.

3.4.6.2 Dividend Coverage

Equity analysts look at the ability of the real estate enterprise to pay out distributions to investors. The ratio used is dividend coverage and is generally stated as FAD/dividends paid. The higher the dividend coverage ratio, the higher is the likelihood that the entity will be able to maintain or increase its dividend.

3.4.7 Cash Accounting versus Cash Flow Statement

The cash flow statement used in accrual accounting is intended to provide the same information to management as the cash method of accounting while providing the insight into the long-term profitability of the business, which is not always present in cash accounting.

3.5 TAXATION

The requirement to pay taxes is a major driver in many real estate decisions. Tax considerations are particularly important to private owners, who are subject to many types of taxation. Many large financial institutions, such as pension funds, may be in a position to avoid taxation.

3.5.1 Income Taxes

Individuals pay taxes on income earned from a trade or business. These taxes are levied by federal, state, and local governments on taxable income. Each taxing entity has a slightly different definition of taxable income, and an individual subject to taxation is responsible for reporting his or her income in keeping with the definitions set forth by the respective taxing authorities.

Owners of property, depending on the structure of the entity in which they hold their assets, may be responsible for paying taxes in the locality in which the asset is located, the locality in which their ownership entity is domiciled, and in the locality where the owners reside. Many investors choose the domicile for their entity, and in some cases the location of their permanent residence, based on tax considerations.

The United States has a progressive tax system that has income tax rates that increase as income levels increase. In looking at most commercial real estate transactions, analysts typically apply the highest combined federal, state, and local marginal income tax rate payable to their projections based on an assumption that property investors are likely to be high net worth individuals with income from many sources.

State and local income taxes are deductible for federal income tax purposes. To

EXAMPLE: CALCULATION OF COMBINED TAX RATE

	Marginal Tax Rate		Effective Marginal Tax Rate
Federal	35%		35.0%
State	10%	10% * (1-35%) =	6.5%
Local	2%	2% * (1-45%) =	1.1%
Combined Effective Tax Rate			42.6%

calculate a combined tax rate, the assumption is made that the highest federal marginal rate is paid on taxable income and that a federal tax deduction is available for the highest state and local income tax rate.

3.5.1.1 Tax Benefits of Leverage
The interest paid on debt financing is deductible, so it lowers taxable income. Therefore, the true cost of the interest payment is the interest paid less the taxes saved by reporting lower income. The amount of taxes saved is equal to the interest paid times the taxpayer's marginal tax rate:

$$\text{Tax savings} = \text{Interest paid} * \text{Effective marginal tax rate}$$

Another way of viewing the impact of taxation on the cost of interest is to calculate the after-tax cost of debt, which is equal to the interest rate paid to the lender adjusted for the tax savings:

$$\text{After-tax cost of debt} = \text{Interest rate} * (1 - \text{Effective marginal tax rate})$$

This assumes that the taxpayer has sufficient taxable income against which to apply the deduction, if not the tax savings may not be realized.

3.5.2 Taxes Due on Sale

When real property is sold, the government taxes any profit made on the sale. This profit, equal to the sale price less the owner's adjusted basis in the property, is subject to taxation.

3.5.2.1 What is Basis?

When an owner purchases a property, the purchase price paid, including any transaction costs, becomes the investor's basis in the property. When an owner improves an asset by investing additional capital, the basis of the property is adjusted or increased by the amount of that additional investment. The sum of the original purchase price plus any additional capital investment is the adjusted purchase price.

Over time, the owner's basis is adjusted downward to account for any depreciation expense taken. Therefore, at any time, an owner's adjusted basis in a property is equal to the purchase price paid for the asset, plus any additional capital invested in the asset, less any depreciation previously taken as a reduction of taxable income.

3.5.2.2 Recapture Tax

Property is expected to decline in value over time due to physical deterioration. For this reason, the government grants a tax deduction for depreciation expense. It is not possible to measure the exact decline in value, so an estimate of useful life set forth in the Internal Revenue Code is applied.

It may turn out that the depreciation expense taken exceeds the true economic decline in the property. If this is true, an asset will sell for more than its adjusted basis. When a property sells for more than its adjusted basis, a part or all of the depreciation is recaptured and is subject to a recapture tax under Section 1250 of the Internal Revenue Code.

The portion of a gain on sale related to depreciation previously taken is subject to tax at the Recapture Tax rate, which is currently 25 percent:

$$\text{Recapture tax due} = \text{Recapture tax rate} * \text{Depreciation recaptured}$$

EXAMPLE

Jon's Law Firm buys a small office building for $1,000,000 and invests an additional $100,000. Over the holding period, the firm takes $250,000 in depreciation expense. The law firm later sells their property for $1,050,000. The recapture tax is calculated as follows:

$$\text{Adjusted basis} = \text{Purchase price} + \text{Improvements} - \text{Depreciation taken} =$$

$$= \$1,000,000 + \$100,000 - \$250,000 = \$850,000$$

If selling price exceeds adjusted basis, then depreciation has been recaptured. Since $1,050,000 is > $850,000, depreciation has been recaptured. Amount of recapture equals the lesser of (sales price − adjusted basis) or (depreciation taken):

$$\text{Lesser of } (\$1,050,000 - \$850,000 = \$200,000) \text{ or} (\$250,000) = \$200,000$$

$$\text{Recapture tax} = \text{Recapture tax rate} * \text{Depreciation recaptured}$$

$$= 0.25 * \$200,000 = \$50,000$$

3.5.2.3 Capital Gains Tax

If a property sells for more than its original purchase price plus the amount of improvements, the seller will not only have recaptured all of the depreciation taken, but — to the extent the sale price exceeds the adjusted purchase price — the seller will also have a capital gain. Capital gains on assets held for less than one year are short-term capital gains, which are subject to ordinary income tax. Gains on assets held for more than one year are long-term capital gains. Long term capital gains are currently taxed at a 15 percent rate.

In this case, the asset has not diminished in value due to physical deterioration. In fact, it has increased in economic value, regardless of its age and physical condition.

If the sales price exceeds the original purchase price plus the cost of improvements, the gain must be apportioned between recapture and capital gain. The amount by which the sale price exceeds the adjusted purchase price is referred to as price improvement and is subject to capital gains tax. The difference between the adjusted purchase price and the adjusted basis is recaptured depreciation and is subject to recapture tax.

$$\text{Capital Gains Tax Due} = \text{Capital Gains Tax Rate} * (\text{Sales Price} - \text{Adjusted Purchase Price})$$

EXAMPLE OF CAPITAL GAINS TAX CALCULATION

In the example above the sale price is $1,250,000 rather than $1,100,000
   Because $1,250,000 is > $850,000 depreciation has been recaptured. Amount of recapture equals the lesser of (sales price — adjusted basis) or (depreciation taken)

   Lesser of ($1,250,000 — $850,000 = $400,000) or ($250,000) = $250,000
   Recapture tax = Recapture tax rate * Depreciation recaptured
            = 0.25 * $250,000 = $62,500

If $1,250,000 is > 1,100,000 then price improvement equals $150,000

   Capital gains tax = Capital gains tax rate * Price improvement
            = 0.15 * $150,000 = $22,500
   Total tax due = Capital gains tax + Recapture tax
            = $22,500 + $62,500
            = $85,000

3.5.3 Other Taxes

In addition to taxes on property sales transactions, there are many other varieties of taxes on real property.

3.5.3.1 Use and Occupancy

Certain jurisdictions charge a tax on users of real property for allowing them to use and occupy the asset, called a use and occupancy tax, which is generally levied by local government.

3.5.3.2 Property Tax

Property taxes are levied by local governments to fund the provision of municipal services and to operate the public school system. These taxes are based on a percentage of the value of the asset. The value is known as the assessed value and the percentage is known as the mil rate. Property taxes are paid in installments over the course of each year.

$$Property\ tax = Assessed\ value * Mil\ rate$$

3.5.3.3 Transfer Taxes

In addition to the tax on the profits from a sale of property, many jurisdictions levy a tax on each transfer of ownership of an asset. This tax is known as a transfer tax and is based on a percentage of the sales price of the asset. Transfer taxes are paid at the time of the transaction. Local custom dictates the apportionment of this tax between the buyer and seller.

3.5.3.4 Deed and Mortgage Recording Taxes

Local jurisdictions charge a tax for recording the ownership of a property on the local register of deeds and for recording the lien of a secured creditor against a property. By maintaining a record of these transactions, the government affords the owner and lender certain rights and protections. These records also inform the public when and if prior claims exist on property. The government typically charges a percentage of the values being recorded. Even though these percentages are usually small, the fee can be a substantial sum for major commercial properties.

3.6 TAX AS A TRANSACTIONAL CONSIDERATION

3.6.1 Tax Deferral as Motivator

The taxes due on the sale of an asset can be quite substantial. In many cases, an investor selling an asset may be unable to reinvest the remaining proceeds of the sale after payment of taxes and replace the cash flow that they were earning on the sold property. This encourages owners to hold properties beyond the point when it might be a good time to sell based on market considerations.

When faced with this situation, owners turn to a number of tax deferral strategies. These strategies are a function of an ever-changing tax code that morphs to fund an ever-increasing level of government expenditures.

3.6.1.1 Refinance versus Sale

An investor may borrow against a property without triggering a sale for tax purposes. If a property has increased in value, the owner may raise the amount borrowed against the asset and is free to utilize the proceeds without realizing a tax consequence. At the end of the transaction, the seller must repay the debt. The taxes due at the time of sale will not be affected by the presence or absence of debt financing.

Owners of strong properties that grow in value over time see ongoing refinancing transactions as a great source of wealth.

3.6.1.2 Exchange versus Sale

If a property owner wants to sell a particular property and replace it with a new property investment, it may be possible for the seller to do so without paying taxes. This can be accomplished under a Section 1031 Like Kind Exchange, which allows a seller to exchange the asset held (relinquished property) with a new asset of a like kind (the replacement property). The seller's adjusted basis in the replacement property is the same as the adjusted basis in the relinquished property.

A 1031 Exchange can either be a direct property for property trade or a three-way trade in which the original asset is sold to a new owner and the proceeds are then used to acquire the exchange property. The three-way exchange is managed by a special third-party intermediary who holds the original proceeds in escrow pending closing on the new acquisition.

To qualify for this special tax treatment, the proceeds from the sale of the original asset must be invested into the replacement property under tightly prescribed conditions and within a limited time period. In a successfully executed 1031 Exchange, taxes are deferred until the replacement property is later sold.

3.6.1.3 Contribution to a Tenants in Common Vehicle

A 1031 Exchange can be used to acquire a fractional interest in a larger asset by acquiring a tenants-in-common (TIC) interest as the replacement property. A TIC interest is a divided interest in a large asset. This interest allows a property owner to exchange a small asset for a share in a large property that may be managed by a professional property management company. The original owner maintains the same tax basis as that in the relinquished property, but is no longer responsible for day-to-day property management.

Although this is an attractive structure from a tax standpoint, there are a number of issues with the TIC structure. Given the diffusion of ownership among many investors, decision making is difficult. If an asset gets into financial distress, there may be no one party with enough of an economic interest to come in and restructure the property's outstanding debt.

3.6.1.4 Contribution to a Real Estate Investment Trust

Owners of larger properties that are of a type and size that makes them attractive to a public REIT may be able to contribute the asset to a REIT for an interest in the REIT's operating partnership. The owner will receive units, or fractional interests, in the REIT's operating partnership (OP units) that may later be exchanged for the publicly tradable shares of the REIT. The former property owners will have a tax basis in the REIT OP units equal to their basis in the former owned asset. Any gain or loss on the transaction will be deferred and recognized at the time the units are exchanged for REIT shares.

3.6.2 Properties in Financial Distress

The value of properties can change substantially depending on both macro and micro economic circumstances. Property owners can find themselves with assets that can no longer support the amount of outstanding debt and may in fact be worth less than the amount of the debt.

In this case, the property owner may face financial alternatives with negative tax consequences when the property must be refinanced. These alternatives may include debt restructuring, foreclosure, and bankruptcy, each of which has complex tax repercussions beyond the scope of this text.

3.6.3 Tax Deferral versus Tax Avoidance

These mechanisms will not ultimately allow the owner to avoid paying taxes. Rather, they will delay the date when the taxes must be paid. Depending on the individual circumstances of the owner, this may be a valuable strategy. Under the current tax regime, if the sale is delayed until the death of the owner, the gain will be part of the owner's estate and may be sheltered from tax by the owner's estate tax exclusion, depending upon the total size of the owner's estate. The property passes to the owner's heirs with a new basis equal to the current market value. This is called a "step up upon death." The heirs can then liquidate the asset without paying any capital gains taxes or enjoy a newly increased basis that can be depreciated, sheltering income received from the property.

Glossary

1031 Exchanges
Above/below-market leases
Accounting
Accounts payable
Accounts receivable

Accrual accounting
Adjusted FFO (Funds From Operations)
Amortization of capitalized costs
Ancillary income
Bank LOC (line of credit)
Basis
Bonds
Capital gains tax
Capitalized expenses
Cash accounting
Cash flow from investments
Cash flow from financing
Cash flow from operations Cash flow statement
Change in working capital
CAM (Common Area Maintenance) reconciliation
Component depreciation
Coverage ratios
Depreciation
Dividend coverage ratio
EBITDA (Earnings Before Interest Taxes, Depreciation, and Amortization)
Expense reimbursements
Expenses
Fixed charge ratio
Funds from operations
GAAP (Generally Accepted Accounting Principles)
Historical cost
Income statement
Insurance
Investment in real estate
Leasehold improvements
Leasing commissions
Liabilities
Long-term
Mortgages
Maintenance
Management Fee
Mortgage recording tax
Net income
Net worth
NOI (net operating income)
NOL (net operating loss)
Notes
Owner's capital
Percentage rent
Prepaid expenses
Property tax
Recapture
REIT (real estate investment trust)

Rents
Retained earnings
Revenue recognition
Revenues
SG&A (selling, general, and administrative expense account)
Short-term
Straight-line rent
Taxes
Tenant allowances
Tenant deposits
Tenant replacement costs
Transfer taxes
Utilities
Working capital

Thought Questions

1. A real estate development company expends large sums to identify properties for future development. Should these costs be expensed in the period incurred or capitalized into a development property asset account?

2. The US government taxes depreciation recapture at a higher rate than capital gains. What do you think the government's rationale is for this tax policy? Do you think the rate should be higher or lower; why?

3. Real estate investors generally seek to delay payment of capital gains taxes. In today's world, is this the correct strategy? What analysis would you suggest to prove your conclusion?

Review Questions

1. Pro Rata Allocation of Expenses
   Harry's Hat Shop operates a 2,000-square-foot store in New Market Mall. There are 100 stores in New Market Mall totaling 400,000 square feet. What is the pro rata allocation of expenses to Harry's Hat Shop?

2. Rent: Gross
   Jon's Law Firm agrees to pay $20 per foot in annual gross rent. Expenses are $5 per square foot. Jon's Law Firm is renting 10,000 square feet. Including expenses, what is Jon's annual payment to the landlord?

3. Rent: Stop
   Bob's CPA Firm agrees to pay $25 per foot in annual rent with a $4 per square foot expense stop. Expenses this year are $5 per square foot. Bob's CPA Firm is renting 50,000 square feet. Including expenses, what is the amount of Bob's payment to the landlord?

4. Rent: Percentage
   Buttercup's Baubles agrees to pay $20 per foot in annual rent with 8 percent percentage rent over a natural breakpoint. CAM expenses are $5 per square foot. Buttercup's Baubles is renting 5,000 square feet.

Buttercup's sales are $1.5 million this year. Including expenses, what is Buttercup's annual payment to the landlord?

5. Rent: Renewal

Jeff's Investment Firm is currently paying $15 per foot in annual gross rent. Jeff's Investment Firm is renting 5,000 square feet. Jeff has the option to renew his lease for a three-year term at a 5 percent rent increase. What is Jeff's new annual payment to the landlord?

6. Rent: Renewal: CPI

Dewie, Cheatham, and Howe (DCH), a local CPA firm, has a gross lease on 10,000 square feet of space in a suburban office building. The lease is now at the end of its first term. It has a renewal option for an additional term that calls for the new rent to be set at the old rent plus an adjustment for the change in the CPI. The CPI Index was at 106.9 at the beginning of the lease term; it is now at 125.4. The original rent was $10 per foot. What is the renewal rent?

7. Rent: Releasing

In the event that DCH does not renew its 10,000-square-foot lease, we will need to release the space. DCH has been in the space for 15 years, and it will need a complete interior renovation. This will cost $25 per square foot. It will also cost 3 percent of the total rent for the new tenant's first term as a leasing commission. What will it cost to release the space to a new tenant for a five-year term at a $20-per-square-foot rent level?

8. Rent: Incentives

The replacement for DCH is Bob's Account Temps (BAT). BAT has agreed to an $18-per-square-foot lease on 10,000 square feet. In order to induce the tenant to sign a ten-year lease, we have agreed to a $5 per foot work letter for tenant specified lighting and a one-time allowance for moving expenses of $20,000. What will these inducements cost us in total?

9. Rent: Straight Line

Dr. Pearl E. White DDS is opening a new dental office on the first floor of Mayberry Mall. Dr. White has agreed to a ten-year lease with a $25-per-square-foot starting rent. The rent steps to $30 at the end of the third year and to $35 at the end of the sixth year. What is the straight-line rent per foot for Dr. White's office?

10. Rent: Straight-Line Rent Receivable

A retail tenant has a ten-year lease with three rent steps:

Year 1, 2, 3	$30 per foot
Year 4, 5, 6	$40 per foot
Year 7, 8, 9, 10	$50 per foot

What is the straight-line rent and what will be the balance in the straight-line receivable account at the end of year 5 (per foot)?

	SL Rent	SL Receivable
A)	50	80
B)	41	0
C)	35	45
D)	41	35

11. Rent: Net Effective

New Shoes Inc. has negotiated a new ten-year lease at the Three Rivers Mall. The lease calls for a gross rent of $30 per square foot on a 10,000-square-foot lease. The tenant has negotiated for one year free rent and a $50-per-square-foot tenant allowance. Leasing commissions are $5 per square foot. Expenses for the property are $10 per foot per year. What is the net effective rent for the space?

12. Rent: Renew versus Releasing

Abe's Furniture Store, a long-term tenant, is at the end of its lease term. Abe currently pays $15 per square foot on 20,000 feet and pays pro rata CAM of $4 per square foot. You offered Abe a five-year renewal at $25 per square foot, with a $5-per-square-foot allowance for brightening up the store. Abe accepted your tenant allowance offer but has come back with a $20-per-square-foot rent counter offer, last and final, threatening to close after Christmas when his current term expires. You believe that if Abe closes, the store will remain vacant for 12 months and you will need to give a new tenant $25 per square foot as a tenant allowance. What rent would the new tenant have to pay on a four-year lease, with pro rata CAM, for you to reject Abe's offer? Assume that interest rates are zero.

13. Expense: Calculation

Newco Real Estate owns a 100,000-square-foot strip shopping center in New Jersey. The center is valued at $20,000,000. Security expenses are $50,000 per year; maintenance costs average $300,000, depending on snowfall. Insurance is $50,000, and administration is $20,000. Next year, the center will need a new roof, at an expected cost of $1,000,000. Annual real estate taxes are currently 2 percent of value. What are the annual operating expenses for the center per square foot?

14. Expense: Stop

Jon has just moved his law firm into new space in Highrise 100, a relatively new class A office building. Jon has agreed to a five-year, $50-per-square-foot rent with a $10 expense stop (set at expected expense level for year 1). In the recent past, expenses at the property have been increasing at 6 percent per annum. If future expenses continue at the same rate of increase, what will Jon's total cost of occupancy per square foot be in the last year of his lease?

15. Expense: CAM

Harold's Video Hideaway sells movies and Hollywood memorabilia in a 1,000-square-foot store at the Starlite Mall in an urban location on the West Coast. The mall has 1,000,000 feet of total gross leasable area, including 450,000 feet of inline space and 550,000 feet of anchor space. Expenses this year are expected to total $20,000,000. In total, the three anchor tenants contribute $2,000,000 to expenses. Assuming Harold pays full pro rata CAM charges, what is Harold's expected total annual CAM contribution? Harold has negotiated a CAM cap of $25 per square foot. Does the cap lower Harold's costs in the current year?

Multiple Choice Questions

1. Which is the proper accounting for a mortgage payment?
   a) Debit: Cash, Credit: Debt Service
   b) Debit: Debit Service, Credit: Cash
   c) Debit: Interest Expense and Mortgage Principal, Credit: Cash
   d) Debit: Cash, Credit: Interest Expense and Mortgage Principal
2. A limited partner in a real estate partnership:
   a) Can lose only the amount they have invested
   b) Can be forced to contribute additional capital
   c) Can manage the affairs of a partnership
   d) Is subject to entity level taxation
3. What is a step up on death?
   a) Free pass though the pearly gates
   b) Increase of basis to fair market value
   c) Increase in estate taxes for family members
   d) Improvement to property management after founder's death
4. Recapture tax is paid if:
   a) Land has appreciated
   b) Sale price is greater than depreciated book value
   c) Sale price is less than depreciated book value
   d) None of the above
5. Capital gains tax is paid if:
   a) Price improvement is greater than zero
   b) Price is greater than depreciated book value, less than original cost
   c) Price is less than depreciated book value
   d) None of the above
6. A cash-out refinancing is:
   a) Subject to tax
   b) Not subject to tax

c) Impacts depreciation

d) Decreases basis

For answers to these Problems and Exercises, please visit the companion website: http://booksite.elsevier.com/9780123786265

CHAPTER 4

Cash Flows and Modeling

4.1 FUNDAMENTAL PRINCIPLES

4.1.1 Revenue

Rent—the periodic payment received from tenants for the use of real property—is the key source of revenue in the commercial real estate business. In many cases, tenants are also responsible for paying their share of the ongoing operating expenses of the property. The financial relationship between the tenant and the landlord is set forth in a legal agreement known as a lease. The key financial terms of the lease are generally summarized in a lease abstract and recorded in an accounting system. The landlord will also use this accounting system to bill and record tenant payments, record and apportion property expenses, and track capital expenditures and property liabilities.

When gathering the required information necessary for the revenue and expense reimbursement portions of a property financial model, the leases or lease abstracts are the primary source for a detailed description of the financial relationship between the tenant and the landlord.

4.1.2 Rent

Rent is a periodic payment received from a tenant for the use of a property. In the United States, rent is typically paid by the tenant on a monthly basis within the first few days of the month.

In the simplest form of rent—base or minimum rent—the amount of the rent payment is set at a fixed level for a given number of years. The particular manner in which rent is quoted depends on the property type.

Residential rent is usually quoted on a per-apartment, per-month basis. To calculate the annual rent from an apartment, multiply the monthly rent by 12.

CONTENTS

An Introduction to Real Estate Finance

> **EXAMPLE**
>
> The rent on an apartment is $1,500 per   × 12 = $18,000/year.
> month. The total annual rent is $1,500/month

In the US, commercial rent for retail, office and industrial space is typically stated as rent per square foot per year even though the rent is due and payable monthly. In Europe, the typical unit of measure is rent per square meter per month.

> **EXAMPLE**
>
> A 2,000-square-foot US retail store has a rent $48,000/year. This rent would be paid by the
> of $24 per square foot. The total annual rent is   tenant at the rate of $4,000 per month.
> $24/square foot/year × 2,000 square feet or

The financial analyst should be careful to clarify any ambiguity regarding a rent structure before building a model, as the rent calculation is a key driver of any property model.

4.1.2.1 Measurement of Space

Rent is usually stated as an amount of money per unit of space per unit of time. For example, an accounting firm rents a 20,000 foot floor in a high rise office building. The rent is stated as $60 per square foot per year. To calculate the rent due per month, the typical period for both rent payments and accounting statements, we must divide the annual rent by twelve months and multiply by the number of square feet leased:

Monthly rent due = annual rent of $60.00 / 12 months * 20,000 square feet equals: $100,000 per month

In this case, the rent is charged on a rentable square foot basis. Rentable space includes the full area space contained within the walls of the building including hallways, mechanical rooms, elevators, etc. In this building, 20 percent of the rentable space is required for these purposes (4,000 square feet) leaving 80 percent of the floor space (16,000 square feet) as usable space, area available to the tenant for its office needs.

The ratio: (rentable space / usable space) − 1 is known as the load factor. In this case:

$$(20,000/16,000) - 1 = .25 = 25 \text{ percent}$$

The ratio: (rentable space − usable space) / rentable space is known as the loss factor. In this case:

$$1 - (16,000/20,000) = .20 = 20 \text{ Percent}$$

4.1.2.2 Minimum Rent Adjustments

Few rental agreements are as simple as those stated earlier. Because most rental agreements are made for a period well in excess of one year, landlords generally seek to have upward rent adjustments built into their leases. The most common type of rent adjustment is an increment to the base rent at a set time in the future.

There are two common forms of base rent adjustments. The most prevalent is to increase the rent by a set amount at one or more predetermined points in the future.

EXAMPLE

The current base rent on Office Suite 17 is $1,000. At the end of year three, the rent on Suite 17 will rise to $1,100.

A more complicated periodic adjustment based on a metric to be calculated in the future. In the United States, the most frequently used metric for rent escalation is the CPI, or consumer price index, as reported monthly by the U.S. government.

EXAMPLE

The current base rent on Office Suite 17 is $1,000. The CPI when the current lease was signed was 100.0. At the end of year three, the rent on Suite 17 will be adjusted by using the following formula: new base rent equals current base rent × (1 + (new CPI/old CPI)). At the end of year three, the CPI is 109.7. The new rent is $1,000 × (1+ (109.7/100.0)) =$1,097.

Another metric used is "market level." In this adjustment, rent is raised to a level typical of the "market" for similar properties at the specified future date. This is a more difficult number to determine because it is subjective and it is typically used in combination with a tenant or landlord option to renew.

EXAMPLE

At the end of the first lease term of five years, the tenant has the option to renew at "market" rent for an additional three-year period.

The implication in this formula is that if there is no agreement on the rent, the tenant can leave and move elsewhere. The actual rent level proposed by the landlord at the time will depend on whether the landlord wants to keep the tenant.

4.1.2.3 Participating Rents

In keeping with the important role that real property plays in enhancing a business's success, many lease agreements call for rental payments that are based in whole or in part on the income earned by the tenant's business. Retail businesses often pay a landlord a percentage of their sales as a part of their rental payment. Hotels and casinos may also include a percentage of their sales as part of their rental payment. A participating rent based on sales performance is known as a percentage rent. The typical formulation for a percentage rent is to multiply the tenant's sales by a set fraction:

$$\text{percentage rent} = \text{tenant sales} \times \text{participation factor}$$

In the most common percentage rent formula, sales below a negotiated level are excluded from the participation calculation. The level of excluded sales is typically known as the breakpoint. Only sales that exceed the breakpoint are included in the participating rent calculation:

$$\text{percentage rent} = (\text{actual tenant sales} - \text{breakpoint}) \times \text{participation factor}$$

If the breakpoint is set as the base rent divided by the participation factor, then the level below which sales are excluded is known as a natural breakpoint:

$$\text{natural breakpoint} = \text{base rent/participation factor}$$

EXAMPLE

Wonderful Clothing Store, which operates in 1,000 square feet pays a percentage rent equal to 6 percent of sales over a natural breakpoint. The store also pays a base rent of $12.00 per square foot. Sales were $300,000 this year. From this information, determine the percentage rent and the total rent payment:

Base rent $= \$12.00/\text{sq. ft.} \times 1,000 \text{ sq. ft.} = \$12,000$

Natural breakpoint $= \$12,000/0.06 = \$200,000$

Percentage rent $= (\$300,000 - \$200,000) \times (0.06) = \$6,000$

Total rent $=$ Base rent $+$ Percentage rent $= \$12,000 + \$6,000 = \$18,000$

4.1.2.4 Forecasting Percentage Rent

As the previous example points out, the level of the rent due to the landlord varies depending on the performance of the tenant. To forecast the rent, it is first necessary to forecast expected tenant sales. This forecast is typically done by reviewing the historic trend of tenant sales in light of current expectations for general economic conditions.

By paying percentage rent, the tenant is transferring part of the risk of its operating business to the landlord. This reduces the tenant's level of fixed costs and increases its level of variable costs. In return for accepting part of the risk of the tenants business, the landlord can participate in the upside of the tenant's business concept. This arrangement can create a symbiotic and mutually rewarding relationship between landlord and tenant.

4.1.2.5 Renewals

Leases are made for fixed increments of time. In modeling a real estate investment, one must make certain assumptions regarding the utilization of space following the end of each lease.

Many leases feature one or more renewal options under specified conditions. In strong real estate markets, with little vacancy, the tenant may choose to exercise the option. In weaker markets, with high vacancy, the tenant may consider the renewal option as a "worst-case" price limit and will seek to renegotiate the rent downward or seek other incentives as consideration for entering into a renewal.

In the event that a tenant terminates its lease, the landlord will face a number of costs. For any period that the space sits vacant and unleased, the landlord will not earn any rent. Once a new lease is signed, either for a new tenant or for the renewal of an existing lease, the landlord will generally owe a leasing commission to the broker that represents the tenant and perhaps an additional commission to the landlord's own broker. In many cases, the landlord will grant the tenant a "work letter" detailing improvements that the landlord will make to the space prior to the date of occupancy or renewal. The cost of the improvements specified in the work letter is known as a Tenant Allowance.

4.1.2.6 Rent Accounting Issues

The straight-line rent method is generally applied when accounting for rental revenues under GAAP. Under this method, the rent payable during the entire term of the lease is aggregated and considered earned ratably over the term of the lease. Any period of free rent used to attract a tenant is included when calculating the term of the lease. Under this method, any changes in the rent

EXAMPLE: STRAIGHT-LINE METHOD

Tenant signs a five-year lease for 1,000 square feet. The landlord gives one year of free rent, so no rent is paid by the tenant during the first year. The rent for the second and third year is $10 per square foot. For the last two years of the lease, the rent rises to $15 per square foot. Under the straight-line method, the rent revenue is modeled as follows:

$$\text{Rent revenue (Straight-line basis)} = (0 + \$10 + \$10 + \$15 + \$15) \text{ per square foot/5 years}$$
$$= \$10 \text{ per square foot per year}$$

	Year one	Year two	Year three	Year four	Year five
Rent (as paid)	Free	$10/sq. ft.	$10/sq. ft.	$15/sq. ft.	$15/sq. ft.
Rent revenue: (credit)	$10,000	$10,000	$10,000	$10,000	$10,000
Cash (debit)	0	$10,000	$10,000	$15,000	$15,000
Straight-line rent accrual (debit)	$10,000	0	0	($5,000)	($5,000)
Straight-line rent receivable (account balance)	$10,000	$10,000	$10,000	$5,000	0

over the full term of the lease are reflected in an "average" rent that is recorded as revenue in each accounting period.

In any period in which the cash rent is less than the straight-line rent, the difference is accrued to a straight-line rent receivable account. In periods where the cash rent exceeds the straight-line rent, the straight-line receivable is reduced by the excess.

Should the tenant vacate early, any straight-line receivable is written off (credit: straight-line rent receivable, debit: lease termination expense).

Leasing commissions and tenant allowances are paid in cash at dates specified in the respective legal documents. For accounting purposes, these costs are capitalized and expensed over the term of the lease. Should the tenant vacate the property early, any capitalized amounts remaining are expensed in full at that time.

EXAMPLE: LEASING COMISSION

In the straight-line period example, the land-lord pays 2 percent of the total rent to the leasing agent as a commission. This commission is paid "up front" when the tenant occupies the space and is amortized over the life of the lease:

$$\text{Commission due} = 1,000 \text{ feet} \times (0 + \$10 + \$10 + \$15 + \$15) \text{ per sq. ft.} \times 2\% = \$1,000$$

	Year one	Year two	Year three	Year four	Year five
Prepaid Expense: Leasing commission: (debit)	$1,000				
Cash (credit)	$1,000	0	0	0	0
Leasing commission expense (debit)	$200	$200	$200	$200	$200
Prepaid expense: Leasing commission (credit)	$200	$200	$200	$200	$200
Prepaid expense: Leasing commission: (account balance)	$800	$600	$400	$200	$0

4.1.2.7 Modeling Rent Revenue

In a complete property model, each space must be considered separately. First, the timing of lease options and expirations must be determined. At each of these renewal points, the tenant's decision to renew or to vacate must be forecast, as well as the terms of the renewal or the new lease.

At each option date, an assumption about the tenant's intention to renew must be made. In strong real estate markets, a renewal at the terms specified in the lease—if they are advantageous to the tenant—is a likely outcome. For this occurrence, forecast the scheduled change in rent and the payment of a leasing commission, if due. In weak markets, consider the strong possibility that the tenant will ask for a rent reduction or decide to terminate the lease.

In the event that a lease termination is expected, the forecast should include a period of vacancy or "downtime" for the space. In many models, standard vacancy periods are used to estimate the time until a space is released. For example, at each lease termination, assume that the space remains vacant for six months. This assumed period of vacancy, with no revenue, is then followed by a new lease at market terms.

A forecast of market terms for a new lease includes:

- Rent levels based on a market forecast for that future time
- Leasing commissions based on market standard rates
- A tenant allowance based on the size of the space and the expected future cost of our standard "work letter"

EXAMPLE

Rent levels: market rents at the beginning of our period are $10/square foot and rents are expected to grow at the CPI. The CPI is projected to grow at a compounded rate of 3 percent per year. This implies a rent level at each future date.

Leasing commission: leasing commissions due are equal to 3 percent of the total rent payable during the new lease term, paid on occupancy.

Tenant improvements: at the beginning of the forecast period, new tenants receive $50 per square foot for improvements.

Historically, this amount has grown with the CPI. The future cost of the current $50 per square foot allowance can be forecast with this growth factor. The future cost of improvements is multiplied by the number of square feet covered by the lease, and this is the forecast tenant allowance.

The last tenant vacated on January 1, 2011, and the space is leased for a five-year term starting January 1, 2012. Market rents on December 31, 2010, were $10 per square foot.

	Dec 2010	Dec 2011	Dec 2012	Dec 2013	Dec 2014	Dec 2015	Dec 2016
Status	L	V	L	L	L	L	L
CPI	100.00	103.00	106.09	109.27	112.55	115.93	119.41
Forecast rent/sq. ft.	$10.00	$10.30	$10.61	$10.93	$11.26	$11.59	11.94
Forecast tenant allowance/sq. ft.	$50.00	$51.50	$53.05	$54.65	$56.30	$57.95	59.70
New rent/sq. ft.			$10.30	$10.30	$10.30	$10.30	$10.30
Tenant improvement/sq. ft.			$51.50				
Leasing commission/sq. ft.			$ 1.55				

Notes: The CPI = starting CPI$\times$ $((1+0.03)^n)$ where n is the number of years. The property is vacant through 2011. The rent for the new tenant is set at the level in effect when the lease is signed (during late 2011) at $10.30, and in this case, stays at that level for the full lease term. The leasing commission is paid up front at $1.55 = 3\%\times$ ($10.30 rent per year $\times$ 5 years). Tenant improvements are also at the CPI-adjusted level in effect when the lease is signed: $51.50.

(website) Application of probability to renewal forecasting

4.1.3 Expenses

The first step in modeling the property expense budget is to make sure that all of the relevant expenses are identified. These expenses include but are not limited to taxes, insurance, utilities, repairs, and maintenance.

The next step in the analysis is to understand the historic costs of these expenses and to evaluate them against market metrics. This step may identify costs that are above or below average and require further study. Aberrant costs on the high side can indicate opportunities for savings or indicate building systems in need of repair or replacement. Lower than expected costs can indicate the existence of long-term agreements that may be maturing and are unsustainable in the current market.

Real estate taxes must be carefully evaluated for the impact of any potential transactions. For example, a property purchase can trigger a municipality to reset that property's appraised value for the purpose of calculating property taxes. The same can occur as the result of a property renovation. In addition, municipalities can have scheduled tax rate increases that should be researched prior to acquiring any new asset. The new buyer may have to increase the real estate tax estimate used in the model.

4.1.3.1 Rate of Cost Escalation

Once the property expenses are fully described and reviewed, they must be forecast forward with appropriate escalation factors. Agreements with business partners, when present, should be used as the basis of the forecast. For example, if a maintenance contract on a piece of equipment calls for a set fee, that fee is used in the projection during the term of the agreement. The market cost for that service for the balance of the forecast period is estimated by applying a growth factor. Many analysts use the CPI as a growth factor. In reality, each type of expense has its own historic growth trend and future forecast which may correlate with the CPI or another metric.

For costs of utilities, such as power and water, current costs are the best starting point. Historic trends in utility unit cost increases modified by known market factors are used to estimate a growth factor. Climate based costs such as HVAC and snow removal can be predicted from historic data and must also be inflated by a growth factor. As with the weather, these amounts are always subject to variability.

4.1.4 Expense Participation

It is customary in many segments of the real estate business for tenants to pay their proportionate share of a property's operating expenses. This agreement is contained in the expense participation clause of many commercial leases.

The types of expenses shared by the tenant as well as the method by which the tenant's share is calculated are enumerated in the lease. Shared expense items typically include the cost of maintenance, repair, and operation of the property (MRO costs), the cost of utilities, and insurance and property taxes. MRO costs generally include cleaning, security, and hospitality services.

The landlord's costs of administering the property, including accounting and management, may also be included. In some cases, the landlord is entitled to charge the tenant for an allocation of the cost of capital expenditures required for the continued operation, or upgrade, of the property.

The tenant's expense participation may be subject to a limit, known as an expense cap. The cap can protect the tenant against a rapid rise in the cost of occupancy under a lease. Caps can shift the burden of expense management to the landlord and impact property profitability when there is volatility in underlying costs (such as the price of energy).

Expense participation takes different forms for different property types. For retail properties, expenses are generally shared pro rata by the tenants based on the square footage they occupy as a percentage of the total square footage of the property.

EXAMPLE: TENANT EXPENSE PARTICIPATION, PRO RATA SHARE

Pro rata share = Tenant's space (sq. ft.)/Total property (sq. ft.)

Tenant A rents a 5,000-sq.-ft. retail store in a mall with 400,000 square feet of shop space. Tenant A is responsible for its pro rata share of expenses =5,000/400,000 = 1.2% of the property's expenses.

The expense level may be subject to a cap. Some landlords have implemented fixed expense levels for given lease terms, taking on the economic risk of operating cost increases themselves.

In office properties, a base level of expense is typically built into the rental rate. The tenant is responsible for paying only any pro rata allocation of expenses above the expense level set in the "base year."

In industrial properties, many leases are structured as "triple-net." (Triple-net structures are used in other property types as well.). In a triple-net lease, the tenant is directly responsible for paying all of the property expenses and returning the building to the landlord in its original condition at the expiration of the lease term. Triple-net leases are most applicable when a single tenant occupies an entire property.

The cost of operating a property is a meaningful part of the tenant's total cost of occupancy. The level of expense participation passed through to the tenant ultimately affects rents as it raises the total cost of occupancy. The tenant is generally indifferent as to the components of its occupancy cost and is only concerned with the total burden the gross rent places on its business. If the landlord operates at a high cost level, it cannot remain competitive in the market.

4.1.4.1 Ground Leases
When a party other than the owner of the building owns the land on which a property is built, the property is said to be held subject to a ground lease. Under a ground lease, the owner of the building must make a periodic payment to the holder of the land. For modeling purposes, the ground lease payment is typically a monthly expense payable in cash. At the termination of the ground lease, any buildings revert to the land owner.

Ground leases are usually made for long periods so that the owner of the improvements (the "ground lessee") can amortize the cost of the buildings. The lease may be structured as multiple successive terms giving the lessee the option to renew. Payments may be set for the entire period of the lease or reset at each optional renewal date.

Typical adjustment factors for payments include the CPI, a factor tied to the market value of the property or the performance of the improvements. For example, if a shopping center is developed on leased ground, the lessor may be entitled to a "participation" payment based on the rental income generated by the property.

At the expiration of the final renewal option, the land reverts back to the lessor. To prevent this from occurring, the ground lessee (owner of the improvements) may offer the lessor a buyout. The typical buyout is set at the net present value (NPV) of the remaining lease payments and the expected terminal value of the improved property at the end of the last renewal period.

$$\text{Value of ground lease} = \text{NPV (Remaining lease payments} + \text{Terminal value of property)}$$

If the ground owner is unwilling to accept a buyout, the ground lessee can try to negotiate for an extension. The extension is important because it is difficult to find financing for any building that is subject to a short-term ground lease.

4.1.4.2 Premature Lease Termination

Tenants who terminate their leases before the end of their stated term may do so because they desire to occupy other space or because their business is failing and can no longer afford the rent.

If the tenant is in default under the lease it is likely the landlord will have built up one or more months of accounts receivable. Once it is clear the tenant cannot pay, the landlord must create a bad debt expense (debit) and reverse the accounts receivable (credit). The same methodology must be applied to any amount remaining a straight line rent receivable.

Unamortized amounts of leasing commission and tenant allowance associated with the defaulted tenant must be reversed (credited) and shown as termination expense. Any amounts recovered from the tenant in the form of a recovery or voluntary payment are treated as lease termination income (credit).

To model the eventuality of bad debt most real estate companies project that bad debt expense will equal a percentage of rent revenue based on historic precedent, typically 1-2 percent of pro forma rent revenue.

4.1.5 The Balance Sheet
4.1.5.1 Working Capital

Working capital is defined as the net of short-term assets and short-term liabilities. The impact of changes in working capital on a company's cash position can be counterintuitive. A company increases current assets by extending credit to its customers. A short-term asset is an expectation that the company will receive cash within a year, but it is not cash. You cannot use a short-term asset to pay a bill. In calculating cash flow, an increase in short-term assets is a "use" of cash. In contrast, a short-term liability is created when the company gives its promise to pay within a year rather than paying a bill in cash. An increase in short-term liabilities is said to be a "source" of cash.

Working capital needs can put financial stress on many businesses. Many companies have problems when their customers ask for credit at the same time that their suppliers are asking for cash. This situation can happen when a company is in a rapid growth mode. The company is making a lot of product and "selling" a lot of product to customers who are using credit. The company ends up with accounts receivable from customers rather than cash. The rapid growth company will attempt to source cash from vendors by purchasing on credit. The vendor may resist allowing a start-up company to purchase using credit. In this case, the fast-growth company can "run out of money."

Thankfully, most real estate companies have limited working capital needs. For the typical real estate company, the largest short-term asset is accounts receivable from tenants. Because Given that most rents are due and payable monthly, account receivable levels are generally limited. Most landlords do not extend credit to tenants and move to evict tenants who do not pay their rent on time.

Short-term liabilities include amounts due to parties that have sold goods and services to the landlord. Payments on property operating expenses are generally due monthly and can involve employee payroll, utilities, and taxes due to government authorities. All of these payees are inflexible, so in property operations, it is difficult to extend payment terms. For these reasons, the typical operator of real estate does not utilize significant working capital.

To model working capital, it is necessary to review each of the individual components and determine which factors drive these numbers. For example, accounts receivable is typically a function of monthly rent revenues. Accounts payable is a function of certain monthly property expenses. With other monthly expenses, such as utilities, there are no payables. (If utility payments are not sent when billed, the lights will go out!).

4.1.6 Capital Requirements

The real estate business is capital intensive and many types of debt and equity financings are used to fund projects and companies. Unlike working capital, these financial instruments are investments with terms of at least one year. This more permanent capital is used to acquire assets, to enhance a property's market position, and to support operations prior to stabilization.

One of the primary reasons that financial models are prepared is to assess a property's capital requirements under various strategic scenarios.

4.2 MODELING DEVELOPMENT AND CONSTRUCTION

Development and construction projects require specialized models. One unique aspect of modeling a development project is that costs are budgeted and incurred over the life of a project, which may include many accounting periods. Costs are aggregated from the beginning of the predevelopment phase. In order to show the progress in completing a project, the physical work that has been completed is reviewed against the project work plan and a "percentage of completion" is calculated. The actual cost for the work completed is compared to the total project budget. The percentage of completion can then be compared to the percentage of total budgeted costs incurred.

For example, 75 percent of the physical work for a $1,000,000 project has been completed. However, 95 percent of budgeted costs have been absorbed. This means that $950,000 has been spent to complete work that was expected to have a cost of 75 percent × 1,000,000 or $750,000. Expected costs of

$750,000 − actual cost of 950,000 = −$200,000, a negative variance, meaning that the project is well over its budget.

While a project is being developed, all direct and indirect costs related to the project including construction, project management, and capital costs are added to the project account "construction in progress" (CIP).

At the completion of a development project or an identified phase of a large project, the asset is put into service and all the related CIP accounts are set to zero. The amounts formerly in CIP are placed in an Investment in Real Estate account.

Operating income and expense reimbursements are budgeted based upon forecast leasing activity. Expenses are forecast based upon existing contracts for goods and services and estimates of utility usage, taxes, and insurance. Once the property is put in service, depreciation begins and interest is no longer capitalized.

In the development and rehabilitation of real estate, working capital can be critical. In many cases, initial-year rents are lowered to incentivize tenants to sign leases at a new property. Current income may not support the property operating costs. In these cases, capital reserves must be available to cover operating income deficits.

4.2.1 Types of Construction Costs

Construction costs are divided into three general types: hard costs (the direct costs of construction), soft costs (professional fees, project management costs, and the costs of the permits), and financing costs (the cost of capital).

4.2.1.1 Hard Costs

Unless a project is built on leased land, a major cost incurred in any development project is the land acquisition cost. In many cases, a development is planned on land that is controlled by the developer through a land option contract. By using an option, the developer does not have to fund the acquisition of a property until the project is ready to begin construction.

Once acquired, land must be prepared to receive the intended buildings and other improvements. This step may require clearing, leveling, filling, and environmental cleanup. These are collectively known as sitework costs. Although geologists generally test a property prior to development, sitework is difficult to budget because it is impossible to anticipate all of the issues that may become apparent once excavation takes place.

In contrast, it is relatively easy to budget the construction of standard types of buildings. For a small risk premium, construction companies will generally give a developer a maximum price contract when building a generic structure on a prepared site. Construction costs will be paid over time as the contractor makes progress in completing the improvements. These are known as progress payments.

Renovating existing structures is more complex and harder to estimate. It may be difficult to determine the current state of the building until renovation is underway, and this difficulty can affect both the timing and the cost of a renovation project.

Once a structure is up, the interior must be transformed or "fit out" for the specific needs of the new occupant. The landlord may finance these improvements for the tenant through a "tenant allowance." This work may be performed by the landlord or by the tenant's own contractor. For modeling purposes, the tenant allowance is assumed to be paid just prior to the start of a lease. Typically, the tenant will then "repay" the landlord for these costs as part of the rent.

4.2.1.1.1 Availability and Cost of Labor and Materials
The availability and cost of building materials can have an impact on your model in two ways. First, and most directly, increases in material or labor costs will affect the cost of constructing a property. Second, and indirectly, the scarcity of materials can delay completion—and in turn the timing of when one can market space to tenants for occupancy (lease-up)—which can increase the amount of the project's capitalized interest.

4.2.1.1.2 Maximum Price Contracts
Developers can shift the risk of increases in labor and materials costs to construction firms through the use of guaranteed maximum price contracts. Under this type of arrangement, the contractor agrees to perform the specified work at a given price. The contractor then hedges materials costs with suppliers and in the commodity markets.

4.2.1.1.3 Change Orders
All construction contracts are subject to additional costs if the specified work is modified during the project, which occurs in almost all cases. Plan revisions are made on site as the work progresses through change orders: written additions to the original work. These are negotiated between the owner's representative and the construction company project manager. Due to their last-minute nature, change orders can be expensive for both the developer and the contractor. When many change orders are required, the costs involved can have a significant negative impact on the profitability of a development project.

4.2.1.1.4 Contingencies
Given the difficulty in accurately estimating construction costs, most models include an allocation for contingencies—costs that are incurred to deal with unforeseen issues as the project is constructed.

4.2.1.1.5 Site Conditions

When preparing a site for construction, soil tests are made to determine the ability of the property to support buildings and what type of foundation will be required. These tests are reasonably reliable but not foolproof, and conditions can be encountered during sitework that were not identified during testing.

4.2.1.2 Soft Costs

Soft costs refer to all of the expenditures for professional services involved in developing a property. Many of these expenditures are predevelopment costs, incurred in advance of acquiring the site on which the development is to take place and well before the start of construction. When predevelopment begins, an asset account is established for the project and costs are capitalized into that account:

> Debit: Asset: Predevelopment: Project X
> Credit: Cash

The key differences between predevelopment costs and construction costs are the source of financing and the risk of loss. Not all projects move from predevelopment to construction. If a project is cancelled after predevelopment work has progressed, the costs incurred are expensed:

> Debit: Terminated project expense: Project X
> Credit: Asset: Predevelopment: Project X

If the project moves forward, the predevelopment costs become part of the construction budget:

> Debit: Asset: Construction in progress: Project X
> Credit: Asset: Predevelopment: Project X

Due to the significant number of predevelopment projects that are never built, lenders are unlikely to agree to fund predevelopment costs and these expenditures are funded from developer equity. It is easier to find external financing for construction-phase expenditures.

4.2.1.2.1 Planning and Entitlements

The intended use of any property has many implications for the local community and its existing infrastructure. These must be considered as part of a planning process involving local, state government, and in some cases federal agencies. Planning costs involve the professional services required to plan the use of the site and the location of the structures on the site. Land planners, lawyers, engineers, and consultants are generally involved in this process. Their fees are part of a project's predevelopment costs.

4.2.1.2.2 Architecture

Architects design structures to facilitate the intended use of a property. During predevelopment, architects develop conceptual drawings and renderings of the desired buildings. If the project goes forward, the architect works with engineering firms to develop detailed construction plans.

Architectural fees for the conceptual design of a property are part of the predevelopment costs. The preparation of construction drawings as well as ongoing work during the construction phase is part of the construction budget.

4.2.1.2.3 Engineering

Many different types of engineering firms are utilized to design aspects of the property infrastructure as part of the planning process that occurs during the predevelopment phase. Professional fees paid to these firms are considered predevelopment costs.

Engineers are also involved in the design of building structural, mechanical, and electrical systems. The cost of this work is part of the construction phase of the project.

4.2.1.2.4 Environmental

Before purchasing a site for development or any existing building, most buyers commission a specially trained scientist or engineer to assess its environmental condition. This is generally referred to as a phase one assessment. If this assessment shows any issues, a further phase two study is required. If significant problems are found, the site or building may require cleanup (remediation).

Property development takes place within a complex set of laws and regulations designed to protect and preserve the environment. As part of the planning process, many localities require the preparation of a study detailing how the development will affect the local environment. This study is generally referred to as an environmental impact study.

Environmental costs can be incurred during planning, at which point they are considered predevelopment, or later, during the construction phase.

4.2.1.2.5 Project Management

Planning for all the phases of a project and the coordination of all of the resources required to implement a complex plan requires skilled personnel with deep knowledge and experience in the development process.

Project management is generally undertaken by the developer or internal staff, supplemented by external resources on very complex projects. The cost of project management is generally calculated as an allocation of corporate resources (specifically the salaries, benefits, expenses, and direct overhead of the development staff). During the predevelopment and construction phases of a project, these costs are capitalized.

4.2.1.2.6 Legal

Legal documents that must be processed during any development project include land purchase agreements, construction contracts, and tenant leases. There are also many regulatory fillings that are a part of the development of any property. All of these documents require the assistance of legal counsel. As with the project management costs, these costs can be internal if the developer maintains inside counsel or external if the developer relies on outside law firms. Even the largest development companies generally rely on the services of highly specialized outside counsel for esoteric aspects of the development process.

4.2.1.2.7 Permits

Government issued permits are required before a developer may proceed with many aspects of a construction project. Permits signify that the appropriate authority has reviewed the proposed work and agreed that the developer may proceed.

Governments charge fees for granting these permits. These fees cover the cost of the government review processes and are in addition to the fees paid to the professionals that write the permit applications. Permit fees are generally part of the construction budget.

4.2.1.3 Financing Costs

Most developers rely on external capital sources to help finance the construction of their projects. In addition to the direct cost of capital, and the interest and dividends paid to capital providers, the cost of securing capital includes fees paid to brokers and capital providers, as well as fees paid to the professionals that are involved in structuring and documenting the transactions. These costs are typically paid "up front" in cash but are then capitalized on the development project's balance sheet.

> Debit: Capitalized financing costs: Development X
> Credit: Cash

In some cases, the financing covers both the development period and the early part of the project's in-service life. If so, the financing costs must be attributed to each period, and—once the property is in service—the costs allocated to the post-completion period are expensed pro rata over the remaining life of the financing.

> Credit: Prepaid expense: Financing costs
> Debit: Financing expense

4.2.1.3.1 Capitalized Interest

While a property is under construction, interest due on construction loans is paid to the provider in cash, but instead of being simultaneously expensed, the interest is added to the basis of the property:

Debit: Capitalized interest: Development X
Credit: Cash

Once the property is in service, interest is expensed as incurred:

Debit: Interest expense
Credit: Cash

4.2.1.4 Post Construction
4.2.1.4.1 Timing of Lease-up

In developing a construction model, the time it takes to lease a property to its stabilized level is known as the lease-up period. During this period, leasing agents and brokers seek tenants to populate the newly constructed or reconstructed space. In the ideal case, all of the space will be leased prior to opening the new property. This rarely happens. Instead, construction is started with an amount of unleased space and agents work to identify and sign tenants until the property is full.

In the property model, the analyst should reclassify the completed space from construction in progress to investment in real estate once it is leased and occupied. In the event that the space is completed and vacant, it can remain as construction in progress for up to one year. Following this lease-up period, the space is considered vacant in service space.

The implication of placing an asset in service is that for accounting purposes, many of the costs that were capitalized during the development period are now expensed. This transition will not have the same impact on the cash position of the property, as many of these costs were paid as they were incurred. For example, interest is paid in cash when due, but is capitalized during construction and expensed when the asset goes into service.

Models of development projects build in a lease-up period based upon an estimate of market dynamics and early indications of tenant interest. If these assumptions are too optimistic and lease-up is extended, the amount of expense capitalized rises and the investment in the project grows, lowering the developer's expected return on investment.

In addition, the developer must support the project with additional cash until the rent stream builds. This can put the project in financial distress.

4.2.1.5 Real Estate as Inventory

Many real estate transactions involve the bulk purchase of property and the future sale of divided interests. Some examples of this include the development of a tract of land into individual housing lots and the rehabilitation of a rental apartment complex into individual condominium units.

In situations in which large properties are being divided into smaller interests for future sale, real estate is inventory that is being processed in a "manufacturing" environment.

When creating a financial model, the analyst must aggregate costs as the property is being improved as well as factor in the cost of the capital that is being invested. The profitability of these types of transactions is a function of the cost at which the product is brought to market as well as the speed of sales.

For example, to improve land for housing, there are the "soft costs" for planning and entitlement as well as the "hard costs" for land clearing, creating the road infrastructure, and bringing utilities to each site. During the development period, there is no income being generated by the property, so the developer must "fund the interest carry": pay from external sources the interest cost on the capital required for the project.

4.3 CASH VERSUS ACCRUAL MODELING

4.3.1 Working Capital

Under GAAP, transactions are recorded when they have economic effect, regardless of whether cash has changed hands. This is referred to as the accrual method of accounting. Income is recorded when earned and expenses are recorded when they are incurred. For example, rent is assumed to be earned when it is due, typically the first of the month, and on this day it is added to revenues on the financial statement. An asset account called accounts receivable is set up to reflect the expected receipt of cash from tenants. Until all the cash is received, net income overstates the cash position.

The opposite situation occurs when a vendor bills for a service at a property, such as landscaping and grounds maintenance. The landscaper comes, cuts the grass, and leaves an invoice with the property manager. Upon receipt of the invoice, the manager enters an expense transaction. Because the vendor has not yet been paid, an entry is recorded to accounts payable. Later, the bookkeeper at the home office issues a payment to the landscaper and reduces the accounts payable liability account. Prior to that time, the net income account will understate the cash position because it will reflect an expense that has not yet been paid.

The above transactions are short term in nature and will ultimately be resolved as funds are received from customers and paid out to vendors.

Money not yet received from tenants can be thought of as a loan to them. Money not yet paid to vendors can be thought of as a loan from them. The net of these amounts is referred to as "working capital" or funds used to support the operating activities of the business. Changes in working capital are either a source of cash for, or use of cash by, the company: a source if vendors are loaning the property more than it is extending to its tenants (working capital is decreasing), or a use if the property is loaning more to its tenants than it is receiving from vendors (working capital is increasing).

Working Capital Item	Impact on Cash Position	
	Source of cash	Use of cash
Short-term assets	Decrease	Increase
Short-term liabilities	Increase	Decrease

When forecasting a property's cash requirements, it is a good practice to project working capital needs.

4.3.2 Noncash Expenses

While working capital transactions begin as noncash transactions, they quickly resolve to cash. For example, as rent checks come in, accounts receivables decline, and as bills are paid, accounts payable decline.

There are other transactions that cause long-term differences between accounting earnings and the cash position. In the real estate business, many long-term investments require up-front cash for long-term benefits. For accounting purposes, assets with a useful life in excess of one year are recorded as long-term assets. As the benefit from these expenditures is absorbed over time, called the useful life of the asset, in each reporting period the asset account is lowered and an expense known as depreciation is recorded.

Depreciation expense is a noncash expense, as the funds used to make the investment were spent in prior periods. For this reason, after depreciation is subtracted, the accounting income on the financial statement of a property is less than the cash actually generated.

Accountants say that without subtracting depreciation, the income generated by a property would be overstated because the property's wear and tear is not expensed. In actuality, many properties appreciate in value over time rather than depreciate. Nevertheless, GAAP accounting requires depreciation, so in order to determine property cash flow, depreciation is added back to net income.

4.3.3 Leasing Commissions and Tenant Allowances

Leasing commissions and tenant allowances are also paid up front and capitalized and then amortized over the term of the lease. Unlike the original property investment, these are recurring costs that occur every year in varying amounts as tenants come and go from properties.

To determine property cash flow, the amortization associated with these costs is added back to income and the actual amounts spent are subtracted from net income.

4.3.4 Non-Revenue-Generating Capital Expenditures

Each year a property requires upgrades to its structure and mechanical systems as well as cosmetic work to keep it fresh and attractive to tenants. This work, though necessary, does not directly create additional revenue. These types of expenditures are referred to as recurring or non-revenue-generating capital expenditures.

For accounting purposes, non-revenue generating capital expenditures are added to the property investment account and depreciated over their useful lives. To determine property cash flow, the depreciation associated with these costs is added back to net income and the actual amounts spent are subtracted from net income.

4.3.5 Revenue-Generating Capital Expenditures

Revenue-generating capital expenditures are capital improvements intended for property improvement or expansion and are added to the real estate investment account. The revenues from this investment will increase property income as lease-up occurs. For accounting purposes, the investment is part of the property account and is depreciated each reporting period.

Revenue-generating capital expenditures are cash costs in the year incurred. To calculate property cash flow, the depreciation related to these expenditures is added back to net income and the cost of these improvements is subtracted.

4.3.6 Stabilized Cash Flow versus Actual Cash Flow

Cash flow models are used for many purposes. To analyze capital requirements, it is necessary to accurately reflect all cash transactions in the period in which they occur. Otherwise, the property may run out of cash. To prepare annual cash flow estimates for use in a discounted cash flow analysis, such as the calculation of net present value, it is also necessary to accurately reflect all cash transactions in the period in which they occur.

There are a number of valuation calculations that use a stabilized view of cash flow to which a perpetuity factor is applied. To stabilize cash flow, recurring expenditures such as leasing commissions, tenant allowances, and recurring capital expenditures are "smoothed": historic trends and future expectations are analyzed to develop average per-year amounts.

Revenue-generating capital expenditures are treated differently. Unlike the other capital expenditures mentioned, the costs involved in revenue enhancement projects are not repeated every year; however, the projects they fund can increase the level of long-term cash flow. To accurately model the impact that these projects have on the value of an asset, expected revenues are added to cash flow and the postproject valuation is calculated.

If the revenue-generating capital expenditure that will boost revenues has not been spent, the cost of the renovation or expansion must be subtracted from the postproject valuation amount.

EXAMPLE

Victory Garden is a 100-unit garden apartment complex currently valued at $20 million, based upon its annual cash flow of $1,000,000. A ten-unit addition of luxury units that will cost $2 million is under construction that will raise cash flow by $200,000 and improve the valuation to $24 million. Assuming that there is no risk in building and leasing this addition, the project valuation is now $22 million ($24 million minus the $2 million yet to be spent). Once the construction is completed (successfully), the value of the property will rise to $24 million.

4.3.7 Tax Issues

Tax expense impacts models based upon GAAP accounting and cash flow.

4.3.7.1 Tax Shield from Depreciation

Although depreciation does not affect cash flow, the U.S. tax authorities allow depreciation to be deducted when calculating taxable income. Thus depreciation creates a "tax shield": a deduction from taxable income that lowers the taxes due. For this reason, it is necessary to calculate a version of pretax income with depreciation properly accounted for so that an accurate estimation of taxes due can be made. The amount of taxes due must be calculated when estimating (after-tax) cash flow.

Not all real estate investors are taxpayers; many institutional investors including pension funds and endowments are tax insensitive. REITs are also typically tax insensitive, as they receive a tax deduction for their dividend payments to shareholders. REIT shareholders are taxed on dividends.

4.3.8 Tax Treatment of a Property Sale

When a property is sold at a sale price that exceeds the holder's investment in the asset, a tax on the gain is due. This gain is called a capital gain and it can either be short-term or long-term depending on the time period the asset has been held.

When an asset is sold, to the extent that the price is greater than the original investment (after subtracting depreciation), the seller has "recaptured" the depreciation. The seller must pay a tax on any amount of depreciation taken during the life of the asset that is recaptured. This amount is taxed at a special rate known as the recapture rate, which is currently 25 percent.

To the extent that the sale price not only exceeds the original investment after subtracting depreciation but also exceeds the original investment price and any capital expenditures, the difference, "price improvement," is subject to tax at the capital gains rate, currently 15 percent for long-term investments.

EXAMPLE

An office property is purchased for $100 million. In case A, it is sold five years later for $110 million; in case B, it is sold for $95 million; and in case C, it is sold for $85 million. What are the taxes payable on sale? Assume that 20 percent of the asset value is attributed to land, the remainder depreciates on a 39.5-year straight-line schedule, the capital gains tax rate on price improvement is 15 percent, and the depreciation recapture rate is 25 percent.

Initial Cost	$100,000,000
Land	$ 20,000,000
Depreciable	$ 80,000,000
Annual Depreciation	$ 2,051,282
Total Depreciation	$ 10,256,410
Tax Basis	$ 89,473,590

	Case A	Case B	Case C
Sale Price	$110,000,000	$95,000,000	85,000,000
Price Improvement	10,000,000	N/A	N/A
Recapture	10,256,410	5,256,410	N/A
Capital Loss	N/A	N/A	4,743,590
Capital Gain Tax	$ 1,500,000	N/A	N/A
Recapture Tax	2,564,103	$ 1,314,103	N/A
Capital Loss	N/A	N/A	Note
Total Taxes	$ 4,064,103	$ 1,314,103	

Note: Unfortunately for the tax payer, capital gains and capital losses are not treated the same. Capital losses can be used to offset capital gains, but if you have only capital losses, there are limits on the amounts that can be used to offset wages and other income. Capital losses in excess of the limit can be carried forward to future years.

4.4 PROPERTY-TYPE-SPECIFIC ISSUES

4.4.1 Hotels

The average daily rate (ADR) is a key metric for a hotel. It represents the average price paid by a guest for a hotel room during a particular interval of time. The revenue model for a hotel will be based on:

$$\text{Hotel room revenue} = \text{ADR} \times \text{Number of rooms}$$
$$\times \text{Projected occupancy rate}$$

Many hotels also offer food and beverage services through onsite restaurants and catering facilities. The revenues and expenses associated with these activities must be added to the room revenues to develop a complete picture of a hotel's performance.

Hotel guests do not pay operating costs separately from their room rate. All property operating expenses are paid by the landlord. The expense model should include all landlord costs and should be based upon historical cost data that is inflated by a CPI growth factor.

Hotel suites must be constantly maintained. This includes basic expenditures for cleaning, touch-up painting, and simple repairs. These costs can be estimated from historic data and are paid and expensed each period.

Units and public spaces must be periodically updated. Renovation costs are capital expenditures and should be based on an initial per-unit/per square foot estimate escalated by the CPI. Unit renovation costs are paid when the work is done but are expensed over their useful life.

4.4.2 Multifamily

Multifamily operators use a concept known as gross potential rent for revenue models. The gross potential rent for a property is the projected rent that would be earned over a specific time interval if the entire property were occupied. This is calculated by multiplying the projected rent for each type of unit by the number of that type of unit. The revenue for all unit types is then summed. A vacancy rate is then applied to the gross potential rent to develop the pro forma revenue forecast.

On the expense side, the cost for refreshing the apartment between tenants is known as the turnover cost. This includes basic expenditures for cleaning, touch-up painting, and simple repairs. Turnover costs are typically estimated by unit type and escalated by the CPI. At lease expiration, a probability is applied to estimate the likelihood of renewal of expiring leases. Units assumed to renew will not have a turnover cost. All units projected to expire are modeled to incur the current turnover cost. In a manner similar to hotel rooms, apartments require periodic renovation which is a capital expenditure expensed over the useful life.

Most property operating expenses are paid by the landlord. If utilities are individually metered to the unit, the tenant often pays. The expense model should include all landlord costs and should be based upon historical cost data inflated by a CPI growth factor.

4.4.3 Retail

Retail revenue models are typically based upon tenant leases that include a combination of base rents, percentage rents, and expense reimbursements.

Retail models are organized by store. At the beginning of the pro forma period, each store will either be leased or vacant. If leased, historic rent and tenant sales data will be available. If vacant, a projection must be made regarding the time it will take to lease the store, its starting rent level, and the landlord's costs, if any, in preparing the store for the tenant, including leasing commissions.

Each existing lease will also have an expiration date in the future. On that date, an assumption must be made regarding the tenant's intention to remain in the space or to vacate. If the expectation is that the tenant will leave, then an estimate of the vacancy period must be made, as well as an estimate of the new tenant's rent and landlord costs. If the tenant remains, a projection must be made regarding the terms of the new lease.

Existing properties will have average base rent data that can be used as a guide for projecting rent levels at the start of the pro forma period. Tenants can typically pay rents that track their sales, so the CPI is a good indicator of how market rent levels will grow over time.

In addition to base rent, many tenants pay some level of percentage rent. Due to this fact, the model also requires an ongoing estimate of tenant sales performance and a formula that tests whether the percentage rent is due in each period.

For some tenants, rent is calculated solely as a percentage of sales. In these cases, the rent will be calculated for each period by multiplying that percentage times the store sales estimate.

Existing tenants will have historic sales figures that can be used for estimating their future sales levels. New tenants that are established operators in other locations will generally have a good estimate of starting sales productivity. The CPI is a good first estimate of the growth rate in tenant sales.

The turnover costs for retail space are based upon historic data for tenant improvements at the property. Future estimates are made by growing this starting level by the CPI. Leasing commissions are calculated as a percentage of the rent expected over the life of the new lease and are payable at opening date of the store.

There are various models of expense participation for retail properties. If the tenant is paying a gross rent, then it does not make a separate payment towards expenses. If a tenant pays pro rata expense participation, then it pays its share of the property operating expenses based on their percentage of the occupied space. There are many hybrid forms of expense participation agreements.

To model expense participation, an estimate must be made for each cost of operating the property. Historic data can inform the starting estimate for each expense item. If these costs are not subject to long-term contracts, then they should be grown over time by the CPI. Once an expense projection is completed, an expense participation model can be developed for each tenant based on its lease terms.

4.4.4 Office

Office revenue models include base rents and expense reimbursements. Models are organized by suite. Space can be rearranged to facilitate tenant needs, but it is not typical to model for that reason unless it is known in advance.

At the beginning of the pro forma period, each office will be either leased or vacant. If leased, the terms of the existing lease will be available. If vacant, a projection must be made regarding the time it will take to lease the space, its starting rent level, and the landlord's costs in preparing the space for the tenant, including leasing commissions.

When each lease expires, an assumption regarding the terms and probability of a renewal must be made. If a termination is assumed, an estimate must be made regarding the projected vacancy period, the next tenant's rent, and costs for renovation.

Existing properties have data on current rent levels for projecting rents at the start of the pro forma period. The CPI is a good growth factor for future projections.

Turnover costs are typically estimated on a per-square-foot basis based upon historic data projected forward using the CPI. Leasing commissions are calculated as a percentage of the full value of the rent expected over the life of the lease. They are payable at the occupancy date.

Office rents typically include a portion allocated to cover building operating expenses. This amount is known as the base year expense estimate or expense stop. If the building operating costs rise in future years, the tenant pays the difference between the base year and the actual expense level. When leases renew, the base year is reset to a new level reflecting the property's then-current operating expenses.

To model expense participation, an estimate must be made for the cost of operating the property in each year. Historic data can inform the starting estimates, and these costs should be grown over time by the CPI or another inflation factor. Each lease must be evaluated in each year of the pro forma to test whether that tenant's expenses have exceeded its base year.

EXAMPLE

The lease of Office Suite 23 calls for annual rent of $20 per square foot with an expense stop of $10. Actual expenses of running the building exceed $10.00 per square foot beginning in the second year of the lease and the tenant is responsible for an additional payment:

	Year one	Year two	Year three
Actual expense	$10.00	$10.50	$11.25
Expense stop	$10.00	$10.00	$10.00
Expense reimbursement	$ 0	$ 0.50	$ 1.25

4.5 BUILDING A SPREADSHEET

4.5.1 Organizational Conventions
4.5.1.1 Worksheet Order
The first worksheet of a property portfolio pro forma model should consist of the table of contents, listing the worksheets that follow. The second worksheet is typically the assumption page, which lists the global variables used throughout the model. The most effective organization is to follow the assumption page with a portfolio summary page. The summary page serves to aggregate the portfolio performance results from all of the individual property models.

Behind the portfolio summary page are the individual property models. Each property should be modeled on an individual worksheet. If it is a very large portfolio, these worksheets can be subtotaled on regional total pages or, in the case of mixed-property-type portfolios, summarized by property type (office, residential, retail, etc.).

4.5.1.2 Local versus Global Variables
When modeling a portfolio, certain general assumptions will have an impact on many individual properties. These include broad market variables such as interest rates and the CPI. These variables are called global variables because they affect the entire model and should be applied consistently across all of the properties. These variables should be stored on a portfolio-wide assumption page.

By storing global variables on a single page, they can be more easily referenced throughout the model and it is easier to run what-if scenarios. If these variables are stored separately on each property's model, scenario construction becomes much more difficult.

Other property variables are specific to one or a small group of properties. These include vacancy rates, rent growth rates, expense growth rates, and other local market statistics. These local variables should be stored on the individual property worksheets because they change from property to property and cannot be set once for an entire portfolio.

4.5.1.3 Individual Property Worksheets

A property pro forma should have a title block with the property name and the date of the pro forma in the upper lefthand corner. Underneath the title block should be the local variables used on the page.

The actual time series pro forma should begin below the listing of variables. The first row of the pro forma shows the periods to be forecast in successive columns from left to right, with the leftmost column being the earliest date and the rightmost column being the latest date. Typical real estate pro forma forecast periods range from five to ten years in length.

Each row in the forecast represents an account. The order of the accounts follows that of the typical chart of accounts. First, the income statement account groups: revenues, expenses, and net income. Second, the balance sheet accounts: assets, liabilities, and net worth. The last group of accounts listed will be the cash flow accounts: cash flow from operations, financing, and investing.

4.5.1.3.1 Net Operating Income

Net operating income (NOI) is defined as property operating revenues minus operating expenses. These quantities are measured without any subtraction for interest, other capital charges, depreciation, or taxes. Stabilized NOI is a typical property valuation metric. It is not a GAAP account. To calculate stabilized NOI, subtractions are made for industry-standard management fees, recurring capital expenses, and in many cases an adjustment is made to bring the property to an agreed-upon occupancy level.

A valuation based upon stabilized NOI divided by cap rate is a view of an asset at a single point in time.

4.5.1.3.2 Discounted Cash Flow

A discounted cash flow (DCF) valuation is based on the free cash flow projected to be generated by the property over a period of time and ends with the liquidation of the asset. Under this method, free cash flow is modeled separately for each year of the projection period. In each year, free cash flow is calculated as forecast property NOI minus the actual amounts of leasing commissions, recurring capital expenditures, and tenant improvements expected in that future year. These annual cash flow estimates are then discounted to the present using a risk-adjusted rate of return.

A critical part of a DCF forecast is the terminal value. The terminal value is the assumed cash proceeds from the sale or liquidation of the property at the end of the forecast period. This amount is added to the estimate of free cash flow for the final year.

4.5.1.3.3 Levered versus Unlevered DCF

The value of an asset is based upon the discounted value of its cash flow before financing costs and is independent of those costs. The value of the equity invested in the property is based upon the DCF net of financing costs. To prepare a levered DCF model, the costs of financing must be subtracted from the operating cash flows. These costs include interest and principal payments on any debt.

If the property owner is a taxpayer, interest payments will reduce the level of taxable income and result in tax savings equal to the taxpayer's marginal tax rate times the interest paid.

Upon the sale of the asset, the remaining principal balance of the debt must be repaid. If the debt is repaid by the seller, it will require a cash outflow. If the buyer assumes the debt, the sale proceeds will be reduced by the amount of the debt. In either case, debt repayment reduces net cash available to the seller.

If the property is sold for a price over its taxable basis, there will also be taxes payable. The taxes due on sale are independent of the manner in which the property is financed. The net proceeds after the repayment of debt and the payment of taxes are available to the equity investors.

4.6 SPREADSHEET ANALYSIS

A basic property pro forma provides a picture of a property operating under a single set of assumptions. With experience, the analyst can become better at choosing assumptions that are reflective of the current operating environment, including rent and expense levels as well as the availability and price of leverage. Estimates are unlikely to be perfect, and further analysis can illustrate the impact on the pro forma if these values are changed.

4.6.1 Sensitivity to Key Variables

Sensitivity analysis can answer many critical questions. Will the property achieve a desired return level if rent growth is less rapid than anticipated? Will the property be able to cover its floating-rate mortgage payment if interest rates rise faster than expected? In each of these situations, the sensitivity of our model to changes in a single key variable is tested.

4.6.2 Scenario Creation

Although it is informative to view the change in the model from altering a single variable, in many cases more than one variable is likely to change concurrently. These variables may be connected by market dynamics that affect both quantities at the same time. For instance, it is likely that rent levels and occupancy rates move together. Landlords lower rents to attract tenants if occupancy is low. Looking at groups of variables moving in tandem can be quite informative.

This type of analysis is called scenario analysis and is accomplished by changing two or more variables at the same time. Investors and lenders like to look at scenarios to see how the performance of an asset or a portfolio is affected by changes in the business cycle. Reviewing the performance of an asset in the face of an economic decline is a scenario analysts refer to as a "stress test."

Glossary

Architecture
CPI (consumer price index)
Cost escalation
Downtime
Engineering
Expense participation
Capitalized interest
Capital requirements
Change orders
Environmental
Financing costs
Fit out
Global variables
Ground leases
Hard costs
Land acquisition
Lease buyout
Lease extension
Lease renewal
Local variable
MRO (maintenance, repair, and operation) expenses
Maximum price contracts
Non-revenue-generating cap ex
Participating rents
Permits

Planning
Project management
Revenue-generating cap ex
Sensitivity analysis
Scenario creation
Site conditions
Sitework
Soft costs
Spreadsheet analysis
Stress test
Total cost of occupancy
Working capital

Thought Questions

1. Under what circumstances are financial models prepared using the cash method more useful than those prepared using GAAP?
2. Under GAAP, commercial properties are depreciated over a 39-year lifespan. Do you agree with this accounting treatment? Explain the basis for your answer. Can you suggest an alternative method?

Review Questions

1. Pro Rata Allocation of Expenses
   Harry's Hat Shop operates a 2,000-square-foot store in New Market Mall. There are 100 stores in New Market Mall totaling 400,000 square feet. What is the pro rata allocation of expenses to Harry's Hat Shop?
2. Rent: Gross
   Jon's Law Firm agrees to pay $20 per foot in annual gross rent. Expenses are $5 per square foot. Jon's Law Firm is renting 10,000 square feet. Including expenses, what is Jon's annual payment to the landlord?
3. Adjustments to NOI: Vacancy Loss
   Marvin Garden's, a 200-unit B-grade apartment complex in Scottsdale, Arizona, is currently 97 percent occupied and has rent revenue of $2,328,000 per year. NOI for the period is $1,500,000. Next year, the property's rents will not increase, and expenses will remain constant. Vacancy loss will be 5 percent of gross potential rent. Estimate the gross potential rent, vacancy loss, and NOI for next year.
4. Adjustments to NOI: Management Fee
   Sleepy Hollow Green is a 500-unit multifamily complex in Harrison, New York. Units rent at an average of $1,000 per month. The property's expenses run at 40 percent of revenues. The complex is typically 90 percent occupied. The owners pay a management fee equal to 3 percent of revenue to Rye Management Company for running the property. How much is the annual management fee? Calculate adjusted NOI for this asset.

5. **Adjustments to NOI: Tenant Allowance**

   Over the next four years, Gateway Towers has 40,000 square feet of leases rolling at flat rents. The owner's predict that tenant allowances on new leases will total $25 per square foot. The property expects to have NOI of $3,000,000. What is adjusted NOI for this asset?

6. **Adjustments to NOI: Recurring Capital Expenditures**

   Science City Industrial Park has 2,000,000 square feet of flex space. NOI for the asset has averaged $20,000,000 per annum. In each of the next five years, management expects to spend $0.50 per square foot on non-revenue-generating capital expenditures. What is our forecast for adjusted NOI?

7. **Interest**

   Peabody Park is a 200-unit apartment complex in Waltham, Massachusetts. On January 1, the owners of the property refinanced their previous ten-year mortgage with a 20-year, 5 percent interest only, $10 million mortgage. What will be the deductible interest expense for the first year of the new mortgage?

8. **Depreciation**

   Stoney Creek, a 300-unit apartment complex in Perth Amboy, New Jersey, was purchased in 1999 for $12 million. Thirty percent of the purchase price was allocated to land. How much depreciation should have been taken in 2010?

9. **Taxation**

   The Gramercy, a 25-story office building in Houston, Texas, was purchased in December 1999 for $25 million. The property was sold on December 31, 2009, for $30 million. Assume that 30 percent of the purchase price was allocated to land. What taxes were due as a result of the sale?

10. **Capital Gain**

    The new owners of Oak Ridge Mall purchased the asset on June 30, 2005, for $35 million. They sold the property for $37.5 million exactly three years later. What amount of the sale proceeds were subject to the capital gains tax?

11. **Recapture**

    The Green Family owned the Stormy Ridge Lodge for 15 years prior to selling it in 2009. They purchased the property for $45 million and then sold it for $42.5 million. Allocate 20 percent of the purchase price to land. Were the Greens liable for paying recapture tax, and if so, for what amount?

12. **General**

    An office building has 10,000 square feet. Average rent is $20 per foot. Average operating expenses are $10 per foot. The average expense stop is $6 per foot. Every fifth year, a 5,000-square-foot tenant comes up for renewal and it costs $25 per foot to replace the tenant (leasing commissions and tenant allowance). Non-revenue-generating capital expenditures is $1 per foot per year. What is the stabilized pre tax cash flow?

a) $105,000
b) $65,000
c) $25,000
d) $5,000

13. Which of the following increases the tenants' cost of occupying space?
a) Free rent
b) Expenses in a gross lease
c) Percentage rent
d) Allowance for tenant improvements

14. Which of the following measures is best utilized to compare leasing alternatives?
a) Base rent
b) Minimum rent
c) Average rent
d) Effective rent

15. Depreciation impacts which of the following?
a) Before-tax cash flow
b) Taxable income
c) Cash flow
d) NOI

16. Which of the following is not subtracted when calculating taxable income?
a) Operating expenses
b) Depreciation
c) Interest
d) Principal

17. A discounted cash flow analysis based on NOI is used to determine which value?
a) Land allocation
b) Asset value
c) Equity value
d) Leverage

For answers to these Problems and Exercises, please visit the companion website: http://booksite.elsevier.com/9780123786265

Property Valuation

CONTENTS

5.1 CAPITALIZED NOI METHOD

5.1.1 Valuation Using Cap Rates

The most commonly used method for valuing a property is to divide its stabilized net operating income by a factor known as a capitalization rate (cap rate).

$$\text{Value of a property} = \text{Stabilized NOI/cap rate}$$

EXAMPLE

Property A has stabilized NOI of $1 million, at a cap rate of 8 percent the property is valued at $1.25 million.

$1.25M = $1M / .08

This equation, dividing a constant annual return by a discount rate, is a form of perpetuity calculation:

$$V \,(\text{Value of a perpetuity}) = C \,(\text{Constant annual payment})/D \,(\text{Discount rate})$$

The presumption is that the property will generate its stabilized NOI forever. The cap rate is reflective of the property type, quality, geography, and market dynamics. It is a singular "figure of merit" that encompasses much of what is known about the real estate market and the competitive position of a particular property.

Stabilized NOI and cap rate are both approximations: the property is not always going to behave as expected, and a single metric, such as the cap rate, can never accurately reflect all the available data about a complex marketplace. Despite these drawbacks, capitalizing stabilized NOI is a method that is easy to understand and apply for property valuation. The results are widely accepted when the method is appropriately applied. The key aspects of this method are set forth in the following subsections.

129

5.1.2 Stabilized NOI

The actual NOI generated by any property varies from year to year due to fluctuations in property revenue and expense streams. Although it is true that certain lease arrangements provide owners with set return expectations, even "triple-net" contracts contain an element of performance risk.

Stabilized NOI is used as a singular representation of long-term property performance. Part of the "art" of valuation is to adjust reported NOI, a "snapshot" of the property's current operating results, and make it a representation of expected future performance. Which types of adjustments are included and the extent to which each is applied can have a significant impact on the property valuation. In a valuation prior to a property sale, each change made to NOI will be negotiated by the buyer and seller.

5.1.3 Typical Adjustments to NOI

The value that an asset can achieve in the market is ultimately dependent on the needs and desires of the purchaser willing to pay the highest price. These individual buyer characteristics cannot be determined in advance. When we develop an estimate of value, we must consider a rational, generic buyer without a particular agenda. In the real estate market, the typical buyer is an institutional, financially driven buyer.

5.1.3.1 Management Fee

We assume the owner will operate the property by contracting for services from third parties on the open market. For this reason, a market management fee is subtracted from NOI to reflect the standard cost of managing the asset. If the NOI as presented includes actual management expenses, these must be adjusted to market standard levels. If management fees are not present, they must be estimated and shown as an expense. Even if an owner will manage the property with internal resources, the market standard management fee represents the opportunity cost of those resources.

5.1.3.2 Vacancy Allowance

Further, it is assumed that this buyer will own the asset in an environment that is reflective of recent historic experience, correcting for any current market inflections that are generally agreed to be short term. To reflect this notion that properties will return to mean performance, a vacancy allowance is subtracted if a property is occupied at a level that is above historic norms.

It is more difficult to adjust for a property that is performing at a below-average occupancy level. There is general agreement that newly signed leases for tenants that are not yet in occupancy should be reflected in stabilized NOI. There is also agreement that leases where notice of termination has been received should be removed. Judging whether the resultant net occupancy level is unreasonably low and should be adjusted upward, and at what hypothetical rent levels, is the job of the analyst.

One should look at current occupancy levels and factors that are having an impact on supply and demand for comparable properties in the national, regional, and local markets to gain guidance on this decision.

5.1.3.3 Capital Reserves
Properties require ongoing capital investment in order to maintain the state of the physical plant. This investment is in addition to the ongoing cost of maintenance and repairs. Most professionally managed commercial properties have an ongoing capital investment program reflected in a non-revenue-generating capital expenditure schedule. These expenditures are called "non-revenue-generating" because they are required to maintain, rather than enhance, the revenue stream from the asset. For example, the replacement of a roof in good condition is a requirement to maintain an asset, not an expenditure that will create additional rent streams or improve rent levels.

5.1.3.4 Leasing Costs
Depending on property type, the costs of leasing space and allowances given to tenants for preparing their space for occupancy may or may not be covered by management fees and ongoing operating expenses. For example, because apartment complexes have many units with relatively short and staggered forms the leasing costs of apartment complexes are generally a part of the typical multifamily management agreement and the cost of minor apartment prep work is generally treated as a regular operating expense.

In contrast, for major office buildings and retail spaces with long-term leases, leasing commissions and tenant allowances are capitalized when incurred and then amortized over the life of each individual lease. Leasing commissions, typically paid at the beginning of a lease term, are based on a percentage of the total rents paid over the life of a lease. Tenant allowances are typically denominated in dollars per square foot and are incurred before a tenant actually occupies the space.

In a cap rate valuation analysis, leasing costs should be modeled in the same manner as capital expenditures. The lease expiration schedule should be reviewed, expected vacancies or renewals listed, and estimated leasing commissions and tenant allowances calculated and aggregated over the investment period. This sum is then divided by the number of years in the investment period to calculate an average annual leasing cost. This cost is a negative adjustment to NOI when calculating stabilized NOI.

EXAMPLE

The 100,000-square-foot Cherry Office Building has Revenues of $3,000,000 and NOI of $2,000,000. It is currently 95 percent occupied in a market in which most similar properties are 90 percent leased. Management fees are 3 percent of revenues. Capital reserves average $1 per square foot per year and leasing costs average $5 per square foot per year. NOI (as reported) is $2,000,000, plus or minus adjustments:

Vacancy (reduce occupancy to 90 percent) $= -(0.05/0.95) \times \$3,000,000 = -\$157,895$

Management fee $(-0.03 \times$ New revenue $= -0.03 \times 0.90/0.95 \times \$3,000,000 = -\$85,263)$

Capital reserves $(-\$1.00 \times 100,000 = -\$100,000)$

Leasing costs $(-\$5.00 \times 100,000 = -\$500,000)$

$=$ Adjusted NOI $= \$2,000,000 - \$157,895 - \$85,263 - \$100,000 - \$500,000 = \$1,156,842$

5.1.4 What Determines Cap Rates

Real estate as an asset class competes with other asset classes such as stock, corporate bonds, and government securities for investor capital. As such, yield requirements for real estate investments are reflective of yields available on competitive investments. These market yield expectations must then be adjusted for the particular risk profile of the property under consideration. In this competitive environment for investment capital, general conditions in the economy and the financial markets form the primary backdrop for cap rates.

5.1.4.1 General Economic Conditions
5.1.4.1.1 Cost and Demand for Capital

Investors invest only when they expect that the returns they make will exceed their cost of capital. Real estate investors facing a high cost of capital will not invest in real property with low returns. If interest rates are high and equity investors demand high current returns, real estate investors will not be able to acquire property unless cap rates are sufficiently high. Property sales will slow down until sellers are willing to drop prices (raise cap rates). When low-cost debt is readily available from lenders and current return expectations on equity are lower, investors will seek to place capital in the real estate market with lower return expectations. This action causes the demand for property to rise and sellers can raise prices (lower cap rates) to reflect that increased demand.

5.1.4.2 Perceived Risks of Asset Class

Historically, commercial real estate has been considered an asset class with stable returns due to the long-term nature of tenant leases. Real estate is also considered to be a good hedge against inflation because as leases expire landlords can raise rents to reflect a rise in other factors of production. These are positive attributes of real property ownership.

On the negative side, direct ownership of commercial real estate can be an illiquid investment. The investment size can be very large, limiting the number of qualified market participants on both the debt and equity side. For this reason, it can take time to market assets and find buyers. Asset transfers are complicated , there are many costs including fees and taxes and ransactions can require a long time to close.

This illiquidity can affect pricing, as investors typically place a valuation discount on illiquid assets. The time lag between when parties agree to a transaction and when a closing actually occurs can make reported pricing slow to reflect market trends.

The factors mentioned are useful in considering real estate as an alternative to other asset classes. Consideration of these dynamics helps us price real estate relative to known market benchmarks such as the yield on ten-year treasury bonds and the implied return on the S&P 500.

5.1.4.3 Unique Attributes of a Market

Along with general financial market trends, the next factor that determines cap rates is the strength of the real estate market in which an asset is located. Real estate located in a market with robust economic growth is generally more valuable than property in a declining market. This comparative assessment applies not only to large geographic regions, such as metropolitan statistical areas (MSA), but also to individual areas within these regions. Properties in markets with strong economies will have better performance than assets in markets with poor growth prospects.

Within a market, property performance is integrally tied to location. There are many determinants of an ideal location, including ease of access, visibility, and proximity to amenities. Identical properties in different locations will trade at different cap rates: the better the location, the lower the cap rate and the higher the price.

5.1.4.4 Unique Attributes of a Property

The primary driver of cap rates is the overall strength of a market. However, within any market, attractive, well-maintained properties with great amenities will trade at lower cap rates (higher prices) than properties that are dated and have deferred maintenance. High-quality properties have the ability to generate higher rents and maintain higher occupancy. Experienced investors will pay less for challenged assets.

Buyers of challenged assets have two basic strategies. The investor can either leave the challenged asset as is or can improve the asset, bringing it to a competitive level by making an additional capital investment. If the investor does not renovate the property, the investor will have less capital invested but the property will experience lower long-term revenue growth. In this strategy, the hope is that the higher initial return will make up for the lower growth and higher risk of a declining market position. In the buy and renovate scenario, the high initial yield will be diluted by the additional capital investment required for repositioning. The investor using this strategy hopes to see an improvement in yield from a higher-quality asset with improved market position. Both scenarios add risk (uncertainty) to the investment horizon, and risk demands additional return.

In contrast, buyers of attractive, stable assets have less risk and more predictable returns. These assets may be attractive to less sophisticated real estate investors who may not have the market acumen or renovation skills necessary to reposition challenged assets. These stable assets are therefore attractive to a broader universe of buyers, are in higher demand, and trade at lower cap rates.

Although doing so is based on some fundamental principles, choosing an appropriate cap rate for valuing an investment is an art, not a science. Different perceptions of a property result in differing views of cap rates and make the real estate market vibrant and exciting—especially for those who are right.

5.1.5 Cap Rate Data from Comparable Properties

Once the stabilized NOI is calculated, the next step is to divide it by an appropriate cap rate to determine the estimated value of the property. Market cap rates are reflective of the general economy, the perception of real estate as an asset class, and the market position for an individual property. Though an analyst could attempt to estimate a cap rate for a particular asset using economic data and contextual information, this is not the typical approach. In general, cap rate estimates are derived from recent transaction data involving properties that are comparable to the one being valued.

For a recent transaction to be relevant, it must have occurred in a time period when market conditions were similar to what they are when we are doing our analysis. In a very stable environment, this can be a year or more. However, in a rapidly changing market, in which major political or financial events have dramatically changed perceptions, only transactions occurring after the market shift are relevant.

When reviewing transaction data to select a group of comparable elements, the most relevant are those for the same property type—that is, retail, office, multifamily, and the like. Within that data set, assets that are similar to the subject property in quality, size, and use are most relevant. For example, if our subject is a 100,000-square-foot suburban office building, then we do not want to compare it to a 50-floor downtown tower, which has different market dynamics and investor groups.

To be most applicable, the data used should come from transactions in the same geographic region as the subject property. This data will reflect the underlying expectations for local economic activity and real property demand. In many large markets, looking at data for submarkets is very important, as economic conditions and activity may differ dramatically across a region.

It is not always possible to access a relevant sample of data that relates to a subject property. The subject asset may be unique, or it may be located in a market with a limited population of similar assets. Even if there are a number of comparable assets, transaction activity may be limited. In this case, we must look to the most relevant data available and extrapolate. For example, if no apartments have traded in submarket X of a medium midwestern city, we can look at similar submarkets of other, similarly sized midwestern cities. If that fails, we can look at data from other regions of the country, and so on.

If we cannot find transactions of similar type assets, we can look to transactions of other property types within the region for comparison. This approach is much less reliable. As our transaction data becomes less relevant, our ability to rely on the cap rate declines.

5.1.5.1 Cap Rates for High-Credit Single-Tenant Properties

In the case of properties that are leased for long terms to high-credit single tenants, the tenant credit quality, rather then the fundamentals of the local real estate market, can drive the cap rate. In this situation, the underlying assumption is that the tenant's ability to pay the rent stream over the lease term is more important to value than the residual worth of the real estate.

When seeking comparable transactions to use in valuing a high-credit single tenant property, the best data will come from recent transactions involving similar properties leased to the same tenant. If comparable transaction data is not available, we can look to alternative sources of corporate credit information. If the company is private, Dun and Bradstreet may be a good source of credit information. If the tenant is a public company, it may be followed by securities analysts who write research reports. If it has publicly issued debt securities, the company may also be followed by a ratings agency such as Standard and Poor's or Moody's and may have a credit rating. The current market yield on the debt can provide insight into the market's view of the tenant's credit quality.

5.1.6 Reconciling the Reported Cap Rate Data

Once we have aggregated a relevant set of comparable transactions, we need to look at how our asset compares to the subject asset in each transaction. This task is easiest if the transactions in the comparable set are from our property's market and we are familiar with them.

First, we need to asses whether the transactions were true "arm's-length" transactions between unrelated parties without major extenuating circumstances. Examples of extenuating circumstances include financial duress of seller, a property in poor physical condition with deferred maintenance, and a property subject to onerous financing and thus limiting the financial flexibility of the buyer or seller.

Second, we need to assess the market attractiveness of our asset against the properties in the comparable set. Is our property best in class and worthy of a premium valuation? Is it one of the less-competitive assets in its market? This analysis can be very subjective, but the analyst should consider the following basic factors: is our property in good physical condition, with market standard amenities, of a desired form factor and with design features in keeping with tenant expectation? Is the asset well located and accessible to transportation? Assessing the relevance of each of these factors to the market viability of an asset is a judgment call.

Such a process can help us decide whether the cap rate reflected by the market transaction data should be applied as reported or whether we should adjust it up or down. An upward adjustment would imply that we think the subject asset is less attractive and presents a greater risk level than those in the reported transaction set. In contrast, a downward adjustment would imply that our asset is more attractive and presents a lower risk than those in the comparable transaction set.

5.1.7 Advantages and Disadvantages of Valuation by Stabilized NOI/Cap Rate

The stabilized NOI/cap rate approach to valuation is compelling in its theoretical simplicity and ease of use. While this method can be quickly implemented to develop a rough estimate of value, it is deceptively complex to apply properly, requiring numerous and subjective modifications to both NOI and cap rate. For this reason, analysts combine the cap rate approach with the discounted cash flow and comparable property methods when performing a complete property valuation.

5.2 DISCOUNTED CASH FLOW (DCF) METHOD

5.2.1 Pro Forma Model of Property Cash Flows

The DCF method values a property by summing the present values of its future cash flows over an investment period and its terminal value (TV), the ultimate sale or liquidation value at the end of that period. The present value of each of these cash flows is calculated at the date of investment using a discount rate based on real estate and capital market factors. The sum of these present values is the value of the asset:

$$DCF = \left(Sum_{(t=investment\ to\ liquidation)}\left(PV_{(r)}(Periodic\ cash\ flow_{(t)})\right)\right)$$
$$+ PV_{(r)}\ Terminal\ value$$

where:
DCF = discounted cash flow
PV = present value
t = time
r = discount rate

Any projection of future events requires many assumptions. The three major elements in a discounted cash flow model are: (a) the annual cash flows during the investment term, (b) the terminal value at the end of the investment period, and (c) the discount rate used to calculate the present value of these quantities. Although the mechanics of this method are straightforward, the art comes from the choice of assumptions.

5.2.2 Annual Cash Flows

The cash flows used in the DCF method reflect our estimate of property performance in each future year of our investment period. Rather than trying to estimate a hypothetical stabilized year's cash flow as we do when applying the cap rate method, in the DCF method, for each year of the model we use the annual cash flow that we expect to take place in that future year.

There are a number of events that affect future year cash flows and drive differences in annual performance.

5.2.2.1 Lease Expirations, Tenant Replacement, and Lease-Up of Vacancy

Commercial property leasing costs are substantial, in many cases over one year's rent, and can skew cash flow in any year. Analysts can look at lease expiration schedules and gain insight into the expected timing of leasing costs. The level of costs is a function of market dynamics and must be analyzed from the perspective of recent experience at the subject property and comparable properties. At each lease expiration, the analyst must predict whether the tenant will renew or vacate. If the prediction is for renewal, the analyst must estimate the new rent, term, tenant allowance, and leasing commission. If vacancy is predicted, the analyst must estimate the period for which the space will be vacant and the terms of the new lease that follows.

5.2.2.2 Forecasting Expenses

In the cap rate model, we use current expense levels in our NOI calculation. In a forward projection, the analyst must estimate changes to the property's expenses over time. For example, the future cost per unit of utilities (power, water) can be estimated by applying an inflation factor to current costs. Usage levels can be estimated based on a review of historic data modified for any proposed operational or system changes that may be planned (assuming that the costs of these changes are also reflected in the capital expense budgets).

5.2.2.3 Non-Revenue-Generating Capital Expenditures

Over time, building systems need replacement. In the cap rate method, we use an annual capital expenditure allowance to adjust NOI. In multifamily properties, the allowance is calculated per apartment per year; in commercial properties, the allowance is calculated per square foot per year. In the DCF method, we look at estimated costs in the year we predict they will occur. For example, if we think the roof will need to be replaced in year five, we put our cost estimate for the repair in year five of our projection.

5.2.2.4 Expansions and Renovations

Part of the value of owning a property is the inherent option to make improvements. If these are a part of our plan for the asset, they should be included in our forecast. Costs should be shown in the year when we predict they will occur and associated revenues should follow based on our plans.

5.2.3 Discount Rates

To consider the value of each future cash flow to the investor at the time of the investment, we must equate that future payment to its current cash value. A dollar in the future is worth less than a dollar in our pockets today, for many reasons. Intuitively, a dollar today can be invested in a risk-free government security and earn interest over the holding period. At the end of the period, you will have that compounded interest as well as your dollar:

$$FV = PV \times ((1 + r)^t)$$

Algebra brings us the following:

$$PV = FV/((1 + r)^t)$$

where:

FV = future value
PV = present value
r = interest
t = time

Each cash flow requires a separate PV calculation using a different "t" reflecting the time of occurrence. The time of each cash flow differs, but most analysts use the same discount rate for all of the cash flows or use different discount rates following the yield curve.

If a single rate is chosen, it is typically the cap rate, as discussed in the prior section. The application of a single rate for a long stream of cash flows is predicated on the notion that real estate is a long-term investment and we will earn a yield on that investment commensurate with long-term rates.

5.2.3.1 Yield Curve–Based Discount Rates

Interest rates differ depending on the term of investment. A graph of investment returns against time is known as a yield curve. Rather than using a single interest rate to discount all investment cash flows, an analyst could apply a different discount factor to each cash flow based on the interest rate shown on the yield curve for securities that mature in the year of that cash flow.

If a yield curve approach is used, an index rate must be chosen. The U.S. Treasury, Swap, and LIBOR (London Interbank Offered Rate) yield curves are typical index rates. A credit spread is then added to the interest rate level on the yield curve that corresponds to each of the model's cash flows.

For example, assume we are using the U.S. Treasury yield curve as our index rate and that we believe that our investment return should exceed that rate by 2.5 percent, reflecting the risk inherent in commercial real estate. To discount our year three cash flow, we would use a discount rate equal to 2.5 percent plus today's yield on a three-year treasury security.

There are arguments for and against using the yield curve as a source of discount rates for a DCF calculation. In most market environments, the yield curve has an upward slope, as investors require higher returns for committing capital for longer time periods. When the yield curve has an upward slope, the application of a yield curve approach will generally result in lower discount factors for short-term cash flows and increase the value of our property.

One can argue that lower discount factors for short-term cash flows is appropriate because we know more about the near future and we can predict these cash flows with a greater degree of certainty than those further in the future. These early-year cash flows are therefore less risky and should be accorded a higher relative value in our analysis.

A contrary point of view would argue that one reason that short-term interest rates are low is because short-term investments rapidly mature into cash and can be reinvested at current rates. Therefore, a short-term investor benefits from liquidity. An investor cannot assume timely liquidity in the real estate market, as property transactions may take months to conclude. Therefore, assuming low short-term interest rates in a real estate DCF calculation may overstate the value of a property.

5.2.4 Terminal Value

The residual value of the property at the end of the investment period is known as the terminal value (TV). The TV is calculated using an estimate of total asset value based on the cap rate method. The stabilized NOI in the final year of the investment period is divided by the exit cap rate, an estimate of the asset's cap rate at the end of the investment period. It is very hard to accurately calculate the TV because it relies on assumptions involving the distant future.

5.2.4.1 Importance Varies with Interest Rates

The TV is typically the largest cash flow in the model. Its relative value to the total investment depends on the discount rate applied. The higher the discount rate and the longer the intended holding period, the lower the impact the terminal value has on the overall investment value. In low-interest-rate environments, the TV is an important driver of total DCF value.

5.2.4.2 Setting the Exit Cap Rate

The starting point for setting an exit cap rate is the cap rate at the time of investment. This cap rate will incorporate our knowledge about the property's market and the competitive position of the property at the date of investment. When setting the exit cap rate, investors typically adjust the initial cap rate for our perceptions about how the market or the property's competitive position will change over time. If the strategic plan for the asset is to move it upmarket through repositioning, a lower exit cap rate is used. In contrast, if the property is in a deteriorating market with releasing risk, the exit cap rate should be moved up to reflect diminished expectations for market conditions at the time of sale.

5.2.5 Issues with DCF Method
5.2.5.1 More Accurate for Properties/Markets in Transition

The DCF method, with its more granular view of an asset, is more accurate for properties that are likely to experience a significant change in their performance over time. This change in performance can come from the implementation of a strategy for changing asset performance or from expected changes in the market and the leases in place. In either case, the DCF method is more accurate for a property in transition.

5.2.5.2 Forecast Error Increases with Time

We must however always keep in mind that the accuracy of any forecast diminishes with time because the future often brings unexpected change. Although we apply our best judgment to fashion a vision of an asset, the future is ultimately unpredictable. Luckily, the further into the future our prediction, the less valuable the cash flow will be to our estimate of value. Later-year cash flows are subject to increasing discount factors due to the higher levels of long-term interest rates and the longer time periods over which compounding takes place.

5.3 COMPARABLE SALES

A very simple, yet very powerful method for valuing real estate is comparing the value of the subject property to that of similar assets that have recently traded in the same or similar markets. In the ideal circumstance, we can establish a value for our target property by comparing it to a sample of recently traded properties of the same type, location, vintage, and condition.

5.3.1 Market Data

There are many sources of data on real estate transactions. In recent years, Internet-based data aggregation companies have been established that attempt to track all commercial real estate transactions by date and location.

These companies gather pricing metrics that can be used in a comparable analysis. The deeper the data set of recent similar transactions and the more stable the economic environment, the more accurate are the inferences that can be drawn. These metrics can answer the key question: at what price have similar assets traded in the recent past?

Once we have established a set of transactions involving comparable properties, we must then establish a basis for comparing our target to those properties in the comparable transaction data set.

5.3.2 Common Denominator

The first step is to pick a few common denominators and calculate pricing benchmarks. The most common way of comparing properties is price per unit of space. The unit of measure varies by property type, with retail, office, and industrial being measured in square feet; apartments in units; and hotels by rooms or "keys." This comparison assumes that comparable properties with similar quality and location will trade at an equivalent price per unit of space, assuming all else to be equal.

Of course, all else is rarely equal.

5.3.3 Adjustments to Comparable Data

Once the price per unit of space is established, one must determine the more subtle factors that distinguish assets from one another.

First, we must adjust for the unique location of each asset: distance from public transportation and road networks, availability of parking, proximity of amenities, and attractiveness of each asset's surrounding environment.

Then we must look at a comparison of the physical condition of each asset, including efficiency of the floor plan, condition of the building (HVAC, electric and vertical transportation systems, age and condition of the roof and paving, and quality of the landscaping). Well-maintained buildings with modern, efficient systems will trade at a premium. In most markets, deferred maintenance costs are direct subtractions from value.

Finally, we must carefully review the status of the current leasing. In general, fully leased buildings with high-credit tenants paying market rents are considered to be lower-risk investments and are attractive to a wider audience of buyers. These buildings will command premium valuations. Buildings with a high level of vacancy present a higher risk profile and attract a more limited set of opportunistic buyers. If the building is in a high demand market or a market in transition, the vacant space may present an opportunity for growth in cash flow, but that opportunity comes with execution risk that typically lowers current value.

5.3.4 Mechanics of Valuation Using Comparable Property Data

If we multiply the quantity of space in our target property by the average price per measure of space, we have the unadjusted value of our asset. Using the previous criteria for comparison, we rate our asset on each of the major factors influencing value. Then these factors are weighted to develop an index of comparison. This index reflects the subjective viewpoint of the analyst and embodies the art of valuation. We can then multiply our unadjusted value by this index. This adjusted value is our best estimate of value by comparison.

EXAMPLE

Master Appraisal Co. has found three comparable properties for the subject office building. Properties A and B are newer and closer to transportation than our subject, Property C is very similar in age and style to our building but has excellent views and has a history of above market occupancy. Their valuation report includes the chart below and concludes that the subject property will trade at a $5 per square foot discount to Property C.

Comparable Property Analysis Prepared by Master Appraisal Co.				
Property	**Subject**	**Property A**	**Property B**	**Property C**
Size	100,000 sq. ft.	75,000	110,000	100,000
Price	Est. $9,000,000	$7,875,000	$13,200,000	$9,500,000
Price/sq. ft.	Est. $90/sq. ft.	$105/sq. ft.	$120/sq. ft.	$95/sq. ft.
Year	1970	2000	2005	1975
Location	Good	Excellent	Excellent	Good
Amenities	Excellent	Excellent	Excellent	Excellent
Finish	Good	Good	Excellent	Good

5.4 COST APPROACH

Another method of valuing a property is the cost approach. In this method, the current cost of replacing the subject property is estimated. This approach draws on construction cost data reported by industry sources as well as land transaction data reported for comparable properties. This approach is informative if the valuation is being performed to settle an insurance claim for a property lost to casualty. In this case, the amount required to rebuild the asset in situ is a relevant number.

In valuing for investment purposes, comparing the market value to the replacement cost informs the buyer of the likelihood of new properties being constructed. If comparable properties are trading at less than replacement cost, developers are unlikely to build new assets. If the market is strong and the value of in service property exceeds the current cost to develop new assets, it is likely that developers will look to build new projects.

5.5 VALUE OF ASSET VERSUS VALUE OF EQUITY

Many students and professionals confuse the value of a property with the value of an equity interest in the property subject to debt financing:

$$\text{Value of asset} - \text{Property debt} = \text{Value of equity}$$

5.5.1 Asset Value Is Independent of Financing

The asset value of a property is calculated as if it were "free and clear" of debt. As discussed earlier, various methods can be applied to develop estimates of value. Each of these methods looks at the amount of net operating income available to support the invested capital. They assume that the property has no current debt or that the existing debt can be repaid. This is known as the free and clear asset value.

Properties are not always debt free. The presence of debt will not typically have an impact on property value if the existing debt has terms reflective of the current market. If the terms of the debt are favorable and it can be assumed by the new owner, then it can enhance property value. The amount of the positive impact will be the present value of the economic advantage provided by the debt. If the debt has unfavorable terms and it cannot be repaid without penalty, then it will lower the value of the property. The negative impact will be: (a) the prepayment penalty required by the lender in order to retire the debt or (b) the present value of the disadvantageous economic terms, whichever is lower.

5.5.2 Equity Value and Returns

The equity value is the free and clear asset value less the mark to market value of any in-place debt encumbering the asset. The mark to market value of the encumbrance includes the current principal amount of the financing adjusted for the difference between the terms of the debt and the terms available in today's market:

$$\text{Equity value} = \text{Property value} - \text{Mark to market value of debt}$$

Investors look at return on equity in two ways. First, they look at the current return available after paying the debt service, including principal and scheduled amortization payments. This is called the cash-on-cash return, the periodic cash flows available to the cash invested. It is generally reported for a single year ("the cash on cash return from property x is y percent") or as the average return during a given period ("the average cash on cash return during the investment period is z percent").

Investors also look at the longer-term returns to equity by using figures of merit such as PV, Net Present Value (NPV), and Internal Rate of Return (IRR). To calculate these metrics, the debt service for in-place financing is subtracted from the property cash flows during the investment period. The metrics calculated are known as the levered PV, the levered NPV, and the levered IRR. The discount rate used to calculate the levered PV and the levered NPV is our expected return on equity. The levered IRR is itself a return metric and is reported for a given period ("the levered IRR during the investment period is i percent").

5.6 IMPACT OF IN-PLACE FINANCING

When looking at in-place debt, we must look at the amount of debt, the interest rate, the amortization schedule, and the maturity.

5.6.1 Above-/Below-Market-Rate Debt

To quantify the impact of interest rates that are off-market, we must discount the scheduled debt service payments by the market interest rate.

The present value of these payments is the mark to market value or fair value of the debt.

Mark to market value $= \text{PV}_{\text{(market interest rate)}}$ (scheduled debt service payments)

If the mark to market value is greater than the current balance, then the debt would trade at a premium. If the mark to market value is less than the outstanding balance, the debt would trade at a discount. The amount of premium or discount is the absolute value of the difference between the market value and the outstanding balance.

EXAMPLE

A property is subject to a $1,000,000 mortgage at 5 percent with an original 30-year term. The current monthly debt service payment (principal and interest) is $5,368.22. After one year, mortgage interest rates have moved up 0.5 percent to 5.5 percent. How will this rate change affect the market value of the mortgage?

First, the remaining principal balance of the mortgage is $985,246.35. The value of the mortgage equals the present value of the remaining 348 mortgage payments discounted at the new interest rate of 5.5 percent per annum = $932,723.52. As a result of the increase in rates, the mortgage has declined in value by $52,522.83.

If we are valuing a property using a single metric like the cap rate, we must adjust our estimate of value by subtracting the debt premium or adding the discount.

If we are using the DCF method, we must develop a levered PV by subtracting the appropriate debt service payment from each periodic cash flow. The amount of this payment will reflect the in-place debt. If the debt is unfavorable, the premium will be reflected in reduced equity returns and a lower valuation. If the debt is favorable, the discount will be reflected in a higher valuation and higher equity returns.

5.6.2 Buyer Concerns About In-Place High Loan-to-Value (LTV) Financing

Many institutional property investors have limits on the amount of leverage they can carry on an individual asset or on a portfolio. They may be unable or unwilling to buy an asset that is highly levered and would require an immediate refinancing in order to comply with their leverage guidelines. Therefore, properties with in-place financing may face more limited buyer interest than free and clear assets. However, in tight credit markets, properties with assumable in-place debt can be very valuable to more flexible buyers with limited cash who require leverage for their investments.

5.6.3 Buyer Concerns About In-Place Low LTV Financing

Buyers who need significant leverage to make an acquisition may find the amount of an existing nonprepayable mortgage too low. To acquire the asset, they will have to increase the amount of equity used to purchase the investment or seek additional debt capital in the form of a junior or second mortgage. Second mortgages are difficult to obtain and carry a higher interest rate than senior secured financings. To raise total leverage to standard leverage levels, the buyer may face interest costs that are higher than market. The higher interest cost will lower the equity returns. If the buyer must use additional equity to acquire the low-leverage asset, the buyer's return on investment (ROI) will also be lower. Although the lower leverage reduces the investment risk, low risk is not the goal of the more opportunistic real estate buyer, and thus the low-leverage asset may have a smaller group of potential investors than the free and clear property.

5.6.4 Buyer Concerns about Timing of Debt Maturity

Lenders want to lend against a property when it is fully leased and those leases have long remaining terms. At this point, the property is most stable and future cash flow is most predictable. Lenders perceive assets as most risky when they are facing considerable lease rollover and are reluctant to lend.

To the potential buyer, rollover may bring an upside in a tight space market. The new owner may need to provide cash to pay leasing commissions and to fit out space for reuse. The tenant turnover costs can be funded with a larger replacement debt financing based upon the new stronger leases.

In contrast, in difficult markets, refinancing with pending lease expirations is very disadvantageous. Lease rollover can result in higher vacancy or tenants renewing at lower rents. This will lower operating income and the new owner may need to reduce the outstanding debt in order to refinance the asset. This will create a cash requirement concurrent with the need to pay turnover costs on any leases that do renew. A buyer who purchases an asset facing this situation needs to go into the purchase expecting to infuse equity into the property.

For these reasons, properties with debt maturing concurrently with major lease rollover present a higher risk profile. They present an opportunity for the well-capitalized investor but will be less attractive to risk-adverse investors with limited capital resources.

5.7 APPRAISAL PROCESS

Banks, insurers, and other financial institutions require independent objective assessments of property value. These institutions use professional appraisal firms for these assessments. The product of the appraiser's work is a written report with an estimate of value. In completing this work, the appraiser may use multiple methodologies for developing his or her opinion of value, including those described in this chapter.

5.7.1 Comparison of Results from Previous Methods

The appraiser often faces a situation in which the different valuation methods lead to different estimates. When this situation occurs, it becomes necessary to reconcile the results and develop a final opinion. This process involves analysis of the results and assumptions followed by the application of judgment as to which result is more representative of the current state of the market. Again, we can see the interplay of the art and science of valuation.

5.7.2 Reconciliation of Differences in Results

Differences between the cap rate analysis and the DCF result from a change in the state of the asset over the holding period that either improves or lowers the value of the property. When this occurs, we must take a hard look at our pro forma model and test all of our assumptions.

If our theoretical constructs—the cap rate and DCF analysis—yield results that differ from the result of our analysis of comparable properties, then we must review the assumptions we used in our models. We must check our operating assumptions to determine whether the subject property's performance is significantly different than that of the other assets in the marketplace. We must determine whether our rents or operating expenses are different from those of the comparable properties and decide whether these differences are sustainable over our investment period. If not, we should adjust our model. If our review of these assumptions does not explain the discrepancy, then we need to reevaluate the discount rate that we have applied.

This reconciliation process is a great way of checking our analysis. An appraiser is trying to determine how prospective buyers will look at a property and what the market will pay for an asset. As an owner, we may be privy to information regarding the asset that colors our viewpoint. As a prospective investor, we may have opportunistic sources of capital that are seeking risk or we may be subject to constraints that influence our valuation. In both cases, we may have a rationale for a different view of the asset than that held by the market. If we reconcile our work and believe that our unique view of value is correct, then we may have a good reason to transact.

Glossary

Appraisal process
Asset value
Cap rate

Capital reserves
Cash on cash return
Comparable sales
Debt discount
Debt premium
DCF (discounted cash flow)
Discount rate
Entity value
Exit cap rate
Forecast error
Levered NPV (net present value)
Levered IRR (Internal rate of return)
LTV (Loan-to-Value)
Management fee
Mark to market
ROI (return on investment)
Second mortgages
Stabilized NOI (net operating income)
Terminal value
Vacancy allowance
Yield curve

Thought Questions

1. When real estate companies rent to tenants, they accept the tenant's credit risk as well as the risk of operating real estate. When a tenant defaults on a lease, the real estate company still has its property. When a tenant defaults on a loan, a lender may have nothing. Should returns on real estate be higher or lower than returns on the tenant's debt securities?

2. Is a multitenant property with staggered lease expirations more or less risky than a single-tenant property with a long-term lease? What factors other than lease term inform your decision?

Review Questions

1. Valuation: Cap Rate

The Crescent Arms is a 15-story luxury apartment building in New Orleans's warehouse district. In 2009, the property had adjusted NOI of $2.5 million. The property was marketed to a broad range of investors and sold for $29.5 million. At what cap rate did the property sell?

2. Valuation: NPV

The owners of the Centre at New Hope purchased the property at the end of 2002. Adjusted NOI for 2003 was projected at $4 million and expected to rise at 5 percent per annum over a seven-year hold period. The property was purchased at a 9 percent cap rate based on 2003 adjusted NOI. The owners expect that they will be able to sell it at the end of the holding period at an 8 percent cap rate. Can the owners achieve a 10 percent return? (Assume the owners are tax exempt.)

3. Valuation: Comparable Property

   Three major class A office properties have recently traded in Baltimore. Building A sold at $300 per square foot, Building B at $250 per square foot, and Building C at $350 per square foot. You believe that your building, a 20-story class A office property with 20,000-square-foot floor plates, has attributes of all three properties. What is your building worth?

4. Which of the following are adjustments commonly made to NOI in a valuation exercise?

   I. Subtract recurring capital expense
   II. Add revenue-generating capital expense
   III. Subtract mortgage principal payments
   IV. Add management fees
   V. Subtract management fees
   a) I, V
   b) II, III
   c) II, III, IV
   d) I, II, IV

5. Which of the following is not a method typically used to value commercial property:

   a) Comparable property
   b) NPV
   c) Adjusted NOI/cap rate
   d) Multiple of after-tax earnings

6. Which of the following is not an appraisal method?

   a) Sales comparison approach
   b) Income capitalization approach
   c) Distressed seller approach
   d) Cost approach

7. Which of the following is not an approach to property valuation based on income?

   a) Gross income multiplier method
   b) Discounted present value method
   c) Direct capitalization method
   d) Future accretion method

8. What attributes of a property would influence the choice of valuation methods used and the accuracy of the resultant valuation?

   I. Future growth in rent
   II. Current property occupancy and cost of lease-up
   III. Expected changes in major leases

    IV. Prospect for overbuilding in the market
    a) I, II, III
    b) II, IV
    c) I, III
    d) All of the above

9. A terminal or reversion value is:
   a) The tendency of property to decline in value over time
   b) The tendency of return on investment in any industry to revert to the average of all industries
   c) The resale price of a property at the end of a financial projection
   d) Purchase price plus growth less depreciation

10. The Return on Equity (ROE) on a levered property investment should be:
    a) $\leq$ Return on Assets
    b) $\leq$ Yield debt
    c) = cap rate
    d) $\geq$ Return on Assets

11. The cost approach to valuation is based on:
    a) Historical cost less depreciation
    b) Historical cost
    c) Replacement cost
    d) Replacement cost less depreciation

12. NOI minus debt service equals:
    I) Cash flow before taxes
    II) Equity dividend
    III) DCF
    IV) NPV
    a) I, II
    b) III, IV
    c) I, III
    d) II, IV

13. In what interest rate environment are terminal value estimates most important?
    a) High rate
    b) Low rate
    c) Declining market fundamentals
    d) None of the above

14. Which is not a real estate valuation method?
    a) DCF
    b) Price earnings
    c) Comparable sales
    d) Capped NOI

15. A property has NOI of $10 million, depreciation of $1 million and similar properties trade at an 8 percent cap rate. What is the value of the property?
    a) $80.0 million
    b) $112.5 million
    c) $125.0 million
    d) $137.5 million
    Adjusted NOI/Cap rate = Value. Depreciation *is not an adjustment to NOI: $10m/0.08 = $125m.

0	1	2	3	4	5	6	7	8	9	10
	4.00	4.12	4.24	4.37	4.50	4.64	4.78	4.92	5.07	5.22
										65.24
(44.44)	4.00	4.12	4.24	4.37	4.50	4.64	4.78	4.92	5.07	70.46
IRR=	12.6%									

For answers to these Problems and Exercises, please visit the companion website: http://booksite.elsevier.com/9780123786265

CHAPTER 6

Capital Markets

6.1 WHY INVEST IN REAL ESTATE?

Investors in real estate may be seeking a property for their own use or may be acquiring property as a financial investment. Both classes of property investors access the capital markets to finance their property acquisitions.

Financial investors deploy capital in order to earn a return. Most investors seek the maximum return possible for the amount of risk they are willing to take. Real estate investments have a number of unique characteristics that make them highly attractive to a large number of investors. For this reason, real estate has historically been seen as an excellent store of value and a wealth creation vehicle for both individual and institutional investors.

6.1.1 Benefits of Adding Real Estate to a Portfolio
6.1.1.1 Diversification
To minimize risk, investors spread their capital across a number of investments so that the failure of any one investment does not jeopardize their entire capital base. This strategy is known as diversification. To be diversified, a portfolio of investments should be associated with multiple aspects of the economy. Otherwise, the investments will have concentrated risk in a single industry and can be severely impacted if the performance of that industry falters.

Diversification across multiple assets (or industries) offers the potential for portfolio returns that are less volatile than those that would be produced by individual investments in any of the component assets. The stability of these returns is attractive to investors, who generally prefer not to be surprised by large, unpredictable swings in the value of their portfolio as the portfolio value appreciates over time.

6.1.1.1.1 Low Covariance with Other Asset Types
When two classes of assets exhibit the same performance characteristics through the course of varying economic cycles, they are said to have high covariance. In contrast, if the performance of these assets differ when faced with the same economic conditions, they have low covariance. You can limit

153

volatility and achieve a diversified portfolio with more stable returns by creating a portfolio of investments with low covariance.

Many investors, both individuals and institutions, have a core portfolio of publicly traded debt and equity securities. Over time, investments in real estate have been shown to have a low covariance with these asset classes and can provide some diversification to these portfolios.

6.1.1.2 Large Investments Are Available

Although it seems an unlikely problem, many institutions have significant sums of capital to invest and find it hard to put their funds to work. It is expensive to build or to acquire major properties. The value of one major office property in a US city can exceed the entire market capitalization of a mid-sized corporation. Thus one can place large sums of capital to work by acquiring a single major property. Corporations are more difficult to acquire and manage than real property. If one attempted to buy all the stock in a corporation, one would also face a number of legal and administrative complications — not to mention the fact that this action would likely drive the price ever higher with each incremental purchase. One would not encounter this situation as the buyer of a single property.

6.1.1.3 Comparison with Debt Investment in Tenant
6.1.1.3.1 Property as Collateral

The return from real estate ultimately comes from rent. Aside from the rent, the tenant's business must pay other operating costs, such as salaries and costs of goods sold. For example, in addition to rent, a grocery tenant renting space in a shopping center must generate enough sales to cover salary expense and costs of goods sold. The tenant must service other continuing liabilities, such as debt payments.

In many ways, the tenant's health affects the strength of the cash flow stream derived from a property. If the grocery store tenant fails, that portion of the property's cash flow stream will cease until that space is released to another tenant.

The landlord in this situation, though suffering a temporary dislocation, is in a much better position than the holders of the tenant's other liabilities. The landlord still has the space to relet. After a tenant's business fails, its other capital providers, such as equity partners or lenders, have let the company use their capital, yet may have nothing left but the paper on which the investment was written.

6.1.1.4 Low Volatility of Returns

By custom, leases used in office, shopping center, apartment, and industrial space are typically written for long periods of time, generally measured in years rather than days or weeks. Due to these long-term agreements, real estate cash flows tend to be steady and predictable over long periods of time, in contrast with the more volatile cash flows generated in many other types of businesses resulting from less predictable (and noncontractual) consumer purchasing behavior.

Upon lease expiration, landlords typically seek a new long-term arrangement at a higher level of rent, which provides returns that track the level of economic inflation over time. Predictable cash flow, with a rising slope, is very attractive to investors who seek a return that will compensate them for the inflation present in most economies.

6.2 TYPES OF REAL ESTATE INTERESTS

6.2.1 Fee Simple

In the United States, the fee simple interest is the most common form of property ownership and is desired by most property investors. This type of interest remains with the owner in perpetuity and is subject only to easements and the claims of the government.

6.2.2 Leasehold

A leasehold interest is the right to use a property, or portion thereof, for a given period of time. The leasehold interest may restrict the use of the asset to certain limited purposes and terminates at a date certain.

6.2.2.1 Ground Lease

A ground lease is given by a property owner to a lessee who desires to use the property for a specific purpose for a given period of time. At the end of the lease, the ground and any improvements made thereupon revert to the original owner.

The lessee under a ground lease may have the right to improve the property by constructing buildings. The ground lessee may seek financing for construction of the improvements from financial institutions. The improvement loan is secured by the right to receive cash flow from the property for the term of the ground lease.

In a subordinated ground lease, the landowner agrees to give the lender who has financed the improvements a senior claim against the land as well. In an unsubordinated ground lease, the rights of the landowner to receive lease payments and to recover the property in the event of a default are senior to any financing placed on the improvements by the lessee. It is always better for the landowner to make an unsubordinated lease; the lessee and lender would rather have a subordinated lease.

A landowner may agree to give a subordinated lease to facilitate the construction of the improvements that will allow the lessee to pay more for the ground lease.

6.2.2.2 Triple Net Lease

A triple net lease is a lease that requires the lessee to pay all of the costs of operating a property. This lease protects the owner from escalating operating costs over the lease period.

6.2.2.3 Sublease

A sublease is a form of lease in which a lessee allows another tenant to use the space it has leased from the property owner. The sublease pays the lessee, who remains responsible for paying the landlord. Subleasing can be very profitable when property demand has increased and the original lessee no longer needs to use the space.

Investors acquire all types of real estate interests, as each can be profitable under the right circumstance. Diligent analysis of all documentation is required so that the investor is aware of the rights and restrictions that apply to the form of interest acquired.

6.3 FORMS OF REAL ESTATE INVESTMENTS

It is possible to make an investment in real estate by acquiring an interest in property or by acquiring an interest in an entity that in turn invests in property.

6.3.1 Direct

In a direct investment, the investor purchases an interest in property and is responsible for the operation of the asset, including its financial liabilities. Day-to-day operational management may be retained or contracted to another party.

6.3.1.1 Investors

Many large investors — including most public real estate companies — have the sophistication and human resources to acquire and manage real estate. Certain large investment firms and financial institutions may acquire direct interests to control the operation and disposition of assets but may outsource all of the day-to-day responsibilities to property management firms.

6.3.1.1.1 Joint Venture

One way that large investors can acquire property is to enter into joint ventures with existing real estate firms. These relationships can bring professional skills and market access to the institutional partner while providing access to capital and economics of scale to the operating partner.

Some real estate firms are reluctant to enter into joint ventures because it inhibits their freedom of action when faced with decisions regarding their assets.

6.3.1.2 Lenders

Lenders can opt to lend directly to property owners and will then have direct ownership of real estate loans and mortgages. Other lenders without the scale, skill, or interest in being a direct lender can purchase interests in mortgage funds or mortgage securities.

One issue with direct investment is liquidity and transaction costs. It may be more difficult to sell real property than to sell real property securities. It may also be more expensive, as there can be many taxes and fees charged on real estate investments.

6.3.2 Indirect

To facilitate greater investment in real estate, securities are issued by real estate companies that reflect the value and cash flow generation of the underlying assets. In many cases, the companies that issue these securities also provide the full array of services to the real estate portfolios that they acquire on behalf of their investors.

6.3.2.1 REITs

Real estate investment trusts (REITs) are widely held entities that invest in real estate and issue debt and equity securities to investors. Many REITs are public companies whose securities are traded on national stock exchanges. A growing number of these companies have large market capitalizations, allowing for liquidity in the trading of their securities.

6.3.2.2 Real Estate Funds

Real estate funds are investment vehicles and are generally structured using some form of tax pass-through entity. These entities are typically structured as limited partnerships on joint ventures in which the general partner receives a promoted interest for providing a wide range of services to investors.

6.3.2.3 Mortgage-backed Securities (MBS) Issuers

Issuers of MBS are typically tax pass-through vehicles that aggregate funds to acquire pools of commercial or residential mortgages. In many cases, the securities of these issuers are publicly traded.

In order to maintain their tax pass-through status, most issuers of mortgage securities serve only to aggregate the cash received from borrowers and to send the requisite payments out to bondholders.

6.4 TYPES OF REAL ESTATE SECURITIES

Real estate securities are financial investments that are derived from an economic interest in real estate. These investments can represent direct financial claims on specific assets or indirect claims through investments in entities that in turn own property.

6.4.1 What Is a Security?

A security is a financial interest in an asset or an entity. There are many types of interests, each with a specified set of rights and in some cases obligations. Ownership of securities may be freely transferable or limited by predefined terms and conditions. In certain limited circumstances, when both the issuers and brokers involved in the transaction have complied with government regulations, securities may be sold to the public and traded on securities exchanges.

6.4.2 Debt

A debt is an obligation of a borrower to repay borrowed funds to the lender under a specified set of conditions known as the terms of the debt. The terms include a set period of time before the debt must be repaid (the term) and the obligation of the borrower to pay the lender interest, a fee for the use of the capital. In many transactions, in order to induce the lender to provide capital, the borrower may agree to additional conditions covering the way the capital will be expended and the borrower's entity will be managed during the term of the debt. There may also be specified consequences to the borrower in the event that the debt is not repaid as per its terms. One typical consequence is that the lender may seize the asset that has been acquired, or enhanced, by the borrower's use of the lender's capital.

6.4.2.1 Debt Basics
6.4.2.1.1 Structure

A security sets forth a series of terms and conditions under which a lender makes a loan to a borrower. In the case of a debt security, these agreements are set forth in a document known as an indenture.

In cases in which the size of the loan is beyond the financial capability of a single lender, a group of lenders is formed to make the loan. This group is called a syndicate, and each lender is known as a participant. These types of loans are known as syndicated loans. In general, each syndicate participant is party to the same terms and conditions, as set forth in the indenture.

Interests in loans are also offered directly to the public through investment bankers. These interests are generically called debt securities. The individual interests may be called bonds, notes, or commercial paper, depending on the terms of the borrowing. The investment banker acts as an agent for the company that is interested in borrowing money (the issuer) and sells the debt securities to investors. The terms of the borrowing are disclosed in the indenture. The buyers of the security are represented in the transaction by a fiduciary known as a trustee. This entity monitors and enforces the terms of the indenture on behalf of the investors, including collecting interest and principal from the company and paying it to the investors.

6.4.2.1.2 Terms

The key terms of a debt security include the amount of the loan, the maturity date, the interest rate, and the collateral, if any, for the loan. Each of these terms may be very detailed. For example, a debt may be repaid through a combination of periodic amortization as well as a final payment of any balance remaining at maturity. Interest rates may be set once at the beginning of a loan (fixed-rate loan) or may be changed periodically based on a publicly disclosed benchmark rate (floating-rate loan).

Finally, the borrower may pledge property as "collateral" to the lenders, which can be liquidated to repay the debt in the event that the borrower does not repay the loan under its terms. This collateral may be pledged solely for the benefit of one group of lenders, or many groups may share the right to proceeds from the specified property. If the property is shared, lenders may then have senior (first priority claims) or junior claims (the right to whatever is left after loans with senior claims have been repaid).

6.4.2.1.3 Covenants

In addition to specifying the terms of the borrowing, lenders may also insist that the borrower agree to operate its business within certain financial metrics and with certain operational constraints. In doing so, the lenders seek to limit the risks taken by the borrower while it is using their capital.

In the event that a borrower does not adhere to the covenants, it is considered to be in default under the loan. A default also occurs when the borrower misses any scheduled payment of interest or principal.

The consequences of a default are specified in the indenture and may range from an increase in the interest rate on the loan to an acceleration of the loan. In the event of acceleration, the maturity date of the loan moves from a future point to the present and the borrower may be forced to pay off the loan immediately. Typically, borrowers are given a grace period to cure any defaults before such serious actions are taken.

6.4.2.1.4 Credit Evaluation and Risk

Before the terms and conditions of a debt financing are agreed upon, the lender or lender's agent must evaluate the credit worthiness of the borrower. This step will determine the terms and structure of the debt financing that the lender is willing to offer.

There are many credit metrics considered by lenders, but the most typical fall into two types: leverage metrics and coverage metrics. A leverage metric looks at the value of a borrower's assets against the total amount of funds that it intends to borrow. The rationale for the leverage metric is that in the event of a default, a lender may need to liquidate the assets of a borrower to reclaim its funds.

The lower the ratio of funds borrowed to assets owned, the greater the amount of "equity cushion" that exists as a buffer between the value of the lender's invested capital and the market value of the assets. The higher the equity, the lower the leverage, and the better the likelihood that the lender will get its money back when the loan matures.

A coverage metric focuses on the level of funds being generated by the business as a going concern against the amounts required to service all of its outstanding debt. The higher the ratio of cash flow available to the amount required to service its debt, the lower the chance that a borrower will default on its loans.

Credit metrics can be viewed for an entire enterprise, including all of its assets, or against a single asset if that asset is itself the subject of a borrowing. Even when lenders are looking at a loan secured by a particular asset, they still care about the financial health of the borrower, because lenders do not want to take over assets. They want to get repaid with interest. Lenders refer to the status of a borrower as sponsorship and say that a loan to a borrower with a good reputation has good sponsorship.

EXAMPLE

Hunter Estates is a new development by the Hunter Property Company (HPC). Hunter has developed a number of successful multifamily projects in the suburbs of New York City. Hunter Estates, at 1,000 units, is the most complex project attempted by HPC. Stagecoach Bank and Trust is considering the construction loan on Hunter Estates. HPC owns the land on which it intends to build the Estates project. HPC has offered to post the land as collateral for the loan.

Stagecoach estimates the land value at 30 percent of the total project cost. Stagecoach estimates that by the end of the first year after completion, project cash flow will reach 1.5 times required debt service and that the project value will be twice the loan amount. At that time, the developer's equity will be 50 percent of project value and the lender's loan-to-value metric will be 50 percent. When this

occurs, Stagecoach believes that HPC can find a long-term mortgage for the project and repay Stagecoach's construction loan.

Although Stagecoach considers HPC a good sponsor, this is the most complex project attempted by this development team and presents significant risk to the lender. Stagecoach, though excited about the project, is asking HPC to guarantee the loan by pledging HPC's interest in Hunter's Run, a much smaller 100-unit completed project that is currently unleveraged, as additional collateral for the loan. Stagecoach has offered to release their lien on this asset once Hunter Estates is 80 percent leased.

HPC, having a good relationship with Stagecoach and being very optimistic about the prospects for Hunter Estates, accepts these terms.

Credit metrics must always be viewed in the context of the industry in which a business operates. In a highly cyclical business, lower leverage and higher coverage may be required, because performance can diminish rapidly during a loan's term. In very stable businesses, it may be possible for a lender to become comfortable with higher leverage and lower coverage.

6.4.2.1.5 Security

In some cases, a borrower may be required to pledge collateral in order to secure a loan. This loan is called a secured borrowing. The lender is said to have a security interest in the asset pledged. A security interest gives a lender certain rights to control the asset in the event that a borrower does not perform its obligations under the loan.

If a borrower's enterprise has great credit, it may be able to borrow funds without pledging specific assets as collateral. This loan is known as an unsecured loan. In the event of a default, unsecured loans are repaid with any assets that are not pledged as security to secured lenders. Remaining funds available after assets pledged to secured lenders have been liquidated and their respective loans repaid, may be used to repay unsecured creditors.

6.4.2.1.6 Seniority

Borrowers may approach different lenders on different occasions to fund an enterprise or an asset. When multiple loans are made against a single source of funds, a hierarchy must be established for repayment in the event that cash flow or liquidation proceeds are insufficient to fund the borrower's obligations.

The terms of each loan state its level of seniority against the claims of other lenders. Claims are repaid first to senior, then junior, and finally to subordinated claims.

There may be multiple loans at the same level, which is often the case for senior loans. In such a scenario, all loans of the same seniority level are paid pro rata, meaning that the sums available are divided ratably over the claims outstanding:

EXAMPLE

It is now five years after the completion of Hunter Estates and HPC, now a public REIT, owns 10,000 multifamily units in the NYC suburbs valued at more than $2 billion. HPC achieved a BBB credit rating, a lower investment grade rating, giving the company access to the public debt market. Stagecoach, still HPC's bank, suggests that HPC issue $100 million of senior debt into what is a very favorable credit market. This will be the fifth offering of Senior Unsecured notes by HPC.

Proceeds from the offering will be used to fund HPC's latest venture, Hunter's Big Game, a proposed ecohousing development. All units at Big Game will overlook a protected reserve featuring exotic animals cloned from DNA extracted from extinct animals found in the melting Arctic icecap.

HPC does not believe that this is the type of project most commercial banks will be interested in financing, so it has decided to borrow funds for this development on the corporate level. If the project is commercially successful, HPC can seek project financing after lease-up is accomplished.

6.4.2.1.7 Bankruptcy

In the event that a loan goes into default and is ultimately accelerated by the lender, the borrower may not be in a position to repay its obligations. In this case, either the borrower or its lenders may put the company into bankruptcy. Bankruptcy is a court-supervised reorganization or liquidation of a borrower's assets in favor of its creditors, meaning that the goal of the process is to maximize the chance that the creditors get repaid.

During reorganization, the liabilities of a company are restructured so that the business is capable of meeting its financial obligations on a going-forward basis. Lenders to a company undergoing reorganization may receive partial repayment of their existing loans, new loans with new terms, or other consideration in place of their current debt.

The court may also determine that the company cannot survive and demand a liquidation, in which case the business's assets will be sold and proceeds used to repay claims in order of seniority.

Lenders try to avoid bankruptcy proceedings because they are time consuming and costly. While the proceedings are occurring, the value of an asset may continue to diminish.

6.4.2.1.8 Foreclosure and Deficiency Judgments

In a secured financing, following a default, a lender may seek to seize the pledged collateral in a proceeding known as a foreclosure.

In some cases, in addition to the pledge of security for the loan, the borrower may have given a guarantee of all or a specified portion of the value of the loan. Such a guarantee typically requires that the borrower must ensure that the specified portion of the loan is repaid, even if liquidation of the asset does not provide sufficient funds to cover that guaranteed amount. A lender can seek a "deficiency judgment" against the borrower through the courts to enforce its right to collect the remaining guaranteed portion of a loan that is not recovered through a liquidation of the collateral.

6.4.2.2 Debt Advanced

Many forms of debt financing are available to owners and developers of real property. The debt financing can be asset-based and tied to a specific property, or entity-based and tied to the general credit of a real estate company, such as a REIT or real estate operating company.

6.4.2.2.1 Asset-Based Financing

Most debt financing for real estate is asset-based, and the type of financing available depends on the type, quality, and maturity of the subject property.

6.4.2.2.2 Land Acquisition

A developer beginning a project needs to finance the acquisition of land. This is the most difficult type of debt financing to obtain, because land held for development does not typically generate cash and the lender has no direct source of interest coverage. Instead, the lender limits the amount of financing that it will give the developer and builds in an amount to cover its interest charges. This is known as an interest reserve.

As the developer draws down the interest reserve, the balance of the loan increases. Over the holding period, the outstanding loan amount rises until the maximum leverage is reached. At this point, the developer must seek outside funding for the carrying costs or liquidate the asset.

To enter into a land financing agreement, the lender and the developer must share the conviction that the land can be developed before the interest reserve runs out.

Given the financial risk involved, developers seek to limit their land holdings. They do this by attempting to get options on land from current owners. The developer must convince the landowner that the owner and developer can both benefit from the increase in value that occurs during a successful development process. The developer also agrees to expend costs on predevelopment planning at no risk to the landowner. This process works best when a developer has little competition. In highly competitive markets, cash buyers may be present that can fund development risk without relying on owner options.

6.4.2.2.3 Construction Finance

As the name implies, construction finance is used to provide capital for the creation of new buildings. In general, commercial banks are the major providers of construction financing. These large banks have the staff and processes necessary to monitor both the capital flows and the work being accomplished during a complex construction project.

During the typical construction project, the developer acquires either a suitable land parcel or an option to buy it. The developer then presents a development plan to the local governmental authorities and requests the preliminary permissions required to undertake a project. At the same time, the developer is working to identify potential tenants to use the space once completed. As the tenants formalize their interest, the developer prepares final plans for government approval.

During this process, the developer will have been negotiating a bank financing package to provide a significant portion of the requisite project costs. The bank will look to the developer to make a substantial equity contribution as well as to give certain guarantees that the project will be completed as designed.

Prior to closing the loan, the lender will require many documents, including proof of government approvals, land acquisition contracts, construction contracts, borrower guarantees, and — most important — lease agreements. These are all required before the bank begins lending.

In a construction loan, funds are advanced over the course of the project in amounts reflecting the work just completed by the contractors. These progress payments are known as loan draws. Draws also include accrued interest. In effect, the bank lends the developer funds to pay the bank its interest.

In certain cases, a construction lender may require that a borrower secure a take-out loan, replacement financing for its construction loan at the end of the development period. This take-out loan can be from another financial institution that will make a permanent loan against the property, or an advance commitment from a prospective investor to buy the asset upon completion.

Construction loans are a very dynamic type of financing in which the originating bank remains highly involved during the life of the loan. As such, they are difficult to trade and there is little liquidity for in-progress construction loans.

6.4.2.2.4 Stabilized Property Debt

The vast majority of financing transactions are done for completed, well leased, and — in most cases — stable assets. These properties have generally achieved targeted occupancy levels and are generating a measurable cash flow stream. At this point in a property's life cycle, its value is easiest to quantify and it will typically support the highest level of long-term financing.

Financing for mature, stable, commercial properties has evolved considerably over the past thirty years. Prior to the 1980s, banks, pension funds, and insurance companies provided most of the long-term mortgage capital for high-quality commercial properties. These assets were known as institutional quality properties because they were typically owned or financed by major financial institutions.

The loans made on these assets came to be known as balance sheet loans because they were an investment owned by, and reported on, the balance sheet of the originating financial institution. This is not to say that these investments were never traded. These loans were often marketed and traded as "whole loans" to other institutions. In cases in which loans were too large for a single institution, "clubs" or "syndicates" of lenders would share in a transaction. The lead institution in such a shared loan situation was known as the agent and the other lenders as the participants.

Starting in the late 1980s, mortgages on commercial properties became increasingly standardized and were bought and sold as commodity-like securities.

In many cases, pools of these mortgages were aggregated and many types of interests in these pools were sold to investors.

6.4.2.2.5 Conduit Debt

Many financial institutions set up groups to originate, pool, and sell investments backed by commercial mortgages. These banks lend money to owners of commercial properties. They then aggregate these loans into large pools and issue securities backed by the interest and principal derived from the loans in the pool. The process of selling securities backed by loans is called securitization and the securities issued are known as commercial mortgage-backed securities (CMBS). The financial institutions that originate, aggregate, and then securitize loans in this manner are called conduit lenders.

6.4.2.2.5.1 CMBS, RMBS, and Structured Products. CMBS became a very popular method of financing commercial real estate, and the amount of CMBS securities originated annually rose to a peak level of more than $230 billion by 2007.

Fueled by relatively low interest rates and high levels of liquidity in the mortgage market, values of commercial properties increased from 2003 to 2008. Many observers also believe that mortgage underwriting standards declined during this period.

Loans on residential properties, including single-family houses are also pooled into many forms of structured securities. Historically, most of these securities were based on pools of conservatively underwritten single-family home mortgages and guaranteed by one of the quasi-governmental housing agencies, Fannie Mae and Freddie Mac. More recently, securitization was applied to a wider range of residential mortgages, some of which were underwritten to lower credit standards, known as subprime mortgages.

The lower credit standards allowed more people to finance the purchase of homes, including increasing numbers of speculators, and raised demand for housing and asset values. When housing prices peaked in 2008 and then began a steep decline, many mortgages went into delinquency, and the securities written against these mortgages suffered dramatic decreases in value. In this respect, the financial crisis was caused in large part by the collapse of the residential mortgage-backed securities (RMBS) market.

6.4.2.2.6 Balance Sheet Debt

The advent of the CMBS market brought changes to the balance sheet lenders that underwrite and hold mortgage debt for their own investment accounts. Historically, pension funds and insurance companies have been the largest balance sheet lenders. These lenders have long-term liabilities to policyholders under annuity and insurance contracts. They can fund these liabilities with long-term mortgage loans.

Balance sheet lenders, once the mainstream lenders for large commercial properties, now tend to focus on providing capital for very large high-quality properties and for high-complexity projects. In these situations, they can charge a premium for their financing over the most competitive rates available, which — before the financial crisis — were typically from those in the conduit market.

For certain high-value properties, the size of the required financing is so large that it might affect the portfolio diversification requirements of many mortgage securitization programs. For these assets, balance sheet lenders can form a group to share the risk of a single large loan.

In the case in which a property is in the process of being renovated or expanded, borrowing from a balance sheet lender can offer additional flexibility when compared to the standardized loans offered under conduit lending programs. As the project progresses, the borrower can enter into dialogue with the lender to respond to changing conditions of the asset and request a change in the loan terms. In contrast, with a conduit loan there is no ongoing lender with whom one might have that kind of dialogue, as the loan has been packaged and sold. In return for the higher level of customer service, balance sheet lenders can charge a higher interest rate than conduit lenders

During much of the 1990s and 2000s, the market for balance sheet commercial mortgages was much smaller than the conduit market. Following the crash and the failure of the conduit market, balance sheet lenders became one of the only sources of liquidity for commercial property borrowers.

6.4.2.2.7 Corporate Debt

Those real estate companies organized as public entities, and some larger private real estate companies, can access the corporate debt market. In this market, a loan is made against the general credit of the company and not against a particular asset. These loans can be secured by a pool of properties, known as a collateral pool, or they can be unsecured, having only a general claim on the corporate assets. In both cases, the debt is generally guaranteed by the company, meaning it has a residual claim on assets in a liquidation.

Corporate debt can be publicly traded or privately placed with financial institutions. Corporate debt can also be structured as revolving credit, in which a company iteratively borrows and repays cash over a period of time — in effect, a corporate credit card. This debt is typically held by groups or syndicates of commercial banks and is short-term in nature (from one to four years). These facilities can be structured as secured or unsecured debt.

6.4.3 Equity

Equity of capital is subordinate to all debt and absorbs the risk of the asset's performance. Unless the debt is not performing, the providers of equity capital determine the direction of an asset or a company.

6.4.3.1 Equity Basics
6.4.3.1.1 Direct Ownership

The most basic form of equity investment in the real estate capital markets is the direct ownership of an asset. The direct investor may provide all of the capital to purchase a property or may lever his or her purchase by using the proceeds from a mortgage as partial payment for the property.

6.4.3.1.2 Partnerships

Partnerships consist of groups of investors that pool equity capital to facilitate the purchase of one or more properties. This purchase may also be levered by the application of the proceeds from one or more mortgages.

There are a number of types of partnerships, reflecting varied relationships among the partners.

6.4.3.1.2.1 General Partnership. Partners in a general partnership contribute funds to purchase a property. Known as general partners and they are all fully liable for the operation and the risk of an asset's performance. They typically participate in decision making in proportion to their investment. A claim can be made against the assets of a general partner for the liabilities of a partnership in excess of the amount of its investment.

6.4.3.1.2.2 Limited Partnership. A limited partnership has two different classes of partners: general and limited. General partners contribute capital, manage the affairs of the partnership and are fully liable for its risks as discussed above. Limited partners also contribute capital but have very little say in the affairs of the partnership. They are granted an interest in the partnership for their capital investment, but — unlike the general partner — they are not liable for the risks of the asset beyond the amount of their invested capital. The purpose of this structure is to allow general partners to aggregate capital for investment without subjecting the nonoperating partners to risks that they cannot control. To reward the general partner for its extra risk and its operational expertise, the general partner may be given a share of the partnership's equity that is disproportionate to the amount of its investment. The general partner may also be paid a management fee for its work.

6.4.3.1.2.3 Master Limited Partnership. In a master limited partnership, the limited partnership interests may be publicly traded on a securities exchange. The partnership's administrator uses sophisticated software to track the partnership's economics.

6.4.3.2 Equity Advanced

Equity structures can become very complex when they are tailored to meet the needs of particular financing sources.

6.4.3.2.1 Joint Ventures

6.4.3.2.1.1 Corporate Joint Ventures. Joint ventures in the real estate field can be done between operating companies who decide to combine their skills to pursue a large or complex project.

When joint ventures are undertaken by real estate operating partners, profits are typically distributed in proportion to each partner's capital investment.

For example: three real estate companies form a joint venture to buy a large property with each partner contributing one third of the equity. Profits would typically be split pro rata with each partner receiving one-third of the profits.

6.4.3.2.1.2 Institutional Joint Ventures. Institutional joint ventures take place between financial institutions, acting individually or in a small group, and a company with real estate operating skills. This allows the operating company to leverage its capital base and work on larger projects. The financial institutions benefit from the expertise of the real estate company with whom they will have a direct alignment of interests. Institutional joint ventures typically involve a single financial institution and a single operating partner. In the most common structure, the operating partner receives a disproportionately large portion of the anticipated profits in return for providing the real estate services to the venture. The operating partner's excess return is known as a promoted return or a promote. It is also referred to as a carried interest. The operating partner may be required to subordinate this disproportionate return to a set return on both partner's actual invested capital known as a preferred return.

6.4.3.2.1.2.1 Club Deals. Club deals are done with small groups of financial institutions acting in concert to fund a project or a portfolio of assets. By acting in concert, they can raise a larger pool of capital and attempt a larger project or gain diversity in their holdings. By participating in a club, an investor can limit its investment in any single asset. Club deals can be hard to manage because each financial institution reserves its right to approve further capital expenditures, refinancing, and the ultimate exit from the asset, which can complicate decision making.

6.4.3.2.1.2.2 Private Equity Ventures. Private equity investors raise funds that are typically directed towards high-return ventures, which are often higher risk than those pursued by most financial institutions. Private equity may invest using their own skilled operatives or in a joint venture format with an operating partner.

When coinvesting with operating partners, private equity investors may give the partners a promoted interest in return for a preferential return on their cash investment.

6.4.3.2.2 Tenants-in-Common

A legal form of property ownership known as tenants-in-common (TIC) allows individual investors to own a fractional interest in a property. They may buy, sell, and finance the property separately from the other owners. The owners agree as a group to hire a management company to operate the asset.

This structure has tax benefits for the owner of a small property that wants to use a 1031 tax-free exchange to convert its investment to a large professionally managed asset without realizing a taxable gain on the sale of its original property. When the interest in the TIC is ultimately sold, the deferred gain is realized unless it can be again rolled into another like-kind investment.

The major issue with the TIC structure is that decision making regarding the asset is complicated by the diffuse ownership structure. If a property requires additional capital or falters and needs to be repositioned, there is little incentive for any individual partner to support the asset unless there is unanimous agreement. In contrast, in a partnership the general partner can make decisions on behalf of the limited partners, and in a corporation management acts for the shareholders.

6.4.3.2.3 Corporations

In addition to partnerships and TIC, many assets and portfolios are held in corporate form. There are many types of corporations, each with different governance structures and tax consequences for the investors. In many cases, the equity raised by these entities is levered with either property- or corporate-level debt. Some of the corporate structures typically used to raise equity and to hold properties are described in the following subsections.

6.4.3.2.3.1 Limited Liability Company. A limited liability company (LLC) is a corporation that acts in many respects like a limited partnership. The LLC elects to be taxed as a pass-through, C corporation, or S corporation. Most LLCs choose to be taxed as pass-through entities with no taxation on the corporate level. Instead, earnings and profits are passed through directly to the shareholders, who are known as members. The liability of a member to the corporation is limited to the amount invested, resembling a limited partnership. LLCs are governed by a manager who acts on behalf of all of the members. The manager may be a member or a third party. In either case, the responsibilities of the manager are outlined in the LLC agreement.

6.4.3.2.3.2 Subchapter S Corporations. Corporations organized under Subchapter S of Chapter One of the US Internal Revenue Code (S corporations) are similar to partnerships in that they are tax pass through entities. Income is recognized and taxes are paid at the shareholder level. Subchapter S corporations are privately held companies owned by a maximum of 100 shareholders, who while free to sell their shares, may have limited liquidity.

6.4.3.2.3.3 REITs. REITs are structured as business trusts or corporations. REITs were created by an act of the US Congress to allow small investors to participate in the ownership of commercial properties. In return for limiting their holdings to real property or mortgages on real property, and for distributing their income in the form of dividends to shareholders, REITs avoid paying tax at the corporate level. REITs may be public companies whose shares are traded on major stock exchanges. They may also be privately held, but all REITs must be widely distributed with more than 100 shareholders. No five shareholders may collectively own more than 50 percent of the outstanding shares of a REIT.

Although the REIT structure has been in place since 1960, this type of investment vehicle did not become popular until the 1990s, when REITs were used to provide liquidity to major development companies that were in need of recapitalization following the real estate recession of the late 1980s.

6.4.3.2.3.4 Real Estate Operating Companies. Real estate operating companies (REOCs) are owners, managers, and developers who have chosen to operate as corporations, some as public corporations, and who have not chosen to operate as REITs. Many of these companies are in businesses that would not qualify for the tax benefits of the REIT structure; others do not need those benefits because they generate depreciation or other tax losses that shelters their taxable income.

6.4.3.3 Hybrid Securities

There are many investors who have a level of risk tolerance that falls between the lower level associated with debt and the higher level associated with equity. These investors are looking for returns that exceed those of pure debt. In return, they are willing to provide more flexible terms and to subordinate their interests to those of the pure debt holders. These securities are known as hybrids because they include aspects of both debt and equity investments. Typical structures include those described in the following subsections.

6.4.3.3.1 Preferred Equity

Preferred equity is entitled to receive "preferred" distributions, which are paid before any dividends payments are made to common shareholders. In the event of a liquidation of an entity, holders of preferred equity are paid out after debt holders but before any payments are made to the common equity.

Most preferred shares are perpetual and do not have a maturity date. Some preferred shares may be converted into common equity shares of the entity; these are known as convertible preferred. If the entity reserves the right to redeem its preferred shares under certain circumstances or at certain times, the securities are known as callable preferred.

6.4.3.3.2 Mezzanine Debt

Mezzanine debt is a hybrid security that is structured as a debt instrument with a set maturity date and a stated rate of interest. Failure to pay the debt on its stated terms is an act of default that can lead to a forced bankruptcy. For tax purposes, the interest paid on this debt is deductible.

Unlike more traditional debt, mezzanine debt is made at a higher loan-to-value ratio and is subordinated to the claims of more senior lenders. In many cases, it is secured by the owner's equity in the property, rather than the asset itself. It may not have the right to receive all of its interest payment in cash but may instead accrue a portion as additional principal. These factors make it a higher-risk profile than traditional debt, although it is still senior to all levels of equity securities.

6.4.3.3.3 Convertible Debt

Convertible debt is traditional entity debt that may be converted into the common equity of the entity under certain circumstances. The ability to convert to equity gives the debt holder a participation in the equity growth of the company while retaining the seniority in liquidation and interest payout of traditional debt.

Convertible debt is used to lower the current cash cost of financing by effectively selling the lender an option on the future value of entity growth. The dual nature of convertible debt as an interest in both debt and equity makes it a desirable hybrid security for many investors.

6.4.3.4 Derivative Securities

Derivatives are securities whose value is derived from the value of other securities or commodity prices. Derivatives can be very useful tools in managing risk. They are also complex financial instruments whose behavior can be counterintuitive to those who do not understand them, which often leads to unintended consequences for those who have not carefully studied these instruments and their behaviors. There are many types of derivative securities, including the following basic varieties.

6.4.3.4.1 Derivatives Security Structures

6.4.3.4.2 Futures

A futures contract is an agreement to deliver a quantity of securities or commodities at a future date. Futures can be bought or sold. When you buy a futures contract, you are purchasing securities for delivery on a date in the future. When you sell, you are agreeing to deliver securities on a date in the future.

Futures contracts originated with agricultural commodities such as wheat, for which farmers financed the cost of planting their crops by selling a futures contract against a portion of their expected harvest. This generated the cash needed to buy seed and fertilizer. By selling futures, the farmers received cash in advance and protected themselves against changes in pricing.

Over time, futures trading expanded to financial commodities such as treasury securities. The willingness to buy or sell an interest bearing security at a future date implies an opinion on the future direction of interest rates. Selling treasury futures can be used to protect against rising rates: buying futures can protect against falling rates.

6.4.3.4.3 Options

Unlike a futures contract, which is an obligation to transact at a future date, an option gives the holder the right, but not the obligation to transact. There are two common types of options contracts: put options and call options.

6.4.3.4.3.1 Put. A put option gives the holder the right to sell a quantity of securities or commodities at a set price until a future date, known as the expiration date. The price at which the securities may be sold is known as the option's strike price.

6.4.3.4.3.2 Call. A call option gives the holder the right to purchase a quantity of securities or commodities at the strike price prior to the expiration date.

6.4.3.4.4 Swap

A swap is an agreement to trade certain types of cash flows during a given period of time. The period of time during which the trades take place is the term of the swap agreement. The parties that agree to the trades are known as counterparties. The quantities involved in the exchange can be based on interest rates, foreign currencies or credit risk.

For example, in an interest rate swap, one counterparty agrees to pay the other a floating interest rate multiplied by a set amount of dollars. The counterparty to the trade agrees to pay the first party a fixed interest rate multiplied by the same set amount of dollars.

EXAMPLE

Counterparty A has a $10 million floating-rate note outstanding with a three-year maturity. Interest on the note is payable monthly at LIBOR plus 100 basis points. Counterparty A would like to fix its rate of interest for the duration of the note. Counterparty A enters into a three-year interest rate swap with Counterparty B, who agrees to pay Counterparty A $10 million times LIBOR/12 each month in return for a fixed payment from Counterparty A of $10 million times 3 percent/12. By entering this agreement, Counterparty A's obligation is now fixed at an annual rate of 3 percent plus 100 Basis Points or 4 percent.

In a foreign exchange swap, each counterparty agrees to pay to the other a set amount of a foreign currency on specified intervals during the term of the swap. This transaction can help parties meet obligations denominated in a foreign currency or repatriate funds from a foreign operation and lock in the conversion rate.

EXAMPLE

The London InterBank Offered Rate (LIBOR) is the rate that banks charge each other for borrowing US dollars. LIBOR is dependent on the term of the loan and is the market base interest rate referenced in many corporate and real estate lending transactions.

The interest rate on many lending transactions is stated as LIBOR plus a credit spread of x basis points. The credit spread is the amount the bank charges the borrower to compensate it for the risk of the loan. The LIBOR rate referred to is typically the one month rate and is a market rate that is constantly changing with economic conditions.

A loan with an interest rate based on one month LIBOR is known as a floating rate loan because the interest rate is reset each month.

An interest rate Swap allows the borrower to "fix" the interest rate for a period of time.

A credit default swap acts to insure a holder against the possibility that the bonds of a particular entity will go into default during the term of the swap agreement. In the event that the bond's issuer defaults, the holder of the credit default Swaps gives the bond to the Counterparty in return for a cash payment of bond's principal amount. The cost of this swap varies with the perceived credit risk of the entity. If the entity covered by the swap appears to be experiencing financial distress, the cost of the credit default swap rises.

6.4.3.4.4.1 Forward Starting Swap. Swaps can begin at the time of agreement or at any future date agreed to by the counterparties. Forward starting swaps can help companies manage risks that they know will be starting at some future point. For example, a company with a maturing note knows that they will have to refinance in the floating-rate debt market. To manage the risk that rates move up, they enter into a orward starting swap in which they agree to pay a fixed rate of interest on the amount of their maturing obligation and to receive payments tied to a floating rate index on the same underlying principal amount. When they refinance, they will pay this floating rate through to their new lender.

6.4.3.4.5 Cap

A cap is an agreement that protects the holder if interest rates rise above a stated level. The issuer of the cap will pay the holder the principal amount of the cap times the amount by which the actual value of the floating rate index exceeds the cap level.

EXAMPLE

One month LIBOR is quoted at 6 percent and Party A holds a $10 million LIBOR cap set at 5% from Bank B. During this month, Bank B pays Party A $10 million times (6% minus 5%) divided by 12 (months) or $8,500.

6.4.3.4.6 Floor

A floor works similarly to a cap except that the issuer pays the holder only if rates fall below the stated "floor" level. If this change occurs, the issuer pays the holder the principal amount of the floor times the amount by which the actual value of the floating rate index falls below the floor level.

EXAMPLE

One month LIBOR is quoted at 4 percent and Party A holds a $10 million LIBOR floor set at 5 percent from Bank B. During this month, Bank B pays Party A $10 million times (5% minus 4%) divided by 12 (months) or $8,500.

6.4.3.4.7 Collar

Caps and floors can work together to create a collar, a range within which a borrower's floating-rate obligation may move. To create this range, the

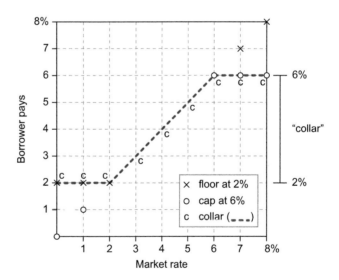

In this example, a LIBOR collar combines a cap at 6%, and a floor at 2%. The borrower will never pay less than 2% no matter how low LIBOR may fall, and never pay more than 6% no matter how high LIBOR may rise. A borrower purchases a cap because it is paying for protection against increasing interest rates. It sells a floor because it is offering the counter party protection against falling interest rates. The cost of the collar is the cost of the cap less the proceeds from the sale of the floor.

borrower buys a cap, which reimburses the borrower if its rates increase over the cap level. To purchase this cap, the borrower must make a payment to the cap's issuer. To pay for the cap, the borrower sells a floor. By selling a floor, the borrower agrees to make a payment to the issuer if rates fall below the agreed floor level. If this occurs, the borrower's reduced loan cost will be given up to the floor buyer. Thus the borrower's effective interest cost will never fall below the floor. The combination of buying a cap and selling a floor creates a "collar."

6.5 REAL ESTATE INVESTORS

There are many types of investors participating in the real estate capital markets. Each class of investor seeks real property investments with different risks and returns. Much of the capital investment in the industry is, however, predicated on the fundamental combination of current cash flow generation and long-term appreciation that have historically defined the real property asset class.

6.5.1 Commercial Banks

Commercial banks source their capital from depositors who are interested in safety and preservation of capital. For this reason, commercial banks, which are highly regulated, look to place their funds in lower-risk investments and are generally providers of short-term financing. They have historically been the providers of choice for construction loans and are also the principal providers of short-term financing facilities (five to seven years or less) to real estate companies. These facilities allow the companies to acquire and reposition properties before seeking longer-term financing. These loans require a high level of service and expertise. For this reason, they can carry fees and interest rates that earn banks a profit over their cost of funds.

Prior to the advent of the CMBS market, commercial banks made balance sheet loans, long-term mortgages on commercial properties for their own investment account. Although they no longer seek to do so for their own account, commercial banks now provide clients long-term mortgage financing (typically 10 year term) through conduit loan programs. In a conduit program, the bank will underwrite the loan and then sell it to investors as part of the collateral pool for a commercial mortgage-backed security. The bank earns fees from the borrower and may profit on the securitization of the loan.

6.5.2 Investment Banks

Traditional investment banks generally source their capital from large, high-net-worth individuals and major institutional investors. These investors have a higher risk tolerance than most bank depositors. Therefore, investment banks can make investments that entail a higher level of risk and return than the commercial banks.

In keeping with their search for higher yields for their sophisticated clients, investment banks will provide high-cost, short-term financing to their best clients to facilitate their large property acquisitions before long-term financing can be secured. These loans are known as "bridge loans" and can be high risk because the client may not be able to find long-term financing on property or portfolio purchased. In addition to bridge loans, and in the same manner as commercial banks, investment banks operate conduit loan programs where they underwrite mortgage loans for packaging and resale as commercial mortgage backed securities.

In addition to making loans to property owners, investment banks can provide equity capital for real property ventures. This capital can be in the form of limited partnership units, joint venture equity investments, or the sale of real estate company equity to investors in the public or private markets.

6.5.3 Insurance Companies

Insurance companies collect premiums in advance of losses and need to invest these funds. In addition, some insurance products, such as whole life policies and annuities, contain investment accounts in addition to providing risk coverage. Many of these insurance polices are long-term obligations for which the insurance company seeks long-term investments.

Insurance companies seek direct investments in real estate and mortgages are secured by real property because they are typically long-term stable sources of cash flow. Insurance companies have long been a primary source of long-term mortgages. In many cases, real estate developers will look for a mortgage from an insurance company to "take out" commercial bank construction financing.

Insurance companies are interested in the combination of cash flow and growth found in direct property investments. They acquire property to provide the long-term income and growth that can support the long-term obligations present in both insurance and annuity contracts.

6.5.4 Pension Funds

Pension funds collect money from employers and employees to fund employee retirement obligations. Pension fund providers look to long-term growth of capital to support the needs of future retirees as the cost of living increases over their working lives. This makes pension funds similar to insurance companies in the desired composition of their investment portfolios.

Pension funds provide long-term mortgage capital and invest directly in real property. In many cases, pension funds invest in joint ventures with real estate operating companies to access transaction flow and the expertise of these companies.

6.5.5 Private Equity Funds

Private equity firms aggregate capital from large individual and institutional investors to invest in major transactions. Because the real estate industry is a major user of capital, large investors generally include an exposure to real property as part of their "alternative asset" strategy. To place this capital, many private equity firms have established an expertise in real estate, which can be through an internal capability or through joint ventures or affiliation with external real estate operating companies.

6.5.6 Sovereign Wealth Funds

Sovereign wealth funds (SWFs) are investment vehicles set up by governments to invest their excess capital. Many of the countries with sovereign wealth funds are rich in natural resources. These funds act as a variant of the traditional private equity firm, investing funds on behalf of their countries in the world capital markets.

Given the large amount of capital aggregated by the sovereign wealth funds, finding appropriate investments in not an easy task. The large capital requirements of the real estate industry make it a natural investment target of these large generators of investment capital.

6.5.7 Individuals

At the peak of the single-family home market, almost 70 percent of American families owned their own home. For the vast majority of these people, their investment in their home was their single largest asset, the store of family wealth.

Beyond their homes, the majority of Americans that save do so through bank accounts and mutual funds. Few Americans own commercial real estate directly, as large amounts of capital and a significant amount of expertise are required to purchase and operate property.

For those that have the capital to allocate to real estate, many individual investors purchase shares of real estate investment trusts that are publicly traded or privately offered through financial advisors.

6.6 CAPITAL MARKET PARTICIPANTS

6.6.1 Functions

There are many active participants in the firms that interact to create the real estate capital markets. Their roles are defined in the following subsections.

6.6.1.1 Principal

Principals are investors who utilize their own capital, or their firm's capital, to buy and sell interests in real estate and securities backed by real estate.

6.6.1.2 Agent

Agents are professionals who act on behalf of principals to facilitate the many transactions associated with the acquisition, disposition, and leasing of property. Agents do not use their own capital to facilitate trade. Agents are also known as brokers.

6.6.1.3 Operator

Operators are responsible for the day-to-day management of real property. Operators can limit their business to property management or provide broader services including leasing, acquisitions, dispositions, development, and construction.

6.6.1.4 Banker

Bankers aggregate capital from depositors and investors. Bankers then invest that capital on behalf of their clients in loans, securities, and operating ventures. Bankers attempt to make a profit between their cost of funds and their investment earnings. Bankers also earn fees by matching investors (capital sources) with companies that need capital to operate and grow (capital users).

6.6.1.5 Trader

Traders buy and sell assets to facilitate a liquid market. They are not investors and do not seek to hold inventory. Securities traders buy and sell stocks and bonds and attempt to make a profit from the spread between the price at which they acquire and sell securities.

Traders can act as principals, buying and selling with their own capital, or as agents, buying and selling on behalf of their clients.

6.7 MARKET STATISTICS

6.7.1 Sources of Capital

The capital invested in the US real estate market comes primarily from US investors with foreign cross-border investments representing an important but limited source of capital.

6.7.1.1 Global

Global investors seek US investment to diversify their domestic and global portfolios. Foreign investors are attracted by the benefits that come with investing in the United States. Relative to many other countries, the United States offers capital markets that are liquid, deep, transparent, protective of the investor, and located in a country with a stable government. Even through the global financial crisis, the United States has retained its perception as a safe haven for wealth.

6.7.1.1.1 Foreign Banks
Many banks domiciled in foreign countries have US real estate lending operations that invest capital in mortgages securing US real estate.

6.7.1.1.2 SWFs (Sovereign Wealth Funds)
SWFs are primarily set up by resource rich nations to invest the funds earned by selling their country's natural resources. Many of these countries do not have domestic economies that can utilize the full amount of capital that they have aggregated. The SWFs attempt to identify investments in which they can recycle their receipts from their natural resource sales and diversify their country's holdings across the global economy. Real property has been a traditional target of SWF investors.

6.7.1.1.3 Investment Funds
Investment management firms have created globally diversified real estate portfolios that are attractive to foreign investors, including non-US corporate and government pension sponsors. The US real estate market has the depth to accept and apply large amounts of capital from these investors.

6.7.1.1.4 Wealthy Individuals
Wealthy foreign investors, especially in countries with unstable political environments or smaller domestic economies, are attracted to the relative stability of the US financial system. The United States makes the investment of large sums of capital attractive to foreigners by affording these investors preferential treatment in the event they seek to immigrate to the United States.

6.7.1.2 Domestic
Most of the capital invested in US real estate is sourced from domestic investors.

6.7.1.2.1 Individual
6.7.1.2.1.1 Personal Use. By asset value, the majority of the US real estate market consists of more than 75 million owner-occupied residential housing units. Many Americans' investment in their house is their principal financial investment. Individuals also invest in properties for use in their businesses.

6.7.1.2.1.2 Retirement Funds. In addition to their direct investment in housing, many individuals invest a portion of their retirement fund in real estate securities. These investors are looking for the growth and income expected from the real estate investment to protect them against the threat that inflation will erode the purchasing power of their savings.

6.7.1.2.1.3 Investments. Many US investors also own mortgage securities, including government-guaranteed home mortgage pools, and interests in commercial properties or funds that invest in commercial properties.

6.7.1.2.2 Institutions

6.7.1.2.2.1 Banks. US banks aggregate deposits from savers and use those funds to make loans to real estate owners. Although many of these loans are packaged and resold to investors, banks still have a significant amount of capital invested in loans secured by real property. Given the large amount of capital required for the US real estate industry, it follows that banks would be a primary source of liquidity to the industry.

6.7.1.2.2.2 Corporations and Institutions. Corporations and institutions invest in real property required for their business activities. For example, service businesses require office space, retail businesses store space, and manufacturing businesses require space for plants and logistics. Operating businesses will either lease or buy their space depending on how important real estate is to the fulfillment of their businesses objectives and how investment in real estate as a use of capital fits into their financial strategy. Many businesses will outsource their real estate requirements to landlords who can lend their economies of scale and process knowledge to the tenant's business.

6.7.1.2.2.3 Pension Funds. There are two types of pension plans: defined benefit and defined contribution.

Defined benefit plans are pension funds that are required to pay income streams to retired employees over long periods of time. The plan sponsor is required to provide the contractual payment stream to retirees regardless of the performance of the plan's investments.

To fulfill this requirement, defined benefit plans invest in assets that will provide inflation protected returns and capital appreciation – qualities that have been demonstrated by real property investment. Property investment has also been shown to be a source of diversification for investment portfolios concentrated in debt and equity securities.

Defined contribution plans include IRA, 401k, and other self-invested retirement schemes. Under these plans, the employee is given money to invest (the contribution) and invests these funds to provide a level of continuing income after retirement. The amount of retirement income is determined by the success of the investor's portfolio.

Defined contribution plans have been a source of funds for the real estate capital markets, as these investors are also driven by the possibility for long-term growth and income offered by real property.

6.7.1.2.2.4 Life Insurance Companies. Life insurance companies receive premiums from policyholders in return for a promise to pay their heirs a settlement upon death. The insurance company charges the policyholder a premium each year that includes an amount to cover the pure mortality risk as well as an amount that is invested on behalf of the policyholder. The investment portion of the policy is expected to grow over time, creating a source of funds for the policyholder upon retirement.

Life insurance policies are long-term liabilities, and insurance companies are always searching for low-risk, long-tenure investments to match their liabilities. Real estate mortgages and equity investments are both used to fund policy liabilities.

Insurance companies also provide investment services to corporate pension investors who create special investment accounts with the insurance company to help fund their pension liabilities.

6.7.1.2.2.5 Mortgage Security Issuers. Mortgage security issuers are pass-through entities that aggregate mortgages and sell investors structured interests in the cash flows generated by these mortgage pools. Prior to 2008, many investors seeking long-term yield driven assets invested in these real estate debt securities because they were relatively liquid and the investor did not need a staff to underwrite the property risk. The financial crisis deeply affected this market and its future remains uncertain.

6.7.1.2.2.6 Government Agencies. Government agencies have a public mandate to help create shelter for the American people. To carry out this objective, they underwrite, guarantee, and fund residential and multifamily mortgages under a number of government-sponsored programs. There is much controversy over the appropriate role of government in the housing market. This ongoing debate has been affected by the poor performance of many of these agencies during the financial crisis.

6.7.2 The Real Estate Industry Is Major User of Capital
6.7.2.1 The Global Demand for Real Estate

The size of the global property market is hard to contemplate without starting our analysis with a few key benchmarks. In the fall of 2011, the population of the world is expected to exceed 7 billion people. Depending on their level of economic development, each person will express some demand for real estate: hence, there are 7 billion points of demand for housing, shopping, and working space, not to mention warehouse space for logistics; institutional space for education, health care and government institutions, and cultural and recreational amenities; and hotels.

6.7.2.1.1 Size of Global Real Estate Capital Markets
6.7.2.1.1.1 Global Commercial Real Estate. At the end of 2010, the Prudential Real Estate Investor (PREI) global universe of commercial real estate contained 55 developed and developing countries with a reported total market

value of $23.9 trillion. This universe includes countries with 4.9 billion of the world's 7 billion inhabitants. PREI estimates that this amount will grow to $47.6 trillion in 2020 and to $97.8 trillion by 2030, with the impetus for the growth coming from developing nations and the Asia Pacific region.

At the end of 2010, DTZ Research estimated the size of the global investment grade commercial real estate market at over $11 trillion. In this analysis, the US market contributes $3.7 trillion, Europe $4.2 trillion, and Asia Pacific $3.5 trillion. Since 2008, Asia Pacific has shown increasing growth, with both the US and European markets declining. DTZ expects almost $1 trillion of additional investment between 2011 and 2013. Between capital spending and change in value, DTZ estimates that the global market to reach $12.9 trillion by year end 2012.

DTZ reports that of the $11.3 trillion total investment in commercial real estate $3.6 trillion is from private equity sources, $0.8 trillion from public equity sources, $1.5 trillion from public debt, and $5.4 trillion from private debt.

Citibank follows 417 global property companies in 34 countries, including 118 US REITs and REOCs. In October 2011, these companies had total equity market capitalization of $1.2 trillion and total enterprise value of $2.2 trillion.

6.7.2.1.1.2 Global CMBS. Mirroring US activity, $251 billion of non-US CMBSs were issued between 2005 and 2007. This amount fell to $14.2 billion total during the following three years (2008–2010).

6.7.2.2 US Demand for Real Estate
In the United States, an average American uses real property across many aspects of their daily life. The US Census Statistical Abstract for 2012 reports statistics that help us put into perspective the demand for real estate:

- Population: There were 308.7 million Americans counted in the 2010 US Census. Through the early part of the century, US population is expected to grow at approximately 1 percent per year.
- Housing: In 2010, there were 117.5 million households, averaging 2.59 individuals each, utilizing a housing unit.
- Retail: In 2008, there were more than 1.1 million stores employing 15.6 million workers.
- Office: In 2008, more than 1.9 million enterprises were involved in information tech, finance, professional services, business management, real estate, and other office-based enterprises employing more than 22 million workers. This figure does not count all of the health care–related use of real estate.
- Real estate business: In 2008, the United States had more than 2 million real estate enterprises, earning over $160 billion in annual revenues, employing in excess of 1.5 million Americans.

For capital markets purposes, the US real estate market is generally classified into three property types: owner-occupied residential, multifamily residential, and commercial.

6.7.2.2.1 Size of US Real Estate Capital Markets

6.7.2.2.1.1 US Residential Real Estate. The US Census estimates that there are approximately 76 million owner-occupied residential units in the United States, and the Federal Reserve estimates the value of these units at $16.2 trillion. This amount represents a significant decline from the 2006 level of $22.7 trillion as a result of the financial crisis.

According to the US Census, approximately two-thirds of owner-occupied US homes are subject to mortgages. As of 2011 Q2 the Federal Reserve estimates, there were $10.4 trillion of mortgages outstanding against one to four family residences in the United States. Of these mortgages, 44.9 percent ($4.7 trillion) were held by government agencies, 24.4 percent ($2.5 trillion) by banks and insurance companies, 22.4 percent ($2.3 trillion) by mortgage trusts, and the balance by individuals and others.

Annual residential mortgage lending peaked at $3.8 trillion during 2003 and is expected to drop to $1.2 trillion in 2011. This decline mirrors the decline in the US housing market, which peaked in 2008.

After subtracting $10.4 trillion of mortgage debt from the $16.2 trillion residential property value, we can estimate remaining owner's equity of $5.8 trillion.

6.7.2.2.1.2 US Commercial Real Estate. The commercial real estate market includes all properties used by businesses and multifamily residential housing. In addition to owner-occupied housing, there are approximately 35 million units of rental housing.

At year end 2010, DTZ research estimated the size of the US investment grade commercial property market at $3.7 trillion. PREI has estimates this same quantity at $6.6 trillion.

6.7.2.2.1.3 Commercial Mortgages. There was approximately $3.2 trillion in commercial and multifamily mortgage debt outstanding at the end of 2011 Q2. This number has remained relatively constant over the past five years. Commercial banks are the largest holders of debt, with slightly over 49 percent. Issuers of structured securities hold 20 percent, multifamily mortgages held by government sponsored entities hold 11 percent, and life insurance companies, state, and local governments and others hold the remaining 20 percent.

6.7.2.2.1.3.1 Commercial Banks. Commercial banks are the largest source of liquidity to the commercial mortgage market. They provide many types of mortgages to owners of multifamily properties, income producing properties, owner-occupied properties, and construction loans.

The Federal Reserve Board shows commercial banks having $1,500 billion of commercial mortgages as of 2011 Q2. Over one-third of the bank lending, $576 billion is on income-producing commercial properties, $216 billion is on multifamily properties, $484 billion is on owner-occupied commercial real estate, and there are $256 billion of construction loans.

6.7.2.2.1.3.2 Life Insurance Companies. Life insurance companies have over $300 billion in commercial mortgages outstanding at the end of 2011 Q2. Over the past seven years, they have provided a more limited but less volatile stream of mortgage capital into the real estate market. Production peaked at $130 billion during the 2005–2008 period, but fell to only $74 billion during the next three years (2008–2010). After the CMBS market closed for a period, life insurance companies became a primary source of liquidity in the commercial mortgage market.

6.7.2.2.1.3.3 Structured Securities. At the end of 2011 Q2, over $629 billion of CMBS remain outstanding, down from a peak of $820 billion at the end of CY 2007.

CMBS issuance in the United States peaked at $230 billion in 2007, closing out a three-year period in which total underwriting exceeded $600 billion. Collateralized debt obligations accounted for another $86 billion during this period, in stark contrast to the following three years (2008–2010), during which only $30 billion of structured real estate debt securities were issued in total. Estimates for production in 2011 are at about $30–$40 billion.

6.7.2.2.1.3.4 Government-Sponsored Entities. Government agencies and government-sponsored entities (GSEs) are a major source of liquidity for all forms of residential housing including multifamily residential housing. At the end of 2011 Q2, these entities had $332 billion in mortgages outstanding against multifamily properties, making them the largest lender in this sector, ahead of banks ($216 billion) and CMBSs ($96 billion).

6.7.2.3 REIT and REOC Debts

Many public real estate companies access the capital markets for corporate debt. Although this debt is not direct real estate debt, it is supported indirectly by the cash flow from real property. The National Association of Real Estate Investment Trusts (NAREIT) reported in October 2011 that its 154 REITs had approximately $438 billion of debt outstanding and average leverage of 48.2 percent.

6.7.2.3.1 Equity Investment

At 2011 Q2, NAREIT reports that there are approximately 154 public REITs with implied total equity market capitalization of $460.1 billion.

Life insurance companies make equity investments in real property through special accounts that purchase direct interests in commercial property. Life insurance companies also invest in portfolios of REIT and REOC securities.

Real estate private equity funds make direct and indirect equity investments in commercial property. They aggregate these funds from institutional investors including pension funds, university endowments, and high-net-worth investors.

Public and private pension funds allocate a portion of their investments, typically less than 10 percent of their portfolios, to alternative asset classes that include direct and indirect interests in commercial real estate.

Glossary

Call option
Cap
Carried Interest
Club deals
Collar
Conduit debt
Convertible debt
Covenants
Credit spread derivative
Floor
Forward starting swap
Futures contracts
Indenture
Interest rate derivative
Master limited partnership
Mezzanine debt
Option
Preferred equity
Private equity
Promote
Property derivatives
Put option
SWFs (sovereign wealth funds)
Swap
Syndicate
TIC (Tenants-in-Common)

Thought Questions

1. What are some of the features of an investment in commercial real estate that make it attractive to investors?

2. Many public real estate companies have the option of seeking either entity or property level debt to finance their capital requirements. Assuming that both are accessible to the company, what are the factors that require consideration when deciding which market to approach?

Review Questions

1. Investment in Real Estate

   Which of the following is not a factor that supports investment in real estate?

   a) Real estate has low covariance with other asset classes.
   b) The real estate industry can facilitate large capital investments.
   c) Debt capital is always available to finance property purchases.
   d) Long-term leases can provide low cash flow volatility.
   e) Tenant credit risk can be mitigated by having real property collateral.

2. Entity Structure

   Which of the following is not a tax pass-through entity?

   a) Limited partnership
   b) General partnership
   c) C Corporation
   d) S Corporation

3. Securities

   Order these securities according to preference in a liquidation:
   I.   Preference stock
   II. Senior debt
   III. Common stock
   IV. Convertible debt
   a) I, II, III, IV
   b) II, IV, I, III
   c) I, III, II, IV
   d) II, I, IV, III

4. Credit Metrics

   Which of the following two credit metrics are defined correctly?
   I.   Loan-to-value (debt/asset value)
   II. Loan-to-value (debt service/asset value)
   III. Debt service coverage (cash flow/interest and principal)
   IV. Debt service coverage (cash flow/interest)
   a) I, III
   b) I, IV

   c) II, III

   d) II, IV

5. Financing Sources

   Match the following items with their most likely sources:

a) construction loan	I. investment bank
b) long-term balance sheet loan	II. CMBS underwriter
c) REIT shares	III. commercial bank
d) stabilized property loan	IV. life insurance company

6. Joint Ventures

   Which types of returns are not typically earned by the operating partner in a joint venture?

   a) Promoted interest

   b) Carried interest

   c) Pro rata interest

   d) Preferred interest

7. Derivatives

   Which of the following are options?

    I. Future

    II. Put

    III. Swap

    IV. Call

   a) I

   b) II, III

   c) II, IV

   d) III

8. Sources of Financing

   US government-sponsored entitites support lending to which property types listed?

   a) Office buildings

   b) Retail centers

   c) Industrial and warehouse

   d) Multifamily

9. Market size

   Which market is larger?

   a) US commercial property

   b) US residential property

10. General
    Match at least five correctly:

A)___	Direct investment	1) Fee interest
B)___	Indirect investment	2) Pension plan based on performance
C)___	Principal	3) Works on their own behalf
D)___	Agent	4) REIT stock
E)___	Ground lease	5) Works on behalf of another party
F)___	Defined benefit plan	6) Right to utilize land
G)___	Defined contribution plan	7) Set monthly pension payment

For answers to these Problems and Exercises, please visit the companion website: http://booksite.elsevier.com/9780123786265

CHAPTER 7

Property Finance: Debt

7.1 TYPES OF REAL ESTATE LOANS

Many types of real estate can be financed using mortgages. The terms and conditions of the loan will vary with the economics of each type of property.

7.1.1 Permanent Loans

Permanent loans are made on properties that generate a stable stream of cash flow. This occurs when a property is physically complete and has reached a level of leasing that is indicative of the demand in its market. At this point in the property's life cycle, the lender can estimate its stabilized NOI and determine the amount of financing that it can support.

7.1.1.1 Commercial Property

Permanent loans are available for commercial properties of all types, including office buildings, shopping centers, warehouses, and industrial spaces as well as more esoteric property types such as health care facilities and biotech research labs. Commercial property values vary from hundreds of thousands of dollars for local assets to billions of dollars for iconic downtown skyscrapers or super regional shopping malls. The loan structures and underwriting criteria used by lenders across a range of commercial properties are surprisingly similar.

7.1.1.2 Residential Property

Residential real estate is generally divided into two broad classifications: multifamily investment property and single-family owner-occupied homes.

7.1.1.3 Multifamily Property

The multifamily properties include garden, mid-rise, and high-rise apartments. In many cases, multifamily projects may include multiple buildings. Loans are available to borrowers who seek to hold the property as an investment as well as to borrowers who seek to sell individual apartments to new owners under a condominium ownership structure.

Multifamily properties held for investment are considered commercial properties. However, because the US government has an interest in promoting the

189

availability of housing for its citizens, government programs exist to provide financing for owners of multifamily property. Many of these programs are administered by the Department of Housing and Urban Development (HUD). Government-sponsored financing programs often require owners to comply with policy initiatives such as making a certain number of apartments available to low-income or elderly residents. Qualifying properties are then granted mortgage insurance that facilitates lower borrowing costs through the Federal Housing Administration (FHA).

7.1.1.4 Home Mortgages

Home mortgages are made to borrowers seeking to purchase primary residences or for vacation homes. There are a myriad of "mortgage products" available to today's homeowner with differing terms to fit the needs of most borrowers.

Unlike commercial mortgages, under which the lender expects that the property will generate cash flow to support the required debt payments, the lender making a home mortgage looks solely to the credit of the borrower to repay the mortgage. The lender does, however, value the home being purchased. In the event that the borrower defaults on the mortgage, the lender will foreclose on the property, selling the home on the open market and using the sale proceeds to repay its loan. The lender will limit its loan amount so that it has a reasonable probability of realizing its full investment in the event that it must liquidate the property.

To enable its citizens to purchase homes, the US government has set up programs to insure investors against homeowner mortgage defaults. The first program was started by the FHA in 1934, following the Great Depression. By providing its sovereign credit support, the government believed that investors would be willing to provide more capital to the home mortgage market at a lower interest cost than would otherwise be the case.

The government credit support is provided in the form of mortgage insurance. To obtain this insurance, the borrower, the property, and the desired mortgage must meet certain qualifications specified by the FHA.

Over the years, private insurance companies that have joined the FHA in the mortgage insurance market. Government-sponsored entities (GSE) like Fannie Mae and Freddie Mac have been created to provide liquidity to the mortgage market by buying and selling insured mortgages.

7.1.1.5 Construction Loans

Construction loans are specifically structured to meet the needs of borrowers who are going to build a property. These borrowers must pay for the ongoing costs of construction over a period of time, typically between six months and three years. While a property is under construction, it does not generate any revenue stream, so the borrower has no ready source of cash for interest payments. During this period, the lender is at risk because its collateral consists of an unfinished property, without tenants, that is not generating any income.

Construction loan programs have been developed to address these issues. Rather than loaning a lump sum to a borrower, lenders advance funds to pay for construction costs as they are incurred. These periodic payments are known as construction draws and are added to the loan balance when they are paid. At the end of each month, interest is charged on the loan, but rather than receiving a cash payment from the borrower, the lender adds the amount due to the outstanding loan balance.

Because the bank is not lending against a completed project, it has only the building in process as collateral for its loan. Construction lenders typically visit the property on a regular basis to monitor activity. While there, they confirm that the project is proceeding on schedule and that the construction draws are being used according to plan.

At completion of construction, the lender expects to be repaid by the borrower from either the proceeds of a permanent loan or from the sale of the newly completed project to an investor. In the event that the borrower believes it will need time after completion to bring the property up to its full cash flow potential, it may request a mini-perm construction loan. A mini-perm loan builds in a postcompletion loan period lasting one to two years, during which the owner can bring the property to stabilization and improve its value before seeking permanent financing.

7.1.1.5.1 Construction Loan Guarantees
Construction lending can present many risks, and lenders may require borrowers to back up their loans with certain guarantees. Under a completion guarantee the borrower asserts to that bank that they will fund costs required in excess of amounts available under the loan to complete the construction of the project. This funding is not a guarantee that the completed project will be successful or that the borrower will be able to refinance the property to repay the construction loan. It does, however, assure the bank that if it needs to liquidate the property to recover its loan, it will have a completed project to bring to market. Banks may also require the borrower to unconditionally guarantee the repayment of part or all of the loan amount. This guarantee is known as a principal guarantee.

7.1.1.6 Land Loans
When security for a loan is limited to an interest in land, it is known as a land loan. Land loans present many challenges to both lenders and borrowers because although land can be intrinsically valuable, it does not usually

generate any cash flow. The borrower must support the loan with cash from other sources. Therefore, in addition to a critical review of the land's value, the lender will look to the borrower's financial capacity as a key source of loan repayment.

In the event that the borrower defaults on the loan, the lender's remedy is to foreclose on the land. The land does not generate any cash flow to help the lender cover its cost of capital. To realize its original investment and lost interest, the lender must sell the land to another user or developer. Doing so may require the lender to sell the property at a discount. Due to the risks involved in land loans, lenders are usually willing to lend only a small portion of the appraised value of the property.

7.1.1.7 Condo Loans

Developers of condominium projects seek financing that allows them to build or acquire multifamily apartments and then to sell the apartments to individual owners. Condo project loans facilitate these sales by allowing the borrower to make a partial repayment of the loan each time a unit is sold. To facilitate the sale of apartments, the borrower pays a prenegotiated release price and the lender releases the apartment to the buyer. The release prices are set at a multiple of the pro rata debt that would be allocated to each apartment based upon cost. In this manner, the loan is paid off well before the borrower has sold all of the condo inventory.

Many banks that make condo loans earn additional fees by offering financing to the condo buyers. These loans are known as end loans. End loan programs benefit all parties: the condo developer, the condo unit buyer, and the lender. The condo developer benefits from having a ready source of financing for buyers, the buyers have a lender who understands the asset they are buying, and the bank makes fee income while converting the condo loan into easily salable mortgages on owner-occupied residential property.

The major risk to the lender is that the condos do not sell in a timely manner and the developer cannot support the expenses of a building full of vacant units as well the debt service on the unsold unit inventory.

7.1.1.8 Bridge Loans

Properties that are in transition require more flexible financing than mature, stabilized assets. Frequently, owners of newly acquired assets may require financing before they have had the opportunity to assess and reposition an asset. In these cases, the borrower may seek short-term financing from a real estate lender who is experienced in analyzing properties in transition and has capital that is open to a higher level of risk in return for higher interest rates. Bridge loans are typically short-term, floating-rate loans held on the balance sheet of the originating lender.

7.1.1.9 Unsecured Loans

Certain large, well-established real estate companies are able to access the bank market for financing that is secured by only their corporate credit. Because these borrowings are not supported by any identified collateral, they are known as unsecured borrowings.

7.2 DETERMINING THE BEST TYPE AND SOURCE OF FINANCING

The type of asset and the purpose of the loan are the first determinants of the type of loan required. Different lenders focus on residential and commercial assets, and certain commercial mortgage lenders may develop a specialty in particular types of properties or assets located within certain geographic regions.

One must then assess the state of maturity of the property. Commercial banks are the typical source of development and construction loans. Properties that are fully leased to high-credit tenants on long-term leases, situated in stable markets and that are in good repair will likely generate strong, stable cash flows. In contrast, new properties that have not yet been established in the market place or older assets in transition that require renovation and releasing may not have stable cash flows. These more challenging assets may generate a lower return at acquisition but may have greater growth potential and may be able to support additional financing as they reach maturity.

Long-term, fixed-rate financing is generally available, and can be optimal, for stable, fully established assets. The stable cash flow from seasoned properties is attractive to institutional and conduit lenders who typically offer advantageous financing terms.

Higher-risk assets are attractive to a smaller subset of the lender community. These lenders must be more sophisticated and able to evaluate the merits of a project repositioning plan and the markets ultimate acceptance of the project. They must also believe in the borrower's ability to execute the plan on time and on budget. A borrower financing an immature property with good future prospects should generally look for short-term financing and plan on refinancing with long-term debt upon completion of the asset's turn around strategy.

In addition to the status of the property, the amount of financing, the length of term sought by the borrower, and the loan-to-value ratio can narrow the universe of potential lenders. Fewer lenders have the financial capacity to make loans on properties over $50 million. In a similar manner, if the term of the loan sought is greater than five years, there are more limited sources of capital as fewer investors are in the market for long-term investment. Borrowers who have limited equity to invest require high loan-to-value financing. There are more limited sources of capital for these higher-risk financings.

7.3 LOAN TERMS

Participants in the real estate finance world use their own lexicon to describe the critical aspects of a mortgage loan. Many of the loan terms also imply conventions governing the relationship between borrower and lender. Understanding these terms and their implications is important when sorting through the different options available to a borrower.

7.3.1 Nominal Amount

The nominal amount is the principal balance due on the loan. In most circumstances, this is the amount originally borrowed, less any principal that has been repaid. However, this description is not always accurate. In a construction loan, for example, the principal balance increases over time as additional draws are made until the full loan amount is borrowed.

A loan balance may also increase if the amount of interest paid in cash currently is less than the total amount owed to the lender. In this case, the amount of accrued but unpaid interest is added to the loan balance.

7.3.2 Maturity

Loans are generally made for specific periods of time. The period of time during which a loan is outstanding is known as the term of the loan. The date at which a loan is repaid in full is its maturity. Some loans may include a provision for an extension at the request of the borrower or conditioned upon the achievement of certain property performance metrics. If a loan has extension provisions, the end of the last extension period is known as the final maturity of the loan.

Mortgages are generally due on sale, meaning that they must be repaid if the borrower sells the property. An assumable mortgage can be transferred along with a property to the buyer and used to finance the purchase of the asset. An assumption provision may require that the new borrower meet certain conditions, including financial metrics such as level of net worth.

7.3.3 Interest Rate

The interest rate is the bank's charge to the borrower for using its funds. The interest rate is applied to the nominal amount outstanding under the loan. In a fixed-rate mortgage, the interest rate is set at the inception of the loan and is not subject to adjustment. Adjustable or variable-rate mortgages have interest rates that are reset periodically to reflect changes in the financial markets.

In some cases, a loan may call for interest to be paid currently at a rate (the current pay rate) that is less than the amount actually owed to the bank (the accrual rate). This arrangement is done to facilitate a borrower who cannot afford to pay the full amount of interest required by the bank. In each period, when the current pay rate is below the accrual rate, the loan principal balance is increased by the difference.

$$\text{Interest Due} = \text{principal balance} * \text{interest Rate}$$

Where:

Principal balance = amount outstanding at beginning of Period
Interest rate = annual rate

7.3.4 Debt Service

Debt service is the required periodic payment to the lender as set forth in the loan document. Debt service includes interest currently payable as well as any amount required for repayment of principal. If the sum of interest and principal due each month is constant, a mortgage is said to have level debt service. A loan may not require the periodic payment of principal. This type of loan is called an interest-only loan and the debt service consists solely of the interest due.

For any period: debt service = interest due + principal due

Example: A 30 year old self-amortizing mortgage with an initial balance of $100,000 at 7 percent interest requires monthly debt service of $665.30.

This calculation can be performed on a spreadsheet. Excel provides us with a simple formula to calculate the payment required for debt service on a self-amortizing mortgage where our inputs are:

RATE = interest rate (annual, expressed as a decimal)
PERIOD = mortgage term (years, expressed as an integer)
PV = mortgage balance (at inception, expressed as a number) and we are solving for:
PMT = debt service payment (monthly, expressed as a negative number)

7.3.5 Amortization

When a loan calls for the periodic repayment of a portion of the outstanding principal, it is said to be subject to amortization and is referred to as an amortizing loan. If the scheduled payments of principal during the term of the loan result in the full repayment of principal coincident with maturity, the loan is said to be fully amortizing (see Figure 7.1). If the loan does not require periodic amortization, or the scheduled amortization payments total less than the amount outstanding, the borrower will be required to make a final, or "balloon," payment of the remaining outstanding principal at maturity.

Loan amortization reduces a lender's risk over time. With amortization, the falling loan balance matches the hypothetical depreciation occurring in the value of property over time, maintaining a constant loan-to-value ratio (LTV).

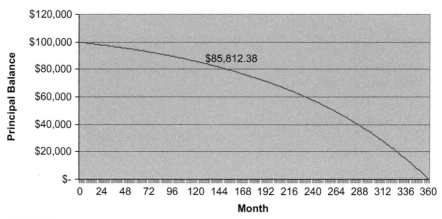

FIGURE 7.1

This illustration shows the remaining principal balance at the end of each month of a level debt service, fully amortizing 30-year mortgage. The remaining principal balance at the end of 10 years (120 months) is $85,812.38.

In general, however, real estate values have risen over time faster than the physical properties have deteriorated. As a result, LTV ratios fall during the life of most amortizing loans.

Most home mortgages are structured as fully amortizing loans with level debt service over the life of the loan. In each month, the payment received by the lender is first applied to interest on the outstanding balance. The residual is then applied to reduce the outstanding principal balance. In each successive month, as the outstanding principal balance falls, the amount of the payment applied to interest decreases and the residual amount applied toward principal repayment increases. The total debt service due each month is calculated so that the final periodic payment completes the amortization of the loan. See Figure 7.2.

Commercial mortgages are also typically structured as self-amortizing, level debt service loans but with shorter terms than the chosen amortization schedule. For example, a typical commercial mortgage may have a ten-year term but may use a thirty-year amortization schedule. As a result, these mortgages have balloon payments due at maturity. In most cases, borrowers look to refinance balloon payments with new mortgages.

Commercial borrowers like longer amortization schedules because they reduce the monthly debt service required on each dollar borrowed. Figure 7.3 shows the remaining principal balance of a level debt service commercial mortgage with a ten-year term using a thirty-year amortization schedule.

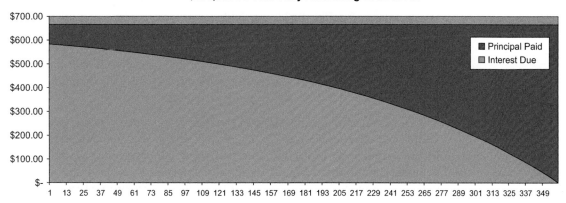

FIGURE 7.2

This illustration shows the allocation of each month's level debt service payment between interest and principal. As the loan matures, principal is repaid, rises and the amount of interest due declines each period.

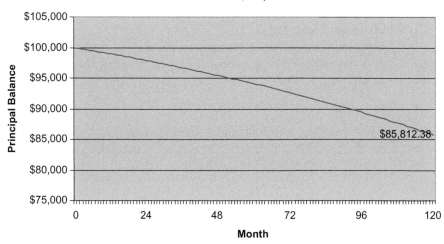

FIGURE 7.3

As a result of amortization, the principal outstanding will have decreased from $100,000.00 to $85,812.38 by the end of the tenth year. If this mortgage were to remain outstanding with the same payment schedule for the next 20 years, it would amortize to a zero balance.

Less frequently, mortgages are structured with fixed periodic payments of principal. In some cases, the frequency of principal payments can be annual or semiannual while the interest remains due monthly. This type of principal repayment schedule is known as "bullet amortization." Following each principal payment, the level of monthly interest due decreases. It then remains level until the next scheduled principal reduction. The total debt service due in any month varies significantly, depending on whether a principal payment is due in addition to the monthly interest payment in that month.

Not all loans require principal repayment prior to maturity. Loans that do not require amortization for some or all of their term are said to be interest-only or to have an interest-only period. Interest-only financing requires lower monthly payments than an amortizing loan with the same principal balance, which makes it easier for a borrower to obtain higher loan proceeds while maintaining the same ratio of cash flow to debt service.

When purchasing a property requiring renovation, a borrower may seek an interest-only loan. This loan makes it easier for the property's lower prerenovation cash flow to cover the debt service. After renovation, as the property's cash flow increases, the loan can call for amortization of the principal balance to begin.

In some loans, the property cash flow cannot support current interest payments, so interest is accrued and added to the loan's outstanding principal balance. This setup is quite typical for construction loans during the period when the property is being built. The buildup of principal over time is known as negative amortization.

7.3.6 Mortgage Constant

In a self-amortizing loan with level debt service, the amount paid to the lender each month is the same. When measured as a percentage of the initial loan amount, this quantity is referred to as the mortgage constant.

The mortgage constant expressed as a percentage:

$$\left(\frac{\sum\limits_{one\ year} \text{monthly principal and interest payments}}{\text{initial principal balance}} \right) * 100\%$$

For example, the $100,000, 7 percent mortgage with the 30-year amortization schedule shown earlier requires level monthly debt service of $665.30:

$$\text{mortgage constant} = \left(\frac{12 * \$665.30}{\$100,000} \right) * 100\% = 7.98\%$$

Extending the amortization period decreases the required principal repayments and lowers the mortgage constant.

The mortgage constant is often compared with the return on investment to determine whether cash flow to equity is improved by adding leverage. The following example demonstrates that if return on investment exceeds the mortgage constant, then leverage increases the return on equity. If the mortgage constant exceeds the return on investment, then leverage decreases return on equity.

Example:				
	(A) No Mortgage	(B) ROI > C	(C) ROI > C, Interest Only	(D) ROI < C
Investment	$ 1,000,000	$ 1,000,000	$ 1,000,000	$1,000,000
Mortgage		$ 600,000	$ 600,000	$ 600,000
Equity	$ 1,000,000	$ 400,000	$ 400,000	$ 400,000
NOI	$ 100,000	$ 100,000	$ 100,000	$ 100,000
ROI	10.0%	10.0%	10.0%	10.0%
Interest Rate		7.0%	7.0%	11.0%
Term	na	30 years	30 years	30 years
Debt Service		$47,902	$42,000	$68,567
Constant		8.0%	7.0%	11.4%
Cash Flow to Equity	$ 100,000	$52,098	$58,000	$31,433
ROE	10.0%	13.0%	14.5%	7.9%

In this example, cash flow to equity is the property's net operating income less the cost of servicing any debt on the asset. Column B illustrates the impact of positive leverage ROI > C on equity returns, column C the enhancement to cash equity returns from a no-amortization/interest-only loan, and column D the impact of negative leverage ROI < C.

7.3.7 Covenants

Covenants are promises made by the borrower to the lender. These promises may cover both financial and operational aspects of the property. The types of covenants made depend on the type of security for the loan. If the loan is secured by a particular asset, the covenants will relate to the financial performance and operation of that asset. Financial covenants may require the property to meet a required level of debt service coverage. If the coverage test is not met, the borrower may be required to reduce the principal balance of the loan. Operating covenants can include requirements to operate and maintain the property in a certain manner and the lender's right to review any alterations to the property or approve major tenant leases before they are signed.

When a loan is unsecured, the borrower's business entity is considered the collateral for the loan and the covenants focus on the financial performance and operations of the entity. In this case, the covenants may require the borrower to remain the direct owner of the entity and to operate the entity within certain financial parameters. These covenants may include maintaining leverage below a threshold percentage of assets and generating cash flow at a minimum multiple of total debt service.

7.3.8 Default

In the event that the borrower fails to meet the agreed-upon covenants, or fails to pay the amounts due on the loan, the loan is said to be in default.

If the borrower does not pay the principal and interest on time, the loan is in monetary default. If the borrower breaches a covenant that does not involve payment of the loan, such as the failure to present critical leases to the bank for prior approval, the loan is in technical default.

The borrower is typically given a short period of time, known as a cure period, within which the borrower can remedy the default, and bring the loan back into good standing. During the period that the loan remains in default, the lender may be entitled to a higher level of interest from the borrower, known as the default interest rate. In addition, the lender may be due service fees, including a significant late charge on any delayed payments.

In the event that the borrower is unable to restore the loan to good standing within the cure period, the lender may accelerate the loan. Acceleration brings forward the maturity of the loan and requires the borrower to immediately repay the outstanding balance and any penalties. Prior to acceleration, the lender may meet with the borrower to negotiate a restructuring of the loan. If the negotiation, known as a workout, is unsuccessful and the borrower is unable to repay or refinance the loan, the lender begins the process of claiming its collateral under the loan agreement through the foreclosure process.

7.4 DETERMINING LOAN AMOUNT

7.4.1 Mortgage Metrics

The amount of money that a lender will advance to a borrower is dependent on two general types of metrics: loan-to-value and debt service coverage. The loan-to-value ratio, also known as the leverage ratio, is the relationship between the loan amount and the market value of the property expressed as a percentage. The lender uses this ratio to determine whether the liquidation of the asset will provide enough cash to repay the loan. The debt service coverage ratio (DSCR) measures the property's cash flow as a multiple of the required cash payments necessary to pay the mortgage. Both quantities are measured over the course of a year. The lender uses this ratio to determine whether the property is generating enough cash to allow the borrower to pay the required monthly loan payments or whether there is a risk of default.

	(B) ROI > C	(C) ROI > C	(D) ROI > C
Investment	$1,000,000	$1,000,000	$1,000,000
Mortgage	$ 600,000	$ 700,000	$ 700,000
Equity	$ 400,000	$ 300,000	$ 300,000
NOI	$ 100,000	$ 100,000	$ 100,000
ROI	10.0%	10.0%	10.0%
Interest rate	7.0%	7.0%	8.0%
Debt Service	$ 47,902	$ 55,885	$ 61,636
Constant	8.0%	8.0%	8.8%
LTV	60%	70%	70%
DSCR	2.09	1.79	1.62

Column B illustrates the impact of increasing the loan amount on the loan-to-value ratio and debt service coverage ratio tests. Because banks usually charge higher rates for higher borrowing levels, Column C looks at the impact of a higher interest rate on these ratios.

For stable properties with steady cash flow, it is not difficult to estimate value, and calculating leverage and coverage tests is comparatively easy and uncontroversial. For properties in transition, estimating stabilized value and cash flow becomes an art form. In tight credit markets, lenders will not recognize the implications of potential positive changes to the property and will calculate ratios based on cash flow and value in place at the time. In easier credit markets, when lenders have capital they want to put out, they will give credit for speculative future changes such as planned renovations in cash flow and value calculations.

When evaluating property projections, lenders will consider the general state of the real estate market, the local market in which the property competes, and the existing and proposed competitive properties in that market. The type of property, the length of its leases, the credit of the tenants, and the historic volatility of its cash flows are also part of the analysis. The lender will "stress test" the borrower's financial projections to see how the property's cash flow is affected by changes in occupancy, rent, and expense assumptions.

When lenders need to invest funds, they will take a more liberal view toward accepting borrowers' optimistic projections for the positive implications of renovation, releasing, and implied improvements in occupancy and rent levels.

7.4.2 Market Credit Metrics

Typically, real estate lenders will lend up to 65 percent of the value of a commercial property (65% LTV) if the stabilized property generates cash flow equal to 1.25 times the required debt service (1.25 times coverage). In periods of easy credit, lenders have been willing to lend up to 75 percent LTV and have dropped required coverage to 1.10 times coverage. The lender's perception of the risks involved in a particular asset modifies the levels of credit metrics that a lender will request. The availability of investment capital in the marketplace modifies the levels of the credit metrics that a lender can achieve before a borrower will seek another capital source.

In some cases, more aggressive loans showing higher leverage and lower coverage may be available from specialized sources at above-average cost. Lenders providing this additional tier of leverage are called mezzanine lenders because of their position at a leverage level above the base loan. The borrower may obtain this capital in the form of a distinct additional "second-mortgage" borrowing, or the primary "first-mortgage" lender may access this capital on behalf of the borrower and then package it into one higher-leverage loan. Having one loan is easier from an administrative standpoint for both borrowers and lenders.

	(A) ROI > C	(B) ROI >C(m) < ROE	(C) ROI < C(m) > ROE	(D) ROI < C(m) < ROE
Investment	$1,000,000	$1,000,000	$1,000,000	$1,000,000
Mortgage	$ 600,000	$ 600,000	$ 600,000	$ 600,000
Mezzanine Debt		$ 200,000	$ 200,000	$ 200,000
Equity	$ 400,000	$ 200,000	$ 200,000	$ 200,000
NOI	$ 100,000	$ 100,000	$ 100,000	$ 100,000
ROI	10.0%	10.0%	10.0%	10.0%
First Mortgage:				
Interest Rate	7.0%	7.0%	7.0%	7.0%
Debt Service	$ 47,902	$ 47,902	$ 47,902	$ 47,902
Constant	8.0%	8.0%	8.0%	8.0%
LTV	60%	60%	60%	60%
DSCR	2.09	2.09	2.09	2.09
Mezzanine:				
Interest Rate		9.50%	11.00%	14.00%
Debt Service		$ 19,000	$ 22,000	$ 28,000
Constant		9.5%	11.0%	14.0%
LTV		80%	80%	80%
DSCR		1.49	1.43	1.32
Cash flow to equity	$52,098	$33,098	$30,098	$24,098
ROE	13.0%	16.5%	15.0%	12.0%

In Column A, our base case, we do not use mezzanine financing, limiting our leverage to 60 percent. In Column B, we add $200,000 of interest-only mezzanine debt at 9.5 percent, an interest rate that is less than both our original ROI and original levered ROE of 13 percent. At this interest rate, the new mezzanine debt offers positive leverage, with ROE rising to 16.5 percent. Column C has the same amount of mezzanine debt but at an interest rate of 11 percent over the property ROI of 10 percent. The mezzanine financing still offers positive leverage because the interest rate is less than the original levered ROE of 13 percent. In Column D, the interest rate on the mezzanine debt exceeds the original levered ROE of 13 percent and the addition of the mezzanine debt now offers negative leverage, reducing levered ROE to 12 percent. Borrowers may take the mezzanine debt, even if it offers negative leverage, because they need the extra capital to acquire the asset or because they are willing to pay a "risk premium" to the mezzanine lender to limit the amount of capital that they have exposed to the project.

7.4.3 Home Mortgage Metrics

A key metric for home mortgage lending is the LTV, the amount of the loan as a percentage of the value of the home being purchased or refinanced. Government policies encouraging homeownership have historically resulted in the availability of higher LTV ratio loans than are normally available in the commercial markets. The prospective homeowner's down payment determines the lender's LTV. For example, a typical 20 percent down payment results in an 80 percent LTV.

Home mortgage lenders look at the ability of the borrower to service the debt on their home by comparing their monthly mortgage payment against their monthly income. This check is a form of debt service coverage test, and it measures the monthly debt service required on a new home mortgage ratio as a percentage of a prospective homeowner's monthly income. Lenders like to see mortgage payments limited to a third of monthly gross income, preferably below 30 percent. Lenders also look at the borrower's total cost of ownership, including debt service on the home and other debt (car, credit card, school), home insurance, and real estate taxes as a fraction of monthly income. This fully loaded coverage ratio gives lenders a more accurate picture of the consumer's ability to finance the cost of their overall lifestyle. Lenders look for this ratio to be below 50 percent — and closer to 40 percent is much preferable.

In the recent period of rapidly rising US home values, aggressive lending institutions made mortgages to prospective homeowners who could not meet standard credit tests. Some of the borrowers failed because of lack of verifiable income. Loans to these borrowers were known as no-income verification loans. Borrowers with poor consumer credit histories were also given mortgages. The lender's credit theory behind all of these loans was that the rapid rise in housing prices would protect the lender in the event of borrower default. The classes of loans that do not meet traditional underwriting standards at the time of their origination are known as subprime loans.

The rapid declines in housing prices that occurred after 2008 resulted in many borrowers defaulting on their mortgages. The high level of mortgage defaults created many problems for the lenders who originated or purchased loans that were underwritten during the postmillennium run-up in housing prices.

7.4.4 Determining Interest Rates

Interest rates on debt used to finance real estate projects are a function of the broader capital markets and the specific risk profile of the individual project being financed. Real estate debt securities compete for investor funds with debt securities offered by companies in other industries and secured by other types of assets. In addition, all commercial debt securities compete with those offered by the US government and other creditworthy sovereign nations.

In the United States, our government securities are considered to be risk free, in that they are not subject to the risk of default presented by any business or real estate project. Therefore, US Treasury securities are priced at the lowest interest rate acceptable to borrowers for the use of their money over time, including the cost of inflation.

US Treasury interest rates vary with the maturity of the security. A graph of US Treasury interest rates versus maturity is known as the US Treasury yield curve. In general, the yield curve is upward sloping, with rates for longer maturities being higher than those for shorter-term loans. In some cases, the yield curve can invert, with shorter-term funds more expensive than longer-term funds.

7.4.4.1 US Treasury Yield Curve

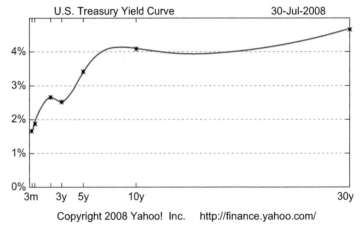

Copyright 2008 Yahoo! Inc.   http://finance.yahoo.com/

FIGURE 7.4

Sample yield curve from Yahoo Finance showing the interest rate on treasury securities graphed against their term.

Fixed-rate loans feature a constant interest rate for their entire term. For most lenders fixed rate loans use the treasury interest rate for a given maturity as a basis for setting interest rates charged to commercial borrowers.

Some borrowers prefer to pay a variable interest rate that resets at specified intervals, known as floating rate debt. To calculate a base rate for variable interest rate loans, the capital markets look to the London Interbank Offering Rate (LIBOR), the interest rate charged by global banks to other creditworthy global banks for borrowing or depositing short-term funds. The most popular term for a LIBOR borrowing is one month.

The interest rate on a commercial loan is generally stated as a base rate and a credit spread. The base rate is tied to a fundamental market rate such as the treasury rate, for fixed-rate loans, or LIBOR for variable-rate loans. The base rate compensates the lender for inflation and loss of liquidity during the term of the loan.

In addition to the base rate, all nongovernment borrowers pay an additional amount of interest for any specific risks related to their particular business transaction. This amount of additional interest, expressed as a percentage of the outstanding loan amount, is known as a credit spread. The total interest rate required by a lender is calculated by adding the credit spread to the base rate.

Example: Interest Rate on a Five-Year Mortgage		
	Fixed Rate	**Floating Rate**
Index	Ten-year US Treasury	One-month LIBOR
Base rate	4.00%	2.46%
Credit spread	2.50%	2.00%
Interest rate	6.50%	4.46%

Interest rates on floating-rate loans are generally lower than those on fixed-rate loans, but are subject to base rate fluctuation. If a property has long-term fixed payment leases, it may be hard for the borrower to fund increased interest payments.

The credit spread reflects the lender's perception of the expected risk in the transaction and builds in a profit for the lender. In a real estate mortgage, this is the risk of the property being unable to generate sufficient cash flow to service the debt and the borrower being unable or unwilling to supplement that amount from other sources.

The level of the credit spread that a lender can charge at the initiation of a loan is a function of the competitive market for capital. In more liquid markets, where investors are eager to lend funds, credit spreads are kept low or "narrow" by competition. When funds are not widely available, credit spreads are higher and are said to "widen."

Adverse economic news can also cause credit spreads to widen. Faced with a greater perception of risk, borrowers may shift their funds to government securities and be less willing to invest in borrowers with perceived business risk. The movement of funds to more secure investments is known as a flight to quality.

The level of risk in debt securities is analyzed by credit research firms known as rating agencies. The most widely known credit rating agencies are Moody's and Standard & Poor's. These agencies assign letter grades ratings to the investments that they analyze with the highest grades awarded being "AAA" or "triple A." Collectively, investments deemed to have a low likelihood of loss and thought to be appropriate for conservative investors are known as investment grade. Lower quality investments are known as high-yield or junk investments.

Investors rely on the ratings published by these agencies to set the level of credit spread required on borrowings. Bank and other intuitional lenders may augment or supplant rating agency analyses with the work of their own credit analysts.

In general, the credit spreads required on investment-grade loans are significantly less than those required on high-yield paper. When there is significant liquidity within the market, spreads narrow (compress) and high-yield borrowers pay less of a premium for their additional risk. When there is less liquidity in the market, or widespread fear of credit problems, spreads widen and low-rated borrowers pay a larger risk premium on their borrowings.

INTEREST RATE DERIVATIVES

Many borrowers have loans with interest rates that use LIBOR as a base rate. Therefore, there is a very liquid market setting the LIBOR level. Because such a large volume of payments are tied to LIBOR, market participants have developed a mechanism for hedging their exposure to the variation in the LIBOR level over time. This mechanism is known as an interest rate swap. In an interest rate swap, party A agrees to pay party B (the swap counterparties) the LIBOR rate times a set notional amount and receives, a fixed interest rate times the same notional amount from party B. Party B pays the fixed interest rate times the notional amount to party A and receives LIBOR times the notional amount from party A. This agreement is in place for a predetermined period of time.

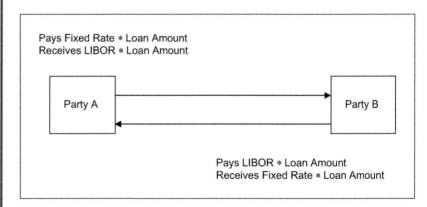

By agreeing to an interest rate swap, a borrower who is required to pay a floating interest rate can know what level of interest payments will be required. In return, a lender of LIBOR-based funds can receive a set rate of return for a given investment period. For each length of agreement, there is a fixed rate at which an interest rate swap can be negotiated. The graph of the fixed rates that counterparties are required to pay to receive LIBOR for each length of term is known as the swap curve, an analog to the treasury yield curve. Rather than using the treasury rate as a base rate, many loans now use the rate from the swap curve. These loans are priced at a spread to the swap rate.

Note: *Bankers quote interest rates as "swaps plus X" or "X over swaps." The X is the credit spread in basis points. If a banker says that a five-year loan will cost 200 over swaps, they mean that the interest rate on the loan will be the fixed rate shown for a five-year LIBOR swap plus 200 basis points (2%).*

7.4.5 Points and Fees

At the inception of a loan, lenders may require a borrower to pay points, an up-front payment equal to a set percentage of the amount to be borrowed. From the borrower's perspective, these payments are additional interest. As an up-front use of loan proceeds, points can be thought of as diminishing the net funds received from the loan, which increases the effective interest rate that the borrower pays.

In addition to interest, lenders also receive processing fees for their work in the initial underwriting of a loan and then for administering the mortgage over its life.

For example, a borrower with $50,000 in cash wants to purchase a $150,000 property and must borrow a net amount of $100,000. The bank requires five points and $2,000 in processing fees. The borrower must then raise its net proceeds to $100,000 plus $2,000 fees or $102,000. It will, however, receive only 100 percent − 5 percent or 95 percent of each dollar of loan amount; the remainder is returned to the bank as points. Therefore, to receive $102,000 net, the borrower must borrow $102,000/0.95 or $107,368.42.

$$gross\ amount\ borrowed = net\ cash\ proceeds\ plus\ fees/100\ percent - points$$
$$\$107,368.42 = \$100,000 + \$2,000/100\% - 5\ percent$$

As shown in this equation, to obtain the required net proceeds of $100,000, the borrower must take a loan out in the amount of $107,368.42.

7.4.6 Credit Issues

Most lenders will tell you that the most important determinant of the success of a real estate project, and therefore the likeliness of loan repayment, is the quality of the project's sponsorship. Sponsorship refers to the ownership group that is borrowing the money to finance the asset. The real estate skills of this group − their financial capacity outside of the subject property, and most important, their personal integrity − are the key ingredients to a successful loan.

The second most important ingredient is the quality of the real estate. The near-term quality of the real estate is derived from the strength of the current tenants and the terms of their leases. Long-term leases with creditworthy tenants give a project financial stability.

The longer-term success of a property is determined by the strength of the property market and the competitive position of the asset within the market. That competitive position will be determined by the quality of the asset's location and the structural integrity, visual appeal, and amenities of the physical structure. It is important to analyze the building as it will appear to tenants, making an independent assessment of the market at the time when the current leases will be up for renewal.

The quality of sponsorship and the value of an asset are both critical determinants of the credit quality of a real estate loan. When a lender seeks a legal right to acquire the asset from the borrower in the event of a default, the property is said to serve as collateral or security for the loan. When a loan is backed by the pledge of an asset, it is known as a secured loan. In contrast, if the loan is made without a direct tie to an asset, it is said to be an unsecured loan. Unsecured loans are generally made only to large public companies and individuals with extraordinary financial profiles.

Even when a lender has a collateral interest in a borrower's property, the liquidation value of the asset may not be enough to assure the lender that the principal and interest due on the loan will be repaid. In this case, the lender will want to have recourse to the borrower's other assets. This loan is known as a recourse loan, and the borrower may be asked to execute a personal guarantee to repay the loan in full. If a borrower has agreed to a recourse loan, in the event that the liquidation value of the collateral is insufficient to repay the loan in full, the lender may seek a deficiency judgment against the borrower. With a deficiency judgment, the lender can look to the borrowers other assets to repay the balance due.

In the event that the lender is satisfied with having the liquidation value of the property as its sole collateral for repayment, the lender will make a nonrecourse loan.

In competitive lending markets, most major real estate loans are made on a secured but nonrecourse basis. In these loans, the lender is entitled to take the property through foreclosure in the event of a default but cannot seek further funds from the borrower. In recent years, lenders have modified this form of loan to permit recourse to the borrower in the event that the borrower has not acted in good faith during the term of the loan.

The situations in which a lender is provided recourse are collectively known as nonrecourse carve-outs. Nonrecourse carve-outs, also known as bad-boy provisions, typically include instances in which the borrower has failed to properly maintain the asset, the property has become environmentally contaminated, or the borrower has misrepresented facts about the property to the lender.

7.5 PROPERTY LIFECYCLE ISSUES

Many real estate loans are made for the long term. Ten-year loans are typical on commercial properties. Home mortgages can be even longer — typically 15 to 30 years. During this period, the property's financial situation can change dramatically.

In the simplest case, assume a property with no cash flow growth but a stable market position, subject to an amortizing loan. Each month, as loan principal is repaid, the property's LTV ratio will slowly decline. In the event that the leases renew at increasing rents, the property's cash flow and its market value will rise over time. The amortizing loan's principal balance falls and the gap between property value and the outstanding loan amount increases at an even faster rate.

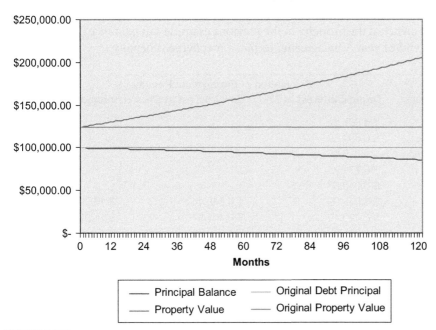

FIGURE 7.5
In this illustration, the borrower seeks to acquire a property that costs $125,000. The lender agrees to make an 80 percent LTV $100,000 loan to the borrower. The borrower supplements the loan with $25,000 of original equity and buys the property. Over the next ten years, the borrower makes $14,800 in principal payments, reducing the loan balance at maturity to $85,200. Assuming that the property's value remains at the original purchase price, the borrower's equity would have risen to $39,800. However, assume the property cash flow grows at 5 percent per annum, creating an increase in market value of $80,000. At the end of year 10, the total borrower's equity would total $119,800 ($25,000 in original equity, $14,800 in principal repayment, and $80,000 increase in market value) against the new market value of $205,000. Until the loan is repaid or refinanced, the borrower cannot use this "stranded equity" in other projects.

In growth markets, borrowers can build up a considerable amount of stranded equity locked into assets subject to long-term loans.

Borrowers have developed a number of strategies for unlocking this built-up equity. The simplest solution is to refinance the loan and to borrow additional proceeds. This refinancing is referred to as a cash-out refinancing.

In many cases, however, commercial loans are subject to steep prepayment penalties. In the case in which interest rates have fallen, the lender seeks to be "made whole" against the prospect of having to relend the repatriated capital at the now lower interest rate. The make whole provision requires the borrower to pay both the present value of the interest differential and a penalty fee. This fee can make the refinancing economically inefficient for the borrower.

The owner of the property in the previous example can refinance the property at the end of year 5 by agreeing to pay a prepayment penalty:

| | Calculation of Prepayment Penalty | | |
Year	Original Interest at 7%	New Interest at 5%	Interest Differential
One	$ 6,967.82		
Two	$ 6,894.39		
Three	$ 6,815.65		
Four	$ 6,731.21		
Five	$ 6,640.67		
Six	$ 6,543.59	$ 4,548.44	$ 1,995.16
Seven	$ 6,439.49	$ 4,451.57	$ 1,987.93
Eight	$ 6,327.87	$ 4,349.74	$ 1,978.13
Nine	$ 6,208.17	$ 4,242.70	$ 1,965.47
Ten	$ 6,079.82	$ 4,130.19	$ 1,949.63
Make Whole			$ 9,876.31
PV (at 5%) of Make Whole			$ 8,727.73

In this illustration, after five years of ownership, a borrower seeks to refinance a loan to take advantage of a drop in interest rates from 7 percent to 5 percent. To repay the loan, the borrower must pay the lender the present value of the "make whole" or interest differential, the amount the lender will lose by reloaning the funds into the lower rate environment. In many cases, the lender will base the interest differential on the treasury rate rather than the mortgage rate, so the lender is not at risk for successfully making a new loan. This arrangement raises the amount of the prepayment penalty significantly.

	Original	End of Year 5: Refinance	End of Year 10: Sale of Asset
Property value	$ 125,000.00	$ 160,419.83	$ 205,000.00
LTV	80%	80%	
Principal balance	$ 100,000.00	$ 128,335.87	
Interest rate	7%	5%	
Balance remaining		$ 94,131.59	
Required prepayment		$ 8,727.73	$ 117,651.30
Owed to lender		$ 102,859.32	$ 117,651.30

(Continued)

	Original	End of Year 5: Refinance	End of Year 10: Sale of Asset
Equity available to borrower		$ 25,476.55	$ 87,348.70
Monthly payment	$ 661.44	$688.93	

At the end of year 5, the borrower obtains a new loan at 80 percent of the then-current value of $160,419. The loan proceeds of $128,335 are sufficient to repay the remaining principal of $94,131 on the old loan, the required prepayment penalty of $8,727, and excess proceeds of $25,476. The monthly cost of the new loan is only $27 per month higher than the original loan payment. The borrower can now use the excess proceeds, reflecting a return of $476.55 over the original equity investment of $25,000, to purchase a new property.

At the end of year 10, the property is sold for $205,000. The new mortgage must be repaid with $117,651.30 of the sale proceeds, resulting in a profit of $87,348.70. In addition to the periodic cash flow from the asset, the borrower has received a total of $112,825.25 on an original equity investment of $25,000.

When prepayment penalties make refinancing diseconomic, the borrower can seek a second mortgage, a loan secured by the residual equity in the property following the assumed repayment of the first mortgage at maturity. The interest rate on a second, or junior, mortgage is typically higher than that paid on a contemporaneous first lien as the lender's risk is higher.

Some first mortgages have a provision against second mortgages because the first mortgage lender does not want to have many parties in interest to a fore-closure proceeding in the event of a default. To work around this problem, borrowers can create entities that hold a number of assets and then borrow against the collective residual cash flow, which becomes available after payment of all mortgage debt service. Many lenders will offer credit lines, or flexible borrowing arrangements, in which the amount of principal can vary over time based on the value of the portfolio's stranded equity and monthly residual cash flow. These arrangements are used to provide real estate investors with access to capital to pursue additional projects.

7.5.1 Troubled Assets

Not all assets continually generate more cash flow. Over long time periods, asset quality can deteriorate and the strength of a location can fall as the center of commerce shifts due to new and competitive development. As a property's market deteriorates, it may be difficult to find new tenants, and those that are found may be willing to pay only a lower rent. As this occurs, cash flow falls off and a property may no longer be able to cover the now partially amortized principal balance. In this case, the borrower may not be able to meet its financial obligations to the lender.

7.5.2 Defaults

When a borrower does not live up to its obligations under the terms of a debt instrument, an event of default occurs. There are two types of defaults under most loan agreements. The first type is a technical default, which occurs when a borrower has violated a loan covenant. An example of a technical default would be the failure of a borrower to maintain an agreed-upon level of debt service coverage on an enterprise level. This violation might occur if the borrower's portfolio suffers the loss of some key tenants and occupancy falls. This drop in income might lead to a decline in interest coverage ratios.

Many technical defaults occur while a borrower continues to make regularly scheduled payments of principal and interest. Were the borrower to stop making the required payments, the loan would go into monetary default.

Most loan agreements contain cure provisions that allow the borrower to remedy the default within a given period of time. If the situation causing the default can be remedied, the loan returns to good standing. If the borrower is incapable or unwilling to cure the default, the bank can initiate a series of actions specified in the loan agreement and ultimately seek the liquidation of the asset to settle its claim.

7.5.3 Workouts

Most lenders do not want to own real estate. In general, they would like to find a way to work with a borrower to restructure a loan so that the borrower can move forward with a property. The process in which the lender and borrower meet to discuss the future of a loan in default is called a workout.

A lender's prospective on a workout is conditioned by the current state of the property markets and the role the borrower has played in the deterioration of the asset. If the market is in a serious decline and the borrower has been diligent in attempting to manage the property, then a lender may agree to restructure a loan, believing that the borrower is the best operator of the asset.

7.5.4 Restructuring

In a restructuring negotiation, the bank may agree to alter the terms of the loan to lower the debt service payments required of the borrower, which may be done by lowering the interest rate or lowering the principal amortization requirement. These changes are usually put in place for a limited period of time and are subject to constant review.

In return for a restructuring, a borrower may be asked to invest outside funds in capital improvements. The borrower may also be asked to have all property revenues sent to an escrow account held by the bank, against which only lender-approved expenses may be paid. The borrower may also be asked to agree in advance to give the property to the lender in the event that the default persists for a period of time. These steps protect the lender in the event that the restructuring fails and the property moves towards foreclosure.

7.5.5 Foreclosure

In the event that a lender has lost faith in the borrower's ability to manage a property, the lender may seek to gain title to the property. Gaining title to the property through the foreclosure process is the lender's first step toward liquidating the collateral in an attempt to pay off its loan.

The borrower may go to court to forestall the taking of the asset, pleading a number of defenses, including lender liability — an assertion that the lender's actions contributed to the decline of the mortgaged asset's value.

In the event that the court approves the foreclosure, the lender is allowed to offer the property for sale to repatriate its principal, interest, and costs. The borrower is then entitled to any residual equity. If the sale proceeds are insufficient to repay a recourse loan, the lender may seek a deficiency judgment against the borrower for any unpaid amounts.

7.5.6 Deed in Lieu

In the event of a failed restructuring, the borrower may decide to give the asset to the lender in settlement of the debt. This process is known as deed in lieu of foreclosure. In this generally amicable proceeding, the borrower relinquishes title in favor of the lender without a lengthy legal process. The lender benefits from gaining control of the asset before its condition deteriorates and the borrower benefits because it is released from further liability.

Glossary

Acceleration
Amortization
Assumable mortgage
Bad-boy provisions
Balloon payment
Base rate
Bullet payment
Cash-out refinancing
Collateral
Completion guarantee
Construction draw
Construction loan
Covenant
Credit line
Credit spread
Cure period
Cure provision
Debt service
Deed in lieu
Default

Deficiency judgment due on sale
DSCR (debt service coverage ratio)
Fees
First mortgage
FHA (Federal Housing Administration)
Fixed-rate loan
Flight to quality
Floating-rate loan
Foreclosure
Fully amortizing loan
High yield
HUD (US Department of Housing and Urban Development)
Interest only
Interest rate
Interest rate swap
Investment grade
Junk
Land loan
Lender liability
Level debt service
Leverage ratio
LIBOR (London Interbank Offering Rate)
Loan-to-value ratio
Make whole provision
Maturity
Mezzanine
Mini-perm loan
Monetary default
Mortgage
Mortgage constant
Mortgage insurance
Negative amortization
No income verification loan
Nominal amount
Nonrecourse carve-outs
Nonrecourse loan
Permanent loan
Points
Principal balance
Principal guarantee
Prepayment penalty
Rating agency
Recourse loan
Restructuring
Second mortgage
Secured loan
Sponsorship
Stranded equity

Stress test
Subprime mortgage
Swap curve
Technical default
Term
Unsecured loan
Workout
Yield curve

Thought Questions

1. Five years ago you invested in a brand-new 100,000-square-foot office building. The building was fully leased to great tenants with ten-year leases. You financed your purchase with a ten-year mortgage at a rate that would be considered high in today's market. You can refinance today and get a new ten-year loan at a lower rate. You will, however, be required to pay your current lender a steep prepayment penalty. You can also wait until the loan comes to term and repay the loan without any penalty. This was your plan until you recently read about a brand-new office park being "discussed" for the old farm just a mile down the road. Coincidentally, this development, if built, could open just as your tenant leases are coming up for renewal. What are your thoughts?

2. Does it ever make sense to give the "keys" back to a lender? If so, under what circumstances?

Review Questions

1. Debt Service

   You just placed a ten-year $15 million CMBS loan on your warehouse with an 8 percent rate and a 25-year amortization schedule. What is your annual debt service?

2. Debt Service Coverage

   New Market Commons has adjusted NOI of $4 million. The bank is willing to make a ten-year 6 percent $20 million loan with a 30-year amortization schedule. What is the debt service coverage ratio?

3. Loan-to-Value

   Upmarket Builders, a builder of fine homes, owns twenty 2-acre lots in a subdivision outside of Princeton, New Jersey. The 5,000-square-foot homes built on these lots will sell for $2 million. Appraisers value the lots at 30 percent of the final home price. Regent Bank is willing to make a land loan at a 50 percent loan-to-value. How much will they lend?

4. Calculating Loan Size (Interest Only)

   A property generates $100,000 in net annual cash flow. The lender requires debt service coverage of 1.25 times on a ten-year interest only loan at an 8 percent annual rate. How much can be borrowed on this property?

5. **Calculating Loan Size (Impact of Amortization)**
   The lender on the property in question 4 also offers a 7 percent loan and requires that the loan follow a 30-year self amortization schedule during its 10-year term. How much can be borrowed assuming the same 1.25 debt service coverage requirement. What will be the remaining principal balance at the end of the 10-year term?

6. **Calculating Loan Size (Impact of LTV)**
   The lender's credit committee believes that no loan should be made at a loan-to-value ratio of greater than 65 percent. Assume that the bank values the property at ten times cash flow. Can the borrower in question 5 borrow the full amount of proceeds available assuming the coverage test of 1.25 percent?

7. **Calculating Amount Available to Borrow and Amortization**
   Bluestone Office Park generates net annual cash flow of $220,000 in year one. The net annual cash flow is estimated to grow at 5 percent per year over the next ten years. The bank offers a 7 percent interest rate on a 10-year loan with 25-year amortization. The initial loan amount is subject to the tighter of (a) 1.1 x coverage test or (b) 70 percent loan-to-value test. Assume the property is always valued at 12 x net annual cash flow. How much can be borrowed? What is the actual loan-to-value at the end of year 5 and at the loan's maturity at the end of year 10?

8. A downdraft hits the real estate market and tenants start leaving Bluestone Park (from question 7) at the end of year 3. Cash flow declines 15 percent year over year in each of years 4 thru 6. Does the property generate enough cash in year 6 to service the debt?

9. **Structuring a Workout**
   You can no longer service your loan on Bluestone Park (from question 8). You use your own cash to support the deficit on the property. At the end of year 6, you are out of cash and approach the bank for a workout. The bank offers to suspend amortization payments and lower the interest rate by 1 percent to 6 percent. Does this help?

10. **Maximum Loan Size**
    The maximum amount that the Stage Coach Bank and Trust will lend is determined by the bank credit committee's loan underwriting standard. This standard looks at the property ability to support a minimum debt service coverage ratio of 1.4 and a maximum 65 percent loan-to-value. The asset presented to committee has adjusted NOI of $5 million. The loan officer believes the property would trade at a cap rate of 8 percent. Loans on similar properties have ten-year terms with interest rates of 7 percent and 25-year amortization schedules. How much will the bank lend?

11. **Debt Service: Impact of Amortization**
    Little John Investors owns a 30,000-square-foot big box store on a triple net lease to King Size Lots. The property is subject to a ten-year 7 percent

interest-only loan with an original principal amount of $5 million. This loan has eight years to maturity. The bank has offered the group a new ten-year loan with proceeds equal to the old loans outstanding balance at 5 percent requiring 25-year amortization. If maximizing annual cash flow for distribution is Little John's only criteria, should they take the new loan?

12. **Home Mortgage Qualification**
You make $50,000 per year and you want to buy a home that costs $250,000. The bank says that you can qualify for a traditional 30-year 7 percent mortgage at 80 percent loan-to-value if the debt service is less than 25 percent of your monthly pre tax income. Do you qualify?

13. **Subprime Loan Underwriting as an Alternative**
The bank (in question 12) offers you a subprime adjustable rate loan with 30-year amortization and a teaser rate of 2 percent for the first two years, maximum LTV of 90 percent. At the end of that period, you can refinance or the rate adjusts to 3 percent over then-current ten-year treasury. The ten-year treasury at the end of two years is forecast to be 6 percent. (At that point, the remaining principal balance will amortize over the next 28 years.) Do you qualify for the teaser loan? How much will your monthly payment rise at the reset date?

14. **Refinancing of a Subprime Loan**
At the end of two years, your income is now $55,000 per year. The value of your house is up to 300,000. Instead of accepting the new 9 percent interest rate, can you refinance with a traditional loan (terms as stated in example 13) in an amount sufficient to pay off your mortgage? What is the maximum amount you can qualify to refinance?

Multiple Choice Questions

1. Which clause allows a buyer to keep the sellers mortgage in place?
   a) Assignment clause
   b) Assumption clause
   c) Due on Sale clause
   d) Acceleration clause

2. A loan secured by property with a further guarantee of payment by the borrower is called:
   a) Stranded equity
   b) Nonrecourse
   c) Covenant of Seisin Mezzanine loan
   d) Recourse loan

3. Which is not an alternative to foreclosure?
   a) Workout
   b) Deed in lieu
   c) Restructuring
   d) Acceleration

4. The amount due to the lender, including costs, less the proceeds from a foreclosure sale equals the amount sought in a:
   a) Cash out refinancing
   b) Deficiency judgment
   c) Junior lien
   d) Make whole provision

5. Which is not a risk associated with mortgage lending?
   a) Obsolescence
   b) Interest rate change
   c) Default
   d) Prepayment

For answers to these Problems and Exercises, please visit the companion website: http://booksite.elsevier.com/9780123786265

CHAPTER 8

Mortgage-Backed Securities

Mortgage-backed securities (MBS) are financial instruments secured by portfolios of commercial or residential mortgages. It is estimated that there are $8.9 trillion in MBS outstanding, accounting for about 25 percent of the total amount of the public and private debt market.[1] The issuers of these securities are typically special-purpose entities whose sole asset is a portfolio of mortgage securities. The special-purpose entity (SPE) collects the cash flow from these mortgages and redistributes it to the holders of the MBS according to the terms of their investments.

MBS are generally sponsored by financial institutions that either originated the underlying mortgages or sourced them in the capital markets. These institutions can also serve as the underwriters of the MBS, structuring the transactions and placing the securities with investors. The sponsoring institution and other financial institutions provide liquidity to the investor community by maintaining a secondary market for the securities.

MBS can be secured by mortgages on many different property types, including single-family homes, multifamily housing, and various types of commercial properties. In addition to commercial and investment banks, there are government and quasi-government agencies that underwrite single and multifamily mortgages and participate in the underwriting of MBS secured by these mortgages (residential mortgage-backed securities or RMBS). The underwriting of MBS secured by mortgages on commercial properties (commercial mortgage-backed securities or CMBS) is the domain of major commercial and investment banks.

CONTENTS

8.1 THE DEVELOPMENT OF MORTGAGE-BACKED SECURITIES

The concept behind MBS is the aggregation of a number of individual mortgages into a portfolio that is used to support the issuance of new classes of securities. These new securities have features that are more attractive to

---

[1] Source: Securities Industry and Financial Markets Association, December 31, 2010. Freddie Mac investor presentation, May 2011 (p. 63).

institutional investors than the direct ownership of individual mortgages. By creating securities that are attractive to institutional investors, more capital is attracted to the mortgage market and the cost of mortgage financing is reduced.

To create MBS, a financial institution acquires a portfolio of mortgages. These mortgages may have been underwritten by that institution or acquired from other originators. This portfolio of mortgages is known as a collateral pool. The mortgages in the pool generate periodic payments of interest and principal that are used to support the issuance of highly structured investment products. The maturity and risk characteristics of these securities are tailored to meet the needs of institutional investors.

The goal of this process is to sell these newly created MBS at a total price that is higher than the cost of aggregating the underlying individual mortgages, and the structuring and issuing of the new securities. This arbitrage and the income from underwriting and originating the mortgages provide a profit incentive to the financial institution. The issuance of MBS also provides a significant source of liquidity for the real estate market.

8.1.1 Development of the Residential Mortgage-Backed Security Market

Prior to the Great Depression of the 1930s, home lending was carried out by banks and savings and loan associations. Loans were made for a short term, generally five years, and were limited to 50 percent of the value of the home. These terms made home ownership impossible for many families, and only a limited portion of American families owned homes.[2]

Under this type of mortgage, the borrower was not expected to amortize the loan but only to make current payments of interest. The borrower had to renew or repay the loan each time it matured. This gave the bank the opportunity to cancel the loan if the borrower's financial status declined.

As there was no market for trading mortgages, banks held mortgages as one of their primary asset classes. The cash flow from these loans provided liquidity for the banks and interest for their depositors.

As unemployment rose during the Depression, many homeowners were unable to repay their loans, which led to the failure of many banks and a decline in available credit in the housing market. The lack of credit and the poor economy combined to cause a steep drop in home values. Without mortgage lenders, home owners with maturing loans could not find a source for refinancing, which reinforced the negative trends in the housing market.

---

[2] According to the U.S. Census, only 45.6 percent of families owned homes in 1920 (Historical Census of Housing Tables, http://www.census.gov/hhes/www/housing/census/historic/owner.html).

In order to address the need for liquidity in the housing finance market, the U.S. government created the Federal Housing Authority (FHA) to insure borrower's mortgage obligations. Borrowers who met defined underwriting criteria and agreed to use certain mortgage documents could purchase mortgage insurance, which served as a government credit backstop to their personal mortgage obligations. With the government guarantee, standardized documentation and underwriting criteria in place, the value of a mortgage could be ascertained and a market for mortgages as investment vehicles developed.

The mortgage market was enhanced by the creation of the Federal National Mortgage Association (Fannie Mae) in 1938 and the Federal Home Loan Mortgage Corporation (Freddie Mac) in 1970: quasi-government agencies that purchased FHA-insured loans from banks and sold interests in these loans to investors. While no longer enjoying the full faith and credit of the US government, these entities are referred to as government sponsored entities (GSE).

In 1968, the Government National Mortgage Association (Ginnie Mae) was created specifically to underwrite MBS that backed by pools of FHA loans. Ginnie Mae securities are structured as fractional, pro rata interests in FHA mortgage pools and carry the full faith and credit of the U.S. government. As all cash flow earned on the mortgages is aggregated and paid through to investors, these securities are known as mortgage pass-through securities (MPTs).

The development of an active market for mortgages allowed banks to sell the loans that they had originated and to relend the sale proceeds to new borrowers. This additional liquidity made home ownership available to more citizens.

8.1.2 Application to Commercial Property Mortgage Lending

As the market for RMBS became highly standardized, the commercial property mortgage market remained more fragmented. Commercial mortgages were underwritten by commercial banks, pension funds, and insurance companies for their own accounts. These loans were known as balance sheet loans because the institution doing the underwriting and origination intended to keep the loan as an asset on their balance sheet.

Each institution applied its own underwriting standards and utilized its own documentation. Transactions were highly structured and customized for each borrower and property. As a result, a high level of real estate expertise was required to participate in commercial property lending, which limited the liquidity in the market. If a lender sought to make a loan in excess of its financial capacity, it formed a syndicate of similar lenders to pool resources. If a lender sought liquidity, it sold its loans to other lenders as undivided whole loans.

Customized financings made it difficult for investors to analyze whole loan portfolios. During the late 1980s, fueled in part by the adverse consequences of the savings and loan crisis, banks began to apply standardized underwriting to commercial property lending. With the end goal of creating a liquid market for commercial mortgage loans, banks began moving borrowers towards acceptance of standard underwriting criteria.

The application of standard underwriting criteria and loan documents to the commercial mortgage space was mediated by the rating agencies. In order to provide credit ratings for MBS, the rating agencies established credit benchmarks for underwriting commercial mortgages and collateral pools consisting of such mortgages.

The borrower's reward for acceptance of the new underwriting criteria was the bank's ability to reduce loan pricing and share the benefits of enhanced liquidity with the borrower. As with residential mortgage securities, the simplest form of commercial mortgage security is the mortgage pass-through, in which the investor owns a fractional interest in the cash flows derived from a pool of mortgages.

8.2 BENEFITS TO LENDERS AND BORROWERS FROM SECURITIZATION

Investors such as pension funds and insurance companies are known as balance sheet lenders because they intend to keep the mortgages they underwrite as investments to match their long term liabilities.

In most cases, banks do not have the long-term liabilities that match the long life of mortgages. Banks underwrite most permanent mortgages with the intention of selling them to other investors. A bank that intends to sell off its mortgage loans is called a conduit lender.

8.2.1 Loan Sales

There are a number of ways in which banks can reduce their investment in a mortgage. In the simplest case, a bank can sell off the mortgage loan in its entirety. This transaction is called a whole loan sale or note sale. The bank can also form a syndicate: a group of banks or other investors that will purchase fractional interests in the mortgage loan. This process, in which a group of banks come together to underwrite a loan, is called a loan syndication. The loan that results is then said to be a syndicated loan. Each bank's share of the loan is known as a participation.

8.2.2 Securitization

A bank may also aggregate a number of loans into a portfolio that can be sold to investors. The bank creates an SPE with the explicit task of owning and administering the loan portfolio. The bank then structures securities to be issued against the cash flow generated by the loans. The structure is reviewed by the credit agencies, which assign ratings to each proposed class of securities before being sold to investors. This process is known as a securitization, because as the investors purchase securities in the entity holding the loans, the mortgages effectively morph into securities.

The investor benefits from the underwriting skills and customer relationships of the bank. The bank works with borrowers to structure appropriate mortgages at market rates and terms. The bank then offers the investors securities that are structured, and in some cases customized, to address focused investment needs.

The bank benefits from fees earned from borrowers for its work on underwriting the mortgages, the process of assessing the ability of the property and/or its sponsor to generate the cash flow required to repay the mortgage. This process is called the origination process.

The bank holds the loans that it has originated on its balance sheet prior to launching the securitization, which is called warehousing the loans. The bank can potentially profit from the spread that it earns between the interest rate on the mortgages and its short-term cost of capital. If the bank launching the securitization has not originated enough of its own loans, it can also acquire loans from other originating banks.

The bank can also profit on the sale of the loans to an SPE if the return on investment demanded by the investors is less than the interest rate underwritten by the bank on the mortgages. The bank can also lose money if the markets move against it. Securities issuers will hedge this risk to protect against losses from changes in interest rates.

8.2.3 REMICs

SPEs that exist for the sole purpose of owning and distributing the cash flows from a pool of mortgages to investors are known as real rstate mortgage investment conduits (REMICs). These entities are typically structured as corporations or trusts. In 1986, the U.S. Congress passed the Tax Reform Act legislation, which allows REMICs that pay all of their cash flow to investors to be excluded from federal taxation. Most U.S. states have also granted REMICs exclusions from state taxes.

The REMIC typically issues many classes of securities, also known as tranches (from the French word for "slice"). Each tranche has rights to a different portion of the cash flow received from the entity's sole asset: its mortgage portfolio.

Following the issuance of securities by the REMIC, the issuing bank or affiliate may also act as a loan servicer, providing administrative services during the life of the loan. The servicer works with the borrowers to handle any issues that arise with the mortgage loans.

In the event that the borrower defaults on its obligations under a REMIC loan, the bank or a third party acts as a special servicer. Unlike the servicer, whose role is purely administrative, the special servicer may negotiate with the borrower on behalf of the investors. If required, the special servicer will ultimately

(A)

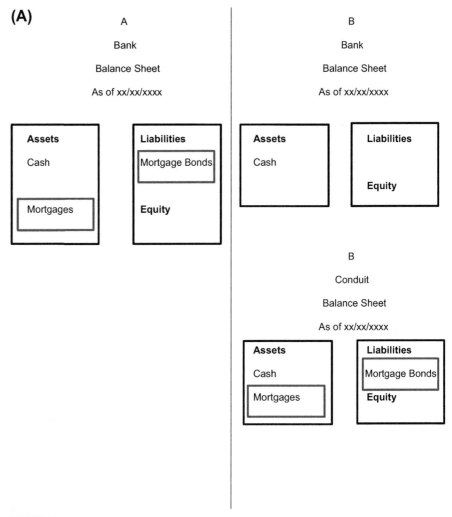

FIGURE A
Both mortgages and liabilities remain on bank's balance sheet. In this situation, bonds issued by the bank may obligate the bank to maintain a certain quantity and quality of mortgages as security for the repayment for the notes. The bank retains the risk of default and prepayment and may be required to restock its mortgage holdings to provide for overcollateralization when required under bond agreements.

foreclose on the underlying property, liquidating it and returning available proceeds to the investors. In cases in which a sale is not immediately possible, the REMIC may hold the foreclosed property as real estate owned (REO).

Banks also make money by maintaining a trading market in MBS. They may act as an agent for investors or buy and sell as a principal for the bank's own account. Maintaining a liquid market gives investors comfort that they can convert their MBS to cash if necessary.

8.3 STRUCTURING MORTGAGE-BACKED SECURITIES

8.3.1 Variables that Affect MBS Performance

Owners of mortgages face a number of risks. Designers of MBS use various structuring techniques to allocate these risks between security issuer and investor, as well as among the various classes of investors.

8.3.1.1 Homogeneity of Collateral Pool

A fundamental risk of property investment is concentration risk. This risk occurs when a substantial amount of a mortgage portfolio's loans are concentrated in either a particular type of real estate or in a limited geographical region. In the case of a portfolio that is concentrated in a single property type, an economic impact on a single industry can have an impact on an entire class of real estate. For example, a decline in consumer consumption can affect retail real estate. In a similar way, a portfolio of geographically concentrated real estate can expose the owner to the risk of a business decline or natural disaster in a particular region. For example, the decline in the U.S. automotive industry has had a negative impact on real estate in Michigan, and Hurricane Katrina has severely affected the real estate market in New Orleans. For these reasons, investors in mortgage securities generally look to invest in diversified pools of mortgages to eliminate concentration risk.

8.3.1.2 Economic Climate During the Period When Mortgages Are Originated

Mortgage underwriters seek liquidity in the secondary market by pooling mortgages and reselling them to mortgage-backed security investors. They are reluctant to hold onto mortgages for long periods of time and absorb risk. They make money on fees and turnover, not investment. For this reason, mortgage pools tend to contain mortgages of a common vintage.

This practice exposes the investor to a number of factors, including the state of the credit market and real estate valuation levels at the time of underwriting. Mortgages underwritten in times of tight credit will generally be underwritten on a more conservative basis than those underwritten during a period of loose credit. Because credit availability also affects valuation, mortgages underwritten during periods of loose credit will generally reflect higher valuations.

8.3.2 Risk of Default
8.3.2.1 Impact of Default

The risk of default is the chance that a mortgagee will be delinquent in paying the principal and interest on a loan or unable to repay the loan when due. Default forces the owner of the mortgage to foreclose on the property and liquidate it to repay the debt. Foreclosure may result in a loss of part or all of the principal and interest that would have normally flowed from the loan. Depending on the structure of the MBS, the risk of default on the underlying securities can be allocated to either the issuer or the investor.

8.3.2.2 Issuer Risk

There are two fundamental ways in which the issuer can protect the investor against the risk of default. The first is collateral substitution, in which defaulted mortgages are removed from the collateral pool and replaced by performing loans, so that the pool always maintains sufficient good collateral to support the outstanding mortgage securities.

The second and more common method is overcollateralization, in which the issuer backs a bond issue or a tranche of a bond issue with more collateral than would be required to repay that amount of securities. This method of credit enhancement is known as external overcollateralization and is typically used in mortgage pass-through securities for which overcollateralization cannot be accomplished within the issue itself.

8.3.2.3 Investor Risk

In the case of a mortgage pass-through bond, the investor owns a pro rata share of a pool of mortgages. If any or all of these mortgages default, each investor is affected and suffers diminished cash flow. Without external over-collateralization, the investors in these securities are affected by any occurrence of mortgage default.

The tranched MBS structure created an economically efficient method to manage investors' risk from mortgage defaults. Most tranched MBS issues are structured with tiers of securities that have prioritized claims on mortgage pool cash flow. Senior classes of securities are overcollateralized because they have a first claim on all of the cash flow generated by the issue's collateral pool. The subordination of the junior tranches provides additional security to the senior classes as the risk of default in the underlying mortgages is allocated first to the junior classes. This practice is known as internal overcollateralization because it is generated through the structure of the issue.

Internal overcollateralization protects the senior investor from the risk that a limited amount of defaults occur in the collateral pool. If the level of default rises and affects an amount of cash flow in excess of that which would have been applied to the subordinate tranches, the senior securities will be negatively affected, which is what occurred during the financial crisis when the levels of default exceeded the level of protection afforded by the junior classes.

8.3.3 Risk of Prepayment
8.3.3.1 Impact of Prepayment
Mortgages are often prepaid when circumstances cause a property owner to sell or refinance an asset. In this case, the mortgage principal reverts to the benefit of the investor, which can be either a positive or negative event depending on the terms of the mortgage and the mortgage interest rate versus the market rate. If the mortgage has a below-market interest rate, the owner of the mortgage benefits by being able to reinvest the returned principal at current higher rates. If the mortgage is paying interest at an above-market rate, the mortgage owner is worse off with an early repayment, as it can reinvest only at lower current rates. Many commercial mortgages and a limited number of residential mortgages call for prepayment penalties that compensate the lender for the risk of reinvestment.

Prepayment can also occur because a mortgage defaults and the underlying property is foreclosed and liquidated, which is known as unnatural prepayment.

8.3.3.2 Issuer
In most cases, prepayment risk is passed through to the mortgage security holder. If the issuer is responsible for maintaining a collateral pool to back a bond issue, then the prepayment risk falls on the issuer. In this case, the issuer will use the proceeds from principal repayments to acquire additional collateral to support the pool.

8.3.3.3 Investor
In mortgage securities for which the investor accepts the prepayment risk, an early repayment of a mortgage generates cash flow that is directed towards the bond owners, reducing their invested principal.

In pass-through securities, this principal is allocated pro rata across all investors. In tranched commercial mortgage securities, the prepayment can be broadly distributed or allocated to specific classes of bonds that are structured to accept early prepayments. In some cases, prepayments are allocated differently depending on whether they are natural or unnatural.

Many RMBS have been structured to have principal-only (PO) securities that are repaid from principal repayments.

8.3.4 Collateral Pool Risk Allocation in Structuring an MBS Issue

An issuer initiates an MBS transaction either to finance a mortgage portfolio or to sell it. In either case, the issue should be structured in a way that minimizes the cost of capital and maximizes the value of the collateral pool. To minimize the cost of capital, the issuer seeks to create a structure that closely meets the needs of the investor.

There are two major forms of risk presented by mortgage collateral: the risk of default and the risk of prepayment. The issuer can agree to accept these risks and shield the investor from this variability. If the issuer retains these risks, for accounting purposes, the issuance is treated as a financing transaction and both the collateral and the securities are reported on the bank's balance sheet. If the issuer passes these risks through to the investor, for accounting purposes, the issuer has achieved a sale of the collateral and neither the collateral nor the securities are shown on the bank's balance sheet.

8.3.4.1 Open System

If the collateral pool functions as an open system, the entity's sponsor must replace mortgages that have performance issues with new collateral. In this way, credit support for the bonds is created and maintained by the issuer's continuing obligation to maintain the pool.

In an open system, the sponsor has "financed" the pool through the issuance of securities and retains a continuing obligation to support the pool. The sponsor retains the performance risk of the collateral and has not sold the mortgages.

If the issuer is maintaining the pool, then the investor is looking to the credit of the issuer to back the investment. In issues of this type, because the credit support is external, the structure of the securities can be separated from the characteristics of the collateral. Simple term notes can be issued.

8.3.4.2 Closed System

If the collateral pool functions as a closed system, the sponsor aggregates the collateral pool at the formation of the SPE and sells the mortgage pool "as is" to the issuing entity, without any continuing obligation. The mortgages allocated to the pool are the same throughout the life of the securities, and the cash flow provided by this particular group of assets is all that is available to the investors. The sponsor's lack of continuing obligation to the SPE allows it to record the transaction as a sale to the new entity.

In the simplest structure, the pass-through security, each investor holds a pro rata interest in the cash flow generated from the collateral pool. When the mortgage pays, the investor receives a set fraction of that payment (less the operating costs of the trust). In this structure, each investor also shares in the collateral default risk.

Within the closed system, there are many ways to differentiate the rights of security holders to benefit from the cash flow generated by the collateral. In a tranched issue, the bonds are organized into a hierarchy by seniority, with the most senior bonds having first claim on the cash flow generated by the pool. In a typed issue, cash flow generated from mortgage interest and principal may be allocated independently to different classes of bondholders. These techniques can be combined into structures in which the cash flow is aggregated by type and then paid through to security holder by level of seniority.

The goal of these more complex structures is to create tiers of securities that are perceived as having less risk and can earn investment-grade credit ratings reducing their interest cost. The presence of these highly rated securities is expected to lower the aggregate interest cost of the CMBS and generate profits for the issuer.

In summary, in open systems the issuer uses MBS to finance its ownership of a portfolio of mortgages; it does not sell the mortgages. The issuer in an open system agrees to provide credit support by replacing mortgages if necessary to maintain the credit metrics of the collateral pool. In closed systems, the risk of ownership of the collateral is transferred to the MBS investors. The risk in these securities may be allocated among classes of investors, but the issuer does not provide credit support.

8.3.5 Common Types of MBS
MBS are classified by the type of collateral that supports the securities issued. The two broad categories of mortgages are commercial mortgages (mortgages made against property used for business) and residential mortgages (mortgages secured by single family homes or multifamily properties). Residential mortgages typically benefit from some form of mortgage insurance provided by government-sponsored housing agencies or private mortgage insurance companies.

8.4 CMBS

CMBS are debt instruments whose interest and principal payments derive from the cash flow on a designated pool of commercial mortgages.

8.4.1 Collateral is a Portfolio of Commercial Mortgages
The issuer of CMBS purchases or originates a portfolio of commercial mortgages that will serve as security or collateral for the payment of the interest and

(B)

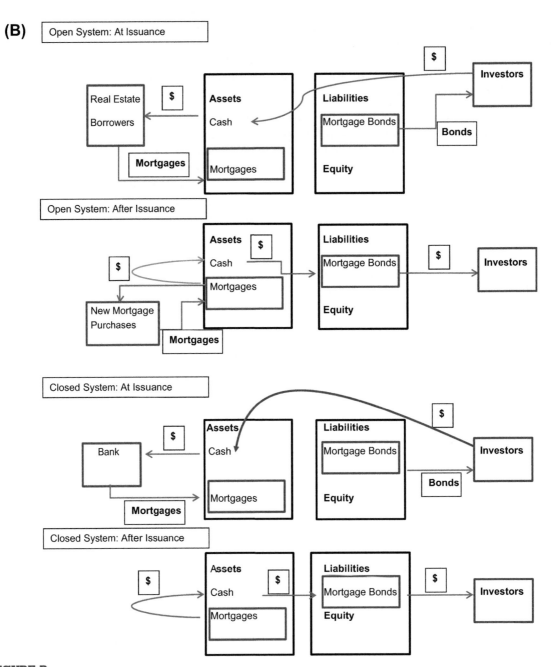

FIGURE B

In case B, the bank has sold the mortgages to a conduit. The conduit has raised the funds to purchase the mortgages by issuing MBS to investors. The investors retain the risk of default and prepayment. This risk may be allocated across different classes of securities.

principal on the debt securities that the issuer sells to investors. The goal of the issuer is to sell its newly issued CMBS at a cost price in excess of the amount that it has paid to acquire the underlying mortgage collateral.

8.4.1.1 Commercial Mortgage Pools

A pool of commercial mortgages will have fewer, larger investments than pools of residential mortgages, and these mortgages will generally have a maximum life of ten years or less. Commercial pools are typically diversified with mortgages on many different types of properties. In some cases, a mortgage pool can consist of a single large asset, which is called a single asset securitization.

The criteria used to underwrite mortgages for the collateral pool is a major determinant of the ultimate credit of the CMBS securities. The properties underlying the mortgages chosen for inclusion, the LTV of the mortgages, the cash flow coverage, and the terms of the mortgages are critical factors in the evaluation of the strength of the collateral. In general, fixed rate commercial mortgages have provisions limiting prepayment. This facilitates modeling expected receipt of principal when structuring CMBS. The more significant risk in CMBS comes from the possibility of borrower default.

8.4.2 Securities Are Notes Paid from Portfolio Cash Flow

Each month, interest and principal payments received from the mortgages are pooled and utilized to pay the current interest and principal requirements of the securities that have been issued.

8.4.2.1 Tranches

The CMBS issuer fashions classes of securities known as tranches. Each tranche participates in the cash flows derived from the underlying mortgages based on a stated formula that defines its rights.

8.4.2.2 Classes of Securities

The participation rights of each CMBS tranche can be based on many factors. The cash flow generated by the mortgages in the collateral pool can be split by time, credit, or source (interest or principal). The particular manner in which the issue allocates its cash flow is to its tranches is known as a waterfall. The most typical structure is a hierarchy in which the most senior classes receive a priority claim on any available cash flow. To assure the investors in the senior classes that they will be repaid, the amount of senior securities issued is limited in proportion to the size of the overall collateral pool. In this way, the senior classes benefit from internal over-collateralization, which occurs when the collateral exceeds the value of the securities that it secures.

8.4.2.2.1 Prioritized Claim on Pool Principal and Interest

Junior classes have a lower priority level and receive cash flow only if it is available after the more senior tranches have been serviced. Investors in these classes take an additional level of risk by subordinating their debt service requirements to those of the senior classes. In return for accepting this risk, the junior investors receive a higher interest rate and are also often given the right to advise the special servicer on the disposition of defaulted mortgages. The tranche with this right is known as the controlling class.

8.4.2.2.2 Seniority can Determine Bond Amortization

In many cases, senior tranches are structured so that they receive a first claim on any cash flow received on the collateral pool. In addition, any principal received from repayment of the mortgages is first applied to repay the outstanding principal balance on the most senior securities. This structure is known as sequential pay. As a result, the senior classes will be retired first and have a shorter duration than the junior classes.

8.4.2.2.3 Junior Classes: Higher Variability/Higher Yield

Junior classes of CMBS securities are repaid once the senior classes have been repaid. Interest payments on the junior classes are also subject to the prior claims of the more senior classes. Losses due to mortgage defaults are first applied to the most junior securities, reducing their outstanding principal balance. Junior classes therefore absorb most of the risk in the typical CMBS structure. As a result of their higher risk, these subordinated classes are structured to receive a higher level of interest.

8.4.2.2.4 Application of Paydown to High-Rated Classes Leads to Yield Creep

In the typical senior subordinate CMBS structure, the first principal repayments received on the mortgage collateral are applied to the repayment of the most senior outstanding debt. As the senior debt (issued at the lowest interest rates) is reduced, the average yield on the remaining outstanding tranches rises. Thus the average cost of capital on the CMBS financing rises over time as an issue matures.

8.4.2.2.5 The Residual Interest Is the Highest-Risk Security

Portfolio risk will have the least impact on senior securities because they have the most collateral supporting their cash flow requirements. In contrast, the impacts of any collateral defaults are first felt by the most junior classes. The most junior class of all is the residual interest. If the issuer of the CMBS were a "real" company, this would be the company's equity. The residual interest has the greatest potential reward from the successful, timely repayment of the mortgages and the greatest risk from any disruption to that orderly payout.

8.4.2.2.6 Structure Cannot Obviate Weak Underwriting Criteria

At the height of the CMBS market, underwriters were making mortgage loans at over 90 percent LTV, with debt service at just over 1 times coverage. These mortgages were placed in collateral pools that backed CMBS in which 70 percent or more of the securities received AAA credit ratings. Looking through the structure to the collateral, a casual observer would say it was as if 70 percent LTV loans were being assigned AAA ratings. This would be a misconception.

The chance that property with a 90 percent LTV loan, generating just enough cash to cover its debt service, will run into financial problems is much greater than that of a more conservatively underwritten loan. If the property has financial problems, an owner with 10 percent equity investment is also less likely to be willing to support an asset than an owner with an investment equal to 30 percent of the property value. For these reasons, the chance of a 90 percent LTV loan failing is greater than a 70 percent LTV loan.

Even if they have the same percentage of overcollateralization, the most senior interest in a pool of highly levered mortgages is not the same as the most senior interest in a pool of more conservatively underwritten mortgages. As recent history has shown, the structure of a CMBS issue cannot replace poor loan underwriting.

8.4.2.3 Role of Rating Agency

Information regarding the loans in the collateral pool, as well as the proposed structure of the CMBS issue, is submitted to the rating agencies that determine the appropriate credit rating for each tranche of the offering. The issuer's goal is to lower its cost of capital by having the largest proportion of the offering qualify for an investment grade rating. Securities that receive less than investment grade ratings are known as B pieces or B notes. There is a limited universe of buyers for these higher-risk securities, and they demand significantly higher yields to compensate for the extraordinary risk.

8.4.2.4 Example CMBS Transaction

> JPMorgan Chase Commercial Mortgage Securities Corp., 2011-C5
> Issue Date: September 16, 2011
> Amount: $1,029,699,910
> Registration Statement: 333-165147

This issue is typical of the post-crisis CMBS offerings. The mortgages in the collateral pool have been originated with more conservative underwriting standards and the senior tranches are supported by significant levels of overcollateralization. This was a notable offering because the senior classes were offered publicly, (rather than through private placements) and because of two interesting large loans in the collateral pool.

Participants:
Underwriters: J.P. Morgan Securities LLC, Goldman, Sachs & Co, Wells Fargo Securities, LLC
Issuing Entity: JPMorgan Chase Commercial Mortgage Securities Corp., 2011-C5
Depositor: J.P. Morgan Chase Commercial Mortgage Securities Corp. (the "Registrant")
Master Servicer: Midland Loan Services, a Division of PNC Bank, National Association
Sub Servicer: KeyCorp Real Estate Capital Markets, Inc.
Special Servicer: Torchlight Loan Services, LLC
Trustee/paying agent: Wells Fargo Bank, National Association
Senior trust advisor: Pentalpha Surveillance LLC

The Depositor aggregates the mortgages from the originators and the securities from the issuer. Upon the offering, the mortgages are placed with the Trustee and the certificates are given to the underwriters for their investors. The offering proceeds flow back to the originators. During the life of the issue, the master servicer, or its subservicer, is responsible for interacting with the borrowers. If the borrower defaults, the special servicer is brought in to work with the defaulted borrower. The Trustee acts for the CMBS holders and in the case of significant financial decisions may be advised by the senior trust advisor on behalf of the investors in the more junior classes.

Collateral:
Originators: JP Morgan Chase Bank, NA and/or Key Bank NA
44 loans on 209 properties
Range of remaining terms: 60 to 120 months
10 largest loans: 61.8% of pool
Underwritten loan-to-value ratio: 59.5 percent
Debt-service coverage is 1.73x
Average interest rate is 5.4%.

Loan concentration:
Hotel 20.3%
Retail 50.5%
Office 16.7%
Mixed use 8.5%
Multifamily 2.1%
Properties are located in 7 states:
Concentration greater than 10%: Illinois 23.4%, North Carolina 11.9%

Largest loans:
Type: Hotel
InterContinental Hotel Chicago (792-rooms)

Balance: $145 million (approx. 50% LTV)
Term: 10 years
Interest rate: 5.61%
Amortization: Interest-only period: 2 years, then 30 years
Type: Retail (bank branches)
Inland American Real Estate Trust
121 SunTrust-100 percent occupied bank branches
Balance $100 million (approx. 50 percent LTV)
Term: Ten years, can be extended for an additional ten years.
Interest Rate: 5.42 percent
Amortization: Interest only for first ten years, then

Tranches:

Class	Investor	Amount	Type	Rating	Rate	Sub Percent	Rate	Life	Principal Return
A-1	Public	$ 49.8	Sr. SP	AAA	Fixed	30.0 percent	1.6001 percent	2.55	10/11– 05/16
A-2	Public	199.7	Sr. SP	AAA	Fixed	30.0	3.1491	4.83	06/16– 10/16
A-3	Public	405.9	Sr. SP	AAA	Fixed	30.0	4.1712	9.79	04/21– 08/21
A-SB	Public	65.4	Sr.	AAA	Fixed	30.0	3.6775	7.17	5/16– 04/21
X-A	Public	807.0	Sr. xs IO		Variable	NA	1.4721	NA	NA
X-B	Private	222.6	Sr. xs IO		Variable	NA	0.3873	NA	NA
A-S	Private	86.2	Sub to A	AAA	WAC	21.625	5.3139	9.89	08/21– 09/21
B	Private	51.5	Sub. SP		WAC	16.625	5.3139	9.96	09/21– 09/21
C	Private	39.9	Sub. SP		WAC	12.750	5.3139	9.96	09/21– 09/21
D	Private	65.6	Sub. SP		WAC	6.375	5.3139	9.96	09/21– 09/21
E	Private	12.9	Sub. SP		Fixed	5.125	4.0000	9.96	09/21– 09/21
F	Private	9.0	Sub. SP		Fixed	4.250	4.0000	9.96	09/21– 09/21
G	Private	16.7	Sub. SP		Fixed	2.625	4.0000	9.96	09/21– 09/21
NR	Private	27.0	Sr. Residual		Fixed	0.000	4.0000	9.96	09/21-– 09/21
R	Private		Residual						
Z	Issuer								

Structure:

This CMBS uses a senior subordinated structure to provide overcollateralization to the senior securities.

The A classes are the senior tranches. These classes have a senior claim on cash flow. Class A 1, 2, and 3 are sequential pay. Class A-SB is amortized at specified intervals. These tranches carry fixed interest rates.

The A-S class is subordinate to the balance of the A tranches and is the last of the A tranches to be repaid. This tranche pays through the average interest earned on the mortgage pool.

X tranches are interest only and are known as the excess interest tranches. They do not receive any payout of principal. They pay their holders the difference between the interest rate earned on collateral and the weighted average interest cost of either the A or B tranches. For the X-A and X-B classes, the notional amount is equal to the sum total of the principal outstanding of either the A or B tranches, respectively.

The X tranches are paid as senior securities along with the A tranches and ahead of the A-S class.

The B tranches (B through G classes) are subordinated to the A tranches. Within the B tranches, the securities pay sequentially in alphabetical order. These classes are attributed losses in inverse alphabetical order. In the event of a collateral loss, the principal amount of the most junior remaining class is diminished first.

The tranches shown as WAC pay out the weighted average interest earned on the mortgage pool times their notional amount.

The R class is the Residual Certificate and receives whatever is left at the end of the Trust after all other classes have been paid. It has no set entitlement to either principal or interest.

The Z class pays out the excess interest on certain loans which by their terms, may be extended past their initial due dates at increased interest rates.

Rating agencies

Moody's, Fitch, Morningstar

8.4.3 CMBS Issuance Process
8.4.3.1 Role of Mortgage Underwriter
The mortgage underwriter works with the property owner, or potential owner, to provide financing that can be used to acquire or refinance

a property. The underwriter is responsible for assessing the financial strength of a property, its physical condition, and it competitive market position. Based on this analysis, the underwriter will determine how much mortgage debt the property can support based on current standards in the credit market. The underwriter will then work with the borrower to document and fund the mortgage.

Unlike residential mortgages, many of which carry insurance, most commercial mortgages do not have independent credit support. Therefore, the key determinant of CMBS credit is the quality of the mortgage underwriting. Analysts assessing the strength of a mortgage portfolio will look at property quality and loan underwriting criteria.

8.4.3.2 Role of Issuer

The issuer acquires mortgages from a group of underwriters and aggregates these into a collateral pool. This collateral pool will serve as security for an issue of CMBS. The goal of the issuer is to create a diverse pool of real estate investments. This diversification is intended to protect the investor from a decline in any segment of the real estate market.

The lender that originated the mortgages may also be the issuer of the MBS securities. In this case, the lender is focused on creating a SPE that will be viewed as independent for tax and accounting purposes. In this way, the SPE can purchase the mortgages from the lender, which can record a sale to the new entity and remove the assets from its balance sheet.

8.4.3.3 Securitization Process
8.4.3.3.1 Creation of SPE

The first step in securitization is to create the SPE that will issue the mortgage-backed securities. The legal form of this SPE is typically a REMIC. The REMIC generally takes the form of a trust and a trustee is appointed to act as the legal representative of the issuer, to hold its documents, and to act on behalf of the security holders if a foreclosure or other major legal action is required.

The sole purpose of the REMIC is to hold the mortgages, its only assets apart from an interim cash position. The liabilities of the entity are the bonds that it issues to investors. The equity interest in the entity is limited and consists of any remaining cash after the MBS are repaid.

8.4.3.3.2 Post-Issuance Administration

At issuance, a master servicer is appointed to administer the mortgage pool, which includes interfacing with the borrowers, receiving and reviewing mortgage compliance documents, aggregating cash flow, and paying the bondholders. The master servicer may work through one or more primary servicers.

In the event of a borrower default, a special servicer is appointed to work out or foreclose on the loan.

8.4.3.3.3 Role of Rating Agency

The role of the rating agency is to provide an objective analysis of the credit quality of the securities issued by the SPE. In order to provide a rating, the agency must understand both the nature of the collateral and the structure of the securities issued—both of these factors can have dramatic impacts on the value of the securities.

The assessment of the collateral is based upon a review of the loan underwriting criteria and their application to each commercial mortgage or pool of residential mortgage. The primary purpose of the analysis is to determine the ability of the properties to generate the cash flows required to service their mortgages, which is not an analysis to determine the growth prospects of the properties but the stability of the cash flow streams under adverse economic circumstances.

Once the collateral is assessed, the rating agency looks at how the cash flows will be applied to service each tranche of debt. A determination is then made as to the level of probability that each tranche of debt will default. The lower the default risk, the higher the rating that will be assigned to the bonds.

8.4.4 Impacts on Borrower
8.4.4.1 Lowest-Cost Execution

Creating a tradable security with a liquid market has increased the flow of capital into the MBS market and lowered the cost of financing for property owners. In return for the lower cost of capital, borrowers must agree to underwriting standards and loan provisions that are in conformity with market norms. This agreement allows the issuers of MBS, known as conduits, to aggregate mortgages with terms that are easily understood by market participants. Using common underwriting criteria further allows the mortgage originators to ensure the likelihood that a mortgage will be able to be sold into a conduit.

8.4.4.2 Least Flexible Type of Loan

In return for efficiency of execution, lenders and borrowers must keep the transaction terms and documents within accepted market norms. Once the loan is underwritten and funded, the borrower will have no ongoing relationship with the originating lender. Instead, the borrower will interact with the loan servicer, an administrative functionary with little ability to modify the terms or conditions of the loan agreement.

These constraints, artifacts of the securitization process, limit the ability of the property owners to make physical or other major changes to the asset after underwriting. For this reason, loans destined for MBS are usually made against mature, well-leased assets for which it is unlikely that the borrower will need to modify the loan before maturity.

8.4.4.3 Strategic Utilization by Borrower

Borrowers seeking mortgage financing can approach many different types of capital sources. Lenders who utilize their own capital to make loans with the expectation of holding those loans until maturity are known as balance sheet lenders.

Historically, insurance companies and pension funds have used their assets, or their balance sheets, to provide mortgage capital to the real estate market. The long term fixed rate nature of commercial mortgages matches the long term fixed nature of insurance company and pension liabilities.

As direct investors in whole loans, these financial institutions can respond to borrowers' needs over the life cycle of a property. For example, if a property needs to be renovated or has an expansion opportunity, the financial institution can respond by altering the terms and conditions of the mortgage to provide additional capital. The presence of a relationship lender who is familiar with the property and the borrower can be very valuable to the owner of an asset in transition. In recent times, borrowers have been willing to pay a premium for the inherent flexibility in this type of lending relationship.

In contrast, the most economic execution of a mortgage financing has typically been through the CMBS market. Because this is an indirect market, there is no continuing relationship between the originating lender and the borrower. The lender, as agent for the future investors, must codify the borrowing relationship into a document that can be executed and interpreted with the exercise of little ongoing judgment. In CMBS, the servicer, who is designated to act on behalf of the investors, is only empowered to enforce the agreement, not to modify it. Only in the event of a default and the appointment of a special servicer can a party negotiate with a borrower on behalf of the investors—and even then, with very limited discretion. In RMBS, the servicer can work with the borrower to try to restructure the mortgage in order to avoid bankruptcy and foreclosure.

For this reason, CMBS financing is best used for mature properties with little likelihood for required lender interaction during the course of the loan. Until recently, however, the depth of liquidity in this market made it the most advantageous source of funds for borrowers with properties generating stable cash flows.

Following the financial crisis, the CMBS market remains limited for new issues. To some extent, traditional balance sheet lenders have begun to provide mortgage capital. Commercial banks, which previously exited the balance sheet lending business, have reentered and added a limited amount of liquidity in the form of balance sheet loans. The lack of liquidity has caused significant dislocation in the real estate market.

8.4.5 CMBS Market Statistics
8.4.5.1 Investors
The variety of bond structures available within the MBS market allows investors to identify securities which closely match their investment needs. Short-term securities are attractive to banks and other financial institutions with short-term liabilities such as deposits. Pension fund and other long-term investors will look for long-term tranches of mortgage securities. Fiduciaries with quality-oriented investment guidelines will seek highly rated tranches with limited default risk. Yield-oriented investors may be more willing to accept variability in repayment speed and higher default risk in return for increased yield.

8.4.5.2 Market Size (1)
The domestic U.S. issuance of CMBS securities rose dramatically over the early years of the millennium. Annual issuance of CMBS reached a peak in 2007 of approximately $230 billion. At that time—the top of the U.S. real estate market bubble—the total amount of CMBS paper in the market place exceeded $2.3 trillion.

Following the failure of Bear Stearns and Lehman Brothers—two major investment banks active in the CMBS market—issuance fell dramatically to $12 billion in 2008 and approximately $3 billion in 2009. The market revived in 2010 to approximately $14 billion and is expected to increase substantially in 2011, reaching an estimated $40 billion.[3]

8.4.5.3 Trends
Ready availability of mortgage capital is also believed to have contributed to the rise in commercial property prices that also peaked in 2008. The tremendous fall in property prices and the concurrent precipitous drop in CMBS values contributed to the financial crisis. These factors combined to substantially close the CMBS market by late 2008. Many of the surviving investment banks shut down their CMBS banking groups laying off most, if not all, of their employees.

The closure of the CMBS market helped create a downward spiral in the commercial property market. The lack of credit in the bank real estate lending market and the closure of the CMBS market combined to reduce the prospects for refinancing maturing notes. This effect lead to widespread fear of fire sale liquidation of property as existing loans came to term. As a result, interest in property investment declined, as did property prices. The decline in asset values pressured the credit quality of existing mortgage debt and created a steep drop in CMBS values.

---

[3] CRE Finance Council, compendium updated October 11, 2011 (New York).

Governments became concerned that without a viable CMBS market, the banking system would suffer catastrophic losses as real estate borrowers would be unable to repay existing debts. This created the need for government intervention to restart the CMBS market. In spring 2009, the government launched the Term Asset-Backed Loan Facility (TALF) program to make loans to investors willing to purchase newly issued and certain existing CMBS that were underwritten according to very strict criteria.

The first issuances that were completed were underwritten at very conservative LTV ratios based on property valuations that were also calculated on a very conservative basis. The success of these early offerings led to the rebirth of the marketplace, in 2010. Securities issued under the new underwriting guidelines are known as CMBS 2.0.

A number of investment banks have restarted their CMBS groups and the market for underwriting loans has again become competitive. Many observers believe that the CMBS market will return as a significant source of liquidity for the U.S. real estate capital markets.

8.5 RMBS

8.5.1 Residential Mortgage Pools

Residential mortgages tend to be written for smaller amounts, as the value of the average house is much lower than the average commercial property. Many residential mortgages have fixed interest rates with terms of either 15 or 30 years. A smaller but growing portion of mortgages have adjustable interest rates that move on a periodic basis to reflect a fixed spread over a market interest rate index such as LIBOR. Per dollar of aggregate pool size, a residential mortgage pool will include a greater number of smaller investments with longer average terms when compared to a commercial mortgage pool.

8.5.1.1 Collateral

RMBS collateral pools consists of mortgages secured by residential properties. The typical pool consists of many small loans secured by one to four family houses and condominiums. These loans may be fixed-rate long-term mortgages (FRM) or adjustable rate mortgages (ARM) that have interest rates that change over time.

The majority of residential loans are underwritten using standards established by the FHA and are known as conforming loans. These standards include limits on loan amount based on geography, income coverage and down payment criteria. If a loan meets these standards, it qualifies for FHA mortgage insurance. Mortgages backed by FHA insurance and mortgage broked security under-written by one of the GSEs are known as agency paper. Mortgages without government backing are known as non-agency paper.

Loans that do not conform are known as nonconforming loans. Loans that are above the FHA principal amount limit are known as jumbo loans. Loans that have low down payments are known as high LTV loans. Loans to nonqualifying buyers with good credit are known as Alt-A loans. Loans that do not qualify because the borrower's credit is poor are known as subprime loans.

Loans that have been outstanding for at least one year and paying on time are known as seasoned loans. Seasoned loans provide the investor with some proof that a borrower can carry the monthly payments on the new mortgage.

8.5.1.2 Prepayments

Residential loans are generally structured as fully amortizing 15- to 30-year mortgages. Each scheduled loan payment includes both principal and interest. Unlike commercial loans, residential mortgages are typically prepayable without penalty. Partial or full prepayments initiated by the borrower are known as voluntary prepayments.

Historically, the average borrower remains in their house for seven years before moving and repaying their mortgage. The actual rate at which a portfolio of mortgages prepays is known as its prepayment speed. The prepayment speed of a mortgage pool is affected by the difference between current rates and the mortgage rate at origination.

If rates fall, borrowers will refinance: this is known as call risk. If rates rise, borrowers will not refinance and may also stay in their houses longer, which is called extension risk. Over time, interest rates also have an impact on the demand for housing. All else being equal, low rates increase prices and high rates decrease prices. The changes in the housing market also affect the ability of owners to sell their houses, which affects prepayment speed.

Prepayment can also occur when borrowers default and the servicer successfully pursues the foreclosure of the property, resulting in the pool's receipt of an early repayment (perhaps at a liquidation value below the amount of the remaining loan principal), which is known as involuntary prepayment.

There are two common measures for prepayment speed: the Constant Prepayment Rate (CPR) and the Public Securities Association (PSA) both compare the performance of a given collateral pool to a standard model and report speed as a multiple of the model portfolio (e.g., 200 percent PSA of 25 percent CPR).

8.5.1.3 Default Risk

Residential borrowers who are unable or unwilling to continue to pay their mortgages may default on their loans. In normal economic environments, defaults are more common in the early months of a mortgage and fall as a loan becomes seasoned and the borrower builds equity. Defaults are more prevalent in ARMs, as the change in rate can increase payments to a level where the borrower can no longer service the loan.

As an analog to the prepayment speed model, the Bond Market Association (formerly known as the Public Securities Association) has developed the standard default assumption (SDA), which serves as a baseline measure of expected portfolio default. The metric for a given portfolio is expressed as a multiple of SDA (e.g., 250 percent SDA).

8.5.2 RMBS Structures
8.5.2.1 Participation Certificates
The simplest type of RMBS structure is the mortgage participation certificate (PC). Under this structure, the certificate holder owns a fractional interest in the cash flows from a portfolio of mortgages. The mortgage remains the property of the issuer/servicer.

8.5.2.2 Mortgage Pass-Through Securities
Similar to the participation certificate is the mortgage pass-through security (MPT). The security owner owns a pro rata share of the cash flow generated by the mortgage pool. In the pass-through structure, the mortgage portfolio is defined at issuance and is sold to an SPE that serves as the issuer. The sale to an SPE qualifies as a sale transaction for the mortgage underwriter.

Ginnie Mae securities are simple pass-through MBS backed by government-guaranteed mortgages. They have long been a staple of both individual and institutional investment portfolios. Ginnie Mae securities are issued by savings banks, commercial banks and mortgage bankers who have aggregated pools of FHA insured mortgages, and—By virtue of the FHA's mortgage guarantee Ginnae Mae securities have the full faith and credit of the U.S. government.

RMBS can also be structured to individually allocate principal and interest streams to different investors. These bonds are called interest-only (IO) and principal-only (PO) bonds. When prepayment speeds increase, PO bonds increase in value as the expected amortization period decreases. The absolute value of the principal returned does not change, but the present value of the stream increases as the average time the principal remains outstanding decreases. The inverse is true of IO bonds. If the mortgage prepayment speed increases, both the aggregate amount and the present value of the interest paid decreases.

	Increasing Interest Rate	Decreasing Interest Rate
Prepayment speed	Slower	Faster
PO value	Lower	Higher
IO value	Higher	Lower

8.5.2.3 Mortgage-Backed Bonds

Mortgage-backed bonds (MBBs) are used to finance a portfolio of mortgages that are owned by the issuer. Bondholders are paid according to the terms of the issue from mortgage cash flow. The mortgage portfolio is structured to generate cash flow in excess of that required to service and repay the securities. The pool is defined at issuance but is subject to change over time if necessary to meet pool criteria as defined in the bond indenture. Although the bondholders have a security interest in the mortgage portfolio, they look to the issuer to pay the interest and principal on the bond. Unlike pass-through securities, these bonds are structured as IO with semiannual payments and full principal due at maturity.

8.5.2.4 Collateralized Mortgage Obligations

Collateralized mortgage obligations (CMOs) are used to finance portfolios of MBS owned by the issuer. The CMO is structured to redirect the incoming cash flow from the MBS to service securities that are structured with maturities that minimize the issuers cost of capital. As with the MBB, the bondholders have a security interest in the mortgage portfolio but look to the issuer to pay the interest and principal on the bond.

MBS Structures

	PC	MPT	MBB	CMO	Sr./Sub
Type	Closed	Closed	Open	Closed	Closed
Cash flow allocation	Pro rata	Pro rata	Indirect	Pro rata	Credit tier hierarchy
Collateral	Mortgages	Mortgages	Mortgages	MBS	Mortgages
Structure	Pass through	Pass through	Bond	Pass through	Pass through
Issuer	Lender	SPE	Lender	Lender	SPE
Lender treatment	Financing	Sale	Financing	Financing	Sale

8.5.3 Collateral Pool Credit Support

Many RMBS either are backed by pools of government-insured mortgages or the MBS issue itself is backed by monocline insurance. In these cases, the variability in issue performance is expected to be primarily a function of the collateral pool prepayment speed rather than the default risk of the collateral. In cases in which the collateral is not government insured, the prepayment risk and the default risk are both significant determinants of issue performance.

In addition to insurance-based external credit support, a number of RMBS structures have been developed that use variants of the senior subordinate credit tiering structure that is prominent in CMBS to generate internal credit support. These structures have helped RMBS issuers achieve sale treatment for their portfolios of nonconforming mortgages.

8.5.3.1 Mortgage Insurance

Mortgage insurance provided by the FHA is the most effective form of credit support, as it carries the full faith and credit of the U.S. government. The GSEs also guarantee MBS collateral, but these guarantees are not full faith and credit obligations of the U.S. government. Private insurers provide private mortgage insurance that guarantees mortgage collateral, but these guarantees are less valuable than those of either the FHA or the GSEs.

8.5.3.2 Monocline-Wrapped Mortgage Securities

In monocline-wrapped mortgage securities, the issuer purchases a credit guarantee on the securities issued from a private insurance company. The financial strength of the insurer is recognized by the rating agencies that grant the issued securities a high credit rating. This rating lowers the issuer's interest rate. The lower cost of financing in turn results in a spread between the cash flow on the mortgage pool and the required debt service on the MBS. This excess cash flow is first applied to reduce the principal of the bonds outstanding and thus improves the level overcollateralization. After an agreed-upon level of overcollateralization is achieved, assuming that the collateral pool is performing well, the excess cash flow provides a profit stream to the issuer.

The monocline-wrapped structure thus combines external (insurance) and internal (overcollateralization via bond principal reduction) forms of credit support.

8.5.3.3 Senior/Subordinate Structure

In the senior subordinate structure, two classes of securities are issued. Each has a different level of priority against the cash flows from the mortgage collateral pool. Depending on the nuances of the structure, the senior class is generally paid before the subordinate classes. In this manner, the subordinate classes provide a form of internal overcollateralization to the senior classes.

8.5.3.3.1 Shifting Interest Structure

The shifting interest structure enhances the credit support for senior classes of RMBS by disproportionately allocating unscheduled principal payments to the senior bond tranches. This structure also features disproportionate allocation of default losses to reduce the principal balances of subordinate classes. Collectively, these actions provide additional credit support to the senior securities.

8.5.3.3.2 Overcollateralization

In the overcollateralization structure, the senior MBS are supported by both the presence of the subordinate classes as well as an additional amount of dedicated collateral (the overcollateralization percentage). Over time, the cash flow generated by the collateral pool in excess of that required to service the bonds is used to repay senior note classes. In this manner, the over-collateralization of the remaining senior classes is enhanced, which is another structure that combines external credit support (excess collateral at inception) with internal credit support (application of excess cash flow to repay senior securities).

8.5.3.4 Example of RMBS Securitization

CWL 2006-7
Issue Date: June 26, 2006
Amount: $1,017,378,100 (approx.)
Registration statement: 333-131591

This RMBS was issued by Countrywide Financial during the peak of the U.S. housing market in mid-2006. Through the credit enhancement structures described here, the issuer was able to issue a large percentage of the RMBS with an investment-grade rating even though the mortgage collateral was from a borrower base with poor credit histories and included junior liens.

Countrywide failed as a result of the financial crisis and was subsequently acquired by Bank of America. This issue and a number of similar Countrywide securitizations are the subject of ongoing litigation brought by the investors against Bank of America, as successor to Countrywide.

Participants:

Issuer: CWABS Asset-Backed Certificates Trust 2006—2007
Depositor: CWABS, Inc.
Sponsor and Seller: Countrywide Home Loans
Master Servicer: Countrywide Home Loans Servicing LP
Trustee: Bank of New York

Collateral:

All of the loans in the collateral pool are first and second mortgages on one- to four-family homes made to credit-blemished borrowers, which means that credit agencies have reported negative information regarding the borrower's credit history. The default rate on loans made to borrowers with negative credit information is expected to be higher than the level experienced on loans made to borrowers with high credit scores.

The collateral is divided into two groups depending on whether the mortgages are conforming or nonconforming:

Loan Group	Property Type	Lien	Interest Rate	Loan Amount
1	One- to four-family residential	First and second lien	Fixed and variable rate	Conforming balance
2	One- to four-family residential	First and second lien	Fixed and variable rate	Nonconforming balance

Prefunding:

Up to 25 percent of certificate sale proceeds can be used to acquire mortgages subsequent to the initial issue date.
Geographic concentrations in excess of 10 percent: California 31.30 percent; Florida 12.85 percent.

Swap:

In this RMBS, the securities issued are floating rate notes based on a LIBOR index. The issuer has arranged an interest rate swap transaction to convert the fixed rate payments received on the mortgages to floating rate payments based on LIBOR.

Credit enhancement:

There are three methods of credit enhancement used in this securitization: overcollateralization, excess interest, and subordination. These enhancements are expected to work in tandem to protect the security holders from defaults in the collateral pool.

Overcollateralization:

The principal of the mortgages and the prefunded amounts exceed the certificate amount by $15.7 million.

Excess interest:

The interest received from the mortgages is expected to exceed the interest due on the certificates.

Subordination:

The Class M securities are subordinate to the Class A securities and only receive principal and interest in the event that the Class A securities have been paid in accordance with their terms. Within the A classes, the 1-A securities have first priority on cash flow from loans in group 1 (conforming). The 2-A securities

Tranches:

Class	Original Balance	Investor Type	Security Type	Last Distribution	Moody's Rating	S&P Rating	Loan Group	Initial Rate
1-A	$313,365,000	Public	Senior/Adjustable Rate	Apr-46	Aaa	AAA	1	LIBOR + 0.130 percent
2-A-1	$246,320,000	Public	Senior/Adjustable Rate	Nov-27	Aaa	AAA	2	LIBOR + 0.030 percent
2-A-2	$56,242,000	Public	Senior/Adjustable Rate	Nov-29	Aaa	AAA	2	LIBOR + 0.090 percent
2-A-3	$137,245,000	Public	Senior/Adjustable Rate	Jan-35	Aaa	AAA	2	LIBOR + 0.150 percent
2-A-4	$85,682,000	Public	Senior/Adjustable Rate	Apr-46	Aaa	AAA	2	LIBOR + 0.250 percent
M-1	$38,628,000	Public	Subordinate/ Adjustable Rate	Apr-45	Aa1	AA+	1 and 2	LIBOR + 0.280 percent
M-2	$34,452,000	Public	Subordinate/ Adjustable Rate	Nov-44	Aa2	AA	1 and 2	LIBOR + 0.300 percent
M-3	$19,836,000	Public	Subordinate/ Adjustable Rate	Apr-44	Aa3	AA	1 and 2	LIBOR + 0.310 percent
M-4	$17,748,000	Public	Subordinate/ Adjustable Rate	Sep-43	A1	AA-	1 and 2	LIBOR + 0.360 percent
M-5	$17,748,000	Public	Subordinate/ Adjustable Rate	Dec-42	A2	A+	1 and 2	LIBOR + 0.380 percent
M-6	$15,138,000	Public	Subordinate/ Adjustable Rate	Sep-41	A3	A	1 and 2	LIBOR + 0.460 percent
M-7	$15,138,000	Public	Subordinate/ Adjustable Rate	Nov-39	Baa1	BBB+	1 and 2	LIBOR + 0.900 percent
M-8	$13,050,000	Public	Subordinate/ Adjustable Rate	Nov-36	Baa2	BBB	1 and 2	LIBOR + 1.100 percent
M-9	$6,786,000	Public	Subordinate/ Adjustable Rate	Aug-36	Baa3	BBB-	1 and 2	LIBOR + 1.900 percent
A-R	$100	Private	Senior/REMIC Residual	Jul-06	Aaa	AAA	1 and 2	N/A
B(1)	$10,962,000	Private	Subordinate/ Adjustable Rate	Jun-36	Ba1	BB+	1 and 2	LIBOR + 2.500 percent
P(2)	$100	Private	Prepayment Charges	N/A	N/R	N/R	1 and 2	N/A
C(3)	N/A	Private	Residual	N/A	N/R	N/R	1 and 2	N/A

(1) Transferred to Countrywide Home Loans, Inc. as consideration
(2) May support NIM (Net Interest Margin) securities that are insured by financial sureties.
(3) Has right to purchase defaulted mortgages for appraised value of home and foreclose.

have first priority from loans in group 2 (nonconforming). Within both the A and M classes, lower numbered tranches are paid first (e.g., 2-A-1 before 2-A-2 and M-1 before M-2). In addition to subordination, this sequential pay mechanism also extends the term of the higher-numbered tranches. Due to their lower seniority and longer term, these more junior securities receive higher interest rates than more senior tranches.

Losses on defaulted loans are allocated first to the most junior tranche in the structure until the principal amount of that tranche has been reduced to zero. As a result of its diminished principal balance after a loss has been allocated, this tranche will also be allocated less interest on an ongoing basis.

Rating agencies:

Moody's, S&P

8.5.4 RMBS Market Statistics
8.5.4.1 Market Size (2)
At the end of 2010, according to the Federal Reserve, the total value of the U.S. housing stock was $16.4 trillion. Residential mortgage debt, including single and multifamily loans outstanding, totaled $10.1 trillion.[4] The amount of mortgage debt peaked at about $12 trillion[5] during 2007 at the height of the U.S. housing market. At the time, approximately $7.4 trillion of residential debt was held by trusts for the benefit of MBS investors. Since that time, the amount of mortgages outstanding has fallen by approximately $800 billion (mid-2011)[6] due to repayment and significant foreclosures.

8.5.4.2 Trends
For the first 50 years of government participation in the mortgage market, underwriting criteria for home mortgages were very conservative. Government-guaranteed loans were not extended to home buyers who did not have down payments and could not meet objective criteria for income and credit history.

As the home market inflated postmillennium, closing out many buyers from home ownership, the government widened its credit criteria to allow underwriting of mortgages to buyers who could not qualify under traditional metrics.

This expanded extension of credit had two major impacts: it supported home price growth and it increased the risk level to the agencies guaranteeing loans.

---

[4] Federal Reserve Board's Flow of Funds Accounts, March 10, 2011, Table B.100 (line #49).
[5] Federal Reserve Board, http://www.federalreserve.gov/econresdata/releases/mortoutstand/current.htm, January 12, 2012.
[6] Federal Reserve Board release date, September 2011, mortgage debt outstanding.

Following the decline in the housing market, which fell 27 percent between June 2006 and March 2011,[7] many borrowers defaulted on their mortgages. As a result, the GSEs suffered tremendous losses and ultimately failed. To prevent the complete disintegration of the U.S. home loan market, the U.S. government was obligated to provide financial support to the GSEs.

To support the housing market, in early 2010 the Federal Reserve completed the purchase of over $1.25 trillion of government agency–guaranteed RMBS.

This de facto call on government credit assurance has brought into question the role of government sponsorship of home ownership via mortgage guarantees and the future of GSEs as fundamental forces in the U.S. home market. In addition, postcrash, there has been a general reversion among housing lenders, including the GSEs, to much more conservative underwriting criteria, which contributes to the continued depression of housing prices.

Glossary

Agency - collateral
ARM (adjustable rate mortgage)
Alt-A loan
Balance sheet lender
Call risk
CDO (collateralized debt obligation)
CMO (collateralized mortgage obligation)
Collateral pool
CMBS (commercial mortgage-backed security)
CPR (Constant Prepayment Rate)
Conduit
Conduit lender
Conforming mortgage
Controlling class
Credit enhancement
Default risk
Depositor
Extension risk
FHA (Federal Housing Administration)
Fannie Mae (Federal National Mortgage Association)
FRM (fixed rate mortgage)
Freddie Mac (Federal Home Loan Mortgage Corporation)
Ginnie Mae (Government National Mortgage Association)
GSE (government-sponsored entities)
IO (interest-only)
Involuntary prepayment

---

[7] The Freddie Mac House Price Index for the U.S./Freddie Mac investor presentation May 2011, page 20

Jumbo loans
Master servicer
Monocline insurance
MBB (mortgage-backed bond)
MPT (Mortgage pass-through security)
Mortgage pool
Non-agency collateral
Nonconforming loans
Overcollateralization
Participation
PC (Participation certificate)
Pass-through security
Prepayment risk
Prepayment speed
PO (principal-only)
PMI
PSA (Public Securities Association)
Rating agency
REMIC (real estate mortgage investment corporations)
REO (real estate owned)
Relationship lender
RMBS (residential mortgage-backed security)
Residual
Sale treatment
Sequential pay
Servicing
Shifting interest structure
Single-asset securitization
SIV (special investment vehicle)
SPE (special-purpose entity)
Special servicer
SPV (special purpose vehicle)
SDA (standard default assumption)
Subprime loans
Syndicated loan
TALF (Term Asset-Backed Loan Facility)
Tranches
Trustee
Underwriting criteria
Warehousing
Waterfall
Whole loan

Thought Questions

1. Which is more important to the value of an investment in MBS: (a) the structure of the securities or (b) the underwriting criteria used to originate the mortgage collateral? Why?

2. A commercial property owner has received financing offers for a property acquisition from both a conduit and a relationship lender. What factors must be considered in choosing the type of lender used?
3. In the years after the Great Depression, the U.S. government considered it good public policy to support homeownership. Do you believe that this is still an appropriate role of the government?

Review Questions

Tranche	Amount	Interest Rate	Expected Principal Repayment Period
A	$ 50 million	4 percent	2010 to 2016
A1	$ 20 million	5 percent	2016
B	$ 30 million	6 percent	2016
R	$100	NA	NA

Collateral Pool
There are ten loans, each with an original principal balance of $10 million. All loans are 6.4 percent seven-year commercial mortgages and were originated on January 1, 2010, with 20-year amortization schedules.

All questions refer to the schedule above.

1) Subordination
   What is the level of subordination of the A1 tranche?
2) Weighted average interest cost
   What is the weighted average interest cost of the securitization?
3) Amortization
   How much of the A tranche will be repaid during the first year of its life?
4) Default
   A single mortgage loan defaults at the end of year four. How much interest does the B trance earn in year five?
5) How much excess interest is generated by the securitization during the first year? Does this amount rise or fall during the expected seven-year life?

Multiple Choice Questions
1) Which of the following protect the owner of the senior tranche of a CMBS?
   I. Overcollateralization
   II. Prepayment speed
   III. Underwriting standards
   IV. Pool diversification
   a) I, II, III
   b) I, III, IV

    c) I, II

    d) II, III, IV

2) Which of the following was not a factor in the early development of the secondary mortgage market?

    a) VA and FHA guarantees

    b) Deregulation of interest rates

    c) Standardized underwriting

    d) Availability of title insurance

3) The primary risk to the purchaser of a MPT containing GNMA securities is:

    a) Early prepayment

    b) Default risk

    c) Over commitment of GNMA backstop funds

    d) Problems with subprime loans

4) Which of the following characteristics of the mortgages in a collateral pool stabilize cash flow?

    a) Limited geography

    b) Varied interest rates

    c) Seasoning

    d) Varied payment patterns

5) Which is not a method for estimating collateral pool prepayment?

    a) Average market

    b) Double declining balance

    c) CPR statistics

    d) PSA model

6) Which are true about MBS?

    I. When interest rates ↑ price drop is > than implied by △ rate.

    II. When interest rates ↑ price drop is < than implied by △ rate.

    III. When interest rate ↓ price rise is > than implied by △ rate.

    IV. When interest rate ↓ price rise is < than implied by △ rate.

        a) I, III

        b) I, IV

        c) II, III

        d) II, IV

7) Rising interest rates will have what effect on RMBS securities?

    a) Extend maturities of IO securities

    b) Shorten maturities of PO tranches

    c) Decrease value of IO tranches

    d) Increase value of PO tranches

8) Which tranche takes the greatest risk in CMBS?

    a) Residual

    b) Senior

    c) Subordinated

    d) PSA

9) Which is true about REMICs?
   a) Tax-free conduit
   b) Owner of residual must consolidate
   c) Can own credit card receivables
   d) Cannot be organized as a trust

10) Which is not a participant in the mortgage securitization process?
   a) Depositor
   b) Balance sheet lender
   c) Special Servicer
   d) Underwriter

11) Which is not a form of credit enhancement?
   a) Monocline insurance
   b) Sequential pay
   c) Loan syndication
   d) Overcollateralization

12) Which risk is associated with falling interest rates?
   a) Call risk
   b) Environmental risk
   c) Extension risk
   d) Default risk

13) Which type of lender is typically involved in the securitization process?
   a) Balance sheet lender
   b) Relationship lender
   c) Conduit lender
   d) Construction lender

14) Which of the following is not an entity involved in supporting the home mortgage market?
   a) Ginnie Mae
   b) Fannie Mae
   c) Freddie Mac
   d) Sallie Mae

15) Which of the following is not a type of MBS?
   a) Ginnie Mae security
   b) Balance sheet mortgage loan
   c) Mortgage pass-through bond
   d) Mortgage-backed bond

For answers to these Problems and Exercises, please visit the companion website: http://booksite.elsevier.com/9780123786265

Property Finance: Equity

9.1 CHARACTERISTICS

There are two aspects of equity that serve to define it as an investment vehicle. First, equity holders own the residual risk—the benefits or losses—from an asset after the more senior classes of security holders have been paid. In return for their acceptance of higher risk, equity investors expect higher returns than debt holders and have the chance to earn the highest returns of any class of investor. Second, equity holders are generally given the right to participate in making the critical decisions regarding the operation and disposition of an investment.

9.1.1 Residual Ownership

When a real estate investment generates rents that exceed property operating expenses, it has positive cash flow from operations. After these funds are applied to interest, amortization of principal, and reserves for ongoing capital requirements, the residual cash—if any—may be distributed to the equity holders. Periodic distributions from the operating income of a property are known as current cash returns.

At the end of a real estate investment, the property is sold and converted into cash. Any appreciation in the asset over the holding period is realized. The cash proceeds from the sale are first applied to repay liabilities in order of seniority. After all of the liabilities have been paid, any residual cash is distributed to the equity investors. This last payment is referred to as the investment's terminal or liquidation value.

Collectively, the current cash returns and the terminal value form the total return to the equity holder. In a pro forma investment model, these amounts are forecast over a period of years and discounted back to the date of investment to calculate figures of merit, such as net present value (NPV) and internal rate of return (IRR).

9.1.2 Unlimited Upside and Downside

Each period, once the senior obligations are met and cash is set aside for ongoing capital requirements, there remains either cash available for

255

distribution to equity holders or a cash deficit. The range of outcomes can be wide and depends on the volatility of the asset's operating performance.

In the case in which current cash flow is insufficient to carry the senior liabilities and the capital required for operating the assets, the equity holders must try to fund additional capital. This capital can be in the form of additional debt or can be equity paid in by either new or existing investors.

When debt funding is increased, existing equity investors find themselves behind any new senior liabilities that have ongoing claims on cash flow. When equity funding is used, new funding may be raised at an entity valuation that differs from the price at which existing equity was sold. If the new issuance price is lowered to attract additional capital, then current equity holders will be diluted. If additional funding cannot be found, the equity holders risk the loss of their entire investment.

The same pattern repeats at liquidation: senior creditors claim fixed amounts. The first available cash from liquidation proceeds must be applied to these fixed obligations. The residual cash, if any, is left for the equity holders.

9.1.3 Absorbing Economic Risk
From a senior lender's perspective, equity capital absorbs economic risk because it does not have a set claim on the cash flow of the entity. It provides capital that can increase the entity's economic activity, generating more cash flow, and building asset value. This value creation lowers the probability that the entity will default on its debt. By cushioning the debt against swings in economic performance, the equity plays a valuable role in absorbing risk for the enterprise. Senior creditors appreciate the added level of safety and typically charge lower interest rates to entities with a higher ratio of equity to capital (lower debt-to-equity ratio).

9.1.4 No Set Maturity Date
Unlike debt, which always has a maturity date, an equity investment does not have a fixed term. Equity investors have accepted the uncertainty of term as part of their investment thesis. Although debt holders can force a sale, the equity holder cannot directly demand a sale or liquidation. However, equity holders can act as a group to take over the management of the entity if current management is not responsive to their desires.

9.1.5 No Set Cash Flow Stream
As mentioned previously, as an equity holder, you can expect a distribution or a dividend but are not guaranteed to receive one. You must look to the cash flow available after fixed costs and reserves for capital expenditures for your

potential source of payout. If the property is not well leased, there may not be enough cash available to make distributions.

9.1.6 Participation in Decisions
Most equity holders have the right to self-determination through entity democracy of one type or another. The specific rights afforded to equity investors depend on the form of entity used to hold the investment.

9.1.7 Assessments
Most equity investments are structured so that the only capital put at risk by the investor is the amount of the investment. The investment can decrease in value, but investors cannot generally be called upon to invest additional capital against their will. However, this is not always the case. In certain circumstances, equity investors may agree in advance to invest further funds if required to support the initial investment. If this is the case, the equity investors are subject to assessment.

9.1.8 Liquidity
Different forms of equity investments offer different paths to liquidity. Private direct investments in real estate offer the most limited liquidity. There is a limited secondary market for interests in private real estate investments. In order to gain liquidity in these investments, an investor must wait until the underlying assets are sold. In contrast, equity investments in public real estate companies are generally highly liquid and are traded on the world's major stock exchanges.

9.1.9 Duration
Corporations are, by definition, of infinite life. Partnerships, however, have a fixed life, at the end of which it is expected that they will liquidate.

9.2 FORMS OF EQUITY INVESTMENT

Business enterprises are organized utilizing common legal structures that have economic, tax, and governance implications for the owners.

9.2.1 Proprietorship
A simplest form of organization is known as a single proprietorship. In this format, a business is owned directly by a single person. The owner receives all the profits and is responsible for all of the legal and financial obligations of the entity. The liability of a proprietor for the actions of a proprietorship is unlimited and extends to the owner's assets outside of the business. All of the profits of the business are income to the owner and are reported on the owner's tax return.

9.2.2 Partnership

A partnership is an agreement among a group of people who desire to share ownership of an enterprise. If the partners are all equal, the partnership is known as a general partnership and all of the owners are known as general partners. Each general partner is responsible for all of the legal and financial obligations of the entity. This arrangement is known as joint and several liability, meaning that each general partner is individually responsible for the entire amount of the liability. In the event that one partner defaults on an obligation, the other remaining partners may be called upon to make up the deficiency.

In addition to sharing financial obligations, partners also have a fiduciary duty to one another. This fiduciary duty obligates partners to act in good faith towards one another and to act in the best interests of the partnership.

Like single proprietors, general partners show the income from a partnership directly on their personal financial statements. They do not pay a separate corporate tax.

A partnership is capitalized from assets and cash contributed by the partners. The value of the contribution is recorded in the partner's capital account.

A partnership agreement documents the structure of the partnership and the relationship between the partners, including the interest in profits and losses of each partner. Partners may own unequal shares of the partnership's profits, losses, and value of the partnership's assets upon liquidation. Partner's shares may also be disproportionate to the amount of capital they contributed to the partnership. Allocations, however, must have substantial economic effect, meaning that their intent must be to alter the distribution of cash rather than solely to create tax benefits for certain partners.

For tax reporting, the income or loss from a partnership is allocated to its partners and affects their personal taxes in the year it occurs, regardless of whether cash is distributed. The distribution of cash from a partnership does not typically lead to a tax event.

The partnership has no obligation to distribute any cash required by the partners to pay the taxes on their share of allocated income; a result can be a situation in which the partner must "come out of pocket" to pay a tax liability, which allows the partnership to retain available cash for additional investment.

9.2.2.1 Capital Calls

Not every real estate investment goes as planned, and occasionally partnerships must reach out to existing partners for supplemental capital to support current investments. In many cases, the general partner will attempt to source this capital by borrowing additional funds, but in some cases, this approach may be infeasible or imprudent because of the financial situation of the asset. A request for additional funding from existing partners is called a capital call. Typically, each partner is asked to invest their pro rata share of the required capital. If the partner invests their pro rata share of the required capital, they retain their same percentage interest in the partnership. If they opt to pay in less than their pro rata share, their percentage ownership will decline.

9.2.2.1.1 Cram Down Provisions

In order to incentivize existing partners to meet capital calls, the partnership agreement often contains a provision under which the general partner can offer new capital providers the right to invest in place of existing investors if those investors do not meet their capital calls. The new investors often receive a disproportionate share of the partnership for their investment, which does not negatively affect partners that meet the capital calls but does affect those that are not willing to invest additional capital. This mechanism is known as a cram down provision for its impact on recalcitrant partners. The ability to offer new investors an incentive to come into a troubled investment can help a general partner attract the capital needed to protect the asset from foreclosure.

9.2.2.2 Dissolution of Partnership

A partnership ends when the investment's value is realized through a liquidation of the partnership's assets or when more than 50 percent of the ownership changes hands within a 12-month period. On liquidation, gains or losses are allocated to the partners according to the partnership agreement.

9.2.3 Joint Ventures

Joint ventures are agreements between financially sophisticated entities to pursue specific goals over a limited period of time. In real estate, joint ventures may be focused on a development project or the ownership of a particular property. Joint ventures are typically structured as partnerships, with each institution retaining a vote in the affairs of the partnership. Major decisions are apportioned by negotiation, rather than voting in proportion to economic interest. This arrangement can constitute an advantage for the operating partner, who might be a minority financial contributor, but is critical to the success of the business and desirous of a larger role in decision making.

The joint venture structure is commonly used by financial institutions that invest capital with real estate operating companies to acquire properties. The investor benefits from the operating skills of the real estate company. The operating partner benefits from the portfolio diversification and economics of scale facilitated by the institution's access to capital. Joint ventures with well-capitalized institutions allow real estate operators to own large iconic assets that would otherwise be beyond their economic reach.

9.2.4 Limited Partnerships

A limited partnership is an arrangement between operating and financial partners to share ownership of an enterprise. The operating partner typically serves as the general partner (GP) of the partnership and has unlimited liability for the operations and liabilities of the partnership. The general partner is responsible for making all operating decisions. In most cases, the general partner also serves as the "tax matters" partner and is responsible for any decisions that affect the tax position of the partnership.

The financial partners—those who contribute cash rather than expertise to the venture—are known as limited partners. Limited partners are not allowed to participate in the day-to-day operation of the partnership, although they may have a say in major decisions. In return for maintaining a passive posture, a limited partner is at risk for only the amount of their investment. They cannot be forced to contribute additional capital to a partnership if it requires additional operating funds or defaults on its obligations. The partnership agreement may, however, allow the economic benefits of the partnership to be reallocated in favor of those partners that contribute additional capital if the partnership requires it. This provision is known as a cram down.

The allocation of the economic benefits in a limited partnership is known as a waterfall. The distribution often favors the general partner out of proportion to its capital contribution. This disproportionate interest can take a number of forms and is intended to reward the general partner for its work in creating and implementing the business plan, as well as for its additional assumption of risk. The GP's additional interest is called a carried or promoted interest.

A limited partnership is taxed in the same way as a general partnership. Taxable income from the partnership is shown on the partner's personal tax return and is not subject to tax at the entity level. Taxable losses, however, are not treated in the same way as income. The amount of losses that may be taken by passive or nonworking partners is limited under the tax code.

Limited partnerships are dissolved in the same manner as general partnerships.

9.2.4.1 Corporations as Partners

To limit the risk entailed in serving as a general partner, a prospective general partner can create a corporation or limited liability company to serve as the general partner. In this way, the liability of the general partner is limited to the capitalization of the corporate entity.

9.2.5 Corporations

Corporations are legal entities, owned by their shareholders, that are set up to conduct a business. Shareholders are entitled to elect a board of directors who govern the corporation and select executives to run the business.

Corporations are entities apart from their owners and have unlimited lives. They are not dissolved unless the board recommends dissolution and the shareholders agree to end the business.

Corporations are required to pay corporate taxes because of their status as separate legal entities. After the payment of taxes, any profits not required for the operation of the business may be retained in the corporation for future growth, used to repay debt, or returned to shareholders in the form of dividends.

In contrast to partnerships, individuals who own shares in a corporation are not taxed separately based on the earnings of the corporation. Shareholders are taxed only when they receive dividends or the proceeds of a liquidation event.

9.2.6 Limited Liability Company

A limited liability company (LLC) has the limitations on personal liability of a corporation as well as the pass-through tax attributes of a partnership. The owners of an LLC are referred to as members. One of the members is selected as the managing member.

9.3 STRUCTURING ISSUES

A number of standard methods for structuring the relationship between the operating and financial partners of a business have evolved over time. These structures and the issues they concern have an impact on businesses regardless of the form of organization but are handled differently depending on the type of enterprise.

9.3.1 Allocation of Profit

In almost all business ventures, the participants must negotiate the allocation of the value created between working and investing partners.

9.3.1.1 Target Returns

A target return is the expected level of return on an investment expected by a financial partner. This return may be stated as an annual return from operating cash flow, in which case it is referred to as the annual cash on cash return: the amount distributed to the investor each year as a percentage of the amount invested. Target returns may also be calculated over the holding period, or "life," of the investment. The target return over the life on an investment typically includes the combination of annual cash distributions and the proceeds realized on the sale of the asset.

9.3.1.2 Preferred Return

To incentivize the financial partner to enter into the partnership, the operating partner may offer a preferred return to the financial or "money" partner. A preferred return is a first claim on profits until a target return has been achieved. The preference may apply to each year individually, in which case the partner with the preference receives all cash distributed until the target return for that year has been achieved. Once the preferred return has been paid, the remaining partners receive the next funds distributed until they have received the same target return on their investment. The remainder is then split according to a prescribed formula.

9.3.1.3 Internal Rate of Return

Figures of merit are metrics used to evaluate the performance or return on an investment over its life. One of the most popular figures of merit is the NPV. The NPV is the sum of the discounted cash flows returned from an investment less the amount of the initial investment. To calculate the NPV, one must choose a discount rate known as a hurdle rate. If the NPV is positive, it means that the investment has a rate of return in excess of the hurdle rate.

An IRR is the discount factor that, when used in the NPV calculation, equates the NPV of the cash flows returned from an investment to the amount of the investment itself. The IRR can be compared to the investor's desired rate of return; if it is higher, the investment exceeds the investor's expectation, and if it is lower, the investment decision must be reconsidered.

Figures of merit can be calculated with or without regard to outstanding debt. If a figure of merit is calculated prior to taking into account debt, it is said to be unlevered. If it accounts for the impact of debt, it is levered. Unlevered returns look at how well an asset is performing without regard to how it is financed and may be an indicator of astute property acquisition and management skills. Levered returns also take into account how well an investor has accessed the capital markets and can be an indicator of financial acumen.

9.3.1.4 Promoted and Carried Interests

In return for its services as investment manager, the operating or general partner may earn a share of the partnership profits that is disproportionate to the amount of the capital it contributes. The most typical form of promoted interest is to grant the operating partner a disproportionate share of profits after the financial partners have achieved a given internal rate of return on their capital accounts. In complex structures, the operating partner's share of distributions can increase as successive levels of overall returns are achieved by the partnership.

9.3.1.5 Deficiency and Clawback

To further incentivize a financial partner, an operating partner may agree to give up a certain portion of its share of return to the financial partner if agreed-upon return thresholds have not been achieved. This type of agreement is known as a clawback provision. The amount of proceeds given up by the operating partner is typically calculated as the amount that, when added to returns already earned by the financial partner, would increase its IRR to a stated target yield.

In the typical case, a clawback provision enforces an investor preference at the expense of any excess profits that have previously been distributed to the GP. In some cases, however, the GP may be asked to repay fees, part of the preference returns on its own investment and return of capital at liquidation in the event that the non-GP investors have not achieved a base level of return.

If the preferred investor does not achieve the target return in a particular year, a number of different solutions can be reached. In most cases, the amount by which the target amount is deficient in any year, plus interest on the amount of the deficiency at the target rate, becomes an additional preferred claim in future years until it is paid. This type of preference is called a cumulative preference. Another way to handle the deficiency claim is to hold it in a suspense account (again with interest at the target rate) until the investment is ultimately refinanced or sold. The provisions to retrospectively bring the investor's return up to the preference rate are known as make whole provisions.

In addition to its preference with respect to annual distributions, a preferred claim may also be entitled to a priority return of capital over common equity on a sale or refinancing of an asset. This is called a liquidation preference.

An equity claim with a preferred return is known as preferred equity. If it has a provision for a deficiency claim, it is known as cumulative preferred equity.

EXAMPLE

The investors in partnership X, including the general partner, have invested $100,000 in their venture. The investors have a preference on profits until an 8 percent annual return on invested capital has been achieved. Any additional profits are allocated at a rate of 20 percent to the general partner and 80 percent to the investor partners (including the GP's pro rata capital contribution). In the event that distributions in any year fall below the preference level, a deficiency is created. Any future profits that exceed that year's preference distribution are first applied to cover any remaining prior period deficiency.

	Year One	Year Two	Year Three	Year Four	Year Five
Profits	10,000	3,000	6,000	15,000	15,000
Investors' preference	8,000	8,000	8,000	8,000	8,000
Investors' excess	1,600				5,600
GP excess	400				1,400
Investor make-whole		(5,000)	(2,000)	7,000	

In year four, the first $8,000 of profit is applied to the annual preference distribution. Of the remaining $7,000, the first $5,000 is "carried back" to restore the year two deficiency and the remaining $2,000 is used to make up for the year three deficiency. Distributions to fulfill prior year deficiencies are referred to as make-whole distributions. In year five, given that all the prior year deficiencies have been made whole, any profits over $8,000 are divided according to the standard 80 percent investor/20 percent general partner split.

In more complex make-whole provisions, investors may be granted interest on delayed preference payments.

9.3.2 Control

The right to control an enterprise may be concentrated in one individual, as in a single proprietor, or divided among separate classes of equity investors.

9.3.2.1 Operating Decisions

Operating decisions cover the day-to-day management of the enterprise. In most corporations, the equity holders do not participate directly in the management of operations; rather, this is the domain of the corporation's executives, supervised by the board of directors. In partnerships, the managing partner makes operating decisions. In limited partnerships, the general partner typically serves as the managing partner.

9.3.2.2 Major Decisions

Strategic decisions regarding the future of the enterprise, including decisions to buy and sell assets, are considered major decisions. In both corporations and partnerships, major decisions are typically made by the equity holders.

9.3.2.3 Debt Financing

The quantity of leverage used to finance the ownership of a property is one of the most important decisions made regarding any real estate investment. Increasing leverage can increase returns but also increases risk. Partners may have different levels of risk tolerance. Some investors see the ability to increase leverage as an opportunistic way to generate cash from their investment. Other investors with limited liquidity may rely on borrowings to provide additional capital. More conservative investors may be adverse to using leverage. The partnership agreement may include reference to a targeted level of leverage and will allocate the right to approve conforming debt financings to the general partner, changing the target leverage level may be a major decision requiring a vote of the limited partners.

In corporations, general guidelines on appropriate levels of leverage and approval of major financing transactions are subject to board control.

9.3.2.4 Tax Decisions

In partnerships, one partner is typically given the discretion to represent the partnership on tax matters. This partner is known as the tax matters partner. Different partners can have different tax positions. For example, one partner can be a tax payer and another partner may be a tax-exempt pension fund. Tax decisions can have major financial impact on certain partners while being of no importance to others.

In corporations, tax matters are typically managed by the Chief Financial Officer and are subject to board control.

9.3.3 Exits and Buy-Sell Agreements

In some joint ventures, an agreement is made in advance as to the circumstances under which one partner can seek liquidity and exit the partnership while another continues to operate the venture. This can be a particularly contentious decision, as a sale may have different consequences for different partners. For example, a sale can have disadvantageous tax consequences for one partner and be economically advantageous for another. A managing partner with fee income in addition to an ownership stake in an asset may want to see a partnership continue, while other partners may want to sell and reposition their capital. Over time, many standard agreements have been developed to control the process of triggering and implementing the sale of partnership assets.

9.3.3.1 Right of First Offer

In a situation in which the partners have a right of first offer, a departing partner may trigger the sale of an asset, but it must offer the remaining partners the right to make an offer to purchase the asset before it is offered for sale to the public. This right is also known as a first look. The selling partner sets a target offer price at which it is a willing seller. In the event that the other partners choose not to buy the asset, it may be offered for sale to the public at the same price. If the price is achieved, the asset is sold to the public buyer. If a lower price is received and the departing partner wishes to accept it, the asset must again be offered to the remaining partners at the lower price before the public bid can be accepted.

This approach is considered an efficient method for orchestrating a sale because the remaining partners always have an opportunity to retain control of an asset. In the event that they choose not to purchase, they are in effect agreeing that the asset is being offered for sale at a price that exceeds their estimate of value. If the asset sells at that price, then all of the partners should be pleased with the result. Buyers in the public sale are willing to consider the investment because they know that the seller has the right to close a sale if the target price is agreed.

9.3.3.2 Right of First Refusal

The right of first refusal is less advantageous to the departing partner than the right of first offer. In a right of first refusal, the departing partner must offer the remaining partner the opportunity to buy the asset at any price agreed to by a bona fide third party. This opportunity is also known as a last look. The prospective buyer in this situation must consider that they may spend a significant amount of time preparing a bid that can be usurped by the remaining partner. This type of buy-sell agreement limits buyer interest in participating in the sale process.

9.3.3.3 Sale by Appraisal

Another common method for price setting between a departing and remaining partner is to have a price set by appraisal. In this structure, the partners are willing to transact but need a price-setting mechanism without taking the asset to market. Each party to the transaction hires an appraisal firm to determine fair value. If the appraiser can agree on a value, then that is the price at which the interest trades. If the two appraisers cannot agree on a value, they choose a third independent appraiser, who sets the price.

9.3.4 Types and Amounts of Fees

Many real estate companies earn fees by providing services to property investors. The provision of these services for unaffiliated parties is known as third-party management. Passive or nonoperating real estate investors can face a wide range of fees charged by their third-party manager.

9.3.4.1 Acquisition

Third-party managers typically charge investors a fee for acquiring properties. This fee covers the manager's cost of sourcing the asset and processing the acquisition. The manager will use this fee to pay a staff of acquisition professionals who review potential transactions and manage the acquisition process, including market analysis, financial analysis, transaction structuring, property due diligence, and review of engineering and environmental reports.

The direct costs of professional services, and other outside costs related to the acquisition, are not typically covered by the acquisition fee and are passed through to the investors.

9.3.4.2 Disposition

In many property companies, the same team works on acquisitions and dispositions. At given intervals, the team will analyze each asset and its market to evaluate the feasibility and profitability of a sale. Once a sale decision is made by the investors, the team gathers and prepares the financial and market information required to create a property sales brochure. The disposition team may attempt to sell the property directly or enlist the services of a property brokerage company to identify a buyer. Disposition fees are typically a stated percentage of the sales proceeds. If an outside broker is engaged to assist with the sale, the broker's fee is paid by the investors in addition to the manager's fee.

9.3.4.3 Financing

To reduce the required equity investment and to increase the return on the equity that is invested, most investors utilize leverage when buying real estate. The manager will work to place that financing, preparing the requisite financial and market analyses that prospective lenders will use to underwrite the property. The manager will then negotiate the terms of the loan on behalf of the investors, in keeping with their targeted leverage guidelines. Once a lender is identified, the manager will file a loan application and take the asset through the underwriting process: agreeing to terms, negotiating documents, and providing the lender with all required due diligence information. The lender will retain appraisers to value the asset and engineers and environmental analysts to review the asset's physical condition. The manager acts as a facilitator during this process.

At the closing of the transaction, the manager typically gets paid a placement fee, calculated as a percentage of the amount of the financing. All direct costs of the loan process, fees charged by the lender, and commissions paid to any mortgage broker are also passed through to the investors.

9.3.4.4 Asset Management

Once a property is acquired, an asset manager is employed to act as a proxy for the investors in preparing and implementing a strategic plan for the asset. Asset managers also oversee the day-to-day operations of the asset by preparing budgets, approving minor capital expenditures, and reviewing leases. Asset managers are paid a fee that is typically related to the value of the asset being managed.

9.3.4.5 Property Management

Property management includes housekeeping, maintenance and repairs, security, and tenant relations. The property manager implements the plan created by the asset manager. Property management is a people intensive business requiring the management and coordination of many different trades and vendors. Property managers are paid a percentage of property revenues.

9.3.4.6 Development

Developers plan and implement the creation of new properties as well as the renovation and expansion of existing assets. The "ground-up" development process starts with the acquisition of a land parcel, followed by the planning and entitlement process, through the construction phase, and ending with the original lease up and tenant fit out. In a redevelopment project, most of the steps are the same except that the developer starts with an existing asset rather than a parcel of land, and creates a repositioning plan for that property. Developers are paid a fee based on a percentage of the project's cost for their work and are often given a share of the development profit.

9.3.4.7 Construction Management

Construction managers coordinate the work of the many trades that are required to build or renovate real estate. Effective construction management can be quite valuable in managing construction costs and minimizing the time it takes to complete a project. Construction managers are typically paid a percentage of the cost of a project as a fee.

9.3.4.8 Fees in a Joint Venture

When a property company enters into a joint venture agreement with a financial investor and invests a share of the capital, it typically absorbs a pro-rata share of the fees charged to the joint venture.

9.3.5 Raising Capital

Soliciting the capital needed for real estate projects is a highly regulated process involving a wide range of professionals, including the property company's financial staff as well as their commercial and investment bankers. The company's principals are supported by many other professionals such as lawyers and accountants.

9.3.5.1 Syndications

Syndicates are groups of banks that come together to place an issue of securities with investors. This is known as a securities offering. Syndicates can be formed for both debt and equity offerings. An equity syndicate is run by a lead "bookrunning" manager. The book refers to the document, now a computer spreadsheet, into which investor interest is recorded. Debt syndicates are run by the "agent" bank, the bank that acts as agent for the lenders who will participate in the offering.

In real estate, finance syndications can also refer to groups of investors that are brought together to finance the equity component of a property investment. These syndicates are typically structured as limited partnerships. Firms that specialized in this type of investment (most commonly in the 1980s and earlier) were known as syndicators.

9.3.5.2 Underwriting

The term "underwriting" comes from the practice of participants in insurance syndicates of writing their names at the bottom of an insurance contract to indicate that they have accepted its terms and a portion of the risk of loss. In the context of a securities offering, underwriters review an investment for suitability on behalf of prospective investors. Once the underwriters have approved a transaction, they have accepted the risk of placing the securities in the market at an agreed-upon price. In recent times, underwriters only sign underwriting agreements after the securities have been placed with investors. Because this step happens simultaneously with the actual sale, underwriters accept little, if any, market risk. Shares issued by publicly listed REITs are generally sold on an underwritten basis.

All public offerings of securities in the United States are regulated by the Securities and Exchange Commission (SEC) and are subject to the Securities Act of 1933 ('33 Act). The '33 Act requires issuers of public securities to file a registration statement, a formal document describing the company and the securities offered, with the SEC prior to issuing securities to the public . It also requires that the buyer of the securities receive a prospectus at the time of sale with information from the registration statement. Public offerings are also subject to the laws of the states in which the securities are offered for sale. These laws are known as the Blue Sky laws (to protect investors from being sold "the blue sky"). If the offering is the first public issuance of equity securities, it is known as an initial public offering (IPO). Once a company has issued public securities, it must conform to reporting requirements under the Exchange Act of 1934 ('34 Act) and prepare periodic financial reports for its shareholders.

In a fully marketed offering, the underwriter arranges for the issuer to meet with a number of prospective investors prior to the offering. These investor meetings are referred to as a roadshow. They are typically one-on-one meetings between company management and individual investors at their offices or group meetings held in major cities. The roadshow gives the investors a chance to assess the company's business plan and management. This approach is used when the company is not well known to investors or has had significant events that may need to be discussed.

For companies that are better known to investors, the overnight offering has become popular. This type of transaction occurs at the end of the business day, after the close of the primary market on which the issuer's securities are traded. This timing prevents existing shareholders from selling shares to reduce the price at which the new shares will be offered. As soon as the market closes, the underwriter calls investors and offers the securities before the market opens for trading on the following day.

For well-known companies with strong investor demand, underwriters may propose a form of overnight transaction known as a bought deal. In this type of offering, the underwriter purchases a quantity of a company's securities at an agreed-upon price, typically at a small discount to the last day's closing price, and reoffers them to the market at its own risk.

In recent years, issuers that require ongoing capital infusion are using a form of continuous sale of equity known as an at the money (ATM) offering. In an ATM offering, the company's underwriter sells shares to investors as part of the regular trading activity in the issuer's shares. The trading volume of the company's stock limits the amount of securities that can be sold; if too many shares are offered, the company risks seeing its stock price fall.

	Fully Marketed	Overnight	Overnight/ Bought	ATM
Investor contact	Road show	Conference calls	Limited	None
Price risk	Issuer	Issuer	Underwriter	Issuer
Capacity	Highest	Moderate	Moderate	Limited

9.3.5.3 Best Efforts Offering

In a best efforts offering, a banker agrees to place an issue of securities but makes no guarantee that the securities will actually be sold and accepts no market risk. In contrast to an underwritten offering, a best efforts offering is a longer process and involves a considerable marketing and sales effort. Real estate partnerships, funds, and private REITs are sold on a best efforts basis.

9.3.5.4 Regulation D Offering

An offering of securities may be exempt from the registration requirements of the '33 Act and the reporting requirements of the '34 Act if it meets certain criteria described in SEC Regulation D (Reg D). Reg D exemptions apply to offerings of limited dollar amounts or offerings that are made to a limited number of accredited investors. Accredited investors include financial institutions and institutional investors, as well as high-income and high-net-worth individuals. These investors are assumed to be able to evaluate the investment proposal without the protections of the '33 and '34 Acts. Many offerings of real estate partnerships rely on Reg D exemptions to avoid the costly public offering process.

9.4 INVESTORS

There are many avenues for investors to source interests in real estate projects and for owners to access the capital they need to build and acquire assets.

9.4.1 Public Markets

A number of different types of equity securities issued by real estate companies are traded on public stock exchanges and are available to both individual and institutional investors. All of these entities are subject to the rules of the exchanges on which they are traded, as well as the disclosure rules of the countries in which they are registered. Many of these securities are analyzed by the research arms of major investment banks and reported on in the financial press.

9.4.1.1 Real Estate Investment Trusts (REITs)

REITs are entities whose primary business is the ownership of debt and equity interests in real property. These entities, typically structured as corporations, agree to limit their investments to real property and to operate within certain parameters in return for favorable treatment under the tax code of their country of origin.

REITs originated in the United States, but similar corporate structures have been adopted by many other countries. In the United States, REITs must be widely held entities investing primarily in equity or mortgage interests in real estate. REITs are not subject to corporate-level tax but are required to distribute substantially all of their annual profits to shareholders. Most U.S. REITs trade on public stock exchanges and are widely held.

9.4.1.2 Real Estate Operating Companies (REOCs)

REOCs are corporations whose primary business is the ownership of equity interests in real property and the provision of services to the real estate industry. These companies are not willing to submit to the restrictive covenants present in the REIT structure. REOCs are able to reinvest their profits and are not required to make annual distributions. In many cases, REOCs have enough tax shelter from depreciation to minimize their tax burden. REOCs include both private and public companies and operate in many countries throughout the globe.

9.4.1.3 Master Limited Partnerships (MLPs)

MLPs are partnerships that issue interests known as units that are registered securities that are traded on public securities exchanges. MLPs invest in real estate and other asset classes. The MLP unit holders enjoy the benefits of the single level of taxation afforded to limited partnerships, in return for which they give up the corporate governance benefits of a traditional corporation.

MLP unit holders receive an annual report from the partnership known as a Form K-1 that reflects the tax activities of their investment.

9.4.2 Private Markets

There are many types of private equity investment vehicles in the real estate capital markets. Investors that invest directly in property and own an interest in an asset are known as direct investors. Investors that purchase interests in entities that own assets are known as indirect investors.

9.4.2.1 Entrepreneurial Limited Partnerships

Many entrepreneurial real estate firms raise capital through the sale of limited partnership interests to small numbers of outside investors. These partnership investments have limited liquidity and uncertain cash flows, so the investors must be willing to forgo liquidity while the entrepreneur attempts to create value.

Many of today's major real estate firms started by acquiring and developing properties that raised capital through limited partnerships. The assets owned by these partnerships can be rolled up into REIT umbrella partnerships, creating liquidity for the investors.

9.4.2.2 Pension Funds and Insurance Companies

Financial institutions seeking long-term investments have often provided private capital through both direct and joint venture investments in real property. These institutions traditionally focus on large, well-located assets in major markets. In many cases, the institutions serve as partners with major property companies to develop and own landmark properties and portfolios.

9.4.2.3 Private Equity

Investment firms that raise opportunistic capital from high-net-worth individuals and financial institutions are referred to as private equity firms. Private equity firms make investments in real property either directly or through joint ventures with property companies. In comparison to pension funds and institutional investors, private equity firms are interested in taking greater risk in order to achieve higher returns.

9.4.2.4 Private REITs

There are many private REITs that invest in property with the goals of creating significant appreciation prior to finding an exit in the public markets or through liquidation. They choose the REIT structure because it provides the benefits of corporate form while having income subjected to only a single level of taxation. Shares in these REITS are typically sold to individual investors through networks of financial planners. They are known as non-traded REITs because their shares are not listed on public stock exchanges and have limited liquidity.

Financial institutions also use private REITs as a means of aggregating capital for property investment. These institutions keep the REIT private so that the shares are not valued by the public market. If the institutions held publicly traded securities, they would be required to state the trading value of those securities on their own financial statements. As that value changes over time, the holder is required to take a gain or loss when they report earnings. This process is called "mark to market" and is required whenever institutions hold securities that are listed on public exchanges.

9.4.2.5 Tenancy in Common (TIC)

TIC is an ownership structure whereby a group of investors each own fractional interests in an investment property. The benefit of this structure is that each owner has a direct interest in real property. TIC investors have generally purchased their interests through a 1031 tax advantaged exchange of interests, which they have held in other properties. The TIC structure facilitates the Section 1031 like-kind exchange rules that provide for the exchange of assets without triggering a tax event when the properties exchanged are of like kind. For example, when someone reinvests the proceeds of an investment sale into a similar investment, they are not taxed on the exchange.

In many cases, the TIC property is a large institutional quality asset managed by a professional company and the properties exchanged are smaller assets managed by individual investors. The goal of the small owner is to use the like-kind exchange to trade up to a better property and to get out of property management responsibilities. In some cases, typically when the property investment is economically successful, the TIC structure can achieve this goal. In other situations, usually with an economically stressed asset, the lack of a single participant in the TIC with a controlling interest can make decision making difficult and affect the ability to restructure an underperforming investment.

9.5 STRATEGIC UTILIZATION OF EQUITY BY THE ENTREPRENEUR

Having an institutional equity partner or access to public equity can accelerate the growth of any entrepreneurial real estate business. An institutional partner can lend credibility to the entrepreneur and bolster its financial position in the eyes of business partners, property sellers, and debt sources. Almost all institutional partners require some control of the venture in return for their investment. The structure of the venture can have significant implications for the entrepreneur.

Accessing the public equity market is a major step for any entrepreneurial company. The governance and reporting requirements that come with acceptance of public market capital are both expensive and challenging, so much so that they are often beyond the capability of most entrepreneurial real estate enterprises.

9.5.1 Control of Business

The real estate entrepreneur's goal is to seek capital to develop and acquire assets without giving up control of either operating or major decisions while accepting only limited personal financial responsibility for the performance of the investment. This state is very difficult to achieve when the equity is sourced from sophisticated institutional investors or through public offerings.

The institutional investors, in turn, typically leave the day-to-day management of property to the operating partner. The institution will seek the right to approve capital budgets and major decisions such as sale or refinancing. In the event that either partner decides to exit the investment, the other partner is often given the initial right to purchase the seller's interest. This agreement is known as a buy-sell agreement.

9.5.2 Implications of Buy–Sell Agreements

In general, the institutional partner in a venture will typically have greater financial resources than the entrepreneur. If both partners agree to a sale, the situation is generally amicable and simple to implement. A buy-sell is typically triggered when there is a disagreement regarding the future of the investment.

Faced with a liquid partner, the entrepreneur must be sure that the buy-sell is not structured in a way that puts it at a disadvantage, which can occur when the institution wants to sell and the entrepreneur wants to keep the property. In this case, the entrepreneur needs time to either find a new partner or to put together the financing to buy out the institution.

Under a right of first refusal, in the case where the institution wants to sell, it must offer the entrepreneur the right to purchase the asset at the price offered by any bona fide third-party buyer. This type of agreement can discourage serious third-party buyers who fear expending resources underwriting an asset they will ultimately not be able to acquire. This reluctance to bid can give the entrepreneur an advantage in putting together a competitive bid.

A right of first offer requires the selling institution to allow the entrepreneur to present an offer to purchase the asset. If the institution rejects this offer, the institution might sell to a third party only at a higher price. This type of agreement puts more pressure on the entrepreneur when attempting to assemble financing, as it is harder to attract a new institution to the property because of the risk that, following a lot of work, the bid might be unsuccessful.

9.5.3 Capital or Control?

Ultimately, most entrepreneurs must trade off aspects of control in order to source capital. For the entrepreneur, the key is to maintain enough flexibility in the venture to enable it to make decisions quickly and efficiently so that it can be competitive in the marketplace. The proactive entrepreneur will also plan for in advance for an exit that protects its interests while still making the venture attractive to institutional capital. Regardless of the flexibility granted by the investor, the entrepreneur and its institutional equity partner must also face the demands of their lenders for control exerted through debt covenants and guarantees.

9.5.4 The Exit
9.5.4.1 Preservation of Tax Position

Once value is built up in a property, entrepreneurs focus on maintaining that value without triggering a tax event. There are a number of strategies that the entrepreneur can use to achieve liquidity for an investment without triggering an immediate tax consequence. Ultimately, however, taxes must be paid.

Preservation of an entrepreneur's tax position becomes an issue in property disposition with institutional investors who may not be tax sensitive. The longer an asset has been held and depreciated, the greater the impact a sale may have on the entrepreneur and the deeper the divide between the institution and entrepreneur regarding the future exit from the venture.

9.5.4.2 Hold and Refinance

The entrepreneur can hold the asset and refinance it instead of selling it. In a refinancing, cash can generally be withdrawn without recognizing immediate tax consequences.

9.5.4.3 Section 1031 Like-Kind exchange

As mentioned earlier, properties can also be exchanged for other like-kind assets. If the seller meets a number of technical requirements, the exchange may be tax free under Section 1031 of the Internal Revenue Code. Tax-free exchanges allow entrepreneurs to change investment strategy without tax consequences. However, in contrast to either a sale or a refinancing, this strategy does not allow the entrepreneur to take out any cash from the asset.

9.5.4.4 Contribution to a REIT Umbrella Partnership

Another exit strategy is to contribute the asset into a REIT via an exchange of the property for partnership interests in a REIT's umbrella partnership. As a result, the contributor receives units in the REIT's umbrella partnership that are economically equivalent and readily exchangeable into shares of the REIT's publicly traded stock. Taxes on gains are not due until the units are actually exchanged for REIT shares.

Glossary

1031 Exchange
'33 Act
'34 Act
Assessment
ATM (at the market) offering
Best efforts
Blue sky laws
Bought deal
Buy-sell
Capital account
Capital call
Carried interest
Clawback
Continuous equity offering
Cram down
Cumulative preference
Cumulative preferred equity
Current cash returns
Direct investors
Figures of merit
First look
Form K-1
General partner
Indirect investor
Joint venture
Last look
Levered returns
Like-kind exchange
LLC (limited liability company)
Limited partnership
Liquidation preference
Major decisions
Make whole provision
Managing member
Master limited partnership
Member
One on one
Overnight offering

Passive investment
Preferred equity
Preferred return
Private equity
Promoted interest
Proprietor
Prospectus
REIT (real estate mortgage investment corporation)
REOC (real estate operating companies)
Registration statement
Regulation D
Road show
Roll up
Right of first refusal
Right of first offer
Secondary offering
Secondary market
Securities offering
SEC (Securities and Exchange Commission)
Substantial economic effect
Syndication
Tax-free exchange
Tax matters partner
TIC (Tenant in Common)
Terminal Value
Umbrella partnership
Underwriting
Unit
Unit holder
Waterfall

Thought Questions

1) Do you think preferred equity should be viewed as debt or as equity? Why?
2) Your company is an established REIT and needs to raise additional equity capital. Your stock is very volatile. Which type of equity offering should you consider, and why?
3) Operating partners can earn returns that are disproportionate to the amount of capital that they have invested in a partnership. These are called carried interests. If this disproportionate sharing results from the sale of an asset, should this income be considered income for services and taxed at full personal income tax rates or should it be considered a return on investment and taxed at capital gain rates?

Review Questions

1. Required Equity
   Greentree Park is a ten-building office park outside of Cleveland, Ohio. The property is valued at $100 million. Bankers have proposed a first mortgage

with an LTV of 55 percent. A financial services firm has offered a mezzanine loan to take the property up to a 75 percent LTV. How much equity will be required from the owners in order to complete the purchase?

2. Cash Return on Equity

Seaside on Dune Road is a 50 unit garden apartment project on Long Island. The project cost $12.5 million to build and is now subject to a 7 year, 8 percent, interest only mini-perm loan in the amount of $9 million that has two years to run. The project shows stabilized NOI of $2 million. What is the cash return on equity (assume no taxes, no cap ex)?

3. Calculation of Income (continuing exercise)

The Freeling Tower, a major office building, is held for a year and one day and then sold. The NOI in year one is $2.5 million.

The original financing is:

$10 million mortgage, interest-only, 6 percent

$5 million mezzanine debt, interest-only, 10 percent

$5 million equity

Assume that the allocation to land is 20 percent of the purchase price depreciable life is 39 years. What is the partnership income?

4. Waterfall from Current Income (continuing exercise)

In question 3, 20 percent of the equity was invested by the GP and 80 percent by the LP. Each year, each party is entitled to a pro rata split of funds available for distribution until a 10 percent return is achieved. The GP is then entitled to a 30 percent share. How much will the GP receive?

5. Proceeds from a Sale (continuing exercise)

The property is sold at the end of one year and one day for $21 million. Upon sale, original equity is returned pro rata if available. Excess proceeds are split pro rata until each party receives a cumulative return of 12 percent. The GP is then entitled to a 30 percent share. How much with the GP receive?

6. Total Cash on Cash Returned (continuing exercise)

What before-tax return will the GP make on its investment?

a) 11 percent

b) 37 percent

c) 49 percent

d) 67 percent

7. Taxation (continuing exercise)

What taxes are payable by the GP and the LPs? Assume an income tax rate of 35 percent, capital gains tax rate of 15 percent, and recapture tax of 25 percent.

8. Partnership Liquidation (continuing exercise)

What is the after-tax cash available to the GP and LPs after taking into account the payment of taxes? What is the after-tax return on investment (for ease of calculation, use one year as the holding period)?

Multiple Choice Questions

1. The responsibility for the management of a real estate partnership rests with the:
   a) limited partner
   b) general partner
   c) syndication
   d) property manager
2. Which of the following participants has unlimited financial responsibility for the affairs of a real estate partnership?
   a) limited partner
   b) general partner
   c) syndicator
   d) property manager
3. Which is not an option for a partnership requiring more capital?
   a) assess limited partners
   b) assess general partners
   c) borrow cash
   d) admit additional partners
4. The opening balance of a capital account is created by:
   a) gain on sale
   b) cash contribution
   c) cash distribution
   d) allocation of losses
5. Which of the following are added to capital accounts?
   a) income and cash invested
   b) income and cash distributed
   c) losses and cash distributed
   d) losses and cash invested
6. Substantial economic effect does not require:
   a) pro rata allocations
   b) allocations that are reflected in capital accounts
   c) liquidations in accord with capital accounts
   d) restoration of deficit capital accounts
7. At the end of a partnership, capital account balances must be brought to:
   a) zero
   b) the amount of original cash investment
   c) the sum of all cash distributed
   d) 10 percent
8. Which characteristics are not shared by both partnerships and corporations:
   a) limited liability
   b) business association

    c) centralized management

    d) objective to carry on the business and divide the gains

9. Characteristics of Reg D offerings generally include all of the following except:

    a) limited to accredited investors

    b) greater than 100 investors

    c) less than 35 investors

    d) exemption from registration

10. In which of the following would an institutional investor generally earn a preferential return?

    a) syndication

    b) REIT

    c) JV

    d) corporation

Reviewers and contributors:

Ian Hunter

Jake Reiter

Edited by Katie Price

For answers to these Problems and Exercises, please visit the companion website: http://booksite.elsevier.com/9780123786265

CHAPTER 10

Capital Structure

The types and amounts of capital that are employed to finance a property are referred to collectively as its capital structure. Today's capital structures can be quite complex and contain many layers of debt, hybrid, and equity securities. Capital structures are typically configured to maximize the owner's return on equity. The capital structure that achieves the maximum return on equity is known as the optimal capital structure. The optimal capital structure can be achieved by combining capital from investors with different risk profiles and return requirements.

Although it is possible to purchase a property entirely with cash, most real estate investors do not employ this strategy. One of the benefits of a real estate investment is the steady stream of cash flow from long-term leases. In many cases, these cash flows can support a level of long-term debt financing, and the typical real estate investor will employ at least one level of leverage when financing an asset. In addition to traditional mortgage debt, real estate owners access the capital markets using a number of hybrid financing structures that combine aspects of both debt and equity securities.

CONTENTS

10.1 THE CAPITAL STACK

10.1.1 Multiple Sources of Capital Are Used to Finance a Property

In many cases, a sophisticated investor will seek multiple levels of financing to aggregate the capital required to purchase an asset. Each level of capital has its own terms and requirements. Collectively, the claims against an asset and the layers of capital are known as the asset's capital stack.

10.1.1.1 Ordered by Seniority of Claims

Each layer of capital comes with a specified set of requirements and claims against the property's current cash flow and liquidation proceeds. The layers of capital can be "stacked," or ordered in terms of seniority. The most senior claim, typically a first mortgage, has the first right to receive operating

281

cash flow and proceeds from a sale or liquidation, but it also carries the lowest return.

10.1.1.2 Claim on Cash Flow

The debt layers of the capital stack have a first-priority, although limited, claim against the cash flow of an asset. The claim must be paid prior to any distributions of cash to equity holders, but the claim is limited to the periodic amount of interest and principal due. After the periodic interest and principal are paid and reserves are set aside for the operation of the asset, any residual is available for the equity holders. The most senior equity claim on cash flow is that of the fixed dividend on preferred stock. In contrast, the dividend on the common equity, if any, has the most junior claim on cash flow in the capital structure.

10.1.1.3 Claim on Liquidation Proceeds

In a sale, the full principal amount of all debt, along with any accrued interest, must be paid prior to any proceeds being distributed to the equity holders. If there are insufficient proceeds to repay all the layers of debt, then they are paid off in order of seniority. Claims that share the same level of seniority are paid pro rata. Once all the debt claims are repaid, the remaining proceeds are paid to the equity holders. If there are multiple layers of equity holders, they too are paid according to seniority, with preferred stock paid first.

10.1.1.4 Temporal Nature of Cash Claims

The claims are not only ordered by seniority but are also temporal. Time of repayment can differ for senior and junior claims. Unless it is in default, a senior claim does not have the right to demand the repayment of principal prior to its maturity. A more junior claim that matures earlier may make such a demand and needs to be satisfied before the more senior claim is due. In a similar manner, because equity holders may have rightfully received annual cash distributions from a property that is ultimately unable to repay its senior debt, they may actually receive payments ahead of senior debt.

10.1.2 Optimization of Capital Structure

There is always a dynamic tension between the amount of debt on a property, the cost of that debt, and the residual return available to the equity. As the amount of debt is increased relative to the income stream of the asset, the lender demands higher and higher returns. The first dollars of senior debt borrowed against a property will typically command a lower return than the average return on the asset. As a result, the presence of the leverage improves the return to the equity holder. This type of borrowing is said to create positive leverage. At some point, the last dollar of debt added to the stack will command a higher return than will ultimately be available to the equity. This type of borrowing creates negative leverage.

WEIGHTED AVERAGE COST OF CAPITAL (WACC)

The WACC is the combined cost of the debt and equity employed to finance a property or entity. It combines the cost of debt and the cost of equity in proportion to the amount of each present on the balance sheet. If the entity is subject to tax, the cost of debt is reduced by the tax rate to reflect the tax deductibility of interest:

$$WACC = (Kd \times D) + (Ke \times E)$$

D = Debt
E = Equity
Kd = Cost of debt
Ke = Cost of equity
t = marginal tax rate

EXAMPLE

Our investment fund is considering purchasing a property for $100 million with $60 million of debt and $40 million of equity.

Our debt is 7 percent interest only. Our equity holders expect a return of 14 percent. What return would the property have to earn in order to cover our cost of capital?

Our WACC is $(0.07 \times 0.6) + (0.14 \times 0.4) =$ 9.80 percent. If we expect that the asset can yield $9.8 million or 9.8 percent on its $100 million asking price, it is a good prospect for our investment fund.

If our fund was a private investor subject to income tax at 35 percent our WACC calculation would be, considering taxes, $(0.07 \times 0.6) \times (1 - 0.35) + (0.14 \times 0.4) = 8.33$ percent.

$$WACC = (Kd \times D)(1 - t) + (Ke \times E)$$

As a private investor subject to taxes, our WACC is lower and we would be prepared to accept an asset with a lower yield.

Property performance changes over time and negative leverage can become positive over the life of an investment if a property's NOI improves. The reverse can also be true: leverage can turn negative if operating performance falls off over time. Because it is impossible to predict the future, it is impossible to know with certainty the impact of every dollar of leverage on equity returns. At any point in time, with a property pro forma in hand, one can evaluate available options for debt financing. There will always be a level of debt capital that maximizes the return to the equity. This level of debt is the optimum capital structure.

10.2 USE OF DEBT TO ENHANCE EQUITY YIELDS

10.2.1 Debt is Lower/"Fixed" Cost

The providers of debt capital can expect a set return consisting of interest during the course of their investment plus the return of their capital at a predetermined maturity date. Debt investors trade off yield for certainty and accept a lower return than equity investors in exchange for the lower risk of their senior position in the capital stack.

10.2.2 Equity Owns Residual Cash Flow

Equity holders own the residual rights to all cash flow and liquidation proceeds after the creditors have been paid. If a property performs well, it may generate cash well in excess of the claims of its debt holders. This excess cash can be distributed to the equity holders or used to repay debt, enhancing the value of the equity interest. Unlike the creditor's claim, the equity holder's claim is not limited to a set rate of return. It is limited only by the performance of the property. The unlimited opportunity for return is the key factor that attracts capital to equity investments.

In any particular period, equity can receive distributions after all required interest and principal payments have been made. As mentioned earlier, because equity holders can receive periodic distributions prior to liquidation, it is possible that they will have received considerable returns from an investment that does not generate sufficient proceeds to repay all creditor claims at liquidation. It is also possible that the property may never generate sufficient cash to pay principal and amortization, let alone current returns to equity holders.

10.2.3 Leverage Causes Yield to Rise on Equity

Leverage is employed to increase the yield on equity. This occurs when the required return to the debt investor is lower than the amount the capital can return when invested in the asset. If the return on the asset (ROA) is greater than Kd the return on equity (ROE) rises. In contrast, if Kd is greater than ROA, the addition of debt to the capital stack causes ROE to fall.

IMPACT OF LEVERAGE

Leverage = $D/(D + E)$

In most cases, increasing the leverage on the property will increase Kd as the lender's risk increases.

If ROA > Kd: Leverage is positive, adding debt improves the return to equity.

If Kd > ROA: Leverage is negative, adding debt decreases the return to equity.

ROA = EBITDA/Total capital

EBITDA = Earnings before interest, taxes, depreciation and amortization. For a property, EBITDA equals NOI less SG&A. Although it does not take into account the claims on funds from capital expenditures or tenant costs, it is one measure of the funds available to service debt.

In the following example, we use the cap rate as a simplified proxy for ROA.

EXAMPLE

We can purchase a $100 million core asset at a 5 percent cap rate (5 percent = Adjusted NOI/Price). We can buy the property for cash (Case A). We have also been offered two loans to consider: $50m at 4 percent (Case B) and $60m at 6 percent (Case C). What is the impact of leverage on return on equity?

CASE A:

Adjusted NOI = $5 million

   Equity: $100 million earns $5 million = 5 percent

   In our base case: without leverage, ROE is the same as ROA.

CASE B:

Adjusted NOI = $5 million

   Debt: $50 million × 0.04 = $2 million

   Equity: $50 million earns $5 million − $2 million = $3 million = 6 percent

   In Case B, ROE (6 percent) is greater than ROA (5 percent) and the leverage is positive. The cost of the debt is less than the return on the asset and adding leverage improves the ROE.

CASE C:

Adjusted NOI = $5 million

   Debt: $60 million × 0.06 = $3.6 million

   Equity: $40 million earns $5 million − $3.6 million = $1.4 million = 3.5 percent

   In Case C, ROE (3.5 percent) is less than ROA (5 percent) and the leverage is negative. The cost of the debt exceeds the return on the and adding leverage reduces the ROE.

In the United States, interest is an expense that can be deducted from taxable income. Therefore, the cost of interest must be measured as the after-tax interest rate. The after-tax interest rate is equal to the actual rate paid on the debt instrument multiplied by 1 minus the investor's marginal income tax rate.

EXAMPLE

The bank rate on an interest-only land loan is 5 percent. The land owner is subject to a 35 percent marginal income tax rate, and interest is a deductible expense. What is the after-tax interest rate?

   I (at) = I × (1 − tax rate)
   I (at) = 0.05 × (1 − 0.35)
   I (at) = .0325 = 3.25 percent

An after-tax interest rate is not the result of the bank changing its expectation for payment. It is the result of the property owner being able to deduct interest paid when calculating income subject to taxation. If the property stops generating income, the tax deduction may be unavailable and the after-tax and pre-tax interest rates become the same.

The deductibility of mortgage interest has the effect of lowering the after-tax cost of debt financing and making it more attractive to the levered investor. To illustrate the impact of the taxation, the above example X is recalculated assuming a 35% marginal income tax rate with a deduction for mortgage interest:

	Case A	Case B	Case C
Debt	$ -	$ 50.00	$ 60.00
Equity	100.00	50.00	40.00
	$ 100.00	$ 100.00	$ 100.00
Interest Rate		4.0%	6.0%
NOI	$ 5.00	$ 5.00	$ 5.00
Interest		2.00	3.60
Income before taxes	$ 5.00	$ 3.00	$ 1.40
Taxes @ 35%	1.75	1.05	0.49
Income after taxes	$ 3.25	$ 1.95	$ 0.91
ROE	3.3%	3.9%	2.3%
Interest		$ 2.00	$ 3.60
Tax Savings		0.70	1.26
AT interest		$ 1.30	$ 2.34
AT Interest Rate		2.6%	3.9%

10.2.4 Exception for "Negative Leverage"

In a case in which the interest rate is greater than the return on assets, the addition of leverage lowers the return on equity. In general, employing negative leverage is not a good strategy. However, there are certain cases in which negative leverage can be useful.

10.2.4.1 Uses of Negative Leverage
10.2.4.1.1 Expect NOI to Grow

An investor may acquire an asset with a view to initiating major changes that will enhance returns over time. This value creation can occur by improving the physical condition of a property, improving its market perception, or by identifying new, more productive spaces that users can then occupy at higher rents.

Although the available leverage for an asset at the inception of an investment may be at yields that will erode immediate equity returns, over the expected life of the investment the leverage may actually become positive as ROA improves.

10.2.4.1.2 Need Cash to Acquire

Accepting a loan with negative leverage may be the only option available to a purchaser seeking to acquire an asset. If the high cost of debt is a function of the state of the property, once the asset is owned, it can be improved to bring up the ROA, creating a positive spread against the cost of debt. If the high cost of debt is a function of the financial market, then once the market improves, it may be possible to refinance the asset at a better interest rate and the leverage may become positive. This is a high risk strategy.

10.3 IMPACT OF LEVERAGE ON RISK

10.3.1 Debt Has First Claim/Requirement Against Cash Flow

Debt capital enjoys a first claim on the cash flow from an investment after the payment of operating expenses. In any period, this claim may be greater than the available cash flow, in which case the equity holders may be required to use cash reserves or to invest additional capital in order to satisfy this claim and avoid default.

10.3.2 Higher Debt Claim Concentrates Operating Risk on Equity

The cash flows generated by most property investments vary with changing economic conditions and as the relative market position of the asset changes over time. In general, the claim placed on cash flow by mortgage debt does not vary with the property's operating performance. Thus, the impact of the variability of the cash flow is concentrated on the residual available to the equity investors.

As the level of leverage increases, the portion of a property's operating cash flow required to service debt increases. In addition to affecting the residual available to equity, the more volatile the operating performance of the property, the higher the probability that cash flow may not be able to cover the debt service. Given the higher level of risk present in high LTV debt, as leverage increases, the debt risk profile becomes similar to that of equity and the returns demanded by lenders increase.

10.4 HYBRID FINANCING FORMS

10.4.1 Mezzanine Debt

Mezzanine debt (mezz) provides an additional level of capital beyond traditional senior secured or first mortgage financing. Mezz is subordinated to more senior debt and generally has more flexible covenants. Senior lenders may have a prohibition against the property owner placing a junior claim against their collateral. For this reason, mezz may be structured as a lien on the investor's equity rather than as a secured claim against the property itself.

As a result, mezz has a higher level of risk than traditional financing and requires significantly higher return. Mezz commonly serves as bridge financing, with a short maturity and an expectation that the mezz will be refinanced once a new capital structure is implemented following asset stabilization or turnaround. As a form of risk capital, the availability of mezz tends to diminish in troubled real estate markets.

10.4.2 Wrap-Around Debt

In many cases, the owner of a property that is encumbered by an existing first mortgage requires additional capital. The owner will approach a new lender that will agree to give a package of financing that is initially a second mortgage during the remaining term of the in-place first financing. When the existing first mortgage becomes due, the new lender advances additional funds to repay it as well. Thus, the new lender has the combined long-term mortgage. This allows the borrower to obtain additional capital and secure a long-term capital commitment in the current financing market. The wrap-around mortgage also provides a way for the borrower to blend the second mortgage risk premium into the long-term cost of the financing package. This type of financing is sometimes referred to as "blend and extend."

10.4.3 Participating Loans

Participating loans give the lender an additional return based on the performance of the underlying asset. This additional return can be based on annual operating performance, proceeds from enhanced valuation at maturity, or both.

The level of participation can be fixed or variable. Fixed participations are generally stated as a set percentage of profits after payment of the base interest rate. For example, the loan earns 5 percent interest plus 25 percent of earnings before taxes. Upon sale of the property, the loan would be entitled to 25 percent of net sale proceeds available after the original principal amount of the debt is repaid.

Variable participations call for the lender to be paid a variable percentage of earnings before taxes and net sale proceeds. The percentage depends on how well the property performs. Typically, the lender earns a smaller fraction of the profit at each higher level of performance, thereby incentivizing the operator to enhance performance.

10.4.4 Convertible Loans

A convertible loan allows the lender to exchange all or a portion of their note for an equity interest in the asset. In this structure, if the asset performs poorly, the lender will seek a return of their principal at maturity. If the asset performs well, the lender will convert their note into an interest in the asset. The lender typically accepts a lower level of current interest in return for the option value inherent in the conversion feature.

Although participating debt has equity-like qualities, it is true debt and failure to make interest payments or to repay principal in a timely manner can lead to a default and the owner's loss of the asset. As debt, the interest paid by the owner is tax deductible.

10.4.5 Preferred Equity

Preferred equity is senior to common equity, receiving dividends and liquidation proceeds before any funds are paid to common equity holders. In return for the more senior claim, preferred holders are typically limited to dividends paid at a stated rate. This rate is generally in excess of the rate paid on the common shares at the time of issuance. The rationale for the higher payment is that the preferred holders do not share in the upside of the asset. Over time, the dividend on the common equity may increase with improved performance, but the preferred divider will always remain the same amount.

Preferred shareholders do not have a debt claim on the asset and, unlike interest payments, dividends are not deductible from taxable income. If there is not enough cash flow available to pay the stated dividend on the preferred equity, the claim may accumulate, in some cases with interest. Securities with an accumulation feature are known as cumulative preferred equity. Although preferred stock may build up a claim against the entity, the claim is still an equity claim and the holders cannot seize the asset or force liquidation.

Some preferred equity structures may include conversion rights. Conversion rights allow the preferred shares to be exchanged into common shares at a set exchange ratio. These structures are known as convertible preferred equity interests.

EXAMPLE OF A CUMULATIVE PREFERRED EQUITY CLAIM

Institutional investors in our property have the right to receive a $5 million annual preferred dividend. In the event that the dividend cannot be paid, it is added to the dividend requirement in successive years, without interest, until it is paid.

Our property loses a major tenant at the end of year one. We find a great replacement

(Continued)

that will pay a much higher rent, but the new tenant will not occupy the space until the beginning of year three.

Year	One	Two	Three	Four
NOI	$10	$4	$10	$14
Interest	3	3	3	3
Cash flow available to equity	7	1	7	11
Preferred dividend due	5	5	9	7
Preferred dividend paid	5	1	7	7
Common dividend available	2	0	0	4

In year one, the $5 million preferred dividend is paid in full. In year two, there is insufficient cash flow available to pay the full preferred stock dividend. The deficit of $4 million ($5 million due minus $1 million actually paid) is carried to the next year. In year three, $7 million is available, $5 million is used to pay the $5 million "current preferred dividend," and $2 million is used to reduce the deficit dividend of $4 million to $2 million. In year four, $11 million is available and used to cover the $5 million current preferred dividend and the remaining $2 million deficit. After these payments totaling $7 million are made, $4 million is available to pay out to the common equity.

10.4.6 Strategic Use of Hybrids

Hybrids are used to provide leverage for common equity holders beyond the level where traditional secured financing sources are prepared to lend. Hybrid security holders are given higher returns for the acceptance of the additional risk that comes with being subordinated to the senior lien holders.

In many cases, senior lenders prohibit the use of hybrid debt structures that are junior to their loans. Although these claims are junior to the senior debt, if the borrower defaults on the hybrid note, the junior lien holder can accelerate its note. This may interfere with the owner's operation of the asset, causing a decline in value that may ultimately affect the security for the senior lien as well.

Hybrid equity securities are even more risky to their holders and hence more costly to the common equity. They are, however, less likely to interfere with the operation of the asset and create less of an impact on senior lenders than junior debt.

Many owners see hybrid securities as interim, or bridge, capital that will be replaced by additional, less expensive, senior debt once a property's performance has improved.

10.4.7 Sale Leaseback

A sale leaseback is a transaction in which a property owner sells his or her asset to an investor and then leases it back from the investor. This allows the property owner to access the capital invested in the asset for other purposes while still maintaining the use of the property. The investor has the benefit of property ownership, including the presence of a ready user for the asset.

Typically, sale leasebacks are completed by corporations that have riskier but more profitable uses for the capital that is invested in their real estate holdings. Corporate headquarters, chain stores, and restaurants are among the types of properties that are candidates for sale leasebacks. A sale leaseback may also include a right for the seller to repurchase the asset at the end of a given period.

The price to reacquire the asset might be set at a low level to encourage the user to repurchase the property at the end of the lease. This is known as a bargain repurchase clause. The presence of a bargain repurchase option lowers the buyer's risk because they know they will have a ready purchaser at the end of the lease. A sale leaseback with a bargain repurchase clause is essentially a collateralized financing transaction rather than a pure real estate investment.

In some circumstances, a property owner requiring cash may choose to refinance the property rather than participate in a sale leaseback transaction. This option is viable, however, only if the owner can both access credit and afford to leave equity invested in the property.

10.4.8 Ground Lease

A landowner may lease a parcel of land under a long-term agreement that allows the lessee to build and utilize a structure on the land. The land lease can be viewed as an additional source of financing for a developer, as the developer does not need to use capital to acquire the land on which the building is constructed. The lessee's requirement to pay land rent is an additional claim on the asset's cash flow that must be covered by net operating income.

In order to construct a building, the lessee must source additional funds, generally in the form of a mortgage on the structure. This loan is generally larger than the value of the land. The bank may be willing to make the loan only if the landowner agrees to subordinate his or her claim on the land to that of the bank. If the land lease is made junior to the bank loan on the structure, it is known as a subordinated ground lease. If the ground lease is senior, it is known as an unsubordinated ground lease.

Unsubordinated ground leases are very safe investments because neither the owners nor lenders on the improvements are likely to lose their assets to the ground lessor through a default. Subordinated ground leases are much riskier assets because in order to preserve ownership of the ground, a lessor may need to repay the first mortgage on the improvements.

A ground lessor cannot depreciate their asset because, by definition, land is not depreciable. Therefore, all of the income from a ground lease is subject to tax. In contrast, the owner of the improvements has a tax-advantaged position in that all of his or her investment is depreciable.

10.4.9 Sale of Partial Interests

It is sometimes advantageous to separate and sell off some of the ancillary rights that come with the purchase of a property. The proceeds from these rights can be used to reduce the capital required to purchase an asset and improve the return on investment. The risk associated with this strategy is that these rights can have strategic or monetary value that is not apparent at the time the property is purchased.

10.4.9.1 Air, Mineral, and Oil and Gas Rights

Air rights are the property owner's rights to develop additional space, typically vertically, on an existing building. These rights can be realized by building additional floors or by demolishing the existing building and building a new taller building. In some locations, air rights can be sold for use at another site.

Mineral rights are the property owner's rights to exploit any minerals that are located on a property. Oil and gas rights are the owner's right to explore for, drill for, and exploit hydrocarbon reserves. These rights are transferable apart from the rights to develop improvements to the land.

10.4.9.2 Water, Riparian, and Littoral Rights

Water, riparian, and littoral rights involve the ability of a landholder to use the water and the shoreline on or adjacent to their property. Riparian rights refer to moving water and littoral rights to oceans, lakes, and ponds. The law regarding these rights is complex and varies with the location of the property. If it is not the developer's intention to use these rights, they can be separated and sold to raise capital. The loss of these rights may compromise the property owner when it comes time to sell, because certain buyers will not be interested in the property without its water rights.

10.4.9.3 "Pad" Sales

In certain situations, small pieces of a property, called pads, can be segregated and sold off as a financing strategy. To accomplish this, the land must first be subdivided into individual lots. For example, a single-family housing developer may sell off a prime corner location to a shopping center developer. The presence of the shopping center is an amenity for the home buyers and a source of cash for the land developer.

10.5 IMPACT OF CREDIT MARKETS ON PROPERTY VALUATION

10.5.1 Availability of High LTV Loans Increases Property Value

The availability of credit has a profound effect on property valuation. In markets in which credit is readily available at low rates and with easy terms, property valuations are generally higher than in economic environments in which interest rates are high and loan terms are more stringent.

In an environment in which credit is readily available, borrowers can purchase assets using a large proportion of debt in the capital stack. This reduces the amount of equity required. If the leverage is available at a positive spread (an interest rate below the return on assets), then the additional leverage raises the return on equity. These high returns come at the price of increased risk, as the higher the leverage level (all else being equal), the greater the chance of financial distress should the property operations or the economy decline.

Credit availability can also impact asset pricing. The same NOI can service more debt as rates fall, without affecting the potential investor's ROE. This can cause asset values to rise and lead to a bubble as was proven in the Financial Crisis.

The availability of credit can be assessed by looking at three factors: required loan-to-value ratios, required debt service coverage levels, and required loan terms.

The loan-to-value (LTV) ratio equals the amount of borrowing as a percentage of the value of an asset. In tight credit markets, banks will lend only 50 percent or less of an asset's value. When credit is readily available, this ratio can climb as high as 80 percent or 90 percent. Normative LTV levels are 60 to 65 percent.

The debt service coverage ratio (DSCR) relates adjusted property NOI to the principal and interest payments required to service a loan. In easy credit markets, lenders will accept a 1.1x ratio (meaning that NOI is 1.1 times required debt service), where property cash flow is only slightly greater than the amount required to service the debt. In tight credit markets, lenders can demand that cash flow is up to twice the required debt service (DSCR = 2.0x). Normative DSCR levels are 1.25x.

As property NOI changes over time, a property's DSCR also changes. If property performance improves, the DSCR increases. If property performance falters, the ratio falls. Loan agreements may call for the periodic measurement of the DSCR, and a borrower may be asked to reduce the outstanding loan balance if the ratio DCSR falls too low. If a reduction is not demanded, the lender may require that cash flow from the property be escrowed until coverage improves.

The DSCR required by lenders also changes due to conditions in the credit markets. By lowering the required debt service, both falling interest rates and longer amortization schedules improve the DSCR. The same property NOI can support much more debt in a credit market with low interest rates and no requirement for amortization (interest only loans). The property NOI, mortgage terms and lender's DSCR requirements may all change significantly during the term of a loan and must be analyzed carefully before replacement financing is implemented.

Economic environments with low interest rates generally have high real estate values. This is because cash flow generating assets are at a premium when bonds offer low returns. High interest rate environments typically bring lower real estate values as cap rates rise and in-place cash flow streams are devalued. In general, LTV and DSCR move inversely and are well correlated. However, this is not always the case.

In an economic decline, real estate can fall out of favor because operations are depressed due to a lack of demand for space, and foreclosed properties add to the supply of space on the market. Real estate valuations can fall even though cash flow is not immediately affected. In this scenario, LTV can be high even though a property retains strong debt service coverage. In an economic boom, the opposite may happen: property may be revalued upward for its potential growth, lowering LTV, before the cash flow is actually in place to improve DSCR.

10.5.1.1 DSCR and Alternative Metrics

There are many types of coverage tests used by financial institutions to review the ability of a borrower to service debt:

- **Interest coverage (EBITDA/interest)**: This test looks at the ability of the borrower to make periodic interest payments.
- **Debt service coverage (EBITDA/interest and principal)**: This test looks at the ability of the borrower to pay both interest and principal payments.
- **Fixed charge coverage (EBITDA/(interest, principal, ground lease payments, preferred equity payments)**: This test is the most comprehensive coverage test, in that it measures a borrower's ability to service all of the regular claims on its cash flow.
- **Debt yield (EBITDA/debt balance)**: This test is a variant on the coverage test that allows the lender to quickly see the maximum level of debt service a borrower could manage. The lender can then compare this to the mortgage constant required to carry a loan in the current market.

> The debt yield divided by the market mortgage constant gives you the DSCR:
> - Debt yield/mortgage constant = DSCR
> - (EBITDA/debt balance) * (1/mortgage constant) = DSCR
> - EBITDA/(debt balance * mortgage constant) = DSCR
> - EBITDA/debt service − DSCR

10.5.1.2 Shifts Best Buyer to Private Market

Public companies with access to the equity market are less reliant on debt financing than private companies with less access to equity. Public companies generally operate at lower levels of leverage than private real estate companies. This is because shareholders in public companies tend to be more risk averse than private real estate developers. For this reason, most public companies are not willing to maximize leverage levels, even when credit is readily available.

When credit markets offer high LTV financing at reasonable interest rates, private companies can "lever up" and become more effective property buyers. In tight credit markets, public companies, with greater access to equity capital and less reliance on debt, are the best buyers.

10.6 IMPACT OF DEBT TERMS ON OPTIMUM CAPITAL STRUCTURE

10.6.1 Debt Service

Debt service is the total periodic cash obligation of the debtor to the lender. In general, this consists of interest and principal amortization payments. In most cases, real estate mortgage payments are based on self-amortizing loans that have level monthly cash obligations. The reduction of the payment between interest due and the principal allocation changes each period as the loan is amortized. Over time, as the principal balance is reduced, the interest component decreases while the principal payment rises.

10.6.1.1 Interest

The interest due in any period is calculated as the loan's principal balance at the beginning of the period times the stated annual rate of interest divided by the number of periodic payments due in the year:

periodic interest due = principal balance at beginning of period

$$\times \text{ (annual interest rate/number of periods per year)}$$

10.6.1.2 Principal

In the typical self-amortizing note, the amount of principal paid down in any month is the amount of the level monthly cash payment made to the lender minus any interest due for that period. The principal balance of the loan at the beginning of the period, reduced by the amount of the principal payment, becomes the beginning balance of the next loan period.

10.6.1.2.1 Required Amortization

10.6.1.2.1.1 Self-Amortization. The most common form of mortgage is the self-amortizing mortgage. This form of mortgage features level monthly debt service payments. The principal reduction that occurs over the amortization period is set to reduce the loan balance to zero by the maturity of the loan.

In many cases, the amortization period used is longer than the stated maturity of a loan. For example, a loan with a ten-year maturity may call for a payment schedule that would amortize the loan over twenty-five years. This is done so that the lender has a lower amount of principal outstanding as the property ages but does not claim all of the available cash flow for amortization.

10.6.1.2.1.2 Sinking Fund. A loan with a sinking-fund typically calls for level amortization payments, rather than level debt service payments. The amount of debt service payable each period is lower than the last, as the interest due on the principal balance outstanding is reduced. Sinking funds are typically set to reduce principal by a set percentage by the maturity of the loan.

10.6.1.2.1.3 Interest-Only Loan. Interest-only loans do not require any principal payments to be made over the life of the loan. This structure results in the lowest level of debt service possible. With a fixed-rate loan, interest payments (and in this case, debt service) on an interest-only loan are the same each period for the life of the loan. The entire original balance of the loan must be repaid at maturity.

10.6.1.2.2 Amortization Requirement Protects Lender Against Value Decline

Lenders typically benefit from amortization. From a lender's point of view the principal amount of the loan is declining while the property is stable or growing in value. This results in an ever-decreasing LTV ratio. Although the credit is improving, the lender is being paid an interest rate reflective of the highest LTV ratio, the level at the inception of the loan.

Many conservative borrowers prefer to have amortizing loans because their obligation to the lender decreases over time, ideally from the cash flow generated by the property. As the loan is paid down, the owner's equity position in the asset increases. Over time, the owner can hold the property free and clear of any debt obligations and enjoy the full use of any cash flow generated. Most opportunistic borrowers typically choose interest-only loans as they would rather control the cash otherwise required for amortization and distribute or reinvest it as circumstances dictate.

10.6.1.2.3 Amortization Competes with Interest as Use of Cash Flow
In challenging economic environments, the cash required to amortize a loan diverts resources from paying interest. A loan with required amortization requires higher debt service payments and has a lower DSCR than an interest-only loan at the same interest rate. This limits the amount that can be borrowed per dollar of property NOI.

10.6.1.2.4 Amortization Requirement Limits Loan Proceeds
When credit is tight, a higher DSCR requirement may constrain the loan proceeds that banks may make available to a borrower. An amortization requirement raises debt service and lowers DSCR. Lenders look at both coverage and leverage tests, and the loan amount is limited by whichever test yields the lesser loan amount.

10.6.1.2.5 Lowers Property Valuation
As the amount of loan proceeds available for a property acquisition decreases, the required amount of equity increases. Unless the leverage is negative, lower loan proceeds will impact the price offered by potential buyers, because reduced proceeds can negatively impact the borrower's return on equity.

In the Financial Crisis, lenders moved away from interest-only loans requiring significant amortization payments, which further accelerated the decline in property values in a market that was already looking to shift capital away from real estate assets. The lower proceeds available not only reduced potential equity returns but also raised fear that sellers, unable to refinance existing loans, would flood the property market with assets, further pressuring and deflating asset pricing.

10.7 DECONSTRUCTING A DEBT QUOTE

Debt quotes can be quite complex, containing multiple options. A borrower must analyze the quote carefully to understand all of its implications and then review it against the particular circumstances of the property.

Example: Bank A offers two term notes. The first, Option A, features a five-year term at 6 percent. The second, Option B, a seven-year term at 8 percent.

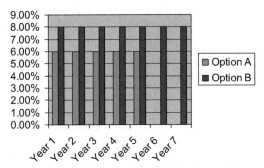

For granting the extra term in Option B, the lender seeks an additional 200 basis points in each of the first five years and then gives us a two-year extension at the 8 percent rate. Here is another way to view the quote:

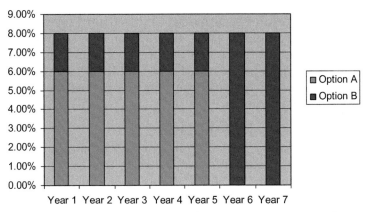

A more insightful way to deconstruct these options is to see them as two sequential notes. The second "extension note" brings the full cost of the first note to the extension period:

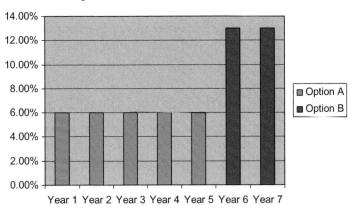

In this graph, we collect all the extra interest being charged for Option B and place it on the two-year extension period. This shows that we are actually paying 13 percent interest for each of the last two years. A more accurate calculation of this effect would include the time value of money, as the higher level of interest in Option B starts in year one, not year six.

Unless the borrower believes that there is a compelling reason for taking the extension, it is hard to justify.

10.7.1 Cost of marginal dollar of debt

Bankers quote mortgage loans in terms of interest rates for loans with specific levels of proceeds. Interest rates increase as the amount of mortgage proceeds loaned increase.

The interest rate quoted can be viewed as the average rate for all of the dollars loaned. By comparing the quotes, we can calculate the interest cost of the marginal dollars offered with each successive level of mortgage proceeds.

Example: the mortgage quote with multiple LTVs. A lender offers Option A with a 50 percent LTV (a $50m loan against a property with a $100m value) and a 6 percent interest rate and Option B with a 60 percent LTV ($60m loan) with an 8 percent interest rate. The analysis is quite similar. First, look at the two quotes side by side. A 50 percent LTV loan is actually five individual loans, each for 10 percent of property value. Option B, the 60 percent LTV loan, is in effect adding an additional 10 percent LTV loan:

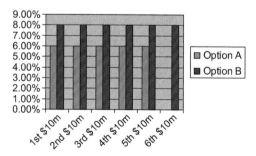

For granting the extra leverage in Option B, the lender seeks an additional 200 basis points for each of the first five loans and then loans us an additional 10 percent at the 8 percent rate. Here is another way to view the quote:

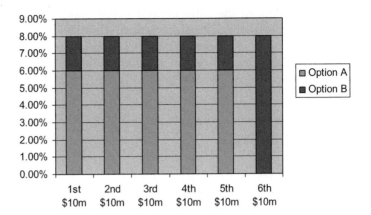

In the following graph, we collect all the extra interest being charged for Option B and place on the last incremental 10 percent borrowing that takes us from 50 percent to 60 percent LTV. This shows that we are actually paying 18 percent interest for the 6th $10m loan.

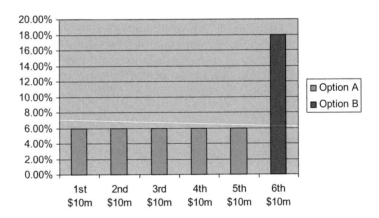

10.7.2 Comparison of marginal debt cost to ROA

Although the average cost of the debt proposed by the lender may be less than the ROA, the cost of the marginal dollar may be well above it. As the cost of the marginal dollar of debt is over the ROA, adding that additional dollar lowers ROE.

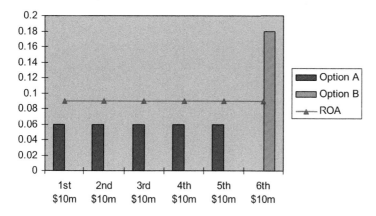

Our analysis assumes that the property owner has the flexibility to use either debt or equity to finance the asset. In some cases, when it is difficult to raise equity, increasing the level of debt may be the only way to finance a project. Although the marginal dollars of debt are expensive, they may be worth it to the property owner.

In Option B of both scenarios, the lender is seeking significant compensation for its higher risk. When the true cost of the marginal term, or the sixth $10 million loan, is analyzed, it may be well above the ROA of the property, and the borrower should in most cases take Option A. This determination, however, cannot be made without a full understanding of the property circumstances. For example, there may be a major lease coming due at the end of year five. If the lease is not renewed prior to maturity, it will make the property impossible to finance. To protect against this risk, the borrower may be willing to pay what appears to be a very high rate for the extra term.

Glossary

Adjusted net operating income
Air rights
Bargain repurchase
Blend and extend
Bridge capital
Capital stack
Capital structure
Convertible loan
Convertible preferred stock
Cost of debt (Kd)
Cost of equity (Ke)
Cumulative preferred equity
DSCR (Debt service coverage ratio)

EBITDA
Ground lease
Hybrid financing structure
Interest only
Leverage
Liquidation proceeds
LTV (Loan to value) ratio
Littoral rights
Mezz (Mezzanine debt)
Mineral rights
Negative leverage
Oil and gas rights
Optimal capital structure
Pad sales
Participating loans
Positive leverage
Preferred equity
Return on assets
Return on equity
Riparian rights
Sale leaseback
Self-amortization
Sinking fund
Subordinated ground lease
Unsubordinated ground lease
Water rights
WACC (Weighted Average Cost of Capital)
Wrap around debt

Thought Questions

1. Does it ever make sense to take a negative amortization loan?
2. Some bankers argue that preferred equity is an inexpensive way to issue permanent capital; others say it is a very expensive way to issue debt. Which do you believe is true?
3. You believe your property is reaching peak cash flow potential. You can sell an equity joint venture interest to a pension fund or increase the amount of the first mortgage outstanding. What are the implications of each of these choices? You read an article in the local paper about a new development that threatens the market dominance of your property. Does this change your choice of financing?

Review Questions

1. An investor group is considering purchasing Warren Woods, a multifamily property with 200 units that are each 1,000 square feet. Rents are running $2.00 per square foot per month. Adjusted NOI is 50 percent of revenues. The property is currently valued at $150,000 per unit. The bank is offering

a loan of $20 million at 6 percent with 25-year amortization. What is the LTV and DSCR?

2. The investors in Warren Woods pay taxes at 35 percent. Assume 20 percent of value is attributed to land and 27.5-year depreciation. What is the after tax return on equity? What is the maximum distribution that can be paid as a percent of equity?

3. An institutional investor offers $5 million of preferred equity at an 8 percent dividend yield. What impact does this have on the original investor group's return on equity?

4. MB REIT owns a shopping center with adjusted NOI of $10 m. Market cap rates for similar properties are 8 percent. The property currently has a $50 million, 7 percent mortgage that expires in six months. The REIT is offered three replacement mortgages $50 million at six percent, $60 million at 7 percent, and $70 million at 8.25 percent. All of the loans are for ten years and are interest only. MB REIT is not a taxpayer. Which loan is best?

5. In the event that the REIT accepts the $50 million loan, a mezz lender has offered a $15 million, ten-year loan at 13 percent, interest only. Is this a better alternative?

6. Grant Industries owns a large warehouse outside of Austin, Texas. The property is currently free and clear of any encumbrances. An investor has offered to purchase the land under the warehouse for $10 million. The investor will charge Grant $75,000 per month rent. At the end of ten years, Grant may repurchase the land at $8 million. Assuming Grant exercises its bargain repurchase option, what is Grant's effective interest cost?

7. Bobby's Bar B Q Shack is a rapidly expanding chain of fast and casual restaurants. The chain currently owns ten locations. Each location costs $5 million to build and generates a stabilized operating profit of $1 million per year. The company would like to build 20 more over the next year and assumes its costs will remain the same. Bobby has been offered a $75 million, three-year bank line of credit at 10 percent and a $75 million, three-year 6 percent convertible mortgage. The convertible mortgage allows the holder to convert $25 million of principal into a 20 percent interest in the company. The market values companies like Bobby's at ten times unit operating profit. Which financing is better?

8. Banco de Poco offers three-year mortgage at 5 percent, a five-year mortgage at 6.50 percent, and a seven-year mortgage at 7.5 percent. What assumption about rates in years four and five would make you choose the five-year over the three-year mortgage? What assumptions about rates in the second five years would make you favor the seven-year mortgage over the five-year mortgage?

9. REIT has an offer of $50 million, five-year financing at 7 percent with 25-year amortization on your property. You have three choices for increasing the financing: $60 million five-year financing at 8 percent with

20-year amortization; add a $10 million preferred equity investment at 14 percent to the $50 mortgage; or add a five-year interest-only $10 million second mortgage at 12 percent to the $50 million mortgage. Which is best?

10. Cherry Towers is a well-leased CBD office building in a major East Coast city. It has never had occupancy below 90 percent; however, leases representing 40 percent of the rentable space are expiring in five years. Oxy Capital Corp, a private lender, is offering a choice of two loans: a three-year, 70 percent LTV loan at 4 percent, and a seven-year 50 percent LTV with financing at 7 percent. Both loans are sufficient to pay off your existing financing and feature a 20-year amortization schedule. Which loan do you recommend?

Multiple Choice Questions

1) Place these claims in order of seniority:
   I. First mortgage
   II. Common equity
   III. Mezz debt
   IV. Preferred equity
   a) I, II, III, IV
   b) IV, II, III, I
   c) I, III, IV, II
   d) III, I, IV, II

2) Which of the following is not typically used as a mortgage covenant?
   a) DSCR
   b) Quick ratio
   c) LTV ratio
   d) Interest coverage

3) Which of the following statements about the impact of adding additional debt are incorrect?
   I. More tax benefit
   II. While I < ROA, ROE increases
   III. While I > ROA, ROE increases
   IV. Distress can result
   V. Credit spread decreases
   a) I, II, V
   b) II, IV
   c) III, IV
   d) I, II, IV

4) One of the following was not a result of the financial crisis:
   a) Interest-only loans
   b) Increased amortization

    c) Higher credit spreads

    d) Lower LTV limits

5) Negative leverage exists when:

    a) ROA > Cap rate

    b) ROA > Cost of debt

    c) ROA > Cost of equity

    d) ROA < Cost of debt

6) If LTV increases and DSCR decreases, what is the impact on the cost of debt?

    a) Decreases

    b) Remains the same

    c) Increases

    d) No impact

7) Increasing the amount of leverage applied has what impact on the risk associated with a property investment?

    a) Decreases

    b) Remains the same

    c) Increases

    d) No impact

8) The purpose of a yield maintenance fee is to:

    a) Protect the lender against prepayment risk

    b) Protect the lender against rising interest rates

    c) Maintain the lender's yield on a loan if issuer credit changes

    d) All of the above

9) Which of the following is not a reason to sell an asset in a sale-leaseback transaction?

    a) Because the property owner does not want to use the space

    b) To transfer depreciation expense to an investor

    c) As an alternative to refinancing the property

    d) To provide financing for a new acquisition

10) If the property ROA is 10 percent, for which Kd is the leverage positive?

    a) 10 percent

    b) 8 percent

    c) 12 percent

    d) 14 percent

11) Common mortgage types include all of the following except:

    a) Interest-only

    b) Fully amortizing

    c) Preferred

    d) Convertible

12) The pay rate _____ exceeds the interest rate in a negative amortization loan.
   a) Never
   b) Always
   c) Sometimes
   d) Not relevant

For answers to these Problems and Exercises, please visit the companion website: http://booksite.elsevier.com/9780123786265

CHAPTER 11

Development Finance

11.1 DEVELOPMENT PROCESS

Creating a new property, from concept through construction to tenant occupancy, is the most creative and complex aspect of the real estate business. The development process involves many different types of professionals working on interrelated tasks that must be achieved in a specific order. Regardless of the type of property being developed, many of the steps in the development process are similar.

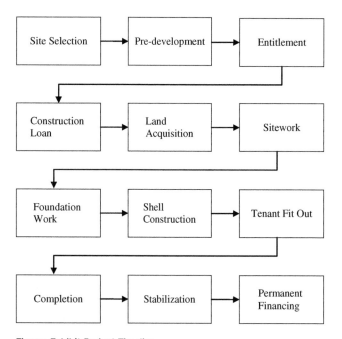

Figure: Exhibit Project Timeline

11.1.1 Concept Development

The concept for a development can be driven either by the requirements of a particular set of users (tenant driven or "build to suit" development) or by the

307

availability of a given site whose owner seeks to find a use that maximizes its value (speculative or "spec" development). The spec developer is betting on the existence of a market for a project in advance of identifying and contracting with specific users.

The number and types of users that must be accommodated determine the scale of a project and help the developer determine the form and the number of buildings required. The scale of the desired project, coupled with an understanding of the permitted development densities in the targeted community, helps the developer set parameters for the type and size of site required.

The process can also be driven in reverse, as when an attractive site is offered to a developer who does not have a particular user in mind. The concept plan for a spec project is then based on the developer's knowledge of the local market and the physical characteristics of the site.

11.1.2 Site Selection

Site selection is the identification of a property that satisfies the minimum requirements set forth in the conceptual plan for a tenant-driven development.

11.1.3 Predevelopment

At the beginning of the predevelopment stage, the developer has only a conceptual plan for an identified site. The developer then works to move from the concept to create a detailed plan for a particular site. Looking ahead to the implementation of this plan helps a developer identify a series of infrastructure requirements.

11.1.4 Entitlement

A property owner's right to use a parcel of land is limited by constraints put in place by local government. Each locality has a zoning code that specifies the uses that are appropriate for properties located within different areas of a community. These limitations govern the type of asset that may be created and the quantity and locations of any structures and improvements. Zoning re-strictions help preserve the character of a particular area and make sure that infrastructure (water, power, sewer, etc.) is available and sufficient for the intended uses.

In many areas, developers are expected to contribute to the costs of building infrastructure in advance of its use. In low-demand locations, the government may make available a package of incentives to parties willing to create economic growth.

Many types of infrastructure are required in order for property to be developed. Most uses require the availability of power and drinking water. The users will create sewerage that must be treated and other waste that must be removed. In many cases, the overall development of the property may have implications for the ecosystem and may require an environmental impact statement. Covering a field with pavement and buildings may create storm water runoff that can upset delicate environments such as wetlands, which house many species of wildlife. In other cases, the reutilization of an environmentally challenged property for a new use is beneficial to the environment but may require environmental testing to certify that remediation of contaminants has been accomplished.

The property being built will also require access from the road network and integration with the public transit system. Some of these impacts will occur at the property's location. Others, such as increased traffic flows, may affect complicated road networks that extend far from the particular site being developed. Traffic mitigation through the expansion of road networks and the installation of signaling networks (stop signs, traffic lights, etc.) is costly and complex.

Property development also has a social impact. Increasing population may require the creation or expansion of first responder networks, health care services, and educational systems. For example, new housing developments aimed at families with children require the creation of additional school capacity. The new neighborhoods may also need fire, police, and ambulance services as well as physicians and hospital beds. Although the ongoing operation of this infrastructure is supported by new property taxes, the developer may need to contribute to its creation.

Approvals

To begin construction of a property, the developer must receive approval of the development plan. Prior to being granted plan approval, the developer must gain permission from many government agencies. Collectively, these reviews, permits and agreements to proceed are known as approvals. Among the many approvals required for a typical development project are:

- **Geotechnical investigation:** Soil conditions, the presence of groundwater, and subsurface rock must be determined prior to preparing a development plan.
- **Environmental:** The property must be assessed to determine if it requires environmental clean up or possess wetlands or endangered species that would be affected by development. Phase 1 environmental surveys and inspections are required to determine the prior site uses and its current status. If environmental issues are found, further Phase 2 testing must be performed and remediation must be planned. The state's department of environmental protection must approve environmental findings. In the case of wetland and wildlife issues, approvals from the U.S. Fish and Wildlife Service or the Army Corps of Engineers may be required.

- **Traffic:** Traffic impact on the surrounding road network and site access must be assessed and if required, proposed improvements must be submitted to the state's department of transportation.
- **Water, sewage, and power:** The requirements for usage must be determined and a request for service placed with the appropriate providers. Lack of available capacity may stall a development project.
- **Zoning:** The proposed development plan must be reviewed to verify that it conforms with the local zoning ordinance. Title reports and American Land Title Association (ALTA) and boundary and topographic surveys are used to determine the current state of the property and existing encumbrances such as utility easements.
- **Development plan:** The reports listed in this box are used to prepare concept and final site plans, including building configurations for submission to local planning authorities.

11.1.5 Preleasing

Preleasing is the leasing of space prior to the start of a construction project. During the preleasing phase, the developer seeks to identify tenants for all uncommitted space. By identifying tenants early, the developer limits the chance that there will be space constructed that remains vacant after completion. Having vacant space postcompletion requires the developer to carry the interest charges, taxes, and operational costs of the unused space. The construction lender will also want to have its loan repaid, and the long-term takeout lender will not make a loan on a property that has limited cash flow. Due to these risks, construction lenders will not agree to fund a project until a given level of preleasing has been achieved. The required level of preleasing is market dependent—typically 70 percent or higher.

The inability to attract tenants to a development may be a function of a poorly conceived project or an indication that the developer has misestimated the market demand for the type of space being created. If preleasing cannot be accomplished, it may be a reason to rethink the project plan, downsize it, or delay it until demand improves.

11.1.6 Construction Contract Negotiation
11.1.6.1 Risk Management

There are three major risks in construction. The first is that the project that actually gets built differs from the one you negotiated. Projects morph as they take form. Features that looked great on a plan may not work in physical form, which can cause the project requirements to change over time. This effect is known as scope creep. The need to change a project while it is in progress leaves, the construction contract open to renegotiation when the developer's leverage is reduced.

The second is that the project is not built on time. In a construction project, time truly is money because the developer is paying interest costs on funds borrowed while the project is not yet generating any income. The longer the project takes, the more it costs. The developer has also made commitments to tenants to provide them with occupancy on a certain date. If the project is not completed on time, there will likely be a requirement to pay penalties to the tenants and they may have the option to walk away from their lease commitments.

The last risk is that the property goes over budget. All construction projects involve uncertainty. Labor and materials prices change over time. The developer may begin building on a site and then discover conditions that were unexpected. To protect against going over budget, projects contain a budget item for contingencies—the myriad unforeseen items that always occur during construction.

11.1.6.2 Construction Contracts

Construction contracts allocate the risk of cost estimation between the developer and the construction company. The major types of contracts are described in the following subsections.

11.1.6.2.1 Lump Sum

In a lump sum contract, the construction company agrees to build a defined project at a fixed price. Cost overruns within the original defined project are the responsibility of the construction company. In the event that the contract can be completed at less than the estimated cost, the construction company retains the savings as additional profit.

11.1.6.2.2 Guaranteed Maximum Price

Many developers look to a construction company to use its expertise in construction methods, cost estimation, and material and labor sourcing to provide a firm bid at which they will build a project, which is called a guaranteed maximum price contract (GMP). Subject to the key term that the project scope remains the same, the contractor agrees to take the risk that the project, as specified, will be built on budget. If the project can be completed at below the estimated cost, any savings are returned to the developer. This situation is considered the most favorable construction contract from the developer's point of view.

11.1.6.2.3 Time and Materials

A time and materials (T&M) contract is typically used when the construction company cannot accurately estimate the costs of completing a given project. In this contract, the construction company is paid for the actual labor and materials required to complete the project as well as a profit margin. It is considered the least favorable option by the developer, who accepts all of the risk of cost overruns. This contract is also known as a cost plus contract.

Comparison of contracts:

Party responsible for	Lump sum	Guaranteed max price	Time & materials
Cost overrun	Contractor	Contractor	Developer
Cost savings	Contractor	Developer	Developer

11.1.7 Sitework

The first stage of sitework is to survey the existing property to determine the soil quality and existing geography. Once the site has been surveyed, the physical work of preparing the land to accept a building can begin.

In many cases, environmental considerations come into play when planning for sitework. One must consider the unique environmental qualities of the parcel and whether it provides a home to wildlife or contains wetlands that host migratory birds or generates runoff that feeds a protected watershed. These conditions may limit the portion of the available land that may be developed. Although these considerations would have been taken into account when the decision was made to purchase the parcel, it is never possible to make an absolute evaluation until you are working on the site.

In other cases, zoning considerations come into play. Buildings may have to be located a certain distance from any edge of a property; this restriction is called a setback. Buildings may have to provide easements for infrastructure features such as power lines or for views (scenic easements). These complicate the ultimate layout of buildings on a site. Land on which structures can be located are called building envelopes.

Once the building sites have been identified, these areas must be prepared to receive the intended structures, which may require the clearing of existing structures or the removal of geologic features such as excess slope or rock. Certain buildings require foundations that entail digging, moving, and relocating dirt. This is expensive work.

Sitework is a risky stage of the project because existing underground conditions, no matter how well they are tested, are never completely knowable. Sitework contractors will usually not accept the risk of cost containment on unexpected site conditions.

An additional part of the sitework process is the creation of an infrastructure layer for the development site. This step includes the facilitation of water, sewer, power, and communications utilities to the building sites. It also involves the creation of access roads that intersect with the public road network.

11.1.8 Pad Delivery

The goal of sitework is to create a pad on which the desired building may be constructed. In a parcel that is being split into individual building sites that will ultimately be owned by different parties, the developer is responsible for delivering the pads to the new user. Once the pads are completed, the developer will turn them over to their new users who will begin construction. If the developer retains ownership, it will continue with the project and construct its own buildings.

11.1.9 Foundation Work/Shell Construction

During the construction phase, a foundation is prepared and the building shell is erected according to the specified plans. This phase involves the completion of the outer shell of the property, the floor plates, and the major interior mechanical systems. These systems include vertical transportation (elevators and escalators); environmental control systems (air flow, heating, and air conditioning); and utility distribution and control systems. These systems may be specified by and for individual tenants or considered part of the common amenities of a multitenant building. Once the building shell is completed, interior spaces are turned over for tenant fit-out.

11.1.10 Tenant Fit-out

During the final stage, tenant fit-out, work is done to prepare the interior environment for its ultimate purpose. This stage is generally tenant-specified, except in multifamily buildings and hotels. A tenant will typically have an interior designer working with the landlord to facilitate turning the raw core and shell into a functional or habitable environment.

The costs of tenant fit-out are generally split between the developer and the tenant. The developer agrees to provide the space in a certain initial condition and then to provide a cash allowance toward the further interior construction needs of the tenant. The tenant may need to add to this allowance, depending on the level of finish and furnishings they require.

For the developer, the fit-out phase ends with the tenant taking possession of the space. Possession occurs at a negotiated time or upon occupancy. Possession is followed by, or concurrent with, rent commencement: the date at which the tenant actually starts paying rent and other occupancy charges.

11.2 KEY PARTICIPANTS

11.2.1 Developer

The developer as the principal actor in a real estate project oversees the creation of the development plan and then manages its implementation. Developers are also the driving financial force behind the project, either providing the equity investment or sourcing it from investors.

11.2.2 Construction Manager

On complex projects, the developer may hire a construction manager (CM) to coordinate all of the tasks and the players required to construct the asset. There are two ways in which CMs can interact with developers. In the first method, the developer uses the CM as its trusted advisor. The developer may empower the CM to make on site decisions that can expedite the completion of the project, rather than having those decisions queued for the developer's approval. In this scenario, the CM is always working to minimize cost and maximize the efficiency of the construction process.

In the second method, the construction manager is at risk, the CM acts as both an advisor and as a general contractor assembling the team of construction trades that will actually complete the project. Under this type of relationship, the CM may execute a GMP contract with the developer, using his or her skills to mitigate construction costs.

11.2.3 General Contractor

The general contractor plans and supervises the actual construction of the project according to the plans and specifications set forth by the architects and engineers. The general contractor also enters into a construction contract with the developer. Typically, this contract is funded by the developer's construction lender. The general contractor hires specialists in the various construction trades and coordinates the staging of their work. These specialists execute contracts with the general contractor and are known as subcontractors or "subs."

11.2.4 Clerk of the Works

The Clerk of the Works (CoW) is generally a degreed accountant with experience in construction accounting who acts as the chief administrative officer of a construction project. The CoW represents the developer by monitoring the progress of the project. The CoW collects and stores all of the project documents, including permits, government approvals, and construction contracts; processes all invoices; records all change orders; and maintains the project accounts on behalf of the developer.

11.2.5 Planners and Architects

Planners help the developer set forth the development concept, size the project based on the land parcel, and determine required uses and zoning. Planners may also lay out the buildings on the site and then work with local officials to get the project approved for development.

Architects work with the developer to take the project forward from the conceptual stage to the actual building designs. They are responsible for creating the construction drawings filed with government agencies and used by the general contractor.

Landscape architects are specialized professionals who work as part of the architectural team to create the outdoor environment and the physical context for a project. Beautiful spaces can be great attractors for customers and increase the value of a project.

11.2.6 Engineers

There are many types of engineers involved in the planning and construction of a development project, as described in the following subsections.

11.2.6.1 Traffic

Traffic engineers estimate the impact on the road network caused by the planned development project. They specify a plan to provide for easy access from the site to and from the existing road network and for improvements to the local road network to support, or mitigate, the additional traffic created by the new development. These projects are called onsite improvements.

On occasion, distant road networks can be affected by a new development. The developer may be called upon to plan for improvements to these roads as well. These projects are called offsite improvements. The developer will be asked to pay part or all of the cost of both onsite and offsite improvements to the road network. These costs must be considered as part of the development pro forma.

11.2.6.2 Civil

Civil engineers plan for the project's infrastructure, including water, sewer, and electric service, as well as for the design of certain aspects of complex buildings.

11.2.6.3 Structural

Structural engineers collaborate with architects to design complex building structures. They work to ensure that building designs can withstand loads and environmental stresses such as wind, climate changes, and earthquakes. In sustainable design, structural engineers work to create structures that minimize the amount of materials used to construct a given building.

11.2.6.4 Mechanical

Mechanical engineers can help developers plan for major building systems such as vertical transportation, including elevators and escalators, as well as for climate control systems including heating, ventilation, and air conditioning (HVAC).

11.2.6.5 Environmental

Environmental engineers test the site for the presence of environmental contaminants. They examine the impact of the planned development on the existing natural environment, including open spaces, waterways, and ecosystems. In renovation and demolition situations, the environmental engineer checks the structure for contaminants that may be released into the ground or air as part of the reconstruction work. Environmental engineers also help plan for the orderly removal of any contaminants found and facilitate the reuse of the existing sites and structures.

11.2.6.6 Geotechnical

Geotechnical engineers assess geologic features of a development site including soil and groundwater conditions. They work with architects, as well as civil and structural engineers to design appropriate structures and construction methods given the observed site conditions.

11.2.6.7 LEED

Leadership in Energy and Environmental Design (LEED) is a term coined by the U.S. Green Building Council (USGBC) to reflect the incorporation of sustainable design principles into both newly constructed and redeveloped buildings. LEED professionals help the development team incorporate these principles into the construction and renovation process. The successful incorporation of LEED principles can result in the building achieving LEED certification which is a criteria used by environmentally conscious tenants, including the U.S. government, when leasing space.

11.2.6.8 Specialized Technical Consultants

There are many specialized technical consultants who are brought into a project depending on its requirements, including acoustical, security, telecommunications, lighting, and parking experts.

11.2.6.9 Local Officials

In the United States, many of the decisions regarding land use are made at the local government level (county, township, city, or borough, depending on the region involved). Local officials acting independently or as part of a geographic region are responsible for providing much of the infrastructure that supports the citizens' quality of life, including schools, hospitals, first responders, local roads, public transportation, and utilities such as water, sewer, and power. As such, these officials attempt to manage demands on this infrastructure by placing constraints on growth where necessary.

Local officials also attempt to manage the quality of the aesthetic environment by aggregating development by use into specific geographic regions and defining the density, heights, building quality, and other factors that create the character of the ultimate property so that it is in agreement with their constituents' vision for their community.

11.2.6.10 Lawyers

Lawyers research and enumerate the transactions and approvals that must be obtained in order to complete a development project. They negotiate agreements on behalf of their clients and the many counterparties that are involved in the project. They document these agreements according to existing legal or regulatory protocol and provide an archival record of those documents for reference as the project matures.

Among the many legal documents required for a development project are the purchase and sale contract, construction loan, building permit, zoning amendments, preliminary and final site plan approvals, traffic approval, building permit, and certificate of occupancy.

11.2.6.11 Construction Lenders

Construction lenders specialize in financing development projects. The typical construction loan provides funds for the construction of the structures and public spaces that constitute a development project. These funds are advanced to the contractors who are undertaking the construction work in the form of periodic draws based on the amount of work that has been completed during the period.

When preparing to lend to a project, the construction lender will work with the developer and chosen contractors to understand the work plan for the development. Once the project has commenced, the construction lender, or their representative, monitors the progress of the project by visiting the site and physically inspecting the work as it is being performed.

The developer pays the lender for the financing commitment and other services provided during the course of the project. At completion, the developer is expected to repay the construction loan with the proceeds from the sale of the project or a refinancing of the stabilized asset by a permanent lender.

Many developers use the services of commercial mortgage brokers to identify lenders who are interested in providing construction loans.

11.2.6.12 Leasing Agents

Developers and financing sources are all interested in the market for potential users of the to-be-built development project. The existence of measurable levels of tenant demand is the greatest indicator of the potential success of a development project. Leasing agents are constantly working to identify businesses and individuals in the market that have a requirement for space. In a similar manner, leasing agents reach out to a network of landlords to determine their available space. The agent acts to match the potential tenant with a space that meets their needs.

The developer employs leasing agents to represent its new projects with prospective tenants. In a typical leasing transaction, the prospective tenant will also retain a separate leasing agent to represent its interests. In major commercial transactions, the agents for the respective parties will work out the details of the lease agreement with the help of legal counsel.

11.2.6.13 Sales Agents

Many development projects are built for sale. Commercial properties can be marketed to investors who seek to hold stabilized assets for growth and income. Multifamily condominium projects are developed for sale to many end users. Real estate brokers are employed to facilitate these sales by marketing the properties, identifying qualified purchasers, and processing transactions.

Some developers like to control leasing and sales efforts and thus employ their own leasing and sales agents, known as an in-house brokerage force. Others like to outsource this work to third-party real estate brokerage firms.

11.2.6.14 Marketing Firms

Marketing firms assist the leasing and sales effort by publicizing the development project and its benefits to potential tenants who may not be known to the leasing brokerage community. The marketing campaign can involve the Internet, traditional direct mail, print advertising, outdoor signage, TV, radio, promotional events, and incentives.

11.3 FINANCING STAGES

11.3.1 Predevelopment

In many cases, during the predevelopment stage the only asset of the project is the intellectual capital of the partners and, as such, the project's financial risk is very high. At this stage, land may be optioned, but it is unlikely to be owned. It is uncertain as to whether appropriate zoning and entitlements will be achieved or whether sufficient tenants will make commitments.

Land Options

A developer expends significant costs to initiate a development project. Without owning the land or having the right to acquire the property, the developer would have no reason to bear these costs.

Under an option agreement, the land owner grants the developer an option to acquire a land parcel at a stated price during a period of time. This time period typically extends from six months to a number of years, depending on the complexity of the project being attempted.

Land owners can benefit from the value created when a developer uses their property as the site of a new project. If the land owner wants to encourage the development process, it will grant the developer an option at little or no cost. If the site has great perceived value and the developer is in competition for the right to develop the property, the land owner may charge a fee for the land option. In some cases, an option includes a "free look" period during which the developer can pursue the project at no cost, followed by paid extension options.

The developer holding the option agrees to use its best efforts to pursue the development, gain the requisite approvals, and bring the project to fruition.

The land option ends at expiration or when the property is acquired by the developer. The land acquisition typically takes place concurrently with the start of construction and may be financed as part of the construction loan.

In some cases in which the certainty of development is high and many developers are interested in the land, the owner may not agree to option the land but may insist that the interested developer acquire the land. This step shifts the entitlement risk from the land owner to the developer.

The land owner may also seek to improve the value of the property by attempting to take it through the approval process at its own cost. The land owner can then sell the entitled property to a developer at a much higher price because the developer will not have to bear the costs and uncertainty of the entitlement process.

During the predevelopment stage, the developer generally commits its own capital to move the project forward. That capital can be sourced from a venture created for this purpose, but it is unlikely to come from a traditional financial institution.

If the development enterprise has other assets, it is possible that a bank will provide financing for predevelopment through a line of credit collateralized by an interest in these other stabilized assets.

In order to conserve this precious venture-level capital, many developers look to their cadre of professionals to lower their fees for work performed at this risk-laden stage of the project. These reduced fee arrangements may include deferred payments until the project begins construction and further rate reductions in the event of project failure. Developers can reward their professionals for this accommodation by providing them with work at premium fees on projects that are successful.

11.3.2 Construction

The construction phase begins with the acquisition of the land or existing structure that is the site of the new project. Depending on the financial climate, the construction lender may or may not be willing to support land acquisition as part of their financing package. In a tight market, the bank may require that the developer acquire the land with its own equity and pledge it as collateral for the construction loan. In easy credit markets, the bank may allow the developer to finance all or part of the land acquisition with proceeds from

Budget								
Year	**One**				**Two**			
Quarter	**One**	**Two**	**Three**	**Four**	**One**	**Two**	**Three**	**Four**
Sitework	$100,000							
Shell construction		$50,000	$100,000	$250,000	$250,000	$150,000		
Retainage	–$10,000	–$15,000	–$10,000	–$25,000	–$25,000	–$15,000		
Tenant allowance						$100,000	$100,000	$50,000
Leasing commission					$50000			$50000
Contingency	$5,000	$7,500	$5,000	$12,500	$15,000	$12,500	$5,000	$5,000
	$95,000	$142,500	$95,000	$237,500	$290,000	$247,500	$105,000	$205,000
Construction loan								
Beginning balance	—	$95,000	$239,400	$339,188	$583,472	$885,141	$1,150,344	$1,278,351
Interest	—	$1,900	$4,788	$6,784	$11,669	$17,703	$23,007	$25,567
Draw	$95,000	$142,500	$95,000	$237,500	$290,000	$247,500	$105,000	205,000
Ending Balance	$95,000	$239,400	$339,188	$583,472	$885,141	$1,150,344	$1,278,351	$1,508,918

the construction loan. Once the site is acquired construction begins. The contractor invoices the developer at regular intervals for the work completed in that period. The developer aggregates these invoices and makes a draw request to the construction lender. The lender may send an inspector to the site to verify that the work has been completed. The construction loan ends at the completion of construction of the project.

11.3.2.1 Construction Draw Schedule
The following example sets forth the budget for a simple construction project. The costs involved are $200,000 for sitework, $800,000 for construction of the building shell, $250,000 for tenant allowance, and $100,000 for leasing commissions. Retainage is an amount set aside from each contractor payment to be held by the developer until the project is completed. A contingency account is provided for cost overruns equal to 5 percent of amounts due for building and sitework. This amount is assumed to be spent during the course of the project.

In this example, it is assumed amounts are billed and paid at the end of each quarter. Interest is also accrued at the end of each quarter on the beginning balance at 8 percent.

The maximum amount that a bank will lend in a construction loan is typically stated as "the lesser of (a) X percent of cost and (b) Y percent of property value at stabilization." It is expected that property value at stabilization will be greater than cost, given that the development process should create significant value. It has been possible at times to borrow 100 percent of cost, most banks like to see significant equity instead by the developer and limit X to 80 percent. The constraint on Y is the LTV ratio available on permanent loans on similar properties.

11.3.3 Take-Out
When the project is completed the developer looks to "take out" the construction loan with permanent financing. The permanent financing, known as a take-out loan, is typically a mortgage provided by a financial institution that provides long-term financing against stable assets. Take-out loans are provided by insurance companies, pension funds, and the CMBS market. If the developer intends to sell the asset, an assumable mortgage may be sought so that the financing can be transferred to the new owner.

If the developer wants to obtain the maximum proceeds from the take-out financing, the property must be substantially leased with creditworthy tenants under long-term leases. If the property has not achieved full lease-up, then the developer can seek short-term financing. Short-term financing, typically at floating interest rates, is usually provided by a commercial bank. In some cases, the construction loan may have a built in provision for a short-term extension upon completion. This type of two-step financing construction loan followed by a short-term mortgage is known as a mini-perm. A mini-perm allows the developer to complete the lease-up of the asset and maximize cash flow before entering the permanent loan market. Having a stabilized property increases the probability that the developer can find advantageous long-term financing.

11.4 GOVERNMENT FINANCE

Governments see a public purpose in the economic activity and social good created by many real estate development projects. To incentivize developers to undertake projects that have uncertain or insufficient economics, governments use a number of financial incentive programs. In the United States, there are programs at the federal, state, and local levels to promote economic development.

11.4.1 Grants

Government grants are gifts of cash made to developers that are applied to reduce project costs. By applying grants, developers reduce the capital they need to source to complete a project and raise the returns on the privately sourced equity. By creating additional support for borrowings, government grants encourage private lenders to fund development projects.

11.4.2 Loan Guarantees

By guaranteeing loans, the government can make capital available to high-risk development projects and reduce the cost of capital needed for the typical development project. In both cases, the government loan guarantee reduces developer financing costs and improves developer economics.

In some cases, the government can charge the developer a guarantee fee that may be supported by the project if it is successful.

11.4.3 Tax-Exempt Bonds

Tax-exempt bonds are securities issued by government entities on behalf of a private project. The interest paid to bondholders is exempt from one or more levels of taxation. Tax-exempt securities are attractive to high-income investors who pay income taxes at high marginal rates. The credit for the bond varies and is typically tied to the success of the project rather than a government guarantee.

11.4.4 Low-Interest Loans

Government entities may lend funds at reduced interest rates to help developers to make their projects economically feasible. The government may use tax revenues to fund these bonds or may borrow in the market to fund the project using the government's own credit worthiness.

11.4.5 Tax Credits

Tax credits are granted to developers in return for their investing funds in qualifying projects. A tax credit allows a tax payer to avoid paying tax on a like amount of income. For example: a taxpayer with income of $1,000 purchases a tax credit of $100 per year for three years. The tax credit reduces the beneficiary's taxable income by $100, from $1,000 to $900. Each year, the holder saves tax equal to $100 times the marginal tax rate of 35 percent or $35. The present value of the three years of tax savings equals:

value of tax credit = PV from date of tax savings back to date of purchase of

(amount of tax credit × highest marginal tax rate)

	Year 1	Year 2	Year 3
Without Credit			
Income	$1,000	$1,000	$1,000
Tax rate	0.35	0.35	0.35
Tax without credit	$350	$350	$350
With Tax Credit			
Income	$1,000	$1,000	$1,000
Tax Credit	(100)	(100)	(100)
Income after credit	$900	$900	$900
Tax rate	0.35	0.35	0.35
Tax after credit	$315	$315	$315
Tax Savings	$35	$35	$35
PV@ 10% = $87.04			

Tax credits are typically transferable and are sold for cash proceeds to taxpayers with high marginal tax rates. The proceeds are used by developers to supplement the private equity in a qualifying project.

11.4.6 Tax Abatements

In order to encourage development, the government may reduce or eliminate the taxes that it would otherwise charge once the project is completed. A typical use of tax abatements is in multifamily housing, where the abatements give real estate tax relief to landlords of newly built or renovated apartments. The tax abatement lowers the landlord's operating costs and in turn improves the economics of a project so that it can be more competitive in the rental market while showing improved returns to the landlord. These higher returns make it feasible for the landlord to finance a project in the private capital markets.

Sometimes tax abatements are offered for projects to be developed in specific areas that are economically challenged. This type of offer can attract development and ultimately job creation to these disadvantaged areas.

11.4.7 Tax Increment Financing

In a tax increment financing (TIF), a developer is allowed to borrow the NPV of the future tax revenues that are expected to be created by a prospective development project. The borrowing creates a capital source that helps the developer pay for the project or improve its economics. Tax revenues collected from activities related to the new project are used to repay the borrowing. From the government's point of view, it is giving away a limited portion of future revenues from a development project that would not have been feasible "but for" the assistance of the TIF program. Once the borrowing is repaid, any additional taxes collected revert to the government.

11.5 DEVELOPMENT RISKS

Real estate development is a capital-intensive business with considerable up-front investment and highly uncertain outcomes. For this reason, investors in development projects demand a return that is well above that offered by the purchase of comparable in-service assets. If premium returns cannot be achieved by developing a new property, then it is better to invest in completed, stabilized properties.

11.5.1 Entitlement Delays

The many approvals necessary for a development project all rely on the somewhat independent actions of many different government agencies. Because these agencies work on their own time schedules, the time required to compete the entire process is difficult to estimate. If a project is delayed, the developer runs the risk of losing tenant commitments or having to pay displaced tenants fines as compensation for missing projected move in dates.

11.5.2 Construction Cost Overruns

At the beginning of a development project, a budget setting forth the expected costs is created by the developer with input from the many professionals working on the project. A critical part of any project is the cost of construction because it is a large proportion of the overall cost.

11.5.3 Unexpected Conditions

Many projects involve preparing a site to receive buildings. On greenfield sites—raw land that has not previously held a structure—this preparation can require excavation and earth moving. It is an expensive process and problematic to estimate because it is difficult to see underground. Brownfield redevelopment involves reclaiming previously developed sites that may have some level of environmental contamination. It can be difficult to judge the extent of the work required to clean up the site and return it to a buildable condition.

11.5.4 Material/Labor Cost Increases

Material and labor costs fluctuate in the marketplace during the course of a construction project. Construction firms use sophisticated models to estimate materials and labor requirements and can use hedging techniques to limit material price changes. For a fee, which may be embedded in the contractor's bid, the contractor generally is willing to offer a maximum price contract for building a project according to a set of detailed specifications.

11.5.5 Scope Changes

The guaranteed maximum price is for building the project to specification. The project requirements often change during construction. There are numerous reasons for these changes. First, the tenants may change their requirements during the construction phase, or the tenants may change and the new tenants may have different requirements. Second, as the property takes physical form it may turn out that the actual product looks different or does not work as well in real life as it did on paper. In either case, and for many other reasons, the developer may need to change the project plans.

Once the developer requests changes, the contractor issues a change order detailing the modifications to the plan and the extra charges, if any, involved. The developer then signs the change order and agrees to the new costs. The banks will also want to see the change order and understand the reasons for the changes. Change orders are typically very expensive, as the developer has limited ability to negotiate in the middle of a live construction project.

11.5.6 Delayed Speculative Lease-Up

When planning a commercial real estate project, most developers begin with a significant amount of preleasing—tenant leases signed ahead of the start of construction. Knowing that there is committed tenant interest and being able to accurately estimate rents reduces the financial risk of the development project. For this reason, most banks require that a set percentage of lease-up is achieved, typically 50 to 75 percent of the to-be-built space, before the construction loan is made. This level of tenant interest gives the bank comfort that the project will be economically viable upon completion.

The stronger the market, the easier it is for developers to lease space. If there is strong demand and little available space, tenants are willing to lease space ahead of construction. In weak markets, unless the project is uniquely attractive, tenants can find space at a discount in existing projects. The lack of preleasing serves as a brake on new development and retards the creation of additional supply.

In the residential market, preleasing is more difficult to achieve. In the rental market, residential tenants typically do not make decisions far in advance of their needs. In the for-sale residential market, prospective buyers may be willing to commit further in advance but may not ultimately honor their commitments if the market declines sharply.

Once the threshold lease-up (or pre-sale level) has been achieved, the project commences. The time it takes to complete lease-up to a stabilized level ultimately determines the cost of the project and its profitability. While the built space sits vacant, the developer must pay both the cost of the interest on the construction loan and the expenses of operating the vacant space. During the construction period, these costs are capitalized (added as an additional capital expense) into the cost of the project. If the time to lease-up exceeds the time originally expected, the project will perform below budget, as the cost of the asset will have increased without a commensurate increase in revenue. In fact, the developer may have to drop pricing expectations if the asset remains vacant for a significant period of time.

Delayed lease-up can also have an impact on the ability of a developer to obtain take-out financing at a level that will allow the repayment of the construction note. If this situation occurs, the developer may have to post additional equity, or the project may fail, in which case the developer will be unable to pay off the construction loan at maturity.

11.5.7 Excessive Interest Carry

If a project exceeds budget for any reason, the construction loan balance will be higher than expected and the interest cost, known as interest carry, may be higher than expected. Interest carry may also be higher than expected if the loan is made on a floating-rate basis and interest rates rise. To mitigate this risk, many developers will agree to hedge the interest rate risk with an interest rate swap. The swap will fix the interest rate for the expected duration of the loan. It is difficult, however, to swap a construction loan because the outstanding amount of the loan at any given time is difficult to determine.

EXAMPLE

The following example illustrates the previous example construction loan, assuming that it is a floating-rate loan at a credit spread of 500 basis points above three-month LIBOR. An increasing portion of the construction loan balance is swapped from LIBOR to a fixed interest rate of 3 percent. All of the swaps are forward starting and terminate at the maturity of the loan at the end of year two.

(Continued)

In each period that a swap is in place, the borrower pays the fixed rate times the amount swapped and receives from the counterparty LIBOR times the same amount. The borrower then pays the LIBOR payment to the bank along with the credit spread. The net result is that the swapped portion of the loan costs the borrower the fixed rate plus the credit spread. On the remaining amount outstanding, the borrower pays LIBOR plus the credit spread.

On unswapped amount:

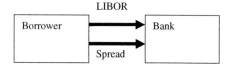

On swapped amount:

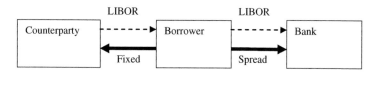

11.6 REAL OPTIONS

It is possible to view many development projects as a series of smaller projects, the success of which informs the decision to build additional space. For example, a garden apartment development may have land available to build ten buildings, each with 40 units. The developer may start by building four buildings and then observe the market reception to the project before deciding whether to continue. By purchasing the land for the expanded project, the developer has created an option to continue the project, known as a real option.

11.6.1 Ability to Continue Development

The opportunity to expand a property exists with many development projects and other existing assets. Although often overlooked because of its speculative nature and lack of near term cash flow, the option for future growth can be quite valuable.

Year	One				Two			
Quarter	One	Two	Three	Four	One	Two	Three	Four
Beginning Balance	–	$95,000	$239,400	$339,188	$583,472	$885,141	$1,150,344	$1,278,351
Amount Swapped	–	–	$200,000	$300,000	$400,000	$500,000	$600,000	$700,000
Swap Pay			3.0%	3.0%	3.0%	3.0%	3.0%	3.0%
Spread			5.0%	5.0%	5.0%	5.0%	5.0%	5.0%
	0.0	0.0	8.0%	8.0%	8.0%	8.0%	8.0%	8.0%
Swap Interest	–	–	$4,000	$6,000	$8,000	$10,000	$12,000	$14,000
Amount Floating	–	$95,000	$39,400	$39,188	$183,472	$385,141	$550,344	$578,351
LIBOR	2.0%	2.0%	2.5%	3.0%	2.8%	3.0%	3.5%	3.5%
Spread	5.0%	5.0%	5.0%	5.0%	5.0%	5.0%	5.0%	5.0%
	7.0%	7.0%	7.5%	8.0%	7.8%	8.0%	8.5%	8.5%
Floating Interest	–	$1,663	$739	$784	$3,555	$7,703	$11,695	$12,290
Total nterest	–	$1,663	$4,739	$6,784	$11,555	$17,703	$23,695	$26,290
Draw	$95,000	$142,500	$95,000	$237,500	$290,000	$247,500	$105,000	$205,000
Ending Balance	$95,000	$239,163	$339,139	$583,472	$885,027	$1,150,344	$1,279,039	$1,509,641

The ability to continue expansion of a successful project after the initial phase has proven successful and the property that has achieved a high degree of market acceptance represents a lower risk proposition to the investor that a new untested project. Hence, all else being equal, the discount rate applied to the analysis of a potential expansion of a successful asset should be less than that applied to the original investment.

11.6.2 Real Options are Undervalued in Acquisition Analysis

When valuing a development project or an in service asset, a value should be attributed to any option to continue development. Given that most real estate trades are based on current cash flow, the opportunity to expand a property beyond its current physical form generally is not taken into consideration when pricing is negotiated. This situation implies that a property with the opportunity for expansion may be underpriced in the marketplace.

Glossary

Approvals
Build to suit
Building envelope
Clerk of the Works
Construction manager
Contingency
Core and shell
Cost plus contract
Entitlement
First responder
General conditions
General contractor
Greenfield
Guaranteed maximum price
Heating, ventilation, and air conditioning (HVAC)
In house brokerage
Infrastructure
Interest carry
Leadership in Energy and Environmental Design (LEED)
Lump sum contract
Mini-perm loan
Offsite improvements
Onsite improvements
Pad delivery
Planners
Predevelopment
Preleasing
Real options
Rent commencement
Retainage
Scope creep
Set back
Shell construction
Signaling network
Site selection
Sitework
Speculative or spec development
Subcontractor or sub
Take-out loan
Tax abatement
Tax credit
Tax incentive financing
Tenant driven
Tenant fit-out
Time and materials contract
Traffic mitigation
U.S. Green Building Council (USGBC)

Thought Questions

1. Farmer MacDonald has had a family farm for five generations but non of the kids has any interest in agriculture. Real Smart Development Company says they can buy the farm for 8 times its value as agricultural land, but only if MacDonad will grant them a no-cost five-year option on the land at that very attractive price. What factors should the farmer consider in making this decision?

2. What are the risks of using a land lease as a financing vehicle? Can these risks be mitigated? If so, how? If not, why not?

3. The City's economic development officer is holding up approval of a TIF package for a proposed waterfront mixed-use development. The program was conceived to help development in economically challenged areas. This is a great project for the City but the most attractive land in the City should support development without government help. Do you think this is an appropriate use of a TIF?

Review Questions

The Center at Cobble Creek is a mixed use project with apartments, office and a retail center. The cost of construction was $200 million, before interest.

1. Cobble Creek was originally financed with $60 million of equity and a construction loan for $140 million. The construction period was eight quarters in length. The construction draws at $20 million each were made at the end of the second through eighth quarters. Interest accrued on all draws at 10 percent, compounded quarterly. Prepare a draw schedule showing interest and principal.

2. The project is expected to show NOI of $20 million in its first year of operation. The property will be managed by a third-party management firm for $500,000. Calculate the expected first-year ROA.

3. At the end of the project, the developers believe the property should be valued using a 6 percent cap rate on the $20 million NOI, without adjustment. How much do they believe the property is worth? What is the value of the developer's equity after repaying the construction loan and all accrued interest?

4. First Bank has proposed a ten-year, 6 percent, fixed-rate permanent loan at $160 million with a 25-year amortization schedule. The ten year treasury bond is currently 3.5 percent. First Bank believes that this is a 55 percent LTV loan. At what cap rate are they valuing the property?

5. Second Bank comes in with a $180 million, seven-year, floating-rate loan proposition with a 20-year amortization schedule. The seven-year treasury is currently 3.0 percent. The swap premium to fix the loan is 1.0 percent. The loan spread is 250 basis points. Second Bank believes the property

should have a 7.5 percent cap rate. Contrast this loan to the First Bank offer in review question 4 by calculating LTV, debt service, and first-year DSCR (based on NOI) for each loan.

6. A joint venture partner approaches and offers $25 million for a 40 percent share of the equity. The partner is a pension fund and would like a convertible preferred stock that pays a 6 percent dividend and converts into a 40 percent ownership interest at the end of a seven-year hold period. Do you accept the offer?

7. Mutual of Atlanta, a large insurance company that buys properties for its real estate investment account, comes forth with an unsolicited bid for the property at $300 million. They can close in 90 days. Analyze the implications of their offer.

8. The site for the Cobble Creek development was priced at $40 million. In addition to an outright sale, the prior land owner originally offered a number of financing alternatives:

   a) An unsubordinated ground lease at $4 million per year
   b) A subordinated ground lease at $6 million per year
   c) Contribution of the site into the joint venture for a 50 percent equity interest
   d) A three-year option at $1 million per year

   Prepare an economic analysis and state the pros and cons of each offer.

9. Assume the following circumstances in review question 8:
   - You have $10 million of capital available to pursue this project.
   - Predevelopment costs excluding land are expected to be $5 million.
   - There is a 40 percent chance the project will progress to construction.
   - The bank will not lend unless you have "control of the land."

   Do these facts affect your decision?

Multiple Choice Questions

1. In which order does a development transaction progress?
   a) site selection, entitlement, construction, tenant fit out
   b) entitlement, site selection, construction, tenant fit out
   c) site selection, entitlement, tenant fit out, construction
   d) site selection, tenant fit out, entitlement, construction

2. Put the following stages of the development process in the correct order:
   A. Entitlement
   B. Site-work
   C. Pre development
   D. Pre-leasing
   E. Shell construction
   F. Tenant fit-out
   G. Pad delivery
   I. C, A, D, B, F, E, G

II. D, C, A, B, E, F, G

III. A, D, C, B, G, E, F

IV. C, A, D, B, G, E, F

3. Which of the following is *not* a type of development financing?
   a) FAR
   b) Construction loan
   c) Take-out loan
   d) Mini-perm

4. Stages of a development project include sale (S), completion and occupancy (C&O), management (M), construction (C), and land acquisition (LA). Place these in the correct sequence.
   a) C, C&O, M, S, LA
   b) LA, C&O, M, S, C
   c) C, LA, C&O, S, M
   d) LA, C, C&O, M, S

5. Which of the following are typical contingencies prior to obtaining a permanent loan commitment?
   a) Exculpation
   b) Lease-up
   c) Approved design changes
   d) Completion by date certain

6. Which category of development costs is least likely to be funded by a construction lender?
   a) Interest carry cost
   b) Hard costs
   c) Land acquisition
   d) Soft costs

7. Feasibility analysis determines whether a project is currently feasible given:
   a) Prevailing market rents
   b) Existing land prices
   c) Financing costs
   d) All of the above

8. Put the stages of the land development process in the proper order:
   a) Contact Broker, Option, Development, Sales
   b) Contact Broker, Development, Option, Sales
   c) Development, Contact Broker, Sales, Option
   d) Option, Contact Broker, Sales, Development

9. Common land financing mechanisms include all of these except:
   a) Purchase for cash
   b) Down payment plus subordinated seller financing
   c) Long-term debt
   d) Down payment plus loan for a percentage of land value

10. Provisions protecting lenders during development include all of the
    following except:
    a) Conversion
    b) Completion bonds
    c) Title insurance
    d) Holdbacks
11. When you look at the pro forma interest carry for a land development
    loan, you must estimate all of the following except:
    a) Amount of draws
    b) Depreciation
    c) Timing of draws
    d) Projected interest rates

For answers to these Problems and Exercises, please visit the companion
website: http://booksite.elsevier.com/9780123786265

Housing Finance

CONTENTS

12.1 HOUSING FINANCE

Residential housing is by far the largest segment of the US real estate market. The provision of housing is a major driver of the US economy and our national investment in housing is a critical part of our country's wealth.

12.1.1 Basic Human Needs

Food and shelter are the two most basic human needs. Most governments consider the provision of adequate housing for all citizens as a key part of their mission and housing receives more government support and faces more regulation than most other property types. One way in which we judge the quality of a government is in its ability to provide for the basic needs of its population.

12.1.2 Facilitates Regional Economic Development

The availability of affordable housing makes an area attractive to workers. Because the cost of housing is a significant part of the typical family budget, it affects the wages required by workers considering relocation. It is easier for a corporation to grow when affordable housing is readily available for new workers. In contrast, workers relocating to regions with high housing costs demand compensation that allows them to manage those costs.

12.1.3 Major Driver of Overall Economy

In the US, housing represents the largest sector of the real estate industry and is a major store of wealth for the nation. The creation and maintenance of our housing stock accounts for a significant portion of our overall economic activity. As we have seen in the Financial Crisis, changes in the level of house prices and homebuilding activity can have a major impact on the country's economic health.

335

12.2 THE ECONOMIC IMPACT OF THE U.S. HOUSING MARKET

In 2010, there were more than 308 million people in the United States, housed in more than 131 million apartments and houses, at approximately 2.35 people per housing unit. The country's population has been increasing at approximately 2.9 million people per year. Applying the current ratio of 2.35 people per unit to projected population increases means that demand for new units is approximately 1.2 million per year.[1] To this demand we must add the requirement to replace the portion of the existing housing stock that becomes obsolete or is destroyed by casualty. This number is estimated at 300,000 per year, leading to total demand of 1.5 million units. Assuming a unit value of $180,000, the U.S. housing stock would be worth more than $23.5 trillion and maintaining the housing stock of the United States would be an approximately $280 billion per year business. Applying an economic multiplier of 2.5[2] to this estimate approximates a total annual impact of the housing industry on the U.S. economy of $700 billion. The housing industry thus accounts for over 5 percent of the country's gross domestic product of $14 trillion.

The decline in the housing values caused by the Financial Crisis has resulted in decreased demand for housing and a profound decrease in housing starts. Many economists see the decline in housing value as having had a critical impact on the wealth of the average American. This decrease in wealth influences consumer behavior and has contributed to the length and severity of the postcrisis economic malaise.

In addition to the diminished value of housing, as a U.S. consumer store of wealth, the decline in housing value has had a severe impact on the value of associated consumer liabilities, residential mortgages, and associated securities. As a result of consumer defaults, these securities have declined in value. This decline in value has affected the U.S. banking system, the financial institutions that held or hold these securities as a store of value, and the U.S. consumer—who is the ultimate beneficial owner of many of these enterprises. The U.S. government, in an attempt to mitigate the impact of this decline in value on the country's financial institutions purchased billions of dollars of mortgage securities, providing liquidity to the banking system. In doing so, the government has absorbed a portion of the impact of the crisis, in effect redistributing it among the country's citizens by raising the national debt.

It is too early to understand the full long-term impact of the financial crisis on the future of the U.S. economy.

---

[1] http://quickfacts.census.gov/qfd/states/00000.html
[2] http://economics.hia.com.au/media/The%20Economic%20Multiplier%20Effects%20of%20Housing%202011.pdf

12.3 HISTORY

12.3.1 The American Dream

Owning a home has long been a fundamental goal of the American family and an iconic representation of the American way of life. The linkage of home ownership to the American Dream was made by James Truslow Adams in his book *The Epic of America*, which was written in 1931 during the heart of the Great Depression.

12.3.2 Rural versus Urban Life

During the late nineteenth century, the country saw a population shift from rural to urban living as America industrialized. An increase in factory jobs attracted agricultural workers and a new wave of immigrants arrived from Europe. Most of these workers did not own their own homes but were renters instead, as reflected in the numbers in the following table:[3]

HOMEOWNERSHIP RATES											
	2000	1990	1980	1970	1960	1950	1940	1930	1920	1910	1900
United States	66.20%	64.20%	64.40%	62.90%	61.90%	55.00%	43.60%	47.80%	45.60%	45.90%	46.50%

12.3.3 Pre-Depression

Prior to the Great Depression, fewer than half of Americans owned their own homes. One of the primary reasons for this low number was the limited availability of mortgage financing. Most mortgages were made by savings and loan associations (S&Ls), a form of bank that accepted consumer deposits and primarily invested in single-family mortgages, and were held by those institutions on their balance sheets. In order to qualify for a home mortgage, a family typically required a down payment of 50 percent of the purchase price. Mortgages were made for short terms—typically five years—and required frequent refinancing and significant amortization.

During the economic collapse of the Great Depression, many homeowners lost their jobs and defaulted on mortgages, leading to the collapse of many banks. In turn, the failure of the banking system further limited the availability of mortgage finance, and even homeowners who could support the payments were unable to refinance their mortgages.

A number of government initiatives were undertaken to support the housing market.

---

[3] Source: Historical Census of Housing Tables, U.S. Census Bureau, Housing and Household Economic Statistics Division. Last revised October 31, 2011.

12.3.4 Post-Depression

The administration of President Franklin Roosevelt initiated a number of housing related programs as part of the New Deal. These programs attempted to address the need for liquidity in the housing market. The focus of these initiatives was to encourage banks to make mortgage loans.

12.3.5 Housing Benefits from New Deal Initiatives

12.3.5.1 Creation of FHA for Mortgage Guarantees

In order to increase mortgage lending, it was thought that banks would need to find a market for their existing mortgage holdings, which would allow the lenders to recycle capital and make more mortgages. The administration believed that a government guarantee would encourage investors to purchase mortgage loans from the banks. The Federal Housing Administration (FHA) was created by the National Housing Act in 1934 to increase home ownership in the United States. The FHA standardized home mortgage underwriting criteria and documentation and provided guarantees for mortgages that had been underwritten using its criteria. Instead of the 50 percent down payments typically required by banks prior to this point, the FHA program set the level at 20 percent of the purchase price. This program provided benefits to home-buyers and mortgage investors. Homebuyers benefitted from improved affordability of housing and investors benefitted from a standardized invest-ment vehicle that was guaranteed by the U.S. government.

12.3.5.2 Fannie Mae Provides Liquidity to Banks

The Federal National Mortgage Association (FNMA or Fannie Mae) was also created to purchase FHA-guaranteed mortgages from banks, providing liquidity to the housing market. FNMA originally accomplished this by using government funds to acquire mortgages. Subsequently, Fannie Mae raised capital by aggre-gating mortgages into pools and selling interests in these pools to investors.

Under the Housing and Urban Development Act of 1968, while maintaining the mandate of providing liquidity to the mortgage market, FNMA became a private corporation without the explicit backing of the U.S. government. At the same time, the Government National Mortgage Association (Ginnie Mae) was created to package and sell interests in mortgage securities backed by the full faith and credit of the United States.

In 1970, the Federal Home Loan Mortgage Corporation (Freddie Mac) was created to add a competitive force in the mortgage market that would keep Fannie Mae from having a monopoly position.

12.3.5.3 Post Depression: Improved Mortgage Financing

As a result of the government's intermediation in the mortgage market, the terms under which home mortgage loans would be made evolved. Rather than the high down payment, fast amortization, and short maturity of loans earlier in the century, FHA placed its insurance on loans with lower down payments that self-amortized over 30-year terms.

12.3.5.4 Improved Affordability of Single-Family Housing

The improvement of the mortgage terms, as well as the lower interest rate encouraged by the government guarantee, decreased monthly debt service payments and made home ownership affordable for more families.

12.3.6 Veterans' Mortgages and Development of Suburbs

Veterans returning from the Second World War were given special incentives to purchase housing. The Veterans Housing Authority (VHA) was created to guarantee loans with modified underwriting criteria that allowed veterans to purchase homes with a down payment of only 5 percent of the purchase price.

Returning WWII veterans, empowered by economic expansion and motivated by their quest to fulfill the American Dream, created increased demand for single-family housing. This demand could not be satisfied by land in central cities and led to the expansion of these urban areas into adjacent and formerly rural areas. These areas became known as suburbs.

12.3.6.1 New Styles of Single-Family Housing

Prior to the Second World War, most housing was individually designed. These custom houses sometimes sharing a common regional or stylistic architectural vernacular creating distinctive neighborhoods.

The intensive demand for housing in the postwar years led to the need for less expensive housing that could be built quickly on small lots. In many cases, large groups of houses were built based on a single design with minor variations in the floor plans. This type of housing became known as tract housing.

12.3.6.2 Facilitated by Transportation

Suburban expansion was further facilitated by the improvement of the U.S. road network and public transit systems that enabled commuting to cities for work.

The interstate highway system, which was completed in the 1950s, created the blueprint for the expansion of major American cities into the suburbs and had a major impact on land values. Land that was easily accessible to urban centers or that was located at major intersections of the newly completed highway system became highly valued and was targeted for development. The same was true for land located in close proximity to suburban rail stations, which facilitated the daily commute into the central city.

12.3.7 The Role of the Savings and Loan Association

In the post–World War Two era, S&Ls became a strong force in mortgage lending. It is estimated that between 1956 and 1979, S&Ls held over half of U.S. single family debt.[4]

The goal of the S&L was to earn a profit on the difference between the interest paid out on its deposits and that earned on its mortgages. This profit was generated because long-term rates were typically higher than the short-term rates paid on the deposit accounts. Rising short-term interest rates in the early 1980s led to an inversion of the yield curve and severe losses at many S&Ls as funding costs rose. The failure of the traditional S&L model led many of these firms to expand into other types of real estate lending, which—along with favorable tax incentives—fueled commercial property development during the early 1980s.

The Tax Reform Act of 1986 put a final end to the S&L era. Prior to the act, real estate investors could deduct losses on real estate projects against earned income. The tax incentive was strong enough to encourage speculative development. When the government's tax policies changed to end these deductions, the value of many commercial real estate projects declined sharply and many loans made by S&Ls defaulted. A crisis followed as many S&Ls failed, ending the industry's role in the residential mortgage market.

One of the many lessons learned from the S&L crisis was that financial institutions needed to pay close attention to matching the duration of assets and liabilities so that they would not face losses as interest rates changed. As a result, many institutions began to focus on selling off their long-maturity loans in the capital markets, which accelerated the development of the mortgage-backed securities market. The seeds of the more recent financial crisis can be found in the creative solutions developed in response to the S&L crisis.

12.3.8 The Era of Mortgage Backed Securities

During the 1990's and early post millennial period, the US market in asset backed securities, including many varieties of mortgage backed securities, grew in size and complexity. Investors, rather than banks and financial institutions, entered the market as many of these securities achieved investment grade credit ratings. This growing market provided liquidity for home mortgages and facilitated an increase in the percentage of US families that owned homes to a peak level of 69.0% in 2004[5].

---

[4] http://www.fanniemae.com/portal/about-us/media/commentary/120811-fahey.html
[5] St Louis Federal Reserve FRED USHOWN data series

12.3.9 The Financial Crisis

Housing prices grew dramatically during the early years of the millennium, fuelled by the widespread availability of mortgage financing at low interest rates. Following the dramatic correction in technology stocks that occurred at the millennium and the political uncertainty of 9/11, Americans saw an investment in housing as a safe and profitable store of wealth with great utilitarian value in an uncertain world.

As the post millennium decade progressed, an excessive extension of credit fuelled an unsustainable rise in housing prices and set the stage for the Financial Crisis. This excessive lending is attributed to a decline in mortgage underwriting standards and the construction of highly complex mortgage securities that were not well understood by either rating agencies or investors. Mortgage bankers faced minimal consequences from the decline in underwriting standards as they were able to find immediate liquidity for their loans through securitization. Investors readily purchased the ever more complex securities that facilitated this liquidity because they offered attractive interest rates in a market that was starved for yield as the US government dropped interest rates to restore economic confidence after 9/11.

In 2008, as an overheated housing market began to decelerate, it became clear that many of the recently placed mortgage loans might default and severely impact the mortgage backed securities market with dramatic consequences for not only the US economy, but for the increasingly connected global economy. The Financial Crisis that followed, and its aftermath, are well documented and beyond the scope of this book. The resulting volatility in housing prices has challenged many American's perceptions about housing as a safe store of wealth and will impact our behaviour over the coming decades.

12.4 SINGLE-FAMILY HOME FINANCING

Single-family housing, in addition to being an icon of the American way of life, also represents the largest store of wealth for the majority of American families. The rhythms of our financial lives are timed by our entry and eventual exit from the housing market. The importance of home ownership to Americans is demonstrated by the fact that interest on home mortgage loans and payments of property taxes are two of the last remaining tax deductions available at all income levels under the U.S. tax code.

12.4.1 Typical American Family Real Estate Life Cycle
12.4.1.1 Starts Out in Rental Apartment
The typical American child grows up in a single-family house. Upon completion of high school or college, one of our rites of passage is for young

adults to move into their own housing unit, usually a rented house or apartment. The exact age at which this event occurs is based on the ability to find jobs that can support the costs of independent living. In times of economic distress, emancipation is sometimes delayed, with deep implications for the rate of family formation, which further retards economic growth.

12.4.1.2 Saves for Down Payment on a Home

Many young adults use their time in rental housing to begin saving for a down payment on a home. Many combine their savings with loans or gifts from family members to save the funds necessary to enter the housing market.

12.4.1.3 Selects House Based on Economic Level and Lifestyle

In addition to the funds required for a down payment, the potential home-owner must be able to service the interest and principal on a mortgage loan. Loan underwriters prefer to see existing debt payments under revolving credit, student loans, and auto loans when combined with the housing expenses expected from the new home—including debt service, taxes, and insurance—to total less than 40 percent of gross income, as demonstrated in the following table.

Example: Sample Home Affordability Calculation		
Gross annual income	$50,000.00	$100,000.00
Gross monthly income	$4,166.67	$8,333.33
Available for debt payments: 40 percent	$1,666.67	$3,333.33
Student and auto loans	$250.00	$500.00
Available for housing	$1,416.67	$2,833.33
Taxes and insurance	$200.00	$400.00
Available for mortgage payment	$1,216.67	$2,433.33
Mortgage amount at 6 percent/30-year term	$202,929.80	$405,859.60
House value (80 percent LTV)	$253,662.25	$507,324.49

12.4.1.4 Obtains "Conforming" Mortgage

Assuming that the potential home buyer qualifies under standard underwriting metrics, there are many banks that will process an FHA-guaranteed loan for the impending house purchase. FHA loans are intended for well capitalized buyers of moderately priced houses. FHA loans are not generally available to the buyer who deviates from any of these norms. These buyers must find a lender who specializes in "non-conforming" loans, meaning loans that do not qualify for FHA financing.

TYPICAL EXCEPTIONS

Jumbo Mortgage

The FHA limits mortgage loan amounts that qualify for guaranteed financing based on home prices in each county in the United States, which is known as the FHA limit. Loans with principal balances above the FHA limit are known as jumbo loans. Jumbo loans are considered to be riskier and lenders making this type of loan typically require higher interest rates.

Subprime and Alt-A Mortgages

Loans made to borrowers whose income, downpayment, credit score and/or documentation are insufficient to satisfy FHA underwriting criteria are known as subprime or Alt-A mortgages. These loans are considered high-risk and are made to home buyers in many situations including those attempting to enter markets where entry-level housing prices are very high. Of the two types of substandard loans, subprime borrowers typically have a credit issue and these loans are generally considered to be higher risk than Alt-A loans.

No-income-verification Loan

These loans are made to homebuyers who cannot document their income. The credit behind the loan is considered to be the sufficiency of the liquidation value of the house to cover repayment of the mortgage principal rather than the sufficiency of the buyer's income to support the ongoing mortgage debt service. In the housing market crash, values decreased precipitously, leaving many loans under secured and many homeowners "under-water" — that is, with little or no equity in their homes. The concurrent loss of employment during the economic crisis led many owners to default on their mortgages. Lenders receiving devalued collateral in foreclosure proceedings suffered severe losses, contributing to the crisis in the financial system.

12.4.1.5 Refinances As/If Equity Grows

Prior to the financial crisis, Americans expected the value of their homes to grow as they moved into their prime earning years. They assumed that greater earnings and the built-up equity in their home would allow them to move from smaller starter houses into larger homes.

If a family was satisfied with their existing house, they would be able to consider withdrawing some of their equity by refinancing their mortgage. This equity could be used to acquire a second vacation house or to provide for the cost of major life expenses such as their children's education or major health care needs.

12.4.1.6 Sells to Downsize on Retirement to Recapture Investment

The wealth of a household is determined by the sum of its housing and financial assets. For many American families, homeownership has provided a stable store of value and represented the largest asset on a family's balance sheet. For many years, this store of value was illiquid and realized only on major life events such as the sale of a family residence upon retirement.

Once a family's children are grown and leave the "nest," many empty-nest couples decide to downsize and sell their homes for smaller living units. For many years, based on more than 70 consecutive years of rising home prices, homeowners expected to realize wealth upon downsizing. They could then use this money for retirement expenses.

12.4.2 Impact of Financial Crisis on Housing as a Store of Value

The increasing sophistication of the housing finance market, triggered in part by the Tax Reform Act of 1986, which eliminated the tax deduction for many types of consumer debt, resulted in the development of home equity credit lines. These loans provided homeowners with the ability to access the stored value in their home equity and encouraged a different view of a family's investment in housing. While home values were rising, access to this increased wealth fueled consumer spending.

The housing market decline in 2008 changed the consumer's perception of the home as a safe and growing store of value. By limiting the availability of mortgage finance and home equity credit, the financial crisis had an immediate impact on consumer liquidity. The decrease in consumer activity affected overall economic activity and contributed to the decline in financial markets. The concurrent decline in housing prices and the value of financial assets further reinforced consumers' perception of declining wealth, diminishing confidence and limiting consumption. The connection between housing values, the value of financial assets, and consumer confidence, expressed as a change in personal consumption, is known as the wealth effect.

Although it is too early to reach conclusions regarding the long-term impact of the financial crisis on the residential housing cycle, one possibility is that the level of homeownership in the United States will decline and more Americans will live in rental housing. This shift, if it occurs, will have numerous social and financial implications.

12.5 MULTIFAMILY

12.5.1 Types of Multifamily Housing

Multifamily housing in the United States is generally typecast by building height.

12.5.1.1 Low-Rise Housing

Low-rise housing is an apartment building typically no more than three stories high. In many cases, these apartment buildings do not include elevators.

Apartment complexes without vertical transportation are known as walk-ups. Given their limited height, low-rise apartments can typically be constructed with wood framing and are less expensive to build than taller structures that require steel structures.

12.5.1.1.1 Garden

The most popular style of low-rise housing is the garden apartment. As the name implies, garden apartments typically include clusters of apartment buildings in a landscaped setting. Residents commonly share amenities such as pools, playgrounds, and clubhouses. Each individual apartment building can include 20 to 40 individual living units with entrances off common hallways. The individual living units are typically laid out horizontally, with all of the space on a single floor. Garden complexes usually have onsite parking adjacent to the individual buildings.

12.5.1.1.2 Townhouse

Townhouse apartments are similar to garden units in their layout and may also share common amenities. The major distinction between garden and townhouse units is that townhouse units typically have separate street-level entrances and in many cases have a vertical floor plan with living space on more than one level.

12.5.1.2 Mid-Rise Housing

Mid-rise apartments are typically buildings of five to ten floors with an entrance lobby on the first floor and then a single-core vertical transportation system serving the living floors, each of which contains apartments that surround a common lobby. This type of building may have service retail or medical office units surrounding the first-floor lobby. The building may share other common amenities such as laundry rooms, party rooms, health clubs, or roof decks.

Mid-rise apartment buildings may have adjacent parking or, in some areas, an underground garage. The height of the mid-rise building requires more complex construction and may increase the cost per unit.

12.5.1.3 High-Rise Housing

High-rise apartments are organized in the same manner as mid-rise apartments, with differences being multiple vertical transportation cores, more sophisticated environmental systems, and a larger tenant base to support additional amenities such as concierge and other hotel-like services.

High-rise structures are more expensive to construct than alternative, lower-height configurations. The construction cost disadvantage is mitigated by the amortization of the land cost over more units. High-rise structures are typically advantageous where land values are high or the land available for development is scarce.

12.5.2 Ownership

In the United States, multifamily housing can be owned or rented by the tenant. The typical lease term for rental housing is one year and the tenant may be subject to annual increases upon renewal.

In certain markets, primarily major urban centers, a portion of the housing stock is subject to limitations on rent increases. These programs are called rent control or rent stabilization. Housing units that are not subject to such controls are referred to as market-rate housing.

12.5.2.1 Rental

Historically, the American ideal has been to own an individual housing unit, typically a detached single-family house. Families and individuals renting housing fall into two groups: those who require transitional housing and those who permanently rely on rental housing.

12.5.2.1.1 Transitional

Transitional housing provides shelter for a diverse group including newly independent young adults, families with very young children, single and newly single individuals, recent immigrants to the United States, returning members of the armed forces, and recently relocated individuals who seek temporary housing prior to purchasing a permanent residence. By definition, transitional housing is used by those groups who ultimately intend to purchase housing units but who have not yet established the economic resources to do so or are in a period of change that requires flexibility.

12.5.2.1.2 Permanent

Permanent users of rental housing can be divided into two groups: those doing so by choice and those by necessity.

Economically disadvantaged individuals or families who cannot afford a down payment or support the cost of owning a home are permanent renters. Those who have little or no income may live in housing that is either owned by the government or supported by government-backed financing programs.

In certain urban areas with extraordinarily high housing costs, many middle-income families (who would in other locations choose to be homeowners) become permanent renters. Major urban areas have middle-income apartment complexes for these families.

12.5.2.1.3 DINC

Dual-income, no children (DINC) couples—a relatively new group of rental housing users—find it appealing to be free of the concerns related to home ownership. This group rents by choice and is focused on finding apartments with quality features and a high-service and high-amenity lifestyle.

12.5.2.1.4 Senior Citizens

Senior citizens may also enter the rental housing market after they have sold a residence. In some cases, they make use of the equity from the sale of their residences to finance the cost of rental housing. In other cases, they may rely on pension income supplemented by Social Security payments to cover rent expenses. Seniors with low incomes can apply for government-subsidized senior housing.

12.5.2.1.5 Impact of Financial Crisis

Many homeowners lost their homes in foreclosure proceedings during the financial crisis. These former homeowners are now renters. They have joined other new entrants into the housing market in giving additional consideration to rental housing as a long-term housing option. The financial crisis, in changing consumer's views on the security of home ownership as a store of value, may have a long-term impact on how new housing market entrants view the attractiveness of homeownership.

At the same time, banks that have acquired rental housing as a result of foreclosure proceedings and investors, seeing an opportunity to acquire rental housing at below replacement cost, are providing a new source of supply for the rental housing market. This development may create a permanent supply of single family homes for rent, separating the lifestyle choice from the economic decisions surrounding homeownership.

12.5.2.2 Owner Occupied

Not all multifamily housing is rental housing. There are two typical forms of owner occupied multifamily housing: condominium and cooperative housing.

12.5.2.2.1 Condominium

Apartment buildings may be divided into individual interests in real estate under a format known as condominium ownership. Each owner of a condominium apartment owns a divided interest in the real property and may borrow against this interest in order to finance the purchase. Owners are subject to a condominium agreement under which they agree to pay a pro rata share of the charges required to operate the building. The individual owner is also directly responsible to the municipality for the payment of real estate taxes.

12.5.2.2.2 Cooperative

In cooperative housing (co-ops), a corporation is formed and becomes the owner of an apartment complex. Each resident purchases a given number of shares in the corporation based on the relative size of their housing unit. The resident enters into a "proprietary lease" with the corporation that gives them the right to inhabit their unit. Each resident is obligated to pay a portion of the expenses of the property based on his or her percentage of ownership. These expenses may include a share of the debt service on any borrowings undertaken by the corporation. In addition, the individual residents may borrow against their "shares and lease" to finance the purchase of their apartment. Thus, the owner of a co-op may be paying multiple levels of debt service.

A housing cooperative is run by an elected board of directors who makes decisions on behalf of the shareholder-residents regarding the operation of the building, the use of the apartments for commercial purposes (rental, home office), and the acceptance of new "owners."

12.5.2.2.3 Comparative Benefits of Co-op versus Condo Ownership

Condominium owners tend to have greater flexibility regarding the use and disposition of their units. Purchasing a condominium unit and then renting it out or using it as a home office does not require the approval of co-op board. Condo owners have a direct interest in real estate that is not compromised by a co-op lease. On the other hand, the residential environment in a condo can be affected by the presence of renters, home office clients, and others who do not have the same level of care as owners. The ability of existing owners to freely trade their units can also result in a group of residents who do not have the financial capacity to operate the building at an appropriate standard and can cause the unit values to fall.

In contrast, many co-op owners consider the controls exercised by their boards a good thing because they maintain the character of a building as a primary residence. Other co-op owners find board restrictions that limit their flexibility in renting or selling their apartments as a major detriment.

In all cases, owners of units in multifamily housing face certain risks that come from their reliance on other owners to finance their individual share of the building's operating and capital expenses.

12.6 HOUSING DEVELOPMENT

12.6.1 Homebuilding

The homebuilding cycle begins with the acquisition of a parcel of land that can be improved and subdivided into lots for new home construction. It ends when the newly constructed homes are sold.

12.6.1.1 Land Acquisition and Development

Homebuilders who intend to build a number of houses in one location must acquire land for development. This land might not yet have the requisite infrastructure required to support homes and might require the creation of a road network or other infrastructure. Purchasing land in advance of home construction requires the homebuilder to pay carrying costs (the cost of interest and real estate taxes during the holding period) and ultimately provides the land inventory for new homes.

During the land development process, the homebuilder must create the required infrastructure necessary to support the new homes. The timing and cost of creating infrastructure can be uncertain due to government administrative delays, scope changes, and construction cost risk. In addition, funding infrastructure costs requires additional carrying charges.

After the infrastructure is completed, the land is subdivided into individual parcels known as improved or building lots. Vertically integrated homebuilders use the improved lots as inventory for new home construction. They are willing to take on the risks of land development in order to increase their potential profits.

Some homebuilders do not develop their own land inventory. They limit their business to building homes on improved lots and are willing to pay more for improved lots; there is less risk because the full cost of the land development process is known in advance.

12.6.1.2 Inventory Financing

Inventory financing is used by the homebuilder to fund the cost of work in progress before sales to homebuyers are closed. Many homes are built based on contracts that have been executed by prospective buyers. These contracts are used by the homebuilder to acquire construction financing to build the new houses. In some cases, however, the homebuilder might build the house prior to having a customer. This type of construction is called building on spec or spec building. The builder takes the risk that the home will sell at a price sufficient to provide a profit.

12.6.1.3 Takeout "End" Loans

Most home purchasers require financing in order to purchase houses. A risk to the homebuilder is the inability to sell the homes because the would-be purchasers cannot obtain financing. To avoid this situation, homebuilders sometimes arrange financing for prospective homebuyers as part of a complete financing package for the development project. Mortgages provided to prospective homebuyers by the homebuilder's bank are known as end loans. By providing end loans to the homebuilder, the bank that has financed the development project transitions their monetary commitment from a commercial mortgage loan into a portfolio of home mortgages that can be sold into the generally liquid residential mortgage market. This approach is very profitable for the bank in that it earns fee income at each stage of the transaction.

12.6.1.4 Development of Mortgage Pools

Mortgage loans from the sale of new homes as well as from purchases of existing homes are aggregated into residential mortgage loan pools that can be used as collateral for residential mortgage-backed securities (RMBS).

Of the 30 million units that are in multifamily structures, more than one million units are public housing owned by the government and provided to families who are living at the poverty level. Of the remaining 29 million units, approximately 15 million have been financed using LIHTC and 7.5 million have been financed using HUD mortgages.

The government supports multifamily housing because it creates an affordable option for those who cannot afford single-family housing. The availability of multifamily housing also facilitates the movements of workers that allow the economy to shift jobs from market to market.

12.6.2 Multifamily

More than one-third of the U.S. population (99.7 million people or 34.9 percent of the population) resides in rental housing. The majority, 57 percent, occupy single-family houses or units in one- to four-family structures, while the balance, 43 percent, reside in multifamily structures with five or more apartments.

12.6.2.1 Construction Loans

Multifamily projects are typically funded using construction loans sourced from commercial banks. These banks have experienced construction lenders who work with developers to create a construction budget and schedule of draws for the expected duration of the project.

During the construction period, the lender periodically visits the project to review progress. The lender ensures compliance with the construction plans and the time schedule furnished to the bank, thus ensuring that the bank's funds are being appropriately spent and that the project is progressing toward completion.

Banks receive fees for their project reviews and premium interest rates for accepting the risks present in construction lending. These risks include whether the project can be completed on time and on budget and the ability of the project to attract tenants that create an income stream sufficient to attract a buyer or support an amount of permanent financing that can fund the repayment of the construction loan.

12.6.2.2 Mini-Perm Loans

A mini-perm loan is a construction loan that extends for a period of time beyond the construction period. During the postconstruction period, the developer leases the apartments and attempts to bring the property to a stabilized level of occupancy. This step maximizes the developer's ability to sell or refinance the property and minimizes the construction lender's risk of a failed repayment.

12.6.2.3 Takeout Permanent Loans

The permanent loan that replaces the construction or mini-perm loan is known as takeout financing because it is used to take out the prior loan. In many cases,

HUD financing is used as permanent financing for multifamily properties. The balance is financed using CMBS or through balance sheet lending by financial institutions.

12.6.2.4 Project Presales

Some multifamily developers are not interested in operating properties and sell their projects upon completion; this is known as a presale. REITs, pension funds, and other financial institutions are typical buyers of newly constructed multifamily properties. In some cases, these institutions agree in advance to buy a property upon completion. Typically, these agreements are conditioned upon the achievement of agreed-upon levels of rent and occupancy. If these levels are not achieved in a set period of time, the buyer's obligation to buy the property expires.

12.6.3 Government Support

The U.S. government supports access to housing and home ownership through a variety of government programs and financial incentives. Many of these programs are housed in the U.S. Department of Housing and Urban Development (HUD). HUD was created in 1965 by the Department of Housing and Urban Development Act as one of the Great Society programs under the administration of President Lyndon Johnson.

12.6.3.1 Mortgage Interest Deduction

The U.S. government supports homeownership by allowing personal income tax deductions for property taxes and interest paid on up to $1 million of mortgage debt. This lowers the effective cost of owning a home.

12.6.3.2 Mortgage Guarantees

The FHA provides a guarantee of principal and interest on mortgages that are underwritten through one of its programs. This guarantee improves the credit of the mortgage securities into which individual home mortgages are aggregated and reduces the borrower's interest cost, which serves to further lower the cost of home ownership for those who qualify for the program.

For those borrowers who do not qualify, there are a number of sources of private mortgage insurance. In return for a fee, these insurers guarantee a mortgage and reduce the interest cost.

12.6.3.3 Low-Income Housing Tax Credits

The U.S. Government makes low-income housing tax credits (LIHTC) available to developers of housing that is at least partially targeted towards low income residents. This housing is typically called 80/20 housing because 20 percent of the units in a LIHTC-financed project must be occupied by families with earnings at or below 60 percent of the area median income. One policy goal of the LIHTC program is to create housing with families of mixed income levels and to avoid aggregating low-income families into housing projects.

If a project qualifies for a LIHTC award, it receives ten years of tax credits in an annual amount equal to 9 percent of the construction cost of the units dedicated to low-income housing and 4 percent on acquisition and rehabilitation of existing housing. These credits can be sold to corporations, which will use them to directly offset taxes due on their taxable income. The value of the credits is the present value of the tax savings discounted at the market's required rate of return.

A developer can apply the proceeds from the sale of the tax credits to offset a portion of the investment required to complete the project, which improves returns. The LIHTC is such a popular program that it is estimated that almost 50 percent of new multifamily housing during the 1990s was financed using LIHTC.

EXAMPLE OF LIHTC FINANCING

In the following example, the developer spends $1,000,000 to build a ten-unit project. Four of the units will be rented to low-income tenants. The project will qualify for annual credits of 9 percent of qualified costs for ten years. The developer will sell these credits and receive 85 cents per dollar of tax credit sold, applying the proceeds to reduce the cost of the low-income units. The result of the subsidy is that the cost of the low-income units is reduced to 43 percent of the actual cost of construction:

Number of units	10
Market-rate units	6
Low-income units	4
Land cost per unit	$35,000
Construction cost per unit	$100,000
Total cost per unit	$135,000
Qualified construction cost	$1,000,000
Low-income units	40%
Cost of low-income units	$400,000
Annual credit %	9%
Annual tax credits	$36,000
Life of benefit	10
Total tax credits	$360,000
Market value of $ of tax credit	85%
Value of benefit	$306,000
Net cost of low-income units	$94,000
Net construction cost per unit	$23,500
Land cost per unit	$35,000
Total cost of low-income unit	$58,500
% of actual unit cost	43%

12.6.3.4 Section Eight

Section Eight housing is a U.S. government program administered by HUD that provides rent subsidies to low-income families, typically at 30 percent to 80 percent of the area median income. Section Eight housing allows these families to occupy market-rate apartments and in certain circumstances to afford the cost of home ownership. The program was an outgrowth of a Depression-era program: the U.S. Housing Act of 1937.

Today, the program is either project based (the subsidy is based upon the tenant's residence in a particular property) or voucher based (a tenant can use the subsidy to access market-rate housing). The program has expanded to provide assistance for low-income veterans, the elderly, and the disabled. Section Eight tenant vouchers are administered through local public housing authorities (PHAs) that operate in many parts of the country.

Although the Section Eight program is no longer available for new development, in prior years, developers received mortgage insurance from HUD that lowered the effective cost of their project. In return for this incentive, the landlord agreed to lease a portion of their apartments for a period of time to Section Eight tenants.

Section Eight tenants pay a reduced rent based on personal income (typically 30 percent). The difference between the agreed (local market) rent and the tenant's actual payment is the Section Eight subsidy paid by HUD.

12.7 IMPACT OF HOUSING DEVELOPMENT ON LOCAL INFRASTRUCTURE

Americans enjoy a high level of basic services that many of us take for granted. We expect our lights to go on when we hit the switch, our taps to provide clean water to drink, and our sewage and garbage to be disposed of without our active intervention. When we dial 911, we expect that the police, fire, or ambulance service we require will be dispatched immediately. These expectations come from the highly developed infrastructure that exists in almost all parts of our country.

12.7.1 Population Growth Requires Public Services

When new communities are built, infrastructure needs to be extended or created. The extension of infrastructure to undeveloped property is expensive and developers are asked to contribute a portion of these costs. Local governments may help fund this expense by financing the creation of public authorities to build and operate public purpose projects. In some cases, such as the interstate highway system, the federal government bears part or all of the construction costs. Homeowners and renters then share the financial burden of maintaining these systems through use and hookup fees, utility bills, and property tax payments.

12.7.2 Transportation
12.7.2.1 Road Access

The sufficiency of the road network that provides vehicular access to a property is a critical factor in any development project. New housing projects often require the creation of internal road networks and may require improvement of the external road network so that it can handle the additional traffic to and from the site.

12.7.2.2 Public Transportation

The presence of public transportation from residential areas to centers of commerce can be a critical determinant of the attractiveness of a housing development. Residents appreciate the ability to find employment and to access critical goods and services without total reliance on their automobiles. Transit-oriented development, the creation of residential and commercial communities around public transit hubs, is a type of sustainable development that has increased in popularity in recent years.

12.7.3 Utilities

Due to the universal requirement for basic public services and the high cost of their creation, many utilities have been developed as monopolies and granted unique protection from competition by the government. In return for this protected position, the government exerts a high level of regulation on these industries, protecting the consumer from the loss of competitive pressure that would naturally limit prices.

12.7.3.1 Power

Power companies generate power by converting nuclear energy, fossil fuel, wind, solar energy, and water pressure to electricity. They then transmit this electricity from the source of generation to the locality where it is consumed over a power grid. At the end point of the grid, the local electric utility distributes it to households and commercial users. Natural gas, used for heating and cooking, is distributed in a similar manner and in many cases by the same utility company.

12.7.3.2 Water

Water companies are responsible for sourcing, purifying, and distributing water for consumption by local residents and industry. To accomplish these services, water companies rely on chemical industry and power suppliers to provide them with the ability to clean and pump their water to end users.

12.7.3.3 Sewage and Garbage Disposal

The collection of waste water is a critical part of our infrastructure, protecting the environment and public health. The capacity of sewage treatment plants and the availability of landfill sites for garbage disposal can be limiting factors on many development projects.

12.7.4 Health and Human Services

12.7.4.1 First Responders

Communities require police protection, fire protection, and emergency medical services. Collectively, the providers of these services are known as first responders. The presence of these services increases quality of life, allows for greater population density, and can affect property value.

12.7.4.2 Education

The quality of education available in a given area has a significant impact on housing values. Public schools within the United States are typically divided into elementary, middle, and secondary or high schools. Many children in the United States are taken to school by bus each day. Long travel times are considered undesirable.

When the school system is at capacity, development may be limited to age restricted housing. Housing developments targeted at residents of ages greater than 55 do not require additional public school capacity.

In addition to public education for children, institutions of higher education include community colleges and four-year colleges and universities, which include undergraduate and graduate education. Institutions of higher education provide the professionals and skilled workers required by industry and are drivers of regional economic development. They also offer cultural amenities that improve the quality of life.

12.7.4.3 Health Care

People require health care services in the form of medical doctors, pharmacies, and hospitals. Communities with high-quality health care are more attractive to residents than those without local medical care. Hospitals offering state of the art care in multiple medical disciplines are generally known as tertiary- or quaternary-care hospitals. The availability of high-level medical care is another quality-of-life indicator considered by prospective residents.

12.7.4.4 Shopping

Americans value convenient access to goods and services. The availability of a grocery store and pharmacy within one to three miles, large-format shopping centers within 10 miles, and regional malls anchored by major department stores within 25 miles are typical.

12.7.4.5 Recreation

The presence of parks and recreational amenities such as community centers and athletic facilities are highly valued amenities. The presence of museums, theatres, and professional sports teams are all considered indicators of a region's quality of life.

Glossary

Age-restricted housing
American dream
Balance sheet lending
Carrying costs
Condominium
Conforming mortgage
Construction loans
Cooperative housing
Custom housing
DINC (dual-income, no children)
Downsize
End loans
Family formation
Fannie Mae
FHA guarantees
First responders
Freddie Mac
Garden apartments
Ginnie Mae
High-rise housing
HUD (Department of Housing and Urban Development)
Infrastructure requirements
Inventory financing
Jumbo mortgage
Low-rise housing
LIHTC (low-income housing tax credit)
Market-rate housing
Mid-rise housing
Mini-perm loans
Mortgage deductibility
Mortgage guarantees
Mortgage pools
Multifamily development
New Deal
No-income-verification loan
Project presales
Public housing authority
Refinance

RMBS (residential mortgage-backed securities)
Section Eight
Self-amortizing
Senior citizen housing
Spec building
Subprime mortgage
Subdivision
Takeout permanent loans
Tax credits
Townhouse
Transit-oriented development
Tract housing
Veterans' mortgages

Thought Questions

1. Do you believe that the government has a role in encouraging home ownership? What are some of the ways in which the U.S. government seeks to make homeownership more affordable?
2. What key historical events shaped the current residential mortgage market?
3. Local governments believe that having attractive housing options for new residents encourages business to locate operations in their region. What are the costs and considerations faced by developers and local governments when considering the creation of new housing units?

Review Questions

1. Maximum purchase price
   In New York City, a young couple should expect to spend 40 percent of their income on housing. David makes $25,000 per year as an opera singer and Penny makes $60,000 as a teacher. Property taxes and condo fees total $1,000 per month. Mortgage rates on 30-year fixed-rate loans are at 4 percent. The couples' parents will gift them the required 10 percent down payment. What can the couple spend on their condo?
2. Amount of tax deduction
   Fred and Wilma have just bought a nice new home in Granite Run on January 1. They financed their home with a $100,000, 15-year, 5 percent mortgage. This will be the second year of their mortgage. How much interest will they pay to their bank? If their marginal tax rate is 35 percent, what is their after-tax interest rate?
3. In addition to their mortgage, Fred and Wilma must also pay property taxes of $5,000 per year (tax deductible) and insurance of $2,000 per year. Property upkeep costs $300 per month on average. What are the average monthly pretax and after-tax costs of homeownership during year 2?

4. Rent or buy

The Andersons want to move to a new apartment in Matrix Cove, a beautiful waterfront development project. Identical rental and for-sale units are available. The monthly rent is $2,000 for their chosen unit. Rents have been rising at 3 percent per year. An identical unit can be purchased for $250,000 with 20 percent down. The balance can be financed at 5 percent for 30 years fixed. Property taxes are $250 per month. Other costs of ownership are $500 per month. Both property taxes and other costs have been rising at 3 percent per year. According to their broker, units have been appreciating at 5 percent per year. Assume income tax rate of 35 percent, capital gains tax rate of 15 percent, and a cost of selling the home of 6 percent of the gross sales price. Should they rent or buy, assuming they will stay in the unit for five years? Does your view change if the house does not appreciate over the five-year period? What if it decreases in value at 2 percent per year?

Multiple Choice Questions

1. Approximately how many housing units are there in the United States as of the 2010 census?
   a) 50,000,000
   b) 131,000,000
   c) 250,000,000
   d) 308,000,000
2. When purchasing, which of the following types of housing does the owner not actually own title to real estate?
   a) Condominium apartment
   b) Cooperative apartment
   c) Single-family house
   d) Townhouse apartment
3. Which of the following apartment types is typically constructed on high-cost land?
   a) Low-rise
   b) Garden
   c) Mid-rise
   d) High-rise
4. Which of the following is not a qualified construction cost for a low-income tax credit?
   a) foundation
   b) roof
   c) land acquisition
   d) plumbing

5. Securities issued by which of the following financial institution are guaranteed by the full faith and credit of the U.S. government?
   a) Freddie Mac
   b) Ginnie Mae
   c) Fannie Mae
   d) Sallie Mac
6. Which of the following would not be used to finance for rental multifamily housing?
   I) Construction financing
   II) Mini-perm
   III) Takeout financing
   IV) Inventory financing
   V) End loans
      a) IV, V
      b) II, III
      c) III, IV
      d) I, V
      e) I, II, III
7. In many cases, new housing developments require additional infrastructure. Who pays the cost of building and supporting the infrastructure?
   a) Developers
   b) Homebuyers
   c) Government
   d) All of the above
8. Which of the following does not represent government support of home ownership?
   a) LIHTC
   b) Section 8
   c) FHA mortgage guarantee
   d) Mortgage interest deductibility
9. Which of the following is/are the key metric(s) used to determine a buyer's ability to afford a home purchase?
   I) Monthly gross income
   II) Real estate taxes
   III) Insurance costs
   IV) Available down payment
   V) Outstanding credit card debt
   VI) Current interest rates
   VII) Price of the home
   VIII) Student loans
      a) I, IV, VI, VII
      b) I, II, III, IV, VI, VII

c) All except VIII

d) All of the above

10. Which of the following does not provide liquidity to the housing market?

a) RMBS

b) Ginnie Mae

c) S&Ls

d) DINC

For answers to these Problems and Exercises, please visit the companion website: http://booksite.elsevier.com/9780123786265

CHAPTER 13

REITs and Real Estate Corporate Finance

13.1 WHAT IS A REIT?

13.1.1 Special-Purpose Entity that Invests in Real Estate

Real estate investment trusts (REIT) are special-purpose entities that focus their investment strategies on the direct ownership of real estate or real estate securities (mortgages or interests in other REIT). The typical REIT investor seeks to achieve a combination of current income and long-term growth to protect against inflation.

Investors purchasing REIT securities, while interested in adding exposure to real estate to their investment portfolio, may not be willing or able to create and manage their own property portfolio. Many REITs are widely held public companies that are traded on major stock exchanges and can provide investors with immediate liquidity, something not available from direct investment in real property.

13.1.2 Corporation or Business Trust

REIT are generally organized as corporations or business trusts. Investors can purchase shares of common stock in REITs that are organized as corporations and shares of beneficial interest in REITs organized as business trusts.

Currently, most REITs are structured as corporations domiciled in either Delaware or Maryland. These two states have well-developed corporate laws that address issues faced by REITs, including consideration of mergers and acquisitions.

13.1.3 REITs Can Invest in Different Types of Real Estate Interests

Congress established the REIT vehicle to allow the small investor to invest in the real estate market. REITs must invest over 75 percent of their assets in either direct equity investments in property or mortgages and mortgage securities. Within these constraints, REITs have exhibited a wide variety of investment philosophies.

13.1.3.1 Equity: Ownership of Property

REITs that primarily make direct investments in real estate are known as equity REITs because they own equity interests in properties.

361

Today's equity REIT is generally a vertically integrated real estate operating company. It provides asset and property management services for a portfolio of properties that it has either acquired or developed. In most cases, the REIT's management also functions as the senior management team for the property operating company.

13.1.3.2 Mortgage: Ownership of Debt Secured by Real Estate

REITs that focus on investment in real estate debt are known as mortgage REITs. REITs can make mortgages, invest in loans secured by real estate, and invest in securities backed by such loans, including CMBS and RMBS. A REIT can make a traditional mortgage loan and earn a base interest rate. In addition, it can also earn additional interest based on the performance of the asset. However, any participation in asset performance must be based on gross revenue rather than net income.

For example, a REIT can make a mortgage to a hotel at a stated rate of interest. It can also earn additional interest or kicker interest based upon the gross revenue performance of the hotel. It may not earn interest structured as a percentage of hotel net income.

The REIT can also have the right to convert all or a portion of its loans into equity interests in the same assets.

13.1.3.3 Hybrid: Own Debt and Equity Interests

A limited number of REITs have portfolios featuring a mix of investment types, including exposure to both real estate debt and equity. These are known as hybrid REITs. During the financial crisis, a number of equity REITs began investing in distressed debt as a way of ultimately acquiring assets at a discount through foreclosure. REITs that were originally mortgage REITs began to foreclose on properties and, at least on an interim basis, had equity positions. These REITs are generally still considered either equity or debt REITs, regardless of their nominal investments in other investment types.

13.1.4 Property Type Focus

In addition to a focus on a particular form of investment—equity or debt—the majority of REITs limit their investments to a particular type of property. At the inception of the REIT market, most REITs had small staffs and were focused either on multiple property types in a single geographic region or on a single property type across a larger geography.

Investors and investment banks organized their portfolio managers, banking coverage teams and research analysts around property types rather than geographies. They believed that the only way these companies could achieve economics of scale was to focus on a single type of property. The investors thought they could assemble a diversified real estate portfolio by purchasing a number of REITs, each focused on a different property type. Therefore, most equity REITs adopted the single property type model.

At the end of 2011, the National Association of REITs (NAREIT), the industry's trade association, reported statistics on 160 companies with a total equity market cap of $450.5 billion. Of these 160 REITs, only 15 companies— representing 6.9 percent of the industry by equity market cap, were characterized as diversified.

The investment breakdown across property sectors by number of companies and total dollars of assets was:[1]

	FTSE NAREIT All REITs		S&P Large-, Mid-, and Small-Cap Indices	
	#	$ (in billions)	#	$ (in billions)
Office/industrial	31	72,344.6	15	58,924.8
Retail	29	106,733.9	19	82,499.9
Residential	19	68,204.8	12	62,603.8
Health care	12	54,622.7	9	52,740.4
Other equity	39	106,073.0	15	83,859.8
Mortgage	30	42,971.7	0	0
Total	160	450,500.6	70	340,628.7

Of these 160 companies, 70 companies with a total equity market cap of $340.6 billion were listed in key S&P indices, including 15 in the S&P 500 Large Cap, 26 in the S&P 400 Mid Cap and 29 in the S&P 600 Small Cap.[2]

13.1.5 Portfolio Geography: from Regional to Global

Since its inception, the real estate REIT industry has believed that local market knowledge is important to successful investment. In the early period of REIT formation, many companies limited their investments to the geographic areas in which they were headquartered. These companies were called "local sharp-shooters" because of their detailed market knowledge.

As REITs grew in size and scale, they extended their reach through diversification into additional geographic markets. In many cases, REITs grew through property acquisition, acquiring assets and staff in additional geographies. In addition, many mergers occurred between public REITs creating larger surviving enterprises. As these companies matured, they proved capable of running multisite and then national investment platforms.

---

[1] NAREIT *REITWatch*, January 2012, p. 27.
[2] NAREIT *REITWatch*, January 2012, p. 27.

In the 1990s, as part of the overall trend towards globalization, and as a result of deep penetration by REITs into available institutional-class assets in the United States, a number of REITs launched international ventures. REITS that launched international ventures included Simon Properties, Taubman, Prologis, Public Storage, and Kimco.

Although U.S. REITs maintain favorable tax status in the United States, they may be subject to foreign taxation and are often exposed to local currency fluctuations.

13.2 REIT QUALIFICATION TESTS

In return for tax benefits, real estate companies choosing to qualify as REITs agree to operate under a series of constraints set out in the REIT legislation. Although some of these constraints have been modified over the past 50 years, many of the original requirements still govern the operation of the modern REIT.

13.2.1 Investment Limitations

13.2.1.1 Asset Tests

The purpose of a REIT is to invest in real estate and real estate securities. Therefore, at least 75 percent of the assets of a REIT must be real property or securities backed by real property such as mortgages, mortgage-backed securities, or shares in other REITS.

Up to 25 percent of a REIT's assets may come from its investment in its taxable REIT subsidiaries. A REIT may also hold cash and short-term marketable securities as interim stores of value.

13.2.1.2 Taxable REIT Subsidiaries

Recent changes to the REIT rules allow REITs to own subsidiaries that invest in businesses that do not qualify under the REIT rules. These investments must total less than 25 percent of the REIT's asset base. The purpose of the REIT taxable subsidiary is to let the company retain control of functions that are integrated with its core business but are not pure investments in real property.

Examples of businesses that are housed in taxable REIT subsidiaries include property management performed for non-REIT assets. This activity leverages the REIT's operating platform but does not generate rental income and is not a qualified real estate investment for a REIT.

13.2.1.3 Long-Term Investment

REITs are intended to be investment vehicles and are expected to be long-term owners of property. They are not intended to hold assets as inventory or to engage in speculative trading (i.e., buying and then quickly selling or "flipping" properties). Transactions that violate this rule are known as prohibited transactions and are subject to a 100 percent tax.

The prohibition on holding real estate as inventory makes it difficult for REITs to buy large land parcels and resell individual lots, sell condominium interests in a multifamily property, or sell time-share interests in a resort. All of these activities are considered participation in a trade or business as opposed to real property investment strategies.

13.2.1.4 Income Tests

REITs must receive over 75 percent of their gross income from investments in real estate. Another 20 percent of their gross income may also come from real estate investments or from dividends and interest on other qualified investments.

Under the REIT qualification tests, income from property must be derived from rents. Rents can include a participation in the gross income of the business operated at the property, but they cannot include an interest in the net income generated from such a business. The difference is based on the fact that the REIT is intended as a real estate investment, rather than a tax-efficient way to hold an operating business. In fact, if a property interest held by a REIT generates income from an operating business, that activity must be held by a special subsidiary created by the REIT known as a taxable REIT subsidiary (TRS), which is subject to normal corporate taxation.

As an example, a REIT can own a hotel and lease it to a hotel operating company for a monthly rent. The REIT may earn, as part of its rent payment, a percentage of the hotel's gross revenues. However, the REIT cannot operate the hotel directly (which would generate net income) or earn a rent payment based on the hotel's profits.

13.2.2 Distribution Requirements
13.2.2.1 Must Distribute 90 Percent of Earnings and Profits

A REIT is required to pay out 90 percent of its taxable income as a shareholder dividend. REITs that meet this payout level are taxed as pass-through entities and afforded tax treatment similar to partnerships, in that they are not required to pay corporate taxes. If a REIT does not make distributions at the 90 percent level, it is required to pay an excise tax and may lose its ability to qualify as a REIT.

13.2.2.2 Difficult to Reinvest Capital Gains

REIT capital gains may be retained by the REIT but are subject to tax at the capital gains rate, or the recapture rate, depending on whether the gain reflects price improvement or recapture of depreciation.

If a REIT distributes its gains to its shareholders, it receives a deduction for the amount of the distribution.

13.2.2.3 Section 1031

In order to preserve their capital base, many REITs attempt to position property sales as Section 1031 exchanges. In doing so, REITs can acquire new assets in place of those sold without recognizing a capital gain. These transactions transfer the REITs existing basis in the sold asset to the new acquisition. This approach defers the recognition of the capital gain on the sold asset and delays the time at which the tax must be paid.

13.2.3 Diverse Ownership
13.2.3.1 Minimum of 100 Shareholders

REITs are intended to be widely held vehicles serving the individual investor and are not intended to be used as personal holding companies. To qualify as a REIT, an entity must have a minimum of 100 unique shareholders. Under the attribution rules, ownership of shares by large financial institutions is attributed to their investors.

13.2.3.2 Concentration of Ownership Limitation

In addition to requiring broad ownership, there are limits on concentration of ownership. Five or fewer individuals may own no more than 50 percent of the securities of a REIT during the last half of any taxable year. This is commonly referred to as the "five or fewer rule."

13.2.4 If Tests Passed, Entity Qualifies as a REIT

If all the tests are passed, the entity qualifies as a REIT and has the benefit of single-level taxation.

13.2.5 Taxation of REIT Shareholders

Shareholders receiving REIT distributions are subject to income taxation. The level of tax is based on the form and amount of the income. If the REIT distributes its net income, the recipient treats it as ordinary income. REIT dividends do not benefit from the lower tax rate on many corporate dividends. If a REIT distributes gains on the sale of a property, these amounts are taxable at the individual capital gain rate. If these gains include recaptured depreciation subject to Section 1250, these gains are taxable at the higher recapture rate. Finally, if a REIT distributes cash in excess of income and profits, this distribution is treated as a return of capital. No taxes are due, but the shareholder's basis in the REIT investment is reduced by the amount of the distribution. The following table summarizes the taxation of REIT income:

Type	REIT distribution requirement	Tax at REIT level	Tax at recipient level
Ordinary income	Must distribute more than 90 percent of earnings and profits, delayed payments are subject to a 10 percent excise tax	None if greater than 90 percent of earnings and profits are distributed; otherwise excise tax	Ordinary income tax
Capital gains	REIT choice to pay tax or distribute	None if distributed, if retained taxed at corporate tax rate	Capital gain: currently 20 percent
Section 1250 recapture	REIT choice to pay tax or distribute	None if distributed, if retained taxed at corporate tax rate	Recapture rate: currently 25 percent

13.3 BENEFITS TO INVESTORS

REIT investors receive many benefits from this form of real estate investment vehicle.

13.3.1 Diversification of Asset Base

REIT investors, particularly individual investors, can participate in the ownership of large portfolios of institutional quality assets that would otherwise be inaccessible to them.

13.3.2 Professional Management

REIT investors benefit from the professional management skills of the REIT management teams, most of whom have long track records in the real estate business. The large portfolios of institutional-grade properties controlled by the REITs can support the expense of these high-quality management teams.

13.3.3 Alignment of Interests

Ultimate authority for the management of the REIT rests with its board of directors. Directors are elected by the shareholders on an annual basis and are responsible for selecting and compensating executive management. Management teams are strongly encouraged to hold stock in their companies and are typically compensated based on the performance of their assets. Thus, the REIT management team's interests are aligned with the interests of their shareholders.

13.3.4 Liquidity through Public Market

Unlike direct property investors, who must find liquidity by selling their assets in the property market, most REIT shareholders are able to find immediate liquidity through the capital markets. This liquidity gives REIT investors the ability to precisely manage their exposure to different types of real estate.

13.3.5 Transparency of Financial Reporting

U.S. REITs that trade as public companies are subject to the reporting requirements of the Securities and Exchange Commission. These companies must report on the assets that they own and on their financial performance on a quarterly basis. Securities analysts follow many of the REITs. They meet with management, visit assets, and write periodic reports on the performance of the companies that they cover.

13.4 CAPITAL REQUIREMENTS

REITs utilize their capital to acquire, maintain, expand, and reposition their assets. As most REITs hold portfolios of large institutional grade properties, they expend large quantities of capital.

13.4.1 Intensive Capital Appetite

REITs are required to distribute 90 percent of all their earnings and profits to their shareholders. Their strict distribution requirements preclude significant reinvestment of capital. Therefore, REITs cannot function like industrial companies that retain earnings to finance future growth; instead, they must frequently revisit the capital markets and seek additional funds from investors. This ongoing requirement to source capital in the marketplace requires REIT management teams to please their investors in order to grow their businesses.

13.4.2 Corporate Finance Alternatives

To satisfy their capital needs, REITs use all of the structures found in modern capital markets.

13.4.2.1 Public Equity

Although it is not required that REITs be publicly held, most REITs have chosen to operate as public companies and their shares trade on major stock exchanges. At the end of 2011, the equity market capitalization of the US public REIT market totaled over $450 billion, with the 150 companies having average equity market capitalization of approximately $3 billion.[3]

13.4.2.2 Public Debt

REITs, as owners of real property, have many options for accessing debt financing. REITs that own property can seek asset-level financing in the

---

[3] NAREIT *REITWatch*, January 2012, p. 1.

mortgage markets. A number of the larger REITs have accessed the public debt market by issuing bonds. Some of these issues have received investment-grade ratings from the major credit agencies.

13.4.2.3 Bank Line of Credit

Most REITs have established lines of credit from commercial banks for interim financing. These credit facilities allow REITs to fund their operating activities, property renovations, and expansions. They also enable the REITs to be aggressive property buyers, as they are able to close acquisitions quickly without the prior need to raise equity or secure long-term debt.

13.4.3 Asset Finance Alternatives

Given the direct ownership of their assets, REITs have many options for property-level financing.

13.4.3.1 Mortgage finance

REITs can seek property debt in the mortgage markets. This debt can be balance sheet debt held by financial institutions such as banks, pension funds, and insurance companies or can be securitized debt raised through the capital markets.

13.4.3.2 Joint Ventures

Certain institutional investors prefer direct property investment over REIT securities. Many of these investors do not have the infrastructure to acquire and manage major properties. These investors can often find REITs willing to acquire properties in joint ownership with them. In a typical joint venture, the REIT acts as the operating partner and earns fees for providing its specialized property management skills. It also has partial ownership of the asset.

Joint ventures can provide many benefits to a REIT. Using joint venture capital may allow the REIT to acquire individual assets of a larger size than would be prudent given the REIT's asset base. Also, joint ventures can increase the number of assets held by the REIT and improve the diversification of its portfolio. By providing fee income, joint ventures can leverage the REIT's existing operating platform to achieve economies of scale in operations.

13.5 THE REIT OPERATING PARTNERSHIP

REITs that have chosen to utilize the operating partnership structure have an excellent vehicle for property acquisition.

13.5.1 Operating Partnership

Operating partnerships are vehicles created to aggregate properties that were originally held by their prior owners in partnership form. In most cases, the

REIT is the general partner and the majority limited partner in the operating partnership. This type of partnership structure is also referred to as an umbrella partnership or an UPREIT.

In this structure, the REIT raises funds in the capital markets and uses those funds to purchase interests in the operating partnership. Each operating partnership unit (OP unit) is economically equivalent to a share of REIT stock. It has the right to receive distributions equal to the dividends paid on a share of REIT stock. In addition, its holder may exchange each OP unit for one share of REIT common stock.

The operating partnership uses the capital to acquire new assets, reposition its existing portfolio, or repay leverage.

13.5.2 Tax-Advantaged Vehicle for Property Acquisition

The UPREIT structure provides a tax-advantaged vehicle that REITs can use to acquire property. An owner of a property held in partnership form can contribute interests in that partnership to the UPREIT in return for a negotiated number of OP units. No tax is due on contribution. The contributor transfers its tax basis from its contributed partnership interests to its interest in the UPREIT. The transferred basis is divided across the new UPREIT units that it receives. The difference between the market value of the units received and the tax basis in the contributed property is the precontribution gain. As long as the asset is held by the UPREIT and the UPREIT units are held, the precontribution gain is not recognized.

If the property is sold by the UPREIT, the original contributors realize the precontribution gain. If this occurs, the holder's basis in the operating partnership units increases by the amount of gain recognized.

If at any time the holder's UPREIT units are exchanged for shares in the REIT, a gain is realized equal to the difference between the holder's basis in the OP units and the current market value of the REIT shares received.

If a contributor dies while still holding OP units, the contributor's heirs receive the units with a new basis equal to the current value of the REIT stock. The step up in basis is added to the estate of the deceased and may be sheltered by the amount of the deceased's estate tax exclusion. When this happens, the heirs can immediately exchange their units for REIT stock and sell them on the exchange with no tax consequence.

This event is considered a major benefit for heirs, especially those who may not be knowledgeable in real estate investment because they do not have the burden of managing the contributed assets or disposing of them to gain liquidity. As a result, older property owners may see the contribution of assets to an UPREIT as an attractive vehicle for estate planning.

13.5.3 Operating Partnership Units as Currency

Given their strategic value as acquisition currency, OP units have allowed REITs to acquire property on favorable terms. Contributors of assets to operating partnerships, motivated by tax benefits, often ask REITs to delay selling the assets that they have contributed for a designated period of time. In the event that the REIT sells before the agreed-upon date, the contributor receives a payment to defray part or all of the tax liability. This payment is commonly referred to as tax protection.

13.5.4 Down REIT

Contributors do not always prefer the operating partnership structure. Some contributors may want the benefits of a venture with a REIT, including professional management and an ultimate exit through REIT shares, but also want to retain the specific economics of their assets prior to their exit. This type of arrangement would be difficult to achieve through the UPREIT structure wherein the acquisition currency is the standard OP unit representing an interest in the REITs entire portfolio.

In circumstances in which the REIT and the contributor wish to isolate the subject properties from the existing REIT portfolio, a separate partnership known as a Down REIT can be created that will hold the contributed assets. This new partnership is separate from the REIT's operating partnership.

The Down REIT is a highly flexible structure. The REIT may use a combination of operating partnership units and cash as its contribution to the new venture. However, within the Down REIT, the contributors can have their economic interest linked solely to the performance of their assets, rather than the entire REIT portfolio.

For example, if the cash return on the contributors' equity exceeds the dividend yield on the REIT shares, the contributors would experience diminished cash flow by contributing their assets to the REIT. Using the Down REIT structure, it is possible for the contributors to receive a preferred claim on the Down REIT partnership's cash flow. In this way, the contributors can earn cash returns that exceed the amount that they would have received in REIT OP unit distributions had they received the equity value of their assets in OP units.

13.6 REIT FINANCIAL STATEMENTS

REITs report their financial performance using generally accepted accounting principals. The financial statements of public REITs are audited by certified public accountants and are filed in the REIT's periodic reports to the Securities and Exchange Commission.

13.6.1 Balance Sheet

The following is the format of the typical REIT balance sheet:

Financial Statements: Balance Sheet

Balance Sheet (as of 12/31/xx)

Assets	Liabilities
Long Term	**Short Term**
Investment in Real Estate	Accounts Payable
Accumulated Depreciation	Other Short Term Liabilities
Net Investment in Real Estate	Total Short Term Liabilities
Current Assets	**Long Term**
Cash	Line of Credit
Marketable Securities	Mortgage Loans
Accounts Receivable	Corporate Debt
Total Current Assets	Total Long Term Liabilities
	Equity
	Retained Earnings
	Paid in Capital
	Total Equity
Total Assets	Total Liabilities and Net Worth

13.6.1.1 Assets

An equity REIT's largest asset is its investment in real estate. In the case of mortgage REITs, mortgages and real estate securities will be the largest asset accounts.

13.6.1.1.1 Investment in Real Estate

Investment in real estate includes the purchase price of properties acquired and the capitalized costs of acquisition. These costs include due diligence and other transaction costs. This account is stated at historical cost, the actual cost incurred to acquire the asset and make any improvements, not the current value of the assets.

Each year the REIT depreciates its assets based on a 39-year straight-line schedule for commercial properties and a 27.5 year schedule for multifamily. Land does not depreciate. Some REITs use component depreciation and apply different depreciation schedules to different parts of the property. The total amount of depreciation taken on all the properties over the period that they have been held by the REIT is shown in the accumulated depreciation account. Comparing the amount of the accumulated depreciation account to the investment in real estate account can give a quick indication of the length of time that the REIT has held its assets. The higher the ratio of accumulated depreciation to investment in real estate, the older the asset base.

13.6.1.1.2 Current Assets

In addition to the long-term assets shown in the investment account, REITs have short-term assets. Operating expenses paid in advance are shown in prepaid expenses and rents expected from tenants are shown in accounts receivable.

An analysis of the accounts receivable account can also be used to uncover any problems in revenue collection. For example, because most tenants pay rent on a monthly basis, if accounts receivable is more than 10 percent of annual revenues, it indicates that there are a significant number of delinquent tenants.

REITs hold their liquid assets as cash and marketable securities. REITs use this liquidity to make investments, pay for capital expenditures, and smooth operating cash needs such as funding payroll, paying fixed charges, and making dividend payments.

Many REITs will show a restricted cash account to reflect escrows and tenant security deposits. This cash is segregated and may not be used for operations.

13.6.1.2 Liabilities
13.6.1.2.1 Long-Term Debt

REITs utilize both corporate- and asset-level debt as financing sources. Unlike private real estate companies that often seek high levels of leverage, public REITs are generally conservative in their application of leverage. Most REITs maintain debt to total market capitalization levels of less than 50 percent.

Asset-level financing typically occurs in the form of mortgage debt sourced from the mortgage backed securities market or institutional balance sheet lenders. This financing is generally fixed rate and for terms in excess of five years. In general, this type of financing is nonrecourse to the REIT with the exception of "bad boy" provisions: as long as the REIT operates the property in a competent manner, in the event of a default, the property is the lender's only collateral for the borrowing.

Shorter-term mortgage financing is available from commercial banks, generally with terms of less than five years. This financing is almost always floating rate; however, the REIT may fix its interest rate by entering into an interest rate swap agreement. This type of financing may have some level of borrower recourse.

First-mortgage financing, regardless of the type and source, typically features LTV (debt divided by the market value of the asset) levels of 65 percent or less. To support a borrower who requests higher borrowing, a lender may package mezz financing as part of the loan and achieve LTV levels of up to 75 percent.

The principal balance of these loans will be shown on the balance sheet in the long-term debt section as mortgage loans.

Larger public REITs may access the public debt market by issuing corporate bonds in the public markets. These bonds typically carry a fixed interest rate, determined by the credit rating achieved by the issuer. A number of large REITs with low overall leverage achieved investment-grade credit ratings (BBB− or better).

REITs also access the bank credit market to obtain revolving credit lines. Revolving lines of credit allow the REIT to borrow and repay funds an unlimited number of times until the maturity date. Lines of credit may be allocated to the REIT on a nonrecourse basis, or may require the REIT to post collateral to secure the line.

13.6.1.2.2 Current Liabilities

Current liabilities are short-term obligations due within one year. Included are accounts payable arising from the operation of the REIT's assets and management infrastructure. Any principal amortization payments on mortgages and corporate debt that are due within one year are also considered current liabilities.

13.6.1.2.3 Equity

REITs typically raise equity capital through broker dealers in public or private stock offerings. The first time a REIT offers stock to the public, it is known as an initial public offering (IPO). When the REIT returns to the capital markets for a subsequent issuance of equity, it is known as a follow-on offering. When the offering consists of shares issued by the REIT, it is called a new issuance. If the offering includes shares that are being sold by existing shareholders, it is called a secondary offering. A new issuance represents additional capital to be used by the REIT while a secondary offering, the sale of already issued shares, has no impact on the company's finances.

13.6.1.2.3.1 Book Value. The amount paid by investors for the shares issued by the REIT is called the gross proceeds of the offering. The net proceeds, the cash received by the REIT for the issuance of the shares, net of the expenses of the offering is shown in equity account of the REIT's financial statement. This amount is added to the company's paid in capital account, which—when combined with retained earnings—equals the equity book value of the company.

13.6.1.2.3.2 Market Value. Once the shares are issued in a public offering, and registered with the SEC, they are known as registered shares and can be listed for trading on a public securities exchange.

Many REITs have operating partnerships that serve as the owners of their property portfolios. In addition to the partnership units owned by the REIT, there may be outside partners who also own OP units. These units are convertible into REIT stock, so when measuring the total common shareholding of the REIT, analysts assume that the operating units will convert to REIT stock.

The sum of outstanding REIT shares and OP units that may convert into REIT stock is referred to as the number of common stock equivalents.

The market value of a REIT is the product of (a) the common share equivalents and (b) the current trading price of the stock.

> **NOTE**
>
> The number of common share equivalents can also be impacted by any securities that have been issued by the REIT that are convertible into common shares. The number of shares for which a convertible security can be exchanged is known as its conversion shares. These are added to the number of common share equivalents. At the same time, the impact of the converted security must be taken into account. If the security was a convertible bond, the interest that would have been paid must be added back to income. If it was a convertible preferred stock, any dividends paid must be added back to FAD. In both cases, the book value of the converted security is added to paid-in capital and removed from its initial account.

13.6.1.3 Income Statement

Financial Statements: Income Statement

Income Statement (for the period ended 12/31/xx)

Revenues
Rents
Expense Reimbursements
Other Income
Total Revenues

Expenses
Real Estate Taxes
HVAC
Housekeeping
Security
Insurance
Total Expenses

Net Operating Income
General and Administrative

EBITDA
Interest Expense
Depreciation and Amortization

EBT
Income Taxes

Net Income

13.6.1.3.1 Revenue

A REIT receives most of its revenue from rent. Rents may be fixed periodic amounts or based on the performance of the tenants. Rents cannot be based on the tenant's net income. Leases that provide for rents that change over time are subject to straight-line rent recognition rules. Under these rules, the average amount of rent paid over the lease term is taken into revenue and the difference between the average and actual cash rent is applied to a straight-line rent receivable account.

A REIT may also receive expense reimbursement revenue from its tenants, depending on the nature of its leases.

REITS, especially mortgage and hybrid REITs, may also receive revenue from interest and dividends earned on mortgages, cash, and marketable securities.

13.6.1.3.2 Expenses

Expenses include the costs of operating the properties: security; hospitality and cleaning; utilities; property, casualty, and liability insurance; and real estate taxes. In many cases, the REIT as landlord is responsible for maintenance of its properties. If the required work is a minor repair, it will generally be expensed. If it has value for greater than one year, it will be capitalized and amortized over its useful life.

13.6.1.3.3 Net Operating Income (NOI)

The net of revenues and expenses equals NOI. This is considered a key metric for REITs because it reflects the pure cash flow generation potential of its assets. Adjusted NOI is a typical valuation metric and is critical to the calculation of net asset value.

13.6.1.3.4 General and Administrative

General and administrative (G&A) costs include the cost of executives, corporate overhead, and operating a public company. Additional costs include professional services used in preparing required public financial statements and shareholder communications; exchange listing fees; transfer agent fees; and other charges related to a company's public securities.

13.6.1.3.5 EBITDA

Earnings before interest, taxes, depreciation, and amortization (EBITDA) is a widely used measure indicating a REITs funds available to service its capital charges. Unlike NOI, which is a property level metric, EBITDA takes into account the substantial G&A burden faced by the REIT.

13.6.1.3.6 Interest Costs

REITs typically use a significant amount of debt capital and pay out a substantial amount of their available cash flow as interest costs. Interest costs have certain categorization requirements, based upon GAAP accounting. Interest costs from debt used to finance operating properties are expensed in the period incurred. Interest costs associated with construction projects are capitalized (meaning that they are added to the project's asset base) instead of being expensed in the current period. Capitalized interest is still paid in cash and must be considered in calculating cash flow metrics.

13.6.1.3.7 Depreciation

Depreciation expenses are based on an estimate of the annual economic decline in asset value due to wear and tear. To calculate depreciation under GAAP, take the amount invested in the asset (net of an allocation for the value of land) and divide it by an estimate of the asset's useful life. GAAP applies a 39-year life for commercial property and a 27.5-year life for residential property. Land does not depreciate.

13.6.1.3.8 Funds from Operations (FFO)

FFO is equal to NOI minus G&A minus interest cost and is a rough measure of a REIT's cash flow. FFO is stated both as an absolute quantity and as a per common share equivalent amount. To calculate the common share equivalent numerator, subtract any dividends paid on preferred shares from FFO and divide the remainder by the weighted average number of common share equivalents.

$$\text{FFO per share} = (\text{Total FFO} - /\text{Preferred stock dividends})/ \text{Number of common share equivalents}$$

Although FFO is a proxy for cash flow per share, rather than earnings per share, it is used by REIT analysts to calculate REIT stock price multiples. FFO multiples are applied to analyst FFO estimates to forecast REIT share price targets. This application is similar to the way corporate securities analysts use earnings per share multiples to forecast price targets for industrial stocks.

13.6.1.3.9 Funds Available for Distribution (FAD)

FAD, sometimes referred to as adjusted FFO (AFFO), is a metric that attempts to reflect the REITs actual ability to generate cash. FAD is used to pay dividends and any excess funds are available for capital transactions. To calculate FAD, subtract non-revenue-generating capital expenditures, tenant allowances, leasing commissions, and capitalized interest from FFO. In addition, it may be necessary to make an adjustment for straight-line rent. If we are recognizing less straight-line rent than the cash rent we are receiving, we must increase FAD. If we are recognizing more straight-line rent than we are receiving in cash, we must diminish FAD.

$$FAD = FFO - \text{non-revenue generating capital expenditures}$$
$$- \text{tenant allowances } - \text{Leasing commissions}$$
$$- \text{capitalized interest } +/- \text{straight-line rent adjustment}$$

13.7 COMMON REIT FINANCIAL METRICS

13.7.1 Net Asset Value (NAV)

A REIT's NAV is the estimated market value of its properties and other assets less the amount of short- and long-term liabilities, as well as the book value of any preferred stock outstanding. This value is typically stated on a per-share basis by taking the total NAV and dividing it by the common stock equivalents.

NAV per share is often compared to the current stock price. If NAV per share is greater than the stock price, the REIT is said to be trading "at a premium to NAV." If NAV is below the share price, it trades "at a discount" to NAV. A stock trading at a discount to NAV implies that if liquidated, the company's assets could be sold, its liabilities and preferred stock repaid, and the balance available for distribution would exceed its current stock price.

$$NAV \text{ per share} = (\text{market value of assets} - \text{liabilities} - \text{preferred stock})/$$
$$\text{common share equivalents}$$

NAV also relates to another metric: implied cap rate. To determine the implied cap rate, divide the REIT's NOI by its total market capitalization.

$$\text{Implied cap rate} = (\text{NOI/total market capitalization})$$

The REIT's NAV equals the sum of the values of all of the REIT's assets. In the NAV calculation, the value of each asset is calculated using actual NOI multiplied by an estimate of the market cap rate. If the REIT's actual stock price equals its NAV per share, the weighted average market cap rate and the implied cap rate will be the same and the REIT stock is trading at its liquidation value.

13.7.2 LTV

Overall, REITs typically keep their portfolio LTV ratio at 50 percent or lower, although REITs may borrow at higher levels on individual assets. This behavior gives the REIT's equity investors comfort that the REIT will not experience financial distress even when the real estate operating environment is adverse.

$$LTV = \text{long-term debt/market value of assets}$$

13.7.3 Debt-to-Market Cap

The sum of a REIT's book liabilities and the market value of its equity is referred to as its total market capitalization. To determine a REIT's debt-to-market cap ratio, divide its debt by its total market capitalization. This ratio is a leverage indicator based on the market's perception of asset value rather than the accounting value of the assets.

Debt-to-market cap = total liabilities/total market capitalization

13.7.4 Available Liquidity

Available liquidity is the amount of capital that a REIT can access in excess of the cash required to cover dividends. Investors use this metric to quantify a REIT's ability to opportunistically invest for growth.

To calculate a REIT's available liquidity, sum cash on hand, securities, and unused credit available from bank lines, to this amount, add any cash flow that the REIT is expected to generate in excess of its dividend requirement (its FAD less its current dividend payout). Available liquidity is compared to known capital commitments, including scheduled mortgage principal payments, announced acquisitions, development and property repositioning budgets, and major capital expenditures.

$$\text{Available liquidity} = \text{cash} + \text{marketable securities} + \text{available line of credit}$$
$$+ \text{FAD} - (\text{preferred and common dividend})$$

A high level of available liquidity is a positive indicator of a REIT's financial flexibility. Available liquidity can support additional acquisitions and revenue-generating capital expenditures and provide the REIT the ability to refinance maturing liabilities in the event that the credit markets become unavailable. In many cases, the REITs available liquidity can be supplemented by project financing; for example, the acquisition of a new asset may be accompanied by the assumption of existing debt, limiting the call on the REIT's available liquidity.

13.7.5 Interest Coverage

A REIT's ability to service its capital charges is a key indicator of its financial health. The typical metric for interest coverage is EBITDA divided by interest expense. DSCR looks at a REIT's ability to pay both interest and regularly scheduled principal amortization payments. DSCR is measured as EBITDA divided by debt service.

Debt yield offers an alternative coverage metric and is measured as EBITDA divided by debt. This ratio can be compared to the mortgage constant on current mortgage financings to give a view of a REIT's ability to refinance its outstanding obligations.

Interest coverage = EBITDA/interest expense

$$DSCR = EBITDA/(\text{interest expense}$$
$$+ \text{scheduled principal amortization})$$
$$\text{Debt yield} = EBITDA/\text{long-term liabilities}$$

13.7.6 Dividend Payout Ratio

Investors measure a company's ability to pay its common dividend by looking at the dividend payout ratio. The dividend payout ratio is calculated by dividing the dividends paid (the product of the weighted average number of common share equivalents and the current per share dividend payment) by either FFO or FAD. REIT dividend payout ratios are expressed as a percentage: the percent age of FFO or FAD that is required to cover the dividend at its current level. NAREIT reports an average FFO dividend payout ratio of 72.4 percent (1994 Q1–2011:Q2).[4] A higher FFO payout ratio (greater than 80 percent) implies that the current level of dividend payout may be unsustainable. A lower payout ratio (less than 60 percent) can imply the potential for a dividend increase in the future. FAD payout ratios are typically lower than FFO payout ratios.

Another common metric is the dividend coverage ratio, which equals 1 divided by the dividend payout ratio.

$$\text{FFO payout ratio} = \text{common dividend rate}$$
$$\times \text{common stock equivalents}/(\text{FFO} - \text{preferred dividends})$$

$$\text{FAO payout ratio} = \text{common dividend rate}$$
$$\times \text{common stock equivalents}/(\text{FAD} - \text{preferred dividends})$$

$$\text{Dividend coverage ratio} = 1/\text{dividend payout ratio}$$

13.7.7 Percent G&A Ratio

The percent G&A ratio, which compares the cost of operating a REIT to its revenue base, measures a REIT's ability to efficiently manage assets. The level of revenues is considered the best denominator for this ratio because it accounts for the scale of the organization. Companies with differing property types, scale, and breadth of geography require significantly different levels of infrastructure and have different G&A percentages.

$$\text{Percent G\&A} = \text{G\&A}/\text{revenue}$$

---

[4] NAREIT *REITWatch*, January 2012, p. 33.

13.7.8 Property Statistics

In addition to reporting on the financial performance of their assets, REITs must give detailed information on the properties in their portfolio. REITs must report this information at least once per year to the SEC in a Form 10-K.

For each property, the filing shows the name, location, size, date of construction, date of last renovation, and current occupancy level. Many companies also list some of each property's major tenants.

13.7.8.1 Occupancy

The occupancy level of the portfolio is a key indicator of market demand for the company's assets. Given the high fixed costs of operating properties, declining or increasing occupancy has significant impact on a REIT's profitability. In addition to an absolute level, the direction of this metric over time has important implications for REIT's future financial performance.

13.7.8.2 Rent Levels and Growth

Rent levels are closely tied to occupancy levels. Landlords with full, stable properties in markets with high demand are in a position to raise rents; those in deteriorating markets must cut rents to compete. Rents and occupancy levels work together to accelerate the direction of a REIT's profitability.

13.7.8.3 Lease Expirations

A typical portfolio has lease expirations equal to 1 divided by the average lease term. Impending lease expirations imply an opportunity for growth in portfolios with high occupancy and rising rents and a significant risk factor in markets with declining fundamentals.

13.7.8.4 Expense Recovery Ratio

Depending on the nature of its leases, a REIT will pay some or all of the operating expenses for its properties. The ratio of expense reimbursement revenue to the total operating expenses incurred is known as the expense recovery ratio. For REITs that charge for expense reimbursement in their lease structures, an ideal ratio is 1 or higher.

13.7.8.5 Same Store Revenue and NOI Growth

Same store revenue and same store NOI metrics illustrate the year-to-year changes in performance of a stable pool of assets. Same store metrics are particularly useful when a REIT has frequent changes to its asset base. The same store concept is borrowed from retail industry, where a standard measure of chain store performance has been to compare the sales of all stores that are open in two consecutive periods. This metric eliminates newly open or recently closed stores. Applying this metric to REIT portfolios allows analysts to look at the growth of revenue and NOI of seasoned properties—those assets that have been in the portfolio for at least two consecutive years.

13.8 CURRENT REIT MARKET STATISTICS

13.8.1 Number of Companies

At the end of 2011, NAREIT listed 160 public REITs with total market capitalization of $450.5 billion. Of this number, 130 were equity REITs ($407.5 billion) and 30 were mortgage REITs ($43.0 billion).

In addition to the public companies, there are an estimated 41 public non-traded REITs,[5] whose shares are sold to the public but do not trade on a public stock exchange. The estimated total capital (historic cost basis) invested in nontraded REITs is $80 billion.[6] There are also private REITs, whose shares are sold only to accredited investors (those with high annual income or net worth in excess of $1 million). Shares of private REITs do not trade and may not be subject to public company reporting requirements.

13.8.2 International Movement

The fundamental concepts underlying the REIT structure, including making commercial real estate investment accessible to the mainstream investor and improving the liquidity of the real estate capital markets, have a universal appeal that transcends national boundaries.

The REIT structure originated in the United States with the 1960 REIT Act; in addition, between 1960 and 2012, 22 additional countries have adopted REIT legislation and 14 additional countries have legislation pending or under consideration.[7]

In 2008, FTSE created the FTSE EPRA/NAREIT Global Real Estate Index to track the global real estate securities market. As of June 30, 2011, the index consisted of 392 companies with net market capitalization of a billion Euros.[8]

13.9 THE NON-REIT REAL ESTATE COMPANY

A number of large real estate companies have chosen to not be structured as REITs. These companies find either that the REIT qualification requirements constrain their operations or that the tax benefit is not helpful to them

---

[5] http://www.reit.com (accessed November 11, 2012).

[6] http://www.bluevaultpartners.com (accessed November 11, 2013).

[7] Cohen and Steers whitepaper Introduction to Real Estate Securities, August 2012.

[8] FTSE factsheet, FTSE EPRA/NAREIT Global & Global EX US Indices, June 30, 2011.

because their taxable income is sheltered by the depreciation derived from their assets.

Non-REIT companies that invest in properties are referred to as real estate operating companies (REOCs). If the real estate company is a service provider rather than an investor for its own account, it is referred to as a real estate services company.

13.10 REAL ESTATE COMPANY OPERATIONS

The goal of a real estate company is to aggregate and exploit a portfolio of real property for the benefit of investors. The level of vertical integration varies widely among industry participants. Highly integrated large public and private firms represent one end of the spectrum. In many cases, these firms rent their operating capabilities to both institutional investors and smaller real estate companies as outsourcing solutions. In contrast, many small firms focus solely on business development functions and purchase all other services from third parties.

13.10.1 Business Development Functions

Business development functions help real estate companies acquire and exploit their assets.

13.10.1.1 Acquisitions

Acquiring assets to build portfolios is a critical function for real estate companies. Acquisition professionals must have a deep understanding of property valuation and the ability to assess the economic health of and prospects for the region in which the assets are located. They must identify key brokers in their desired markets and maintain strong relationships with them so that they are aware of any properties that are offered for sale. Seasoned acquisition professionals can identify desirable properties that are not currently for sale and negotiate off-market transactions.

Once a target property is identified, an acquisition professional reviews property operating, legal, and financial data in a process known as due diligence. Once a buyer and seller agree to transact, the acquisition professional prepares an offer letter, followed by a purchase contract. Acquisition professionals are also responsible for closing the purchase transaction. In many cases, they also integrate the new asset into the company's property management regime.

13.10.1.2 Development

Development professionals are responsible for the creation of new properties from concept through construction. Development projects can be undertaken on behalf of a building's user to meet known tenant demand or to opportunistically address a perceived market need (spec development). Development professionals identify parcels of land for new construction or existing buildings to be reutilized. With architects and planners, they then create a concept for the new use, obtain government permits and entitlements to undertake the project, and implement the plan with a construction contractor.

Development is a high-risk, high-value undertaking that creates a growth vector for many real estate companies.

13.10.1.3 Asset Management

Asset managers act as the owner's proxy to implement plans that maximize the value of each property in the portfolio. This strategy extends from the commitment of resources to rehabilitate and reposition an asset to decision making regarding rent levels and leasing commitments. The asset manager determines when a property has reached its peak and should be sold so that the capital can be repositioned into new properties with greater growth prospects.

13.10.1.4 Leasing

Leasing agents are the real estate company's sales force. The leasing agent attempts to match potential tenants with the company's available inventory of rentable space. By interacting in the marketplace, the leasing agent gains insight into supply and demand for space. Thus the agent can help the asset manager to set appropriate lease terms, including rent levels and amenity packages, to maximize the property's returns.

13.10.2 Marketing

Real estate companies use their marketing function to enhance their company's reputation as well as to clearly position their properties in the marketplace. Property marketing professionals analyze regional demographics and competitive properties to help tenants understand property attributes. They then prepare sales materials for use by leasing agents in approaching tenants.

Corporate marketing helps enhance the reputation of the company in the marketplace by convincing its customers, business partners, employees, and capital sources of its expertise and capability to complete its projects. Because many real estate projects involve large amounts of risk capital, the real estate firm's ability to perform is crucial in competing for new business.

13.10.3 Property Management

Most real estate companies provide property management services. Property management entails the operation and maintenance of the physical plant;

the provision of housekeeping, security, and landscaping services; the leasing of the property to tenants; and the accounting for the rents and expenses.

Real estate firms that develop, own, and manage their own assets are known as owner/operators. Those that provide these services to other property owners are known as third-party management companies. To provide these services, companies maintain a staff of professionals in each of the disciplines mentioned. The overhead of the company includes professional salaries, benefits, and office space as well as information technology (IT) and human resource management costs. Depending on the company's level of vertical integration, it may directly employ workers or hire employees through specialized outsourcing firms.

13.10.3.1 Third Party Management

In return for property management services, non-operating owners generally pay a management fee based on a percentage of total property revenue. This fee is typically paid on a monthly basis. Owners are directly responsible for the operating costs of their properties and all on-site personnel, even if they are employees of the management company.

Some property management firms provide leasing services; others outsource them to local providers. Owners typically pay leasing commissions on a per transaction basis at the beginning of the lease based on a percentage of expected rent over the lease term.

13.10.4 Financial Functions
13.10.4.1 Budgeting

Real estate companies prepare operating budgets for the properties they manage, including revenues, expenses, the payment of capital charges (interest), the provision for recurring and nonrecurring capital expenditures, and tenant costs including leasing commissions. In addition to property level budgets, companies need to prepare their own budget for the provision of management services.

13.10.4.2 Treasury

The treasury function facilitates cash management including the collection of rent and the application of funds to pay operating expenses. Companies with large property portfolios operating across a wide geography may have accounts at many banks and require sophisticated treasury management systems for aggregating, investing, and disbursing cash. Modern systems can integrate the company's cash management processes directly with its banks, tenants, and vendors.

13.10.4.3 Finance

Although the treasury deals with short-term liquidity issues, the company's finance function is responsible for its long-term capital position. Real estate companies tend to have large capital requirements and must interact with a broad spectrum of banks and financial institutions.

13.10.4.4 Investor Relations

Most real estate companies rely on outside capital from public and private sources to grow their asset base. These capital providers require information regarding the company and its assets prior to investing. They also need a continuing stream of updated data once an investment has been made. The packaging and distribution of information about a public company is subject to strict regulations, including SEC Regulation FD (fair disclosure) adopted in October, 2000. A violation of any of the many rules can result in civil and criminal penalties to the company and its executives. To properly market the company to potential investors, the investor relations professional must combine a deep knowledge of the company's business operations, accounting conventions, and financial performance. This information must be communicated to potential investors with sensitivity to the strict regulatory environment surrounding investor communications.

13.10.4.5 Accounting

The accounting function aggregates transaction information from the operating and financial functions and uses the data to prepare financial reports and analysis. Most large real estate companies use sophisticated enterprise resource planning software to manage their financial reporting. In many public companies, the accounting function is divided between the property accounting function, which focuses on operations, and the corporate accounting function, which focuses on the preparation of GAAP financial statements.

13.10.4.6 Internal Audit

The internal audit group works with the company's accountants to ensure that all transactions are accurately reported and classified appropriately on the financial statements. To accomplish this, the internal audit group randomly tests the reporting system against original transaction documents to verify accuracy and compliance with Sarbanes-Oxley regulations. In some cases, visual observations are made of facilities to verify occupancy, completion of construction work, and presence of supplies and equipment. Third parties are often contacted to verify transaction activity and ensure that proper purchasing procedures have been followed.

The internal auditor is often called upon to investigate whistleblower reports and other complaints of violation of corporate policies. To maintain independence from management, the internal auditor has a direct reporting relationship to the audit committee of the board of directors.

13.10.4.7 Information Technology

REITs are constantly expanding their use of information technology. Enterprise resource planning (ERP) systems are widely employed for transaction processing and financial reporting.

These systems now integrate with portfolio management, project management, human resource management, and tenant service request tracking systems. In many commercial real estate firms, customer relationship management (CRM) software now manages the leasing "sales" cycle. Hotel and residential real estate firms employ software-based models for occupancy and rent optimization.

The modern real estate company also uses the Internet and social media to interact with internal and external constituents, including employees, tenants, business partners, and capital providers. This outward-facing infrastructure makes the corporate network more susceptible to security threats which must be constantly monitored and deterred.

Business intelligence tools are being incorporated into the IT infrastructure to analyze the transactional data, bring it to the executive's desktops, and help them make real-time decisions.

In most real estate companies, the interaction between IT and financial reporting is most critical, and for this reason, in many companies the IT department reports to the CFO.

13.10.5 Administrative Functions
13.10.5.1 Human Resources

The typical real estate company employs a broad cross section of employees, ranging from highly compensated business development executives to hourly workers who perform asset-level hospitality and security functions. Identifying, hiring, and managing such a diverse group of employees is challenging. Creating compensation and performance management systems for these multiple-level firms is complex.

Many real estate companies also operate across a wide geography. Benefit packages must be implemented, using many local providers that adhere to different regulations. In many areas, unions may represent groups of workers, adding an additional layer of complexity.

In addition to facing many operational challenges, today's human resource professional operates in a highly regulated and litigious environment, which makes attention to detail and systematic record keeping key success factors.

13.10.5.2 Legal

The legal team at a modern real estate company manages corporate, asset, and leasing transactions. For public real estate companies, the legal team must also deal with public securities filings and compliance issues. Due to the wide range of transaction types and venues, as well as the need for peak staffing to accommodate transaction activity that may vary over time, many real estate companies employ both internal and external counsel. The internal general counsel coordinates all of the firm's legal activities.

13.10.5.3 Risk Management

In the past decade, the role of risk manager has evolved from a focus on property casualty insurance to a wide view of the totality of risks facing a real estate enterprise. These include a broader range of insurable risks: personal lines, liability, property and casualty, directors and officers, and environmental and terrorism risk insurance, combined with a focus on loss prevention and business continuity planning. In the face of the many natural and manmade disasters that have taken place since the millennium, boards of directors have begun to focus on enterprise risk management as one of their key areas of oversight. As a result, the modern enterprise risk manager is a senior member of management and, in some cases, is directly accountable to the board.

13.11 HISTORY

On September 14, 1960, the U.S. Congress passed the REIT Act which allowed for the establishment of real estate investment trusts. This legislation was created to give individual investors the opportunity to participate in the ownership of commercial properties. Prior to the creation of REITs, most commercial properties were owned by institutions, wealthy families, or partnerships of wealthy individuals. Only the very wealthy could own large commercial properties due to securities legislation that limited participation in limited partnership investing to high net worth individuals. Small investors did not have access to an investment vehicle in this asset class.

Under current U.S. tax law, partnerships are allowed to pass through income and losses to shareholders without entity level taxation. To accomplish economic equivalence with partnerships, REITs receive a deduction from federal income tax for all dividends distributed to shareholders. Shareholders of REIT securities are therefore only subject to a single level of taxation: personal income tax on distributions received.

To qualify for this special tax treatment, REITs were required to follow a number of rules covering the composition and management of their investment portfolios and the distribution of earnings to their shareholders.

13.11.1 Original Conception as a Real Estate Mutual Fund

At its inception in 1960, many of the REIT rules were originally modeled after those in the Investment Company Act of 1940, which governed "40 Act Companies," commonly referred to as mutual funds.

Mutual funds are investment vehicles that allow small investors to own fractional interests in large portfolios of professionally managed securities. The mutual fund is considered a passive investment vehicle and pays no entity-level tax. The portfolio manager of a mutual fund may not take an active role in the management of the companies in which it invests. The mutual fund portfolio manager decides on the composition of the portfolio only.

At its inception, the REIT was thought of as a mutual fund that would invest in real property assets rather than equity securities. The function of the REIT was viewed as portfolio management rather than real estate operations. The role of the REIT management team was to acquire and dispose of properties. Third-party property management companies, which—unlike the REIT—would be subject to entity-level taxation, were to manage operations. Violation of the many rules limiting the operating activities of REITs could result in the loss of REIT status and its tax advantages.

There are a few major structural differences between REITs and mutual funds, which have existed since inception. Unlike mutual funds, which hold publically traded securities and are redeemable each day at NAV, there is no independent method for the real-time valuation of a REIT's assets and no assurance that the REIT shares will trade at NAV.

Additionally, REITs do not include any immediate link between portfolio manager performance and compensation. Mutual funds are open ended, meaning that the investor can seek redemption at will: if the mutual fund manager underperforms, the holders can redeem at NAV, forcing the contraction of the fund and a decline in compensation. In a REIT, which is a "closed-end" vehicle, the shareholder does not have an ability to transfer the shares back to the manager at NAV and force liquidation. The shareholders of publicly traded REITs can trade their shares on the stock exchange but cannot force the REIT to redeem shares and liquidate.

13.11.2 Third-Party Management Inhibited Growth of the Industry

As the REIT concept developed over time, the REIT's passive management structure was seen as one reason why the REIT industry experienced slow growth. During the 1970s and early 1980s, financial institutions, including major insurance companies, set up mortgage REITs to provide capital for real estate loans. In this early version of commercial mortgage securitization, the financial institution underwrote the loan and then funded it with the REIT's capital. This meant that financial institutions earned underwriting and management fees without retaining any risk.

Many of these early mortgage REITs had financial problems. The separation of the management company from the REIT, a function of the legislative mandate, led to some abusive practices and was seen as contrary to the interest of the investing public. In some cases, substantial management fees were paid without regard to asset performance. Management teams could prosper while shareholder value diminished. Self-management, in which the interests of the REIT's management team were economically aligned with the interest of the shareholders, was seen as a better model.

13.11.3 Evolution to a Vertically Integrated Real Estate Company

The Tax Reform Act of 1986 granted REITs the ability to manage their own properties. This step was the key to REITs gaining the ability to vertically integrate into the management of their own assets and to develop assets for their own portfolios. Bankers and analysts quickly promoted the vertically integrated REIT, seeing it as the most appropriate structure to align the interests of management and shareholders.

13.11.4 End of Tax Shelters Became an Impetus for the Modern REIT

The Tax Reform Act of 1986 also ended the era of real estate tax shelters. Tax shelter investments were highly levered, meaning that a small amount of equity capital controlled a large amount of property. Accelerated depreciation and high interest costs created investments that showed tax losses. The tax losses were used to offset taxes due on income earned from unrelated activities. In this way, the tax savings generated a return in the form of tax relief.

Sponsors known as real estate syndicators acted through, and sometimes as part of, major securities brokerage houses and organized these tax shelter investment partnerships.

Properties developed as tax shelter investments were frequently built without regard for tenant interest or economic demand. Instead, the development was driven by the creation of tax losses. When tax reform passed in 1986 and the tax shelter market closed, there was a precipitous drop in the value of these assets, many of which were called see-through buildings, because they had no tenants.

These buildings had little economic value, so when investors lost the economic benefit of the tax deductions, they withdrew from the tax shelter partnerships.

As the partners withdrew, the partnerships defaulted on their property- and partnership-level debt.

Defaults on tax shelter partnership debt shook the banking system, especially in the fast-growing south and southwest areas of the country, where many of the properties were located. The banks liquidated the assets after foreclosure, further depressing the real estate market. As a result, many of the banks that had real estate loans concentrated in the fast-growing sun-belt states failed.

13.11.5 Tax Shelter Development in the 1970s and 1980s

In 1989, the banking system's bad debt issues led to the passage of the Financial Institutions Reform, Recovery, and Enforcement Act (FIRREA) and the creation of the resolution trust company (RTC), which aggregated bad debt, foreclosed on property, and sold the distressed assets to new investors. The low prices at which these properties were trading kept the property markets depressed through the early 1990s.

13.11.6 Operating Partnerships Emerge

As a result of credit market conditions, it was generally difficult to find liquidity in the real estate capital markets in the early 1990s. Many large family-owned real estate companies were facing significant difficulty in obtaining refinancing for maturing loans and were thus threatened with the loss of their assets.

As property values declined well below replacement costs, contrarian investors started to look for a way to reenter the real estate market. The REIT structure, with its favorable tax treatment and public market liquidity, was considered ideal.

The public REIT market presented an opportunity for large property owners to find capital to repay the debt against their properties. The issue for these owners, many of whom had fully depreciated assets, became how to position the REIT as a vehicle that could acquire properties in a tax efficient manner without triggering gain recognition.

13.11.7 The Roll-Up

It was, and still is, typical for private real estate owners to hold their assets in individual property partnerships to avoid linking the assets together in the event of project failure or mortgage default. However, to attract public investors, many properties must be aggregated into a single vehicle with scale.

The aggregation of multiple assets held by separate partnerships into a single entity is known as a roll-up. In order to accomplish a tax efficient roll-up, a newly formed REIT would be organized whose sole asset is its interest in a master partnership. Into this master partnership, the family or group undertaking the roll-up (the sponsor) contributes interests in each of their single property partnerships. In return for these property-level partnership interests, the master partnership, known as an umbrella or operating partnership, issues the contributors OP units.

Each OP unit is designed to be economically equivalent to one share of REIT stock. In return for their assets, the contributing property owners are given units in the operating partnership. These units retain the same tax basis that the investor had in the contributed asset. The units can ultimately be converted into shares in the public REIT. Unfortunately, converting the operating partnership units to public REIT stock triggers the recognition of any taxable gain. However, the contributors control when they convert their units and, at any time they desire, have immediate liquidity by selling their REIT shares on the stock exchange.

In addition to the sponsors whose holdings were large enough to initiate their own REITs, the ability to affect these tax-advantaged transactions attracted additional property sellers to these newly created operating partnership REITS. The ability to hold REIT operating units and to convert at will to publicly traded shares is attractive to many investors who use the method for estate planning. Upon the death of the unit holder, the unit tax basis is stepped up to market value and the gain is taken against the decendent's estate tax exclusion. The heirs can then convert the units to public shares and obtain liquidity without further tax consequence.

In addition to obtaining properties in exchange for operating partnership units, REITs using this structure can issue shares to the public for cash. The funds raised are used to purchase additional limited partnership units. This approach maintains the one-to-one correspondence between the number of units held by the REIT and the number of shares it has outstanding. In turn, the operating partnership uses these funds to acquire additional assets and/or to help reduce the existing debt on its owned assets.

13.11.8 Era of the Entrepreneurial REIT

As a result of the operating partnership structure, many real estate entrepreneurs found a new home in the REIT marketplace. A further step to facilitate the entrepreneurial REIT was taken in 1993, when taxable REIT subsidiaries were created to allow REITs to perform services related to their assets. This allowed many vertically integrated private real estate companies to seamlessly transition to REIT form.

During the mid-1990s, many of the former scions of major real estate families reemerged as CEOs of public REITs. The nature of the industry evolved to reflect their business acumen and aspirations for growth. Removed from the need to individually finance each asset and with access to the equity capital markets, these newly public REITs had the potential to grow rapidly. Investors interested in moving capital into a recovering real estate market fueled the industry's growth.

The REIT structure evolved alongside rapid technological shifts, led by the invention of the Internet. In the late 1990s, the emergence of the Internet and its ancillary technologies shifted investor focus from real property into the virtual realm and led to a slowdown of the REIT market.

The REIT market remained quiet as the U.S. economy was hit with two consecutive blows: the technology stock bubble in 2000 and the terrorist attacks on the World Trade Centers in 2001.

In order to restart the economy, the postmillennial period was marked by low interest rates. The low interest rates, combined with a reversal of investor preference for virtual assets, reignited the growth of the REIT market, a hard-asset industry with relatively high dividend payouts.

As the industry grew, the largest REITs became world-class companies and entered the S&P 500, marking the maturity of the industry in the eyes of the investment community. This acceptance of REITs allowed pension funds and other conservative financial institutions to increase their allocation to real estate securities and further increased the flow of capital into the industry.

At the same time the REIT market was growing, so was the demand for direct investment in property. Private equity funds sought to arbitrage the asset value of REITs against their stock prices by buying REITs and liquidating their assets. This development led to a flurry of consolidation as REITs were liquidated into a private real estate market fueled by the availability of high leverage and loose credit standards.

13.11.9 Strong Enough to Weather the Storm

In 2008, the Financial Crisis abruptly ended the expansionary real estate market. The flow of capital to the real estate market and transactional activity ceased. Asset prices fell precipitously as capital became scarce. Lower asset values raised apparent leverage levels. Many REITs suffered financial distress as liabilities matured into a market with little liquidity. REITs came under pressure to deleverage their balance sheets by raising equity. In parallel to the developments of the early 1990s, REITs were again seen as vehicles to provide capital to a distressed real estate market. Investors seeking a contrarian investment recapitalized a number of REITs, positioning them as asset aggregators, in expectation that many opportunities to buy properties from distressed sellers would emerge.

This recapitalization of the REIT industry created a perception in the marketplace that the REITs would become aggressive buyers of distressed real estate. In an ironic way, the anticipated REIT demand for property served to stabilize the property market and made the opportunistic purchases sought by the REITs more elusive then anticipated. As the industry neared its 50th anniversary in 2010, the fact that investors saw REITs as the agent of choice in a period of risk indicated to many investors that the industry had reached maturity.

Glossary

Adjusted NOI
AFFO (adjusted FFO)
Alignment of interests
Attribution rules
Available liquidity
Balance sheet debt
Bank line of credit
Board of directors
Business trust
(business intelligence)
Common stock equivalent
CRM (customer relationship management)
Debt yield
Distribution requirement
Dividend coverage ratio
Dividend payout ratio
Down REIT
Equity REIT
Earnings and profits
ERP (enterprise resource planning)
Enterprise risk management
Expense recovery ratio
Excise tax
Five or fewer rule
FIRREA (Financial Institutions Reform, Recovery, and Enforcement Act)
Follow-on issuance
FAD (funds available for distribution)
FFO (funds from operation)
G&A (general and administrative expense)
Gross proceeds
Hybrid REIT
Implied cap rate
Income test
IPO (initial public offering)
Investment Company Act of 1940 (40 Act)
Local sharpshooter

Master partnership
Mortgage REIT
NAV (net asset value)
NOI (net operating income)
Net proceeds
New issue
Off-market transaction
Operating partnership
OP unit (operating partnership unit)
Owner/operator
Pass-through entities
Percent G&A
Pre-contribution gain
Prohibited transaction
REIT (real estate investment trust)
REOC (real estate operating company)
Real estate services company
Real estate syndication
Registered shares
Regulation FD
RTC (resolution trust company)
Roll-up
Secondary issue
See-through buildings
SEC Form 10-K
Self-management
Shares of beneficial interest
Sponsor
Tax shelter
TRS (taxable REIT subsidiary)
Tax protection
Tax Reform Act of 1986
Third party management
UPREIT (umbrella partnership REIT)
Whistleblower

Thought Questions

1. Hyper Development Company ("HDC") builds and sells condominiums at vacation destinations on three continents. An investment banker recently proposed that Hyper HDC restructure as a REIT. What could they have been thinking?
2. Jack McKaid has built a great private real estate company in the warehouse business. He has always dreamed of taking his company public as a REIT. While preparing for the public offering, he is approached by one of his competitors, who proposes making a significant but non-controlling investment in Jack's business. What factors should Jack consider?

Review Questions

For questions 1 through 5, use the following information:

East REIT

Income Statement

(For period ending December 31, 2013, in millions)

Revenues	$200
Expenses	$130
General and administrative	$5

Balance Sheet

(As of December 31, 2013, in millions)

Assets		Liabilities and Net Worth	
Investment in real estate (net)	$1,000	Liabilities	$400
		Long-term debt	
		Total Liabilities	
		Equity	
		Common shares	$600
Assets	$1,000	Total Equity	$1,000
		Total liabilities and net worth	

The debt is interest only with a 5 percent coupon rate. There are 10 million shares outstanding. The shares trade at $80 per share.

1. Calculate NOI.
2. Calculate FFO.
3. Calculate FFO per share.
4. Calculate interest coverage.
5. Calculate debt-to-market capitalization.

Multiple Choice Questions

1. Which of the following is not true about REITs?
   a) Must have at least 100 owners
   b) No five or fewer individuals can own greater than 50 percent
   c) Must pay out 75 percent of earnings and profits
   d) Can have up to 25 percent of assets in a TRS
2. Publicly traded REITs are subject to all of the following except:
   a) SEC disclosure requirements
   b) Generally accepted accounting principles
   c) Special real estate principles
   d) Exchange listing requirements

3. Which of the following asset allocations is not possible for a REIT?
   a) 100% CMBS
   b) 30% industrial stock
   c) 25% of a taxable subsidiary
   d) 95% real estate

4. Equity REITs generally concentrate their investment focus by:
   a) Property geography
   b) Property type
   c) Life of investment
   d) All of the above

5. The REIT concept is:
   a) Used in many countries
   b) Limited to companies owning U.S. assets
   c) Declining in appeal to the capital markets
   d) Limited to companies listed in the United States

6. Which of the following is not a major source of REIT capital?
   a) Public market equity
   b) Mortgage financing
   c) Issuance of corporate debt
   d) Investment of after tax profits

7. REITS may invest in assets at which stage of completion:
   a) Land
   b) Projects under development
   c) Construction completed with cash flow
   d) All of the above

8. Funds available for distribution is primarily an indicator of:
   a) Ability to cover interest payments
   b) Ability to cover common dividends
   c) Ability to finance property development
   d) Ability to issue new equity

9. An umbrella partnership allows all of the following except:
   a) Liquidity for owners of privately held properties
   b) Unit holders who can request REIT stock
   c) Sale of real estate as inventory
   d) Tax efficient acquisition of property

10. What is the fundamental measure of REIT operating performance?
   a) Net income per share
   b) DSCR
   c) FFO per share
   d) IRR

For answers to these Problems and Exercises, please visit the companion
website: http://booksite.elsevier.com/9780123786265

CHAPTER 14

Corporate Real Estate

14.1 FUNCTION

In addition to being an asset class for investment, real estate plays an important role in implementing the strategic plans of many corporations and institutions. To this end, many corporations have a real estate or facilities department that is responsible for providing physical space for the operation of the business.

In order to accomplish this mission, the corporate real estate department must assess the space needs of the organization and identify appropriate and optimal locations for each type of property. The department must negotiate to lease, acquire, or develop the required facilities; arrange for the fit out of the space; and prepare for the relocation of staff and equipment to the new location. Once the new space is occupied, the department must maintain the space while it is in service. At the end of its useful life, the department must refit or sell the space, and, if required, begin the space acquisition process again.

For an increasing number of businesses, real estate is critical to the establishment of brand identity. A wide range of factors—including the location, design, and environmental standing of key properties—can have a major impact on the success of the corporation.

14.2 GOALS

14.2.1 Location
As with all real estate, corporate properties benefit from locations best aligned with their intended use. This alignment occurs when the chosen location has attributes that reinforce the key elements of the company's strategic plan.

14.2.2 Zoned for Intended Use
Well-planned development typically involves allocating contiguous land for common usage. For instance, residential and industrial uses are typically physically separated to enhance the aesthetic of the residential environment and to provide the requisite infrastructure to support industry. Companies with manufacturing and warehousing requirements have an easier time acquiring permits and entitlements when they locate in an area zoned for industrial property.

399

However, not all property types benefit from isolation and homogeneous zoning. For example, although major retail complexes benefit from collocation in shopping districts (increasing the efficiency of the customer's shopping trips), retail shops can also integrate well in mixed-use developments that also include office and residential property.

For non-industrial uses, many corporations find that locations in mixed-use developments provide attractive amenities to both customers and employees.

14.2.3 Access to Factors of Production

The ideal location for any business asset is one that is accessible to its key factors of production, including labor, materials, utilities, and transportation.

14.2.3.1 Skilled Labor

For manufacturing or service businesses that rely on skilled labor a location in any area that has a deep pool of talent can be a determinant of success. For this reason, business activity in particular industries is clustered around communities with deep pools of talent with related skills.

For example, high technology corridors exist around major universities. The growth of the well-known Silicon Valley near Palo Alto, California, is based in large part to the talent attracted to Stanford University in Palo Alto. The same can be said regarding the Route 128 technology corridor outside of Boston, Massachusetts, which grew out of the talent attracted to both MIT and Harvard.

Talent can also aggregate around unique and successful businesses. An example would be Microsoft, which has attracted workers skilled in computer software development to Seattle, Washington. The presence of large numbers of skilled workers can lead to entrepreneurial activity, including the creation of ancillary businesses, spinoffs, suppliers, and even competitors.

14.2.3.2 Materials for Use in Manufacturing

For manufacturing companies, especially those dependent on low value to weight raw materials, locating adjacent to raw materials is important. A proximate location ensures a low cost of transportation, which in turn can lower the cost of the final product, making it more competitive in the marketplace. For businesses creating products with low value to weight, local customers or efficient access to low cost shipping is critical.

For example, it is difficult to justify shipping either paper products or simple aggregates over long distances, as their value to weight ratio is low. In contrast, the cost of shipping diamonds is low relative to their value and diamonds are processed far from the site of the mine and far from the end user. In fact, diamonds are processed in locations where skilled cutters and polishers are available at the best labor rates because the required skill is unique. The materials and labor costs are far more important determinants of the final product's value than the cost of transportation.

14.2.3.3 Utilities such as Energy, Telecom Bandwidth, Water, and Sewer

Many industries are dependent on the availability of utilities. Where utility availability and cost are key inputs, a wide range of industries emerge around locations where the utility is available in quantity and at competitive cost.

For example, the production of aluminum from the ore bauxite requires copious amounts of electricity and tends to be located where electricity is plentiful and cheap. The same is true of companies operating large amounts of computer equipment for data processing and storage. The power demands of major server farms and data warehouses may be unsupportable in certain areas, setting a constraint on location.

Access to telecommunications bandwidth is another constraint facing companies dependent on Internet connectivity. Companies that depend on high speed and high-throughput internet service tend to acquire space for their equipment in data hotels, which are specialized buildings that have controlled temperature environments, access to power, and a connection to the optical fiber networks that transmit data signals.

Water is a key requirement for many industrial uses, including power generation. Water is used as the source of power in hydroelectric plants and is used to cool nuclear reactors that operate at very high temperatures. Access to water is thus a constraint for locating this type of commercial activity.

The ability to treat and dispose of sewerage can also be a constraint on industrial activity. Large farms and food processing facilities can generate significant amounts of waste that present a challenge to the local environment. For these activities, the availability of waste treatment facilities with sufficient capacity becomes a critical determinant in choosing a location.

14.2.4 Ability to Ship Goods

Many businesses are dependent on access to trucking, rail, and shipping to move products to and from warehouses. For these companies, proximity to good transportation infrastructure is critical. For users sensitive to logistics, locations that are close to ports, rail lines, and the interstate highway system are more highly valued than those with less efficient access that adds time and cost to the movement of goods. Locations where multiple types of transportation are accessible are called intermodal transportation hubs. These are ideal locations for warehouse facilities.

14.2.5 Customer Access

For a service or retail business to be successful, it must be easily accessible to customers. In the retail business, minor nuances in location, such as the side of the road on which a store is located, the presence of a traffic light at an adjacent intersection, or the visibility of the store from adjacent roads can dramatically affect sales productivity.

Professional service businesses with highly compensated knowledge workers and unique skill sets tend to aggregate in Class A office buildings in central business districts (CBD). These areas offer a quality of space that is attractive to both the professional service worker and the executive level customer base that seeks the hotel, restaurant, and other amenities typically found in these locations.

14.2.6 Corporate Image

For many companies, the choice of location can communicate a statement about the corporate brand and the intended market position of the company.

14.2.6.1 The Corporate Office

Service businesses attempting to serve a high-net-worth clientele attempt to locate in Class A office space in CBD locations. They look for high-quality buildings with numerous amenities and distinctive architectural features. Large companies may seek to have a noted architect create an individual building for their principal use that attempts to reflect the corporate identity.

For the past 100 years, major U.S. cities such as New York and Chicago have been noted for their renowned eponymous skyscrapers housing many world famous companies. The Chrysler Building in New York City with its gargoyles in the shape of 1927 Chrysler car hood ornaments and its elevator grills taken from hub cap designs represents one of the best known examples of "corporate" architecture integrating a distinctive brand into its design.

Buildings housing high-end corporate headquarters and professional service firms feature numerous amenities. They typically offer limited access via an elegant lobby with a security check-in. Each floor may also have elevator lobbies that lead to secure reception areas. Core mechanicals will also be protected and have limited access. Restrooms will be of high quality and may have entrance security.

Interior design can also be used to inform a customer about a brand. Furnishings and architectural details carry out the theme. For example, established firms may use wood-paneled walls with founder's portraits and antiques to show stability. Consultants imply modern thinking with sleek, trendy environments including contemporary furnishings and space layouts.

Conference rooms and common spaces also reflect a corporation's mission. Individual office or workspace design reflects both the stature of the individual and the expected time that the professional and the client will spend in the space. Senior executive offices may be larger and include conference tables and sitting areas to host client meetings.

14.2.6.1.1 Alternative Work Environments
The advent of the Internet has led to major changes in the work environment. The classic office environment has been altered due to changes in the lifestyle and aspirations of the younger generation.

The Internet start-ups of the late 1990s reflected the work-hard/play-hard ethos of the young founders. The workspaces were often based on flexible, open plans without many walls. They were easily reconfigurable and were said to encourage creativity and cooperation. These work environments were informal and included many recreational amenities for employees that spent long hours at work. The employee's dedication to the job blurred the distinctions between workplace and home. The media coverage of these evolutionary workspaces made this type of start-up look and feel familiar.

Conversely, homes began to look more like workspaces. Improved telecommunications made working from home or another offsite location a real possibility for many service workers. The home office became a reality for many service workers who spent long hours on the road. These workers now rarely had to come into the central corporate office. Employees who split their work hours between their office and home or other location became known as telecommuters.

Although telecommuting workers spent much time away from the office, they would still use the central corporate location for tasks requiring face-to-face interaction, such as group project meetings and training. When in house, many of these workers were assigned temporary quarters, often stocked just-in-time with their personal effects. This practice became known as hoteling.

14.2.6.1.2 Sustainability
At the same time as these trends were taking hold, growing environmental concerns led to an increased focus on the impact that the built environment was having on carbon consumption. Studies claimed that over 38 percent of U.S. energy consumption went toward lighting and heating buildings. This finding lead to widespread focus on corporate sustainability and the growth of the green building movement.

The green building movement focuses on environmentally sound construction and operating standards that reduce energy consumption and improve indoor and outdoor environmental quality. The U.S. Green Building Council (USGBC) developed a set of standards known as Leadership in Energy and Environmental Design (LEED) that ranked properties on their adherence to sustainable practices.

LEED principles are based on conservation of energy and water, reduction of greenhouse gases and landfill waste, and improvement of health and safety for occupants. Buildings that comply with these principles are ranked using a point system. Many corporate space users and the U.S. government use LEED ratings as a criterion when selecting buildings to occupy.

14.2.6.2 The Campus

World-class technology businesses with knowledge workers drawn from prestigious universities see their corporate location as an extension of the worker's academic milieu. Google, Microsoft, Oracle, Bell Labs, and Xerox have all used the "campus" metaphor to refer to the collections of low-rise suburban buildings that form their corporate workspaces. This type of environment communicates the companies' core values to both employees and customers.

In many cases, the aggregation of workers drawn to a high-growth technology company can have a profound impact on the local economy. The growing technology company seeds ancillary economic development, as many business partners in the key company's supply chain set up offices nearby. In addition, a second wave of growth occurs as employees with entrepreneurial ambition leave the mother company to form spinoffs, leveraging the deep local talent pool and resources.

14.2.6.3 Retail Stores: Brand in a Box

For many years, retail businesses relied heavily on their physical space to communicate their brand to consumers. The quality of the finish used at their stores, along with packaging used for products, implied the positioning of the goods purveyed.

Major stores were curators of goods and the customers were collectors. For apparel, the provenance of Saks Fifth Avenue and Neiman Marcus were as important as the brand name on the item's label. Mass communication and the wide promotion of brand-name goods allowed the value retailer to sell goods based on their own merit and to not associate that value with the store in which they were sold. Value merchants informed the consumer that the goods spoke for themselves and that the sales environment was in fact costing them money they did not need or want to spend.

Since the advent of mail order shopping in the late 1880s, catalog retailers have used a print document to take the place of the physical environment and to create a sales thesis behind a collection of goods. The catalog offered the convenience of at-home shopping and delivery to the house. Starting in the mid-1990s, the Internet delivered the catalog online, and innovators such as eBay and Amazon added interactivity; an ever-evolving combination of intelligence, community involvement; and more efficient fulfillment methods to improve the sales process.

Today's best brands and the most forward-thinking merchants, designers, and landlords seek to integrate the unique sensory aspects of physical space with the effectiveness of the Internet to create a fully integrated brand profile for the consumer, which has become known as multichannel retailing.

Apple is a great example of the new multichannel retailer that has captured the imagination of the global consumer. The Apple Store, with its unique architecture, beautiful design, and ability to cross-sell from physical and virtual space creates a 360-degree environment surrounding its high-end, well-informed customer base.

14.2.7 Flexible Occupancy Terms

The rapidly evolving world described in the previous section creates an inherent volatility in business. Corporate real estate strategies must demonstrate an ability to accommodate growth, downsizing, or change in use. In the past, corporate users sought long-term leases to protect against expected price escalation. In the recent past, however, many corporate space users, fearing functional obsolescence, sought to limit the risks inherent in a long-term real estate strategy and opt for short-term flexible leasing.

Short-term leases create financial risk for landlords as real estate investments require the commitment of large amounts of capital, often financed with long-term fixed-rate debt. Landlords attempt to minimize their financial risk by looking for long-term leasing commitments from tenants to match their long-term liabilities.

For many years, real estate investments with long-term leases have been able to support high levels of debt. The availability of leverage has lowered the landlord's required return on assets. This leverage cannot be supported with more volatile rental streams. Reducing the level of leverage used in financing properties requires additional equity and raises the overall cost of capital.

Since the Financial Crisis, the commercial real estate market has remained weak in many markets. In soft markets, landlords seek to accommodate tenant demands for more flexible lease terms. As market equilibrium returns, landlords will need to pass on the true cost of flexible leases to tenants by raising rental rates. Tenants will either agree to these higher costs or be priced out of their spaces when their leases come to term.

14.3 STRATEGIC REAL ESTATE FINANCING FOR CORPORATIONS

14.3.1 Form of Ownership (Rent or Buy)

Businesses have many options to consider in addressing their real estate needs. They can seek to rent existing space from a landlord or to sublease that space from another tenant. They can also choose to acquire existing space that they will own and operate as a corporate asset. Finally, they can acquire land for development or redevelop existing property. There are a number of factors that affect property ownership decisions.

14.3.1.1 Qualitative Issues

As discussed previously, for many companies, control of appropriate real estate is a key part of their business strategy. In today's world, companies have many new options that have an impact on their requirement for real estate.

Companies in manufacturing, distribution, and retailing can use just-in-time sourcing and supply chain management tools to reduce inventory levels and the associated space requirements. Businesses with a service component can choose to outsource functions to third-party providers or to allow their own workers to telecommute. Both options decrease the company's internal need for office space.

In many cases, the preferred mode of operation is to outsource all nonstrategic operations to high-quality, low-cost providers. These providers minimize cost and improve quality by having a deep focus on providing a single service. Using outsourced services allows the corporation to focus only on the most critical aspects of value creation.

Beyond the economics of property ownership, the question of corporate focus on the core business is also an issue to be considered when deciding whether to acquire real estate. Owning and managing property—even for corporate use—can be complex, time consuming, and a distraction to management.

14.3.1.1.1 Does the Company Have Capital?

Assuming that a company has access to the full range of possible real estate solutions for their needs (rent, buy, develop, redevelop), a number of financial decision criteria must be assessed. Given the capital requirements involved in property ownership, access to capital, cost of capital, and the competitive uses of available capital are typically major factors in the rent/buy decision.

Many businesses do not have access to the capital required to pursue a real estate ownership strategy. They may not have the resources available to invest or access to the credit required to leverage the equity that they do have. These companies must look to rent space from a property owner.

In the case in which the company has access to capital, the next consideration is whether the capital can be better applied to another use. For example, a well-established landlord may have access to capital at a lower rate than the typical entrepreneurial firm. The landlord may be willing to pass this lower cost of capital to the space user.

Although this choice may at first appear irrational on the part of the landlord, remember that the landlord is only giving the tenant the use of the space; if the tenant fails, the landlord's risk is the frictional cost of repositioning the space. This is a different risk than the risk that the tenant will succeed in business.

From the tenant's point of view, renting space can be an effective way for a small company to "borrow" money. The tenant is using the landlord's capital to pay for a factor of production over the period of the lease.

In contrast, the landlord must "price in" or consider the probability of tenant failure when calculating the cost of renovating existing space for use by a tenant with a low credit rating. In strong markets, landlords may require tenants with weak credit to post some form of credit support to back their lease commitment.

14.3.1.2 Quantitative Issues

Through accident of history or prior business strategy, many corporations have acquired a significant portfolio of real estate. These companies must assess, on a continuing basis, whether to maintain ownership of their properties.

For many companies, their real estate holdings may represent a lower risk asset class than their core businesses and demand a lower cost of capital. The market may not be properly assessing the company's real estate exposure when applying a cost of capital to its shares. Thus, the company may consider divesting its properties by selling them to a third-party investor. The capital formerly invested in properties can be applied to other corporate purposes, used to pay down debt, or returned to shareholders.

For some companies, the sale of real property is a way to bolster the growth rate of the business. As properties are sold, the company's asset base shrinks. Growth and profitability in the core business are concentrated over a smaller remaining asset base. Proceeds from the property sales may be used to fund growth of core operations.

For other companies, selling off properties is a way to improve financial flexibility by reducing leverage. Although owning leveraged properties may have been an opportunistic strategy for a company in a period of easy credit, a highly leveraged balance sheet may look very risky to investors in the post–Financial crash Crisis era.

Many corporate property sales are purely financial transactions. Despite moving the property off the company's balance sheet, the company may still maintain the use of the property by entering into a lease transaction with the buyer. In this case, the day-to-day operations of the company are not altered in any way.

14.4 FINANCING STRUCTURES

14.4.1 Property Sale Leaseback

One of the most common financing strategies used in corporate real estate transactions is the sale leaseback. As the name implies, the corporation sells an asset that it owns to a real estate company and leases it back for a period of time. The transaction is typically used to free up capital the corporation has invested in the property for other purposes. One of the key factors to evaluate in considering sale leaseback transactions is the company's alternative uses of capital and the impact the transactions may have on financial flexibility.

Sale leaseback transactions also have tax and accounting implications. For accounting purposes, there are two kinds of sale leaseback transactions: operating leases and capital leases.

14.4.1.1 Operating Lease

To structure a sale leaseback as an operating lease, the company must meet a number of criteria. The lease term of an operating lease is subject to limitation and the property must be transferred to the new owner without the seller either (a) regaining ownership of the property or (b) retaining the right to repurchase the asset at a bargain price at the end of the term.

If the sale leaseback meets the operating lease criteria, the asset column of the balance sheet reflects the transaction by replacing the investment in real estate with the net cash proceeds from the sale. The amount of net proceeds will equal the sale price less the amount of debt repaid and taxes paid. On the liability side, the debt associated with the property is removed.

Any gain on sale is reported on the income statement. Interest expense on the property debt will cease as will depreciation on the property asset. In each period during the term of the operating lease, these expenses are replaced by lease expense.

14.4.1.1.1 Example of Operating Lease

Xco, a major retailer, completes a five-store sale leaseback with Real Investco. Real Investco agrees to buy the properties from Xco and lease them back to the retailer under a ten-year lease with a five-year option to renew. During the term of the lease, rent will rise each year at the CPI and the lessee will remain responsible for all of the costs of operating the properties.

A short-term lease without an option to repurchase will likely qualify as an operating lease; a long-term lease with a bargain option to repurchase will not.

14.4.1.2 Capital Lease

In a capital lease, the corporation may be able to structure a longer lease and retain the right to regain possession or repurchase the building at the end of the lease period. However, in a capital lease, the seller receives what many would consider less favorable accounting treatment. It retains the property as a leasehold asset on its balance sheet and the matching liability is calculated as the present value of the payments due on the lease.

In each period, the leasehold asset is amortized. As the lease payments are made, a portion of each payment is applied to reduce the lease liability and a portion is expensed as interest.

14.4.1.2.1 Example of Capital Lease

Xco, a major retailer, completes a five-store sale leaseback with Real Investco. Real Investco agrees to buy the properties from Xco and lease them back to the retailer under a twenty-year lease with a five-year option to renew. During the term of the lease, rent will rise each year at the CPI and the lessee will remain responsible for all of the costs of operating the properties.

At the end of the lease period, Xco will have the right to repurchase the properties at a significant discount on the price at which it originally sold the properties.

A long-term lease or a lease with a bargain repurchase option is typically treated as a capital lease.

14.4.1.3 Taxation

A sale leaseback that results in an operating lease is typically treated as a sale for tax purposes. If the property is sold at a gain, then the seller will have to pay taxes. Future lease payments will be deductible expenses. If the sale leaseback results in a capital lease, the transaction may be characterized as either a sale or a mortgage financing, depending on the specific circumstances. If treated as a mortgage, the seller would be able to continue depreciating the property and deducting the portion of the lease payment attributed to interest; the portion attributed to repayment of principal would not be deductible.

	Operating lease	Capital lease
Structure:		
Treatment	"Sale"	"Financing"
Term	Short	Long
Repurchase option	Market	Bargain
Accounting:		
Asset	None	Leasehold
Liability	None	PV of payments
Income	Gain on sale	None
Expenses	Lease payment	Amortization of leasehold interest
Taxation:		
Income	Gain on sale	None
Expenses	Lease payment	Amortization of leasehold interest

NOTE: FUTURE OF LEASE ACCOUNTING

The future of lease accounting is being reviewed currently by the Financial Accounting Standards Board (FASB) and may be changed in the near future. Readers should refer to http://www.fasb.org for current information and additional details.

14.4.2 Property Sale to REIT

If a company (Use-Co) has a significant number of properties then it can consider forming a property company (Prop-Co) to take title to those assets and sell a substantial interest in those assets to the public. The property company may take the form of a real estate operating company or elect to qualify as a real estate investment trust. Use-Co will then lease the properties from Prop-co. The strength of Use-Co's credit and the value of the assets to other users will determine the cost of funds to Prop-Co and the lease payment required from Use-Co.

14.4.2.1 Implementation

Prop-Co raises funds in a public offering and uses those funds to buy properties from Use-Co. Use-Co enters into a lease with Prop-Co for the continued use of the previously owned assets.

To accomplish the divestiture of the assets, the owner creates a new company, Prop-Co, to hold the properties. Prop-Co raises capital from public or private sources to acquire an interest in the assets along with the former owner's real estate operating group. The seller may retain a partial interest in Prop-Co and distribute some or all of Prop-Co's shares to its shareholders. This form of transaction is known as a spinoff. Use-Co can also divest its property holdings by selling its entire interest to the new investors.

Prop-Co can limit its business to the ownership of properties leased to Use-Co, or it can have a broader business plan in which it seeks to acquire property from other users. This strategic choice will depend on the strength of the original Use-Co brand and whether Use-Co is growing and will have additional assets for Prop-Co to acquire.

The taxation of spin off transactions is complex. There are a limited set of circumstances under which spin-off transactions can be accomplished on a tax-free basis. A full discussion of spin off taxation is beyond the scope of this text.

14.5 ALTERNATIVE CAPITAL SOURCES FOR CORPORATE REAL ESTATE

Landlords and localities can be a source of financing for growth. A landlord's investment in space allows a corporate space user to conserve capital that can then be directed to other uses. This ability can be especially important to start-up companies and small businesses that cannot access the capital markets on their own. In this case, the landlord can serve as a financial intermediary, bringing the tenant capital at the landlord's cost rather than tenant's cost. The landlord uses its right to take back the space as collateral for the tenant's performance. The value of the right to reclaim the asset depends on the strength of the property market.

14.5.1 Government Capital

Governments consider encouraging economic development to be one of their primary functions, based on the belief that economic growth positively affects all citizens by improving the quality of life. In many cases, economic growth is based on creation or enhancement of the built environment that provides shelter for citizens, facilitates commerce, and creates educational and cultural amenities. One of the principal benefits of growth through property development is direct and indirect job creation. Direct job creation occurs as construction and development firms build and rehabilitate property. Indirect job creation follows from the activities that take place in the new space. For these reasons, governments use their fiscal powers to encourage sustainable development.

14.5.1.1 Economic Development Initiatives

Governments have created many types of programs that create incentives for development that is considered to have a public purpose. These incentives generally rely on the government's ability to spend its capital or alter its tax policies to favor specific types of development.

14.5.1.1.1 Tax Abatements

A tax abatement program reduces or eliminates the real estate taxes that would otherwise be due on a targeted class of property. By lowering the tax burden and thus operating costs, the targeted property becomes more economically competitive compared to properties facing the full tax burden. The benefit can be passed through to tenants, facilitating occupancy at below-market rates, making the targeted property attractive. This step can also drive cost-sensitive property users to new markets. In the case in which the targeted property can command market rates, the benefit of the tax reduction can allow the developer to support the higher cost of repositioning underutilized properties for new uses.

Example: Iron City wants to encourage the redevelopment of its many closed steel mills. It offers a ten-year abatement of property taxes to any development project that converts an old industrial site into a new retail or industrial use.

14.5.1.1.2 Tax Credits

Tax credits are government-issued rights that can be used in place of cash to pay an existing tax liability. The credits are typically transferable and are sold to end users who have known tax liabilities. In many cases, the credits related to a particular project are issued over a period of years and can be sold to an end user for their present value. The sale of the credits produces funds that can be used to reduce the cost of the project.

In the United States, tax credits have been used for many purposes. The Federal Historic Preservation Tax Incentives program, established in 1976, uses tax credits to encourage the rehabilitation of existing older buildings. The New Market Tax Credit (NMTC) program established in 2000 has been used to encourage development in economically challenged areas.

14.5.1.1.3 Tax Increment Financing (TIF)

Tax increment financing (TIF) programs allow the government to retask the new taxes created by a targeted development project to the repayment of a bond. The bond proceeds are made available to the developer to reduce the project's cost. The government's rationale for the TIF program is that the taxes would not exist if the new project were not built, and the new project would not be economically viable without the subsidy created by the TIF. After the TIF bond is repaid, the future tax benefits revert back to the government.

14.5.1.1.4 Industrial Development Bonds (IDB)

Industrial development bonds (IDB) are bonds that are issued by economic development authorities on behalf of developers of targeted projects. The bonds do not have government credit behind their interest or repayment obligation, but the interest received by the investor is free from taxation, which reduces the cost of financing the development.

Similar types of bonds are also issued to finance other types of development projects such as construction of hospitals and college dormitories.

14.5.1.1.5 Loan Guarantees

The government can extend its credit to reduce the cost of financing by agreeing to guarantee the interest and principal repayment for a targeted development project. This approach reduces the developer's funding cost, and the loan guarantee can make funds available that would otherwise be inaccessible because of the risk of the targeted project.

14.5.1.1.6 Grants

Grants are direct payments made by the government that are used to offset the cost of the development. Grants are the most direct form of government sponsorship.

14.5.1.1.7 Enterprise Zones

Enterprise zones are designated geographic areas that a government has targeted for economic development. To encourage development within the enterprise zone, the government will work to assist developers by coordinating the availability of many types of support programs into a compelling financing package. The local government's economic development officials typically coordinate the structuring of the financing package.

14.5.1.2 Leveraging Relocation
14.5.1.2.1 Job Retention/Creation

Governments seek out opportunities for economic development by encouraging companies to relocate to their city or state. They encourage relocation by offering packages of financial incentives that will benefit the targeted company. Incentives used for relocation can be in the form of a job creation tax credit, offering a set amount of tax credits for each new job brought to the new location.

In some cases, companies already operating in the government's region are offered packages of incentives to remain at their current location. This program may be in response to an incentive package offered by a neighboring region to encourage the corporation to move.

There is significant competition between regions to attract growth companies because of the myriad of benefits they can bring to a community.

14.5.1.2.2 Future Tax Revenues

Governments believe that attracting companies to their region will improve their economic growth prospects and lead to significant future tax revenues.

These revenues will repay the government's investment in the financial incentive package.

14.5.1.2.3 Economic Multiplier Effect

When looking at the impact caused by the relocation or retention of a business, the government conducts an economic impact study (EIS). Such a study seeks to identify the direct and indirect consequences that the business will have on the local economy. A business has many direct impacts on the economy by hiring workers, purchasing goods and services, and creating tax revenues for local and state government. In addition, the business creates second-order effects when its workers and suppliers also spend their funds in the local economy. The sum of the economic activity generated as a function of the original company's revenues is called the economic multiplier.

14.5.1.3 Landlord Capital
14.5.1.3.1 Third-Party Financing

The corporate property user can view its landlord as a source of third-party capital for its business. The landlord invests its funds to provide the tenant with the space that it requires and, in many cases, to furnish that space to the tenant's unique requirements. This arrangement allows the corporate space user to retain its capital for its core business. The rent required by the landlord for its role as a space provider may be lower than the costs that the tenant would have to incur were it to furnish its own property.

14.5.1.3.2 Landlords' Cost of Capital May Be Lower

At times, landlords are able to access capital at a lower cost than their corporate tenants and can pass those savings on in the form of lower occupancy costs.

14.5.1.3.3 Risk May Be Less

The landlord holds the property in its portfolio and can reposition a building to another user in the event that a tenant ceases to pay rent. The landlord's business is structured to effect these transitions efficiently. This reduces the risk of failure of any specific tenant. Rather than being the sole property asset of a corporate user, the properties remain part of a larger portfolio. The bankers providing capital to the landlord see additional security in the broader and more diverse holdings of the typical property company. This reduction of risk helps to lower the landlord's cost of financing, and this lower cost can be shared with the tenant to reduce its occupancy costs.

14.5.1.3.4 Landlord Has Core Competence in Real Estate

Given the changes in the real estate industry, today's landlord is likely to be a large vertically integrated company and have the ability to develop and manage its own properties. Its core competence is real estate. All but the largest corporate property owners are unlikely to achieve the scale and competency of a specialized real estate company. For this reason, many corporate property users see the real estate company as an efficient outsourcing solution.

If the corporate property owner needs new facilities, the real estate company can bring experience in the development and construction of complex facilities including cost estimation, project design, and construction management.

Once the new property is completed, the real estate company, experienced in building management, can bring operational economies of scale to the corporate space user. Many property management companies have deep supply chains, sourcing the goods and services required to maintain property at lower costs than would be available to the owner of a single asset. These companies use complex software for building management that allow them to measure and optimize the productivity of each property. They can effectively allocate costs across a portfolio of facilities owned by many different users and reduce costs.

EXAMPLE

Prop-Co has created an energy efficiency engineering group that reviews and optimizes power purchasing and usage reducing portfolio energy costs. The cost of this group is significant. Prop-Co can amortize if over a very large portfolio of properties.

14.5.1.3.5 Landlord Incentives

Landlords seeking to attract tenants can provide a compelling set of incentives. For tenants currently occupying space under an existing lease, the new landlord can agree to a lease buy-out. In a lease buy-out, the new landlord relieves the prospective tenant of financial responsibility by paying the remaining rent due to the tenant's current landlord. The new landlord may also offer to pay the tenant's cost of relocation including the cost of moving. The new landlord may also offer the prospective tenant an allowance to renovate the new space and/or give the tenant a period of free rent at the beginning of the new lease. The combination of these incentives can be quite compelling to the corporation seeking to relocate.

The new landlord views the cost of these incentives as an investment in the acquisition of the new tenant and its prospective long-term lease, which will generate years of future cash flows. The new landlord's risk is that the incentives require it to expend significant capital at the time the tenant first takes occupancy, while the new landlord's economic benefit may take years to achieve and is subject to the risk that the tenant may or may not remain solvent for the term of the lease.

The new landlord's willingness to provide incentive packages depends on the competitive dynamics of the property market and its cost of and access to capital.

Glossary

corporate sustainability
data hotels
economic development
EIS (economic impact study)
economic multiplier
Enterprise Zone
functional obsolescence
green building
greenhouse gases
hoteling
historic tax credit
IDB (industrial development bonds)
interactivity
intermodal transportation hubs
job creation tax credit
just-in-time
landfill waste
LEED (Leadership in Energy Environmental Design)
lease buy-out
loan guarantee
multi-channel
new market tax credits
outsource
Real Estate Investment Trust (REIT)
Real Estate Operating Company (REOC)
sale leaseback
spinoff
supply chain management
sustainable development
tax abatements
TIF (tax increment financing)
telecommuters
USGBC (U.S. Green Building Council)
value retailer

Thought Questions

1. You are the CEO of New Corp, a tech start-up located next to Ivy University in a suburb of a major coastal city in the northeast. Red State, in the deep south, has sent their Secretary of Economic Development to visit to convince you to locate in the South. The incentive package is compelling. What factors should you consider?

2. SuperApp is a next-generation Internet company that serves 100 million unique customers every day. People depend on SuperApp having near 100-percent availability of its services. The company's technology center is said to use more electricity than many small countries. SuperApp has

outgrown its current headquarters and needs to move. Right out of business school, the CEO asks you to prepare a whitepaper on what needs to be considered in any such move.

3. ValueCo is a large retailer suffering from a downturn in sales. It operates a portfolio of 800 stores across the United States: half are leased, most at below-market rents, and the balance have been owned for an average of 20 years. The new CEO has been tasked with turning around the company. As vice president of real estate, you must think through what you can do to contribute to the turnaround.

Multiple Choice Questions

1. Which is not a government incentive used for corporate relocation?
   a) Loan guarantee
   b) Economic impact study
   c) New Market Tax Credit
   d) Tax incentive financing
2. Which is a method used by corporations to reduce the amount of property on the company's balance sheet?
   a) Sale leaseback
   b) Industrial development bond
   c) Historic tax credit
   d) enterprise zone
3. Which of the following did not result from the Internet?
   a) Multi-channel retailing
   b) Telecommuting
   c) Value retailing
   d) Just-in-time sourcing
4. Which is not a factor in choosing a corporate location?
   a) Access to transportation
   b) Sufficient utilities
   c) Availability of skilled labor
   d) Availability of greenhouse gasses
5. Landlords can supply which of the following incentives for corporate relocation:
   I) job creation tax credit
   II) access to lower cost capital
   III) moving allowance
   IV) tenant allowance
   V) lease buy-out
   a) I, II, III
   b) II, III, IV, V
   c) I, III
   d) II, IV

6. The economic multiplier is a measurement of which of the following:
   a) The sales of a relocated company/the government incentives provided
   b) The rent paid by the new company/the landlords lease incentives
   c) The total economic activity generated by the new company/the new company's revenues
   d) The historic tax credit/the cost of building renovation
7. Shoppers' Paradise, a major retailer, has excellent locations and owns its stores subject to mortgage financing. There is a new competitor, Buyers' Heaven, and the company requires capital to renovate its stores. Which is the best strategy for Shoppers' Paradise to use?
   a) Approach its landlord for tenant allowances
   b) Approach its bank for a secured credit line
   c) Enter into a sale leaseback transaction
   d) Ask the local government for property tax abatements
8. Dewie, Cheatem, and Howe is a major law firm with more than 200 partners. Its lease in its West Coast high rise is expiring next year and it is considering moving out of Major City to EdgeBurb, a short commute near where most of its high-net-worth partners and customers live. EdgeBurb has no income tax; Major City does. Which of the following can Major City offer directly to the law firm?
   a) Space in an enterprise zone
   b) Industrial development bond financing
   c) Historic tax credit
   d) Tax increment financing
9. LEED is a rating system for buildings that includes all but one of the following criteria:
   a) Conservation of energy and water
   b) Improved property NOI
   c) Improvement of health and safety for occupants
   d) Reduction of greenhouse gasses and landfill waste
10. Why might a company decide to rent from a landlord rather than own its properties?
    a) The company has limited access to capital.
    b) The company's capital can be better applied to another use.
    c) The landlord may have access to capital at a lower rate than the company.
    d) All of the above.

For answers to these Problems and Exercises, please visit the companion website: http://booksite.elsevier.com/9780123786265

CHAPTER 15

International Real Estate

15.1 OVERVIEW

This chapter looks at the risks and rewards of ownership of property in a foreign country as a real estate investment strategy.

The defining quality of real property is that it cannot be moved. Its location never changes. Property that is located outside of an investor's domestic market is subject to the property laws, taxation, and customs of that foreign country. Many countries, including the United States, place additional burdens and regulations on foreign property owners. In addition, in some cases the investor's home country may impose additional conditions and restrictions on the ownership of foreign property by its citizens.

This complexity can be difficult to master, but for those investors who are able to surmount the challenges of cross-border investing there can be many benefits. Investing across borders can provide investment opportunities that are unavailable in one's own market and can add diversification to a geographically concentrated portfolio.

15.2 REWARDS

Given the complexity of cross border property investment, one would attempt to enter foreign markets only for a positive economic benefit in excess of the potential risks. There are a number of benefits that are intriguing enough to encourage investors to cross borders.

15.2.1 Exposure to Higher Growth Markets

For investors in any country, foreign real estate markets that are growing at faster rates than their domestic market. This growth may mirror a rapid expansion of the target market's underlying economy buoyed by population growth, exploitation of natural resources, or unique technological skills. By moving capital into the higher growth market, the foreign investor can increase the value of an investment more rapidly during the holding period.

Developing countries may provide stronger economic growth prospects than fully industrialized nations. This rapid growth may in turn create strong demand for real estate and the prospect for rapidly rising rents. Thus, cross-border investing from an industrialized country such as the United States into a developing nation may provide the opportunity for greater returns than are present in our developed market.

The rapid growth in developing nations may not be sustainable in the long term, and investment in these countries may also expose the investor to a number of risk factors that may be present in developing nations.

15.2.2 Ability to Transfer Process Technology

Process technology, developed in one economy to address a particular set of needs or desires present in that market, may have broader applicability than just the initiating country. This technology—whether it is based on design, construction, management, or financial innovation—can create a competitive advantage for the investor who brings it into a foreign market.

15.2.3 Political Stability and Rule of Law

Throughout history, investors facing challenging domestic political situations look to transfer wealth to countries that have stable political institutions and legal systems that respect the private ownership of property. These target markets, by representing a stable home for wealth from unstable countries, benefit from the economic growth created by capital influx.

15.2.4 First Mover Advantage

The first mover can have a unique advantage in defining the market place. Products or processes that have reached maturity in one market can be launched quickly and capture market share while new competitors struggle to catch up.

First mover advantage in cross-border real estate investing can come from bringing new property types to a market that did not have them, as well as the new to market tenants that utilize them (an example would be the first outlet mall in China). First mover advantage can also come from process technology transfer: examples include introducing new construction methodologies and financing techniques into a developing market.

15.2.5 Diversification

In addition to greater growth prospects, many global investors seek diversification through cross-border investing. Investing in foreign countries exposes the investor to the local economy, which may move in a cycle that is different from that of the investor's home country. Foreign markets may present investment opportunities when the domestic market is in a cyclical decline.

With increasing globalization, many countries' markets are becoming intertwined, and economic cycles are now more likely to move in tandem. As was shown during the recent financial crisis, globalization may have limited the benefits of diversification through cross-border investment. Investors are currently asking whether global investment actually provides the diversification they seek in return for the additional logistical burden, complexity, and risk of a multinational investment portfolio.

An astute investor must always ask whether the potential for higher returns is worth the risk and the extra effort required when managing an international portfolio. The logistical challenges to managing an international portfolio are significant and should be undertaken only if the investor is certain of a net benefit.

Does the potential for growth and diversification compensate for risk?

15.3 RISKS

15.3.1 The Complexity of Understanding Multiple Markets

The intellectual effort required in order to understand property markets in multiple countries should not be underestimated. Each country has its own laws and customs surrounding the ownership of real property as well as its own financial system governing capital transactions.

15.3.1.1 Laws

Each country has its own set of property laws that must be taken into account when considering making an investment. Owning, managing, and developing property in multiple locations under different legal regimes adds a significant level of complexity to an investment portfolio. Real property is particularly complicated, as the asset is immovable and it is impossible to decide to exit a market without disposing of the asset. An unfavorable change in law cannot be avoided by deciding to relocate the business.

15.3.1.2 Customs

Different cultures may have different views towards property ownership. Not all countries hold property rights in high esteem, and understanding the local viewpoint is a necessary prelude to investment. In some countries, property is considered communal, to serve the common good; individual ownership is not permitted or is permitted only under limited circumstances. At the other extreme, property ownership may be limited to the sovereign or to a designated class of land owners. This protocol can change over time. If a nation moves to control private property, the land it claims has been nationalized; in contrast, if the country sells off its land to individuals or corporations, that land has been privatized.

Nationalization may occur, as it does under eminent domain in the United States, with appropriate compensation to the former private owner. In some cases, however, there is no compensation paid and the former property owner can face a total loss of investment.

Many countries may have a negative view of foreign ownership of property, which can stem from a belief that foreign property ownership may undermine national sovereignty. Both laws and custom can impede the foreign owner that attempts to compete to purchase property. This issue may be significant if the targeted property or intended use has particular nationalistic significance.

15.3.2 Real Estate Market Standards
15.3.2.1 Survey

A survey is a complete physical description of a parcel of land. This description is used to describe the location, features, and boundaries of land parcels and can also include information about land use, including prior ownership and agricultural cultivation.

A survey can also identify the location of any easements that have been granted to government, utility, or private users, as well as the location of infrastructure such as power, water, and sewer.

Governments use surveys to inventory their land. This inventory can be used as the basis for tax assessment and political subdivision. This land inventory is stored in a register, sometimes called a cadaster, that can be used by cartographers as the basis for the creation of maps.

It is less risky to invest in a country where land is owned under a universally accepted system that records formal definitions of land parcels. This arrangement allows foreign buyers to legally identify the parcel of land that is being purchased.

In the United States, the Bureau of Land Management has worked since 1785 to survey 1.5 billion of the approximately 1.8 billion acres in the country.

15.3.2.2 Titles and Recording

A fundamental construct for a functioning real estate market is a system to record property ownership. This system should include a survey methodology and a process for recording the title: the current and previous owner of a parcel of land.

The legal document that represents the ownership of land is known as a deed. The deed references a parcel of land defined by a survey. Any limitations on the use of the property through contract or governmental assertion, as well as easements granted to third parties, should be recorded as part of the deed. Recording a deed may be subject to a tax.

The owner of the land described under the deed is said to hold title to the property. The holder of title to the property is recorded in the title registry. Title to the property may be transferred. The historical record of the ownership of a property is called the chain of title. In many cases, a change in title is subject to a tax.

Having a universally respected system for recording survey, deed, and title protects potential investors against claims of ownership from third parties without status. Without a respected title system, foreign property owners can be at a disadvantage in a property ownership dispute with a local claimant.

15.3.2.3 Title Insurance

The inability to prove ownership limits the ability of a prospective owner to find financing for an acquisition. Banks are unwilling to extend credit against an asset for which ownership is subject to question. In general, banks require title insurance as a predicate to financing. Title insurance companies research the chain of title of a property to determine whether it can be transferred to a new owner free of existing claims. The title insurance company requires a robust legal system in order to assess the risks of contested ownership against which they are providing insurance coverage.

15.3.3 Logistics

15.3.3.1 Time Zones

At a minimum, running a business across multiple continents involves maintaining operations outside of normal business hours at the home office. It is also possible that it will require local presence in foreign countries. Active communication with a home office is difficult if the field has the majority of its business day while the home office is asleep.

15.3.3.2 Managing Multiple Sites

Managing in multiple locations is much more complex than operating out of a single location. Deciding which functions to centralize and which to place in satellite offices can be difficult.

Operating locally with personnel in the field provides more insight into the market and can be invaluable in providing visual confirmation of business conditions. It is harder to take advantage of economies of scale when many functions are duplicated across field offices unless each office is large enough to independently generate scale.

For example, when accounting is aggregated in a single office, employees can work on data from multiple sites and avoid downtime during the monthly rent receipt and payables cycles. But accountants in a central office cannot visually confirm the rent roll, nor will they witness the arrival of shipments of goods and the provision of services. Deciding on the level of onsite accounting is typical of the personnel decisions that come with multisite and multinational growth.

15.3.3.3 Compliance with Multiple Regulatory Systems

Most legal systems include regulations on the construction of buildings and the operation of real property. These regulations can include building and life safety codes. They can also include deep provisions for tenant rights that may go as far as implying equitable rights for renters. These rules can present an economic burden and affect property owner's rights. Understanding the regulatory climate is a predicate to investment in a foreign country.

15.3.4 Geopolitical Risk

One of the key risks facing investors in foreign real estate is the possibility of a change in government leading to conditions that are unfavorable for business and economic development in general or for the local real estate market in particular.

Changes in government can have an impact on local policies regarding property ownership. These changes can restrict all private property ownership or can be directed toward foreign ownership of property depending on the ideology of the new government. Communist and socialist regimes can favor governmental and communal ownership of property; nationalist regimes can favor limits on foreign ownership. Some governments have acted against their core ideology to promote private property ownership as a means to encourage economic development.

15.3.4.1 Government Stability

The stability of local government is a key factor in assessing a foreign real estate investment. If we can gain an understanding of the real estate market dynamics, and we have reason to believe that the government is stable, then we can make a reasoned judgment about the political risks. In contrast, if the government is fragile, the current status of the property markets are less relevant because there can be no assurance that the environment will remain constant.

15.3.4.2 Local Property Law

In most countries, local political forces control property development and usage. Local popular opinion towards land development and usage has an impact on the value of a potential acquisition. The value of an asset can change significantly if its zoning and entitlements are affected by local authorities.

15.3.4.3 Local Tax Law

Local tax laws can have a large effect on the economic outcome of a development or investment plan. Tax incentives can be used to encourage development and repositioning of properties. Tax increases can reduce or destroy the value of an investment. Stability of the tax code allows owners and developers to accurately assess investments; variability in the tax code induces risk that reduces values.

In a number of respects, the U.S. government has negatively affected foreign investment in U.S. real estate through unfavorable tax legislation such as the Foreign Investment in Real Property Tax Act (FIRPTA), which mandates withholding on certain property-related income.

15.3.5 Financial Risk

15.3.5.1 Maturity of Financial System

A mature financial system has many components that facilitate capital investment. These components include a stable currency that allows foreign investors to predictably translate local returns into their home currency.

15.3.5.2 Local Capital Market

Developed countries typically have robust banking systems that are able and willing to provide credit to property investors. The ability of financial institutions to extend credit to real property owners is contingent upon the existence of a legal infrastructure that protects private ownership of property and respects the potential claims of lenders. If a lender cannot exert remedies in court against defaulted borrowers, they will not extend credit.

15.3.5.3 Repatriation of Profits and Investment

Some countries limit the repatriation of investment returns made inside their countries. The governments that pursue this policy reason that limiting the repatriation of investment returns encourages the local reinvestment of profits. These limitations may however have the opposite result by diminishing the level of foreign investment and slowing down economic development.

15.3.5.4 Currency Risk
15.3.5.4.1 Local Financing
15.3.4.4.1.1 Financing Should Match Rent Stream to Avoid Currency Risk. The existence of local capital markets and financial institutions willing to make property loans allows investors to incur liabilities in the same currency as they will receive their rent payments. This is also the currency in which most operating expenses will be paid. Further, this is the currency that they will likely receive upon the sale of their asset to a third party. This setup minimizes the amount of cross-border currency movements.

There will be cases in which a reference currency will supplant the local currency for business transactions. In some countries, rents are pegged to or paid in a reference currency such as the U.S. dollar. If the landlord receives U.S. dollars rather than local currency, then having major liabilities in dollars will prevent currency conversion risk.

Even if it is desired to finance a project in local currency, the local financial infrastructure may not be able to support the amount of borrowing required. In this case, it may be necessary to borrow overseas to finance foreign projects. The lender in this circumstance may require the corporate guarantee of the parent company rather than subsidiary operating in the foreign country where the investment is to be made.

15.3.5.4.2 Hedging Opportunities

Investors with predictable cash flow streams can hedge their exposure to a foreign market with currency swaps. Using currency swaps, the foreign investor can receive a fixed amount of his or her home currency for each specified amount of local currency generated by the foreign property investment. This type of hedging transaction can limit the risk from currency exchange rate changes.

15.3.5.4.2.1 Cost of Hedging Currency Risk. The cost of a currency swap is determined by the volatility of the exchange rates and the relative interest rates between the two countries.

Countries with weak economies or those built on a narrow industrial base can have volatile exchange rates. The volatility of the exchange rates can make hedging currency risk expensive and lowers investor returns.

15.3.5.4.3 Capital Repatriation

It is difficult to hedge against the risk that a country closes its doors to cross-border capital transactions. In some countries where it is not possible to export currency, the currency can be converted into salable products that can then be exported. These products can be sold in the investor's home country for local (home market) currency.

15.3.6 Asset Protection
15.3.6.1 Presence of First Responders

An investment in property is protected by the presence of first responders such as firefighters, emergency medical services, and police. Without these services, the property may be subject to loss or damage from fire, theft, and vandalism. The provision of these services—while generally available in urban areas of developed nations—may not be universally available in rural areas or in developing nations.

15.3.6.2 Availability of Property and Casualty Insurance

The availability of property and casualty insurance may be limited or nonexistent in areas without a first responder infrastructure. If the insurance company cannot count on the risk to the property being mitigated by first responders, it may not be able to afford protection. In turn, the lack of insurance protection can make financial institutions unwilling to extend property financing.

15.3.6.3 Building Codes

Building codes are regulations that govern the design and construction of structures with the goal of protecting the occupant's life safety. Building codes may be set at the local or national level and reflect the geography of the building's location and the types of risk it may face, including the likelihood of flood, fire, and earthquake.

The building codes may affect the types of materials used in construction and may vary depending on local architecture and available materials. They also reflect the types of risks most likely to cause damage to the property. For example, in areas of flooding, property may need to be raised above ground, and in areas of seismic activity, additional structural support may be necessary. These conditions and the design features required to mitigate them can significantly increase the cost of construction.

15.4 INVESTMENT STRUCTURE

15.4.1 Direct Investment

A direct investment in foreign property requires an investor to identify, purchase, operate, and ultimately sell an asset in a foreign market, which requires a prospective owner to project his or her operations into a new market; acquire an in-depth understanding about a foreign country's property laws, regulatory environment, and business customs; and project their current corporate culture and success factors into a new environment.

15.4.1.1 Operations

15.4.1.1.1 Requires Structured Communication

Successful businesses manage to extend their corporate culture and business processes across borders and time zones, which is not easy to accomplish. It is easy for distant sites in a multisite enterprise to disengage. Regularly scheduled communication through email, conference calls, and in-person visits can help enfranchise personnel at distant locations and extend the corporate brand and culture.

15.4.1.1.2 Understanding of Local Business Practices

To be successful as a multinational corporation, the foreign operating units of the business must be sensitive to local business practices while not diluting the aspects of the brand that are universal and the underpinnings of the company's success. Understanding of the local culture can come through study and immersion prior to entering a market, partnership with local businesses, and the engagement of local employees.

15.4.1.1.3 Understanding Local Logistics

Efficient property management requires establishment of relationships with many service providers. These service providers maintain building systems, provide housekeeping and security services, and maintain the property grounds. In order to offer competitive occupancy costs, a property owner must access these services from reliable providers at a low relative cost. Not all markets have local sources for all of the services required. If the required services are not available locally, the foreign investor must either train local people to provide the required services or source them externally.

15.4.1.1.4 Initial Loss of Scale until Local Portfolio Grows

Until the local portfolio reaches scale, the entrant into a new market must try to find scale through outsourcing. Outsourcing can give the foreign property owner the economics of larger domestic service providers to keep property operating costs down.

If operating at scale is not possible, the cost structure of the foreign investor may preclude it from effectively competing in the foreign market against more efficient domestic real estate owners.

15.4.2 Indirect Investment

It may be easier for the new investor entering a foreign market to gain exposure to the targeted property market by purchasing securities issued by property companies that are active in that market. It can also participate in property funds offered by private equity investment managers.

15.4.2.1 Operations

15.4.2.1.1 Liquidity Is Easier than Selling Assets

Finding liquidity in traded securities of foreign property companies is generally easier than buying or selling real property. Many global stock brokerage firms now maintain active markets in securities issued in many foreign countries. These firms can facilitate the ownership of foreign securities in a home country account. They may also provide securities research reports on individual corporate performance and economic developments that may affect the real estate industry in that country.

15.4.2.1.2 Data Sources and Transparency

Reporting requirements for public companies vary from country to country. Depending on your country of residence, your target market may have greater or less robust disclosure requirements. Financial reporting may adhere to international standards such as International Financial Reporting Standards (IFRS) and may allow direct comparison between corporations across many nations.

Data on the trading history of securities listed on a foreign exchange may be available online or may be difficult to access. The status of the local securities exchange's reporting infrastructure should be evaluated in advance of making an investment.

15.4.2.1.3 Ability to Trade in Quantity

The presence of an active investment community and the willingness of market makers to commit capital determine the ability of investors to purchase and liquidate positions in reasonable time periods and without dramatic price movements. The depth of the market is a function not only of the infrastructure but also of the security being traded. Securities with large market capitalizations usually have deeper markets.

As a rule, institutional investors generally avoid markets that are illiquid. The lack of institutional participation makes it difficult for companies to raise capital. Companies domiciled in countries with weak capital markets may have to seek financing from abroad.

15.4.2.1.4 Transaction Costs

Transaction costs tend to be higher in illiquid lightly traded markets. Global firms are likely to have limited connectivity with these markets, and the lack of liquidity will limit transaction price competition. In well-developed markets, there are many securities firms that collectively create a competitive marketplace.

15.4.2.1.5 Regulatory Limits

Some countries limit ownership of certain classes of securities to their own citizens.

15.5 PARTICIPANTS

Investors may spend many years understanding a foreign market before making their first capital investments. They can seek to enter a new market by forming a partnership with a local company or employing local talent in their own operation. In other cases, the foreign investor hires local professionals such as lawyers and accountants. In each case, the investor is seeking to understand the new market from a local point of view as a means of mitigating risk.

15.5.1 In the Target Market
Upon entering a new market, the real estate investor will seek out some or all of the following.

15.5.1.1 Local Joint Venture Partners
At its heart, real estate is a local business. It is place based and it is hard to understand the value of an asset without understanding it in the context of its role in the local community. Many foreign investors seek local property companies with deep market knowledge to provide entrée. The local property company can benefit from the foreign partners' capital access or unique process technology.

15.5.1.2 Local Financial Institutions
Local financial institutions may not be as large or sophisticated as those in the investor's home country. They may, however, be much better at understanding supply and demand in the local property market. They will also have prior knowledge and experience with a broad segment of local regulators. Local banks can be invaluable in mitigating risk from lack of market experience.

15.5.1.3 Local Lawyers/Brokers
Local lawyers and brokers are at the heart of transaction flow in most property markets. They see and participate in the deal flow and have an understanding of local pricing and usage metrics that is invaluable to the foreign investor.

15.5.1.4 Multinational and U.S. Professional Service Firms with Local Offices
In many cases, major multinational professional service firms with global practices can help foreign firms enter new markets. They are likely to have well-connected local staff that can provide market, political, and cultural input. In addition to providing the specific service rendered by the firm (law, accounting, etc.), the cross-border professional services firm can help the foreign company accelerate their entrance into the new marketplace.

15.5.1.4.1 Understand Implications of Global Operations
Global professional service firms are also well versed in the logistical and other challenges of running multisite businesses operating in both the home and the target market of the client. This experience can be invaluable.

Glossary

Cadaster
Compliance
Currency hedge
Currency risk
Deed
Developing markets
Diversification
First mover advantage
FIRPTA (Foreign Investment in Real Property Tax Act)
Geopolitical risk
Globalization
Government stability
IFRS (International Financial Reporting Standards)
Logistics
Nationalization
Privatization
Repatriation
Technology transfer

Thought Questions

1. You work for a U.S. major consulting firm. The partner in charge asks you to consider your company's first overseas property investment, an office building in a major European city to house your new headquarters. What factors should you consider in choosing a location?

2. The new People's Republic of the Sahara is a former European colony with a history of political strife. Massive quantities of natural gas have been discovered and the capital city is undergoing rapid growth. You work at a private equity shop and your global alternative asset fund manager thinks that this is a good time to enter the country's property market. How do you get started?

3. You have just received a capital allocation for $50 million from a family office to invest in real estate either domestically or overseas—your choice—but your performance will be measured against a global property index. What are your considerations?

Multiple Choice Questions

1. Overseas investment can provide which of the following benefits:
   a) Diversification
   b) Exposure to growth markets
   c) Access to additional assets
   d) All of the above

2. Which of the following is not a particular risk of international investing:
   a) Geopolitical
   b) Seismic

    c) Currency

    d) Nationalization

3. Which of the following is not involved in land registration?

    a) Title

    b) Repatriation

    c) Deed

    d) Survey

4. Global property investment is always more profitable than domestic investing: true or false?

5. Intrinsic to a strong securities market are all of the following except:

    a) Liquidity

    b) Transparency

    c) Volatility

    d) Regulation

6. Which of the following is a regulation that affects the willingness of foreign investors to invest in the U.S. property market:

    a) FIRPTA

    b) IFRS

    c) GAAP

    d) USBLM

7. Which of the following strategies can protect against currency risk:

    I) Currency swap

    II) Mortgage and rent payments in the same currency

    III) Mortgage and rent payments in different currencies

    a) I, III

    b) I, II

    c) II, III

    d) All of the above

8. Introducing new business practices to a market is called X and generates Y:

    I) Market transparency

    II) First mover advantage

    III) Technology transfer

    a) I, III

    b) I, II

    c) II, III

    d) III, II

9. Access to foreign real estate investing can be achieved through all of the following except:

    a) A global property fund

    b) A cadaster

c) A partnership with local developer

d) Publicly traded securities

10. In order to provide mortgage financing, which of the following is not required?

a) Property and casualty insurance

b) Title insurance

c) First responders

d) Rapid economic growth

For answers to these Problems and Exercises, please visit the companion website: http://booksite.elsevier.com/9780123786265

Index

Note: Page numbers with "f" denote figures; "t" tables; "b" boxes.

Printed and bound by CPI Group (UK) Ltd, Croydon, CR0 4YY

08/05/2025

01864769-0001